OPERATION TEXAS STAR

The Last American Battles of the Vietnam War
April – September 1970

John G. Roberts

DEDICATION

To the men of the 101st Airborne Division (Airmobile), be they Grunts, Red Legs or Rotor Heads, who gave of themselves so unselfishly for their buddies, their unit and their country. And to my wife and partner Shari who knows all about PTSD and its long-term effects. As William Shakespeare once wrote in Henry IV: "In thy faint slumbers I by thee have watched and heard thee murmur tales of iron war." JGR-2017

ISBN: 9781549742316
Copyright © 2017 John G. Roberts
All Rights Reserved

Other books by John G. Roberts
Mighty Men of Valor: With Charley Company on Hill 714-Vietnam 1970
'A Damn Big Fight': Crazy Horse, Custer and Sitting Bull at the Little Bighorn

"We are not about to send American boys 9 or 10 thousand miles away from home to do what Asian boys ought to be doing for themselves."
Lyndon B. Johnson, 36th President of the United States
1964 campaign speech at Akron University

"We did not choose to be the guardians at the gate, but there is no one else."

Lyndon B. Johnson, just prior to ordering 210,000 US troops to Vietnam.

"What we need is a term like 'Vietnamizing' to put the emphasis on the right issues."

Secretary of Defense Melvin Laird to President Richard M. Nixon, 1969

TABLE OF CONTENTS

Glossary of Military Terms and Boonie Rat Slang

Chapter 1 – Vietnamization

Chapter 2 – The Tactical Situation in I Corps, 1970

Chapter 3 – The Opening Moves

Chapter 4 – Building Ripcord

Chapter 5 – The Fight on 'Re-Up Hill'

Chapter 6 – Hill 714

Chapter 7 – Firebase Granite – Part One NVA Target of Opportunity

Chapter 8 – Firebase Granite – Part Two

Chapter 9 – Hill 882

Chapter 10 – "Hard Luck Alpha" at Firebase Henderson

Chapter 11 – The NVA Quicken the pace

Chapter 12 – Hill 902 – A Night of Terror

Chapter 13 – Ripcord Under Siege – Part One

Chapter 14 – Hill 1000 – An Exercise in Futility

Chapter 15 – Hill 805 – A Desperate Battle

Chapter 16 – Ripcord Under Siege – Part Two

Chapter 17 – Into the Storm

Chapter 18 – Ripcord Under Siege – The Final Day

Chapter 19 – Picking Up The Pieces

Chapter 20 – Firebase Barnett and 'Comeback Ridge'

Chapter 21 – "But What Good. . .?"

Infantry Weapons of the Vietnam War

Bibliography

GLOSSARY of MILITARY TERMS and BOONIE RAT SLANG

A-Gunner The assistant machine gunner.

Airmobile A technique for mass movement of troops and equipment using helicopters. A unit trained in the use of airmobile tactics.

AK-47 The *Avtomat Kalashnikova* type 47 assault rifle caliber 7.62mm by 39mm. Can be fired either semi or fully automatic.

AK-50 Same as above but with folding 'wire frame' stock; favored by NVA sappers because of its compact size.

Air Medal A medal awarded to helicopter crewman and airmobile infantryman after a certain number of combat assaults; or, for valor with V-device.

AO Designated area in which a unit carried out combat operations.

ARA Aerial rocket artillery; usually a AH-1G Cobra attack helicopter

Arc light Term used to describe a high-altitude carpet bombing mission by B-52 bombers.

ARVN Army of the Republic of Vietnam

A Shau Valley A forty-kilometer (25 mile) long valley on the western border of Vietnam (Thua Thien Province) and Laos. A main branch of the *Ho Chi Minh Trail* ran through the valley.

'Aw Shit' Valley G.I. slang for the A Shau, the scene of many battles.

B-52 A large, high-altitude jet bomber used by the U.S. Air Force for strategic bombing missions.

bird A helicopter or any type of aircraft.
booby trap A concealed explosive device set to explode from a pressure device, trip wire or command detonation. Now referred to as an 'improvised explosive device.'
boonies G.I. slang for the jungle or unpopulated countryside.
boonie hat A soft hat with a full brim worn in place of the steel helmet to break up the outline of the human head.
boonie rat G.I. slang for an infantryman operating in the jungle.
Buck Sergeant (E-5) The lowest-ranking NCO, often used as a fire team leader or squad leader.
bunker A fortified fighting position usually with overhead cover.
bunker complex A mutually supporting group of bunkers sometimes connected with each other by trenches or tunnels.
bunker line Individual defensive bunkers placed around the perimeter of a firebase or base camp.
butter bar A second lieutenant, named for the gold bar indicating his rank.
CAR-15 The carbine version of the M-16 assault rifle.
C-4 A plastic explosive. Used to destroy enemy bunkers, knock down trees or cook you C-rations.
C-rations Canned rations that served as the boonie rat's primary source of food in the field or on a fire base. There were twelve meals to a case, a four-day supply of food. A case weighed twenty-five pounds. Also called *Charlie rats.*
C.A. Combat assault. The movement of troops by helicopter into enemy-controlled territory.

canopy A distinct layer of jungle foliage; single, double or triple canopy.
Charlie Oscar G.I. slang for the commanding officer of a unit.
Charley or Charley Cong G.I. slang for a Vietnamese guerilla soldier.
Charley-Charley or C&C bird Command and Control helicopter used by unit commanders to control combat assaults or troop movement on the ground.
cherry A soldier freshly arrived from the states and newly assigned to a unit.
CIB Combat Infantry Badge; awarded to infantry soldiers who have served in actual combat.
claymore A command detonated anti-personnel mine named after a Scottish broad sword. Convex-shaped plastic case contains about 700 .32 caliber steel balls propelled by C-4. Used for ambushes or perimeter security.
click See *klick*.
Cobra Nickname for the AH-1G assault helicopter based on the UH-1 Huey. Usually armed with a 7.62mm mini-gun, 40mm grenade launcher and 2.75-inch rockets.
Combat Medic Badge Awarded to aid men (medics) who serve in combat with infantry, artillery or armored units.
Cong 'Red', or communist.
CONUS Continental United States.
C.P. Command post; the position within a perimeter occupied by the platoon leader/company commander and the medic, RTO's and the artillery F.O.
CS Tear gas in aerosol or crystalized form.

DDP Daylight defensive perimeter. Used as a base for security patrols searching for the enemy's presence or to receive resupply.
DEROS Date estimated rotation overseas. The date a soldier left Vietnam to return to the United States or vice-versa.
det cord A hollow cord filled with an explosive used to connect separate explosive charges, tipped with a blasting cap.
deuce-and-a-half All-wheel drive (ten wheels), two-and-a-half-ton capacity truck. Used to carry cargo, personnel or tow artillery pieces. Sometimes had an M55 Quad 50 machine gun mounted in the bed.
DISCOM Division support command.
DMZ Demilitarized zone. During the Vietnam War, a 100-kilometer long, two-kilometer wide zone along the 17th parallel separating South Vietnam from North Vietnam.
'Doc' G.I. slang for a combat medic, as in 'Doc Jones or 'Doc' Brown.
DOW Died of Wounds
drag Rear security; the last man in a file of moving troops.
Dust Off As in *Eagle Dust Off;* an unarmed Huey air ambulance equipped to evacuate wounded troops from the battlefield.
EOD Explosive ordnance disposal
E-1 Pay grade for private, recruit
E-2 Pay grade for private
E-3 Pay grade for private first class
E-4 Pay grade for corporal or specialist fourth class
E-5 Pay grade for sergeant or specialist fifth class
E-6 Pay grade for staff sergeant or specialist sixth class.

E-7 Pay grade for sergeant first class.
E-8 Pay grade for first sergeant or master sergeant.
E-9 Pay grade for sergeant major or command sergeant major.
E-club A bar/snack bar where the lowest four enlisted ranks party.
ETS Estimated time of separation; the date a soldier is discharged from the service.
FA Field artillery.
FAC Forward air controller, the pilot that serves as an airborne liaison between ground units and fighter-bombers.
FDC Fire direction center; controls the aiming of the guns, angle of fire and fall of artillery shells.
firebase Fire support base. A semi-permanent artillery/mortar position supporting an infantry battalion, usually on a hilltop, within a barbed wire perimeter containing the artillery FDC and the infantry TOC and secured by an infantry unit.
FNG Fucking new guy. See *'cherry.'*
FO Forward observer. An artillery officer of sergeant attached to an infantry unit in the field; used to control the called-for artillery or mortar fire. Pronounced *'foe.'*
frag Fragmentation grenade; either the M-61 'pineapple' grenade or the M-67 'baseball' grenade. The later versions had a segmented wire coil compressed inside the body for greater fragmentation.
Freedom Bird Any aircraft used to fly a soldier home from overseas, usually a chartered civilian airliner.
freeway G.I. slang for a wide, well-used trail through the jungle. Usually indicated the presence of a large enemy unit. Also called a *'high-speed trail.'*

Gook G.I. slang for any Asian, usually used to refer to the enemy. Possibly derived from the Korean word *'miguk'* meaning 'country' or 'countryman.' The term has been in use by U.S. troops since the early twentieth century in the Philippines, Nicaragua, Korea and Vietnam.

grunt G.I. slang for an infantryman serving in the field.

gun bunny Infantry slang for an artillery crewman.

gunner The artilleryman who fires the howitzer, an M-60 or M-2 machine gunner or an M-79 grenade launcher gunner.

H&I fire Harassing and interdicting fire. Artillery or mortar fire used to disrupt the enemy's movements at night, sometimes fired at known or suspected trails or enemy unit positions.

HE High explosive; indicates a type of artillery or mortar round.

Hill xxx Hill plus a number used to indicate an individual hill or the hill's height in meters above sea level. Hill 937 indicated Dong Ap Bia (Hamburger Hill) at 937 meters (3073 feet) above sea level.

hooch or hutch A peasant's bamboo hut, a poncho shelter or a barracks at a base camp.

horn A radio or a radio handset as in, *'get on the horn.'*

hot LZ A landing zone where the enemy is waiting to fire on the helicopters and troops as they land.

Huey A Bell utility helicopter, type 1, model D or H; the standard troop-carrying, air ambulance or cargo helicopter.

in country The state of having entered Vietnam to serve your tour of duty; as in *"How long you been in country?"*

KBA Killed by artillery [fire].

KCS *Kit Carson Scout.* An enemy soldier who has surrendered to U.S. troops and has volunteered to serve as a scout for a U. S. unit.

KIA or KBHA Killed in action or killed by hostile action. Indicates official status of a soldier killed by the enemy in combat.

kill zone The area of an ambush where most of the fire is concentrated.

klick G.I. slang for a kilometer (1000 meters or .62 miles)

M-72 LAW Light anti-tank weapon; a rocket-propelled grenade. Because there were no enemy tanks in the 101st AO, they were used against bunkers and trench lines. Like the RPG but the M-72 cannot be re-loaded.

light on the skids Describes a helicopter that does not fully land, the pilot keeping the helicopter ready for instant take off.

log bird Logistics bird. A Huey being utilized in a resupply/cargo mode; an *'ass and trash'* mission.

LOH Light observation helicopter. A Hughes Aircraft OH-6 Cayuse sometimes armed with a 7-62mm mini-gun.

LP Listening post; usually three men with a radio positioned 50 to 100 meters outside an NDP to give warning of an approaching enemy.

LT G.I. slang for a first or second lieutenant, pronounced *'ell-tee.'*

LZ Landing zone. Any area large enough for helicopter to land, usually a clearing in the jungle wide enough to accommodate a Huey's 44-foot rotor span.

MA Mechanical ambush.

M-16 A light assault rifle, caliber 5.56mm with a 20-round detachable magazine; can be fired semi or full automatic. Carried by U.S. forces and their allies.

M-60 Light machine gun, caliber 7.62 x 51mm belt fed modeled after the German Wehrmacht MG-42 from WWII.

M-79 A grenade launcher, caliber 40 x 46mm break action, breech loaded. It fired He, WP, flechette, illumination or buck shot rounds. The HE round had to travel a minimum of 13 to 16 meters before arming itself.

MACV Military Assistance Command Vietnam

mad minute Firing all weapons in a unit for about one minute. A defensive action by a unit that suspects enemy presence around a perimeter.

meter A length of measurement equal to 39 inches or 3.28 feet.

MOS Military occupational specialty. Describes a soldiers' job. An example is an MOS of 11B10 (light weapons infantry), 11C10 (mortar crewman) or 11B40 (light weapons infantry sergeant).

NCO Non-commissioned officer. Sergeants in pay grades E-5 through E-9.

NVA North Vietnamese Army.

OCS Officer candidate school.

old man G.I. slang for the commanding officer of a unit.

one twenty-two A 122mm Katyuska tripod-launched rocket with an effective range of 11 kilometers or about 7 miles.

OP Observation post. A position taken away from the main troop position during daylight hours to give warning of approaching enemy.

OPCON Operational control. The headquarters which controls the movements of a unit, i.e.; 2-506 was under the OPCON of the 3rd Brigade during Texas Star.
P-38 G.I. slang for the small can opener packed in every box of C-ration.
pathfinder A soldier trained to control the flight of helicopters into and out of an LZ, firebase or base camp. Also called *blacks hats* because of the black baseball caps they wore.
PAVN People's Army of Vietnam. Formal name of the NVA.
Phantom Nick name for the F-4 fighter-bomber.
PFC Private first class; also, *proud fuckin' civilian.*
penetrator A torpedo-shaped device that can be lowered on a cable from a medevac helicopter through thick jungle canopy to evacuate a wounded man. I can carry three troops.
PX Post exchange, An army department store.
pink team A pair of helicopters, usually a Cobra and a LOH, used to scout out and then attack enemy troops or positions.
PRC-25 Portable radio communication, model 25. Called the *prick 25* by those who had to carry it, the radio weighed over 23 pounds and had a range of 3 to 4 miles under ideal conditions.
PRC-77 Portable radio communication, model 77. An up-grade of the PRC-25 with solid state electronics, could be used for encrypted, secure radio communication.
PZ Pickup zone. An area designated for helicopters to land and pick up troops for air movement.
red team A pair of Cobras used in a ground support role.

recon by fire Advancing while in a line abreast firing weapons to keep the enemy's heads town or to provoke them to fire back revealing their positions.
REMF Rear echelon mother fucker; a soldier stationed at a base camp as opposed to a grunt out in the jungle.
RIF Reconnaissance in force. A squad or larger patrol sent out from the main unit to scout terrain or locate the enemy.
ROTC Reserve Officers Training Corps. A program of military instruction at a college or university in which students receive a reserve commission upon graduation.
RPD *Ruchnoy Pulemyot Degtyaryova.* A Russian-made light machine gun, caliber 7.62 x 39mm, drum or belt-fed.
RPG Rocket propelled grenade. A Russian or Chinese-made shoulder-fired, tube-launched, fin-stabilized reloadable rocket with an effective range of 100 meters. Fires a B-40 rocket.
RTO Radio-telephone operator. The soldier responsible for carrying and using the radio.
Shake-n-bake G.I. slang for a graduate of the NCO Course and Army Infantry School, Fort Benning, Georgia or another military post depending on the MOS. Soldiers graduated as an E-5; the honor graduate received the rank of E-6.
sit rep Situation report, periodically sent by radio to advise higher headquarters of a unit's status.
Six Radio designation for the commanding officer of a unit.

Slick A Huey helicopter without machine gun or rocket pods attached to the fuselage. Used for troop movement or cargo, it had two M-60's mounted in the doors.
Snake G.I. slang for an AH-1G Cobra attack helicopter.
SOI Signal operating instructions for radio communications.
SP4 Specialist fourth class. An E-4, equivalent to a corporal but not considered an NCO.
SSG or SSGT Staff sergeant. An E-6, often used as a platoon sergeant or platoon leader in Vietnam.
TOC Tactical operations center, usually on a firebase; The headquarters for the infantry battalion operating around the firebase.
TOT Time on target. An artillery fire mission where shells are fired to hit the target at the same instant.
USARV United States Army Vietnam
Victor Charley Viet Cong or VC. A Vietnamese communist guerilla fighter. The phrase Viet Cong means *red Vietnamese* or Viet Communist.
WIA Wounded in action
WP White phosphorous or *willie pete.* An artillery round, rocket or bomb producing bright white smoke when it explodes. Used to mark a target or start a fire in the jungle.
XO Executive officer. The second in command of a military unit.

Chapter 1
VIETNAMIZATION

"Defeat doesn't finish a man, quit does. A man is not finished when he's defeated. He's finished when he quits." -- Richard M. Nixon, 37th President of the United States

Richard Milhous Nixon (1913-1994), while campaigning for the US presidency in 1968, promised voters that, if he were elected, he would end the Vietnam war and bring the troops home. Nixon took office in late January 1969 and in March of that year, Secretary of Defense Melvin Laird told President Nixon *"what we need is a term like 'Vietnamizing' [in order] to put the emphasis on the right issues."* Nixon liked the term and the United States policy for ending its' participation in the war in Southeast Asia officially became known as "Vietnamization."

Accordingly, President Nixon declared the first reduction in US troop strength in June 1969 – 25,000 soldiers were to be withdrawn by July. This left more than one half million troops still in Vietnam, so Nixon announced that a further 60,000 men would be withdrawn by December 1969.

In line with the reduction in troop numbers, the United States began meetings with the North Vietnamese government in Paris, France to negotiate a peace settlement. In Paris, the US negotiators developed and used a tactic known as the 'Madman Theory', an attempt to frighten the Hanoi government into a speedy peace settlement. The 'Madman Theory' was quite simple. It was an attempt to convince the North Vietnamese government that President Nixon hated communism so much and believed in the 'Domino Theory' so strongly that he was willing to use nuclear weapons against the North if they continued to prolong the war. The North Vietnamese discounted this ploy and the Paris peace talks dragged on for another three years.

There is little doubt that President Nixon developed and then implemented Vietnamization in response to increasing political pressure in the United States. The process of Vietnamization had three parts – first was the gradual withdrawal of US troops from South Vietnam; second was to continue and then increase the funding of the Army of the Republic of Vietnam (the ARVN) to the point that it could assume even more responsibility for the conduct of the war against the North. The US Army would train the ARVN to fight their own war in their own country. Third, the United States would honor all its treaty agreements.

Almost no one believed that the ARVN was then capable of turning back an all-out attack by the People's Army of Vietnam (the PAVN), more popularly known as the North Vietnamese Army or NVA. The ARVN had been relegated to and had been used as a secondary, back-up force after the US build up began in 1965. Most of the senior US military commanders believed that the ARVN, as it was in 1969, would only be able to maintain the *status quo* once all US troops were withdrawn. No one thought the ARVN had any offensive capability. Most assumed that the US would have to increase the level of training and supply the ARVN with more modern equipment if they were to have any hope of becoming a fighting force that could hold its own against or defeat the well-trained and increasingly well-equipped NVA.

Accordingly, at the direction of the White House, Secretary of Defense Laird prepared a specific time table for the orderly withdrawal of US combat troops in South Vietnam. Those US forces that remained in South Vietnam during the withdrawal process were to assume an advisory and support role to the ARVN and the South Vietnamese civilian government.

The US withdrawal began on July 1, 1969 with more withdrawal dates over the next three years – December 1970; June 1971 and December 1972. Many of the top military commanders were unhappy with the decision to withdraw US fighting forces; they believed that all they had fought for since 1965 would soon be lost. They knew the ARVN alone would not be able to defend South Vietnam against a combined NVA-Viet Cong attack like the one that occurred during Tet, 1968 and that the result would be the expansion of communism throughout southeast Asia – the very thing the US had fought against since the French were defeated in 1954.

From a purely military point of view, Vietnamization was foolish. But from a political standpoint, it was very understandable. The long, drawn out war had become extremely unpopular in the United States and elsewhere. Nixon's reputation would be greatly enhanced if he could manage to be the president who successfully guided the US out of the quagmire of the Vietnam War. President Nixon believed that Vietnamization would ensure that the ARVN would be left with more than sufficient training and support for it to be successful. Nixon needed to withdraw US forces for compelling political reasons but, on the other hand, he did not want to become known as the man who had abandoned the ARVN to stand alone against a strong enemy like the NVA.

To bolster the ARVN and serve as a first line of defense, the US Army began to recruit, organize and train civilian defense groups. The US unit that assumed most of the responsibility for training civilians at the hamlet/village level was the 5th Special Forces Group (the Green Berets). This unit had been in-country since 1962 with their primary mission being the creation and training of civilian security forces. Over the years, the Green Berets had worked with the Civilian Irregular Defense Group (CIDG), the National Police Field Forces and the Peoples Self Defense Force. These groups were mostly local villagers, familiar with the areas they would patrol and defend. Initially, they received 8 weeks training but as Vietnamization took effect, their training period was increased resulting in many of these units being up-graded to Ranger companies and battalions and attached to existing ARVN units. They were also formed into Regional and Provincial Forces. The CIDG training and subsequent transfer to the ARVN was completed by 1971 and the 5th Special Forces was withdrawn to the United States.

Despite these efforts, ARVN performance continued to be erratic and ARVN commanders often called for and relied on US combat forces to bail them out. The first big test for Vietnamization occurred in 1971 with Operation Lam Son 719. By then, US troop levels had been reduced to about 156,000. Lam Son 719 was an attack by ARVN forces into Laos with the goal of severing the Ho Chi Minh Trail. The incursion was a disaster for Vietnamization. The ARVN forces were routed and driven in total disarray back across the border. The next trial by fire for the ARVN came in 1972, during the so-called Easter Offensive. The NVA surprised ARVN forces by attacking into the northern provinces of South Vietnam with a conventional invasion of armored forces and ground troops. ARVN forces were only able to halt the invasion and push back the NVA when the US intervened with massive air strikes against NVA armored columns. The city of Quang Tri was destroyed in the heavy fighting just south of the DMZ.

Vietnamization ended on January 23, 1973 when a peace agreement was reached and a cease fire was declared between North and South Vietnam. The agreement stated that **all** US military forces had to leave South Vietnam and that no further military aid could be given to the South. The North agreed to uphold the cease fire, return all US prisoners of war to US control and end the infiltration of NVA forces into the South. On March 29, 1973 the United States Military Assistance Command, Vietnam was shut down and an era had ended.

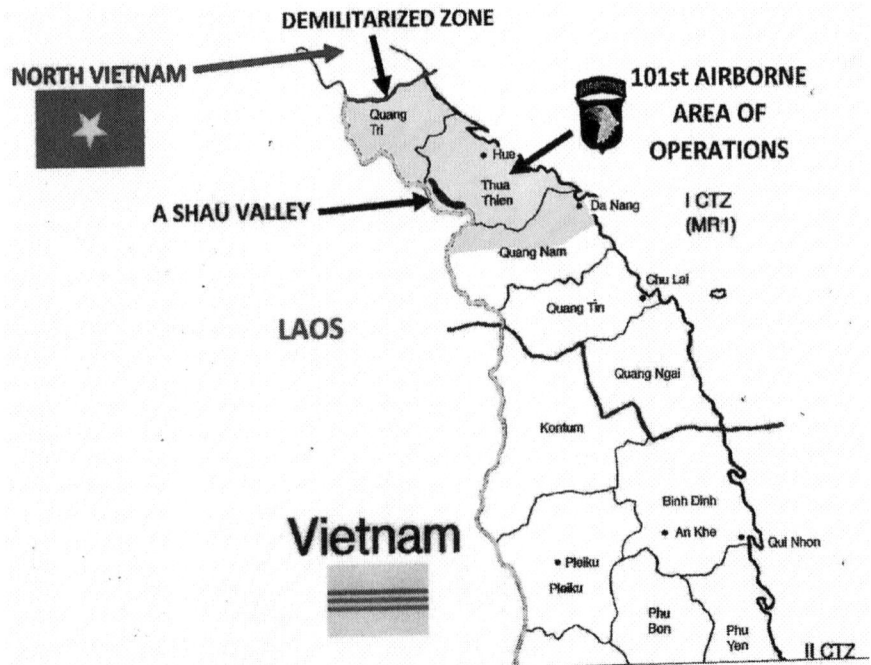

The above map illustrates the five northern-most provinces of South Vietnam which comprised I Corps Tactical Zone, re-named Military Region 1 in July 1970. The 101st Airborne's primary Area of Operations was in Quang Tri and Thua Thien Provinces and the northern portion of Quang Nam Province, shown shaded in light blue. The A Shau Valley is shown in green on the eastern border of Thua Thien Province with Laos.

Chapter 2
THE TACTICAL SITUATION IN I CORPS – 1970

"We are swatting flies in the South when we should be going after the manure pile in Hanoi." -- US Air Force General Curtis E. LeMay

In the spring and summer of 1970, the over-all strategy for the US Army in Vietnam and in I Corps (pronounced eye core) particularly was support for the on-going process of 'Vietnamization'. For this process to succeed, US forces had to buy time for the ARVN to recruit/draft new soldiers and to train them to proficiency with the newly-issued modern equipment flowing into the country. To this end, the US Army attacked NVA forces in their base areas along the Cambodian and Laotian borders and the 'Warehouse Area' in the infamous A Shau Valley. Enemy troop concentrations, once located, were attacked with air strikes, artillery and ground troops with the goal of destroying or dispersing them. These battles were conducted in the jungled, mountainous interior as far away as possible from the population centers in the lowlands along the coast of South Vietnam.

US and ARVN forces, in a long overdue attack, crossed the Cambodian border with South Vietnam on April 29, 1970 with the goal of destroying NVA base areas and troop concentrations. Before this, US policy had forbidden air strikes or ground attacks on these 'sanctuary areas' in Cambodia. Fully aware of this, NVA planners had taken advantage of this policy to build huge, protected logistical centers to support their war effort in South Vietnam. NVA troops would cross the border into South Vietnam, attack US and ARVN soldiers and base camps, then retreat into Cambodia where they were protected from retaliatory attacks. In World War II terms, this was the same as sending American troops to fight in Europe but forbidding them to cross the border into Germany to attack and destroy the heart of the problem.

The American publics' outrage and heavy Congressional pressure forced President Nixon to cancel the Cambodian 'incursion' and pull back US troops by June 30, 1970. Even though the operation had been largely successful, locating and destroying huge amounts of logistical supplies, the anti-war factions continued to accuse Nixon of 'widening the war'. To placate these very vocal anti-war critics, Nixon sped up the scheduled withdrawal of US troops from South Vietnam. However, President Nixon did not change his orders for US forces to aid the Republic of Vietnam in the Vietnamization process.

During the spring and summer of 1970, the only offensive campaign planned for the whole of South Vietnam by the US Military Assistance Command Vietnam (MACV) ordered the 101st Airborne Division, supported by the 1st ARVN Infantry Division, to attack NVA 'warehouse areas' located on the eastern side of the A Shau Valley near Co Pung Mountain, in the A Shau Valley itself and those portions of the Ho Chi Minh trail entering Quang Tri and Thua Thien Provinces from Laos. There was very little reliable intelligence regarding NVA troop concentrations in those areas.

The Paris Peace Talks had been in session for over a year so the North Vietnamese, wanting to negotiate from a position of strength, kept up the process of 'liberating' more and more areas of South Vietnam. The north's strategy did not include withdrawal of any troops from the south or any slackening of military operations.

The US plan included a requirement that ARVN and US forces operating in the mountains to the northeast of the A Shau Valley make a concerted effort to locate and destroy the large supply caches in the warehouse area and cut the communication lines of the 29th and 803rd NVA Regiments. To support these efforts, Fire Support Base (FSB) Ripcord was scheduled to be re-opened in March 1970. Ripcord had been designated as the key forward operations base during the planning for the 101st Airborne's summer campaign. FSB's Airborne, Bradley and Kathryn were scheduled to be opened, but only Kathryn was occupied though it was too far away to support operations around FSB Ripcord. The division commander had decided not to occupy Airborne and Bradley after the 3rd Brigade of the 101st encountered fierce resistance during the re-opening of FSB Ripcord. He did not want to spread his meager resources too thinly across the five northern-most provinces of I Corps.

Major General John M. Wright, commanding the 101st Airborne Division, ordered MACV's Operation Texas Star to begin on April 1, 1970. The 101st was to coordinate its operations with the ARVN 1st Infantry Division. In preparation for the start of Texas Star, patrol and reconnaissance actions began in March. The area of operations (AO) for the division was in the mountainous jungles of western Quang Tri and Thua Thien Provinces between the Song Bo and Rao Nai Rivers and the Laotian border. The mission was to engage the NVA in these remote areas to prevent attacks on the ARVN controlled population centers along the coast.

The main combat forces of the 101st Airborne Division were organized into three infantry brigades, each brigade normally having three infantry battalions. This force was airmobile and could be moved around the battlefield very quickly by the three helicopter battalions of the 101st Aviation Group. In 1970, three infantry battalions (1-327, 2-327, 2-502) were assigned to the first brigade, primarily operating in the southern part of Thua Thien Province, ranging into Quang Nam Province when necessary. One of the 1st Brigade's battalions was always committed to the Division Reserve as the Ready Reaction Force. The three infantry battalions (1-501, 2-501, 1-502) of the 2nd Brigade were assigned to pacification duties in the populated parts of eastern Thua Thien Province. The three infantry battalions of the 3rd Brigade (3-187, 1-506, 2-506) operated mostly in the northern and western portions of Thua Thien and Quang Tri Provinces.

The combat units of the division were ably supported by the 326th Engineer Battalion, the 326th Medical Battalion, the 501st Signal Battalion, five battalions (105mm and 155mm) of tube artillery and the 77th Aerial Rocket Artillery (Cobra helicopter gunships). Naval and Air Force fighter bombers, Air Force flare ships and 'Spooky' gunships armed with batteries of mini-guns were on call.

Because of the withdrawal of both the 1st and 3rd US Marine Divisions and the removal of the 1st Cavalry Division (Airmobile) from the northern provinces of South Vietnam, the 101st Airborne Division was left with a very large area of operations. The only other American combat unit in northern South Vietnam was the 1st Brigade (mechanized) of the 5th Infantry Division. Because this brigade was mechanized (tanks, armored personnel carriers and self-propelled tube artillery) it was necessarily confined to operations in the built-up areas. Due to the lack of improved roads, the 5th Infantry could not operate in the interior of I Corps. In an area where once three full US divisions had been heavily engaged, there was now only one US division and the number of NVA units operating against that division was rapidly increasing.

The NVA had moved engineer troops equipped with heavy road building equipment into the A Shau Valley and the 'Warehouse' area. The engineers could repair damaged or destroyed bridges and roadways nearly as fast as the Air Force could locate and bomb them. The NVA were experts at camouflage and many of the roads and paths making up the Ho Chi Minh Trail were so well hidden that it was nearly impossible to detect them from the air. And, as the U.S. Air Force was learning, how do you 'destroy' a dirt road?

North Vietnam's Central Committee of the Communist Party issued Resolution 18 in early 1970. In part, the resolution directed NVA forces to: *"Seize the initiative by launching a continuous series of attacks to kill large numbers of enemy troops and destroy large quantities of enemy military equipment and to resolutely defeat the enemy's tactics of 'garrisoning the high ground,' and 'keeping our forces at arm's length.' Our combat opponents in this effort would be the U.S. 101st Airborne Division and the puppet 1st [ARVN] Division. . .We would intensify the movement to shoot down enemy aircraft."* Hell On A Hill Top – page 43.

South Vietnam was made up of 44 provinces, but most of the American deaths and casualties in the Vietnam War were incurred in I Corps. Fifty-four percent (more than 31,000) of the 58,000-plus deaths in the Vietnam War were killed in the four northern-most provinces of South Vietnam. Arrayed against the 101st were two full NVA divisions: the 304B Division that had defeated the French in 1954 at Dien Bien Phu and the 324B Division. Each of these divisions had three full infantry regiments plus supporting artillery, anti-aircraft, engineer and Sapper battalions. So, in the spring and summer of 1970, the 101st Airborne Division, along with the ARVN 1st Division, faced the maelstrom of combat in the forbidding jungle covered mountains of northern I Corps alone.

Chapter 3
THE OPENING MOVES

. . . the last great Division fight of the war in Vietnam was a tactical success **attributable solely to the soldiers on the ground** *but a shameful operational and strategic blunder."* Brigadier General (ret.) James E. Mitchell, US Army

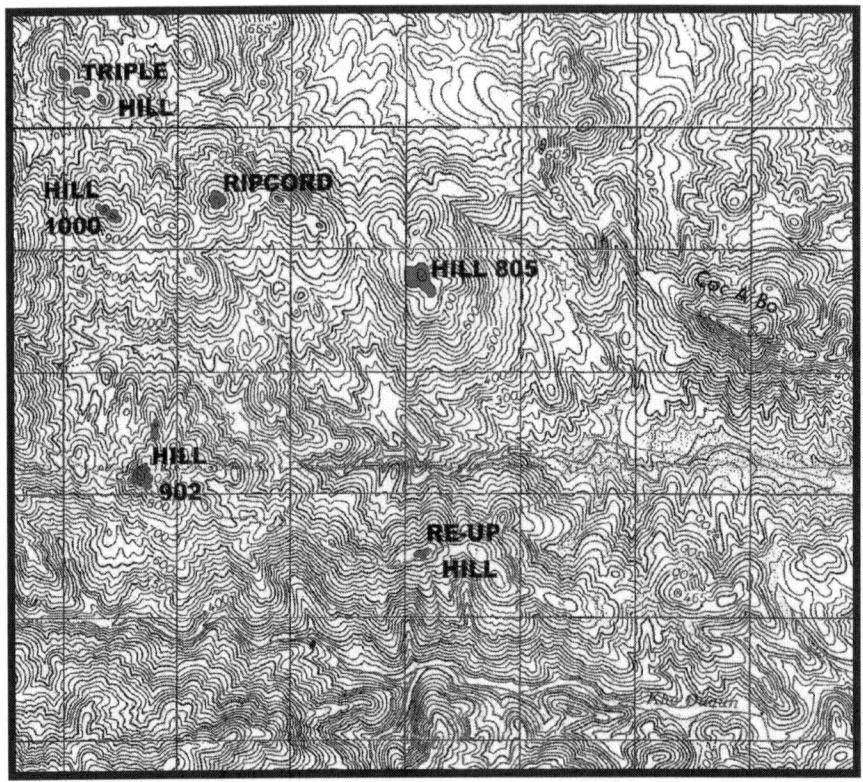

Enhanced detail from topographical map sheet 6441-4, series L7014, A Luoi District, Thua Thien Province, showing US positions outlined in blue with suspected or known NVA positions outlined in red. Map from authors collection. Enhanced map © 2017.

Air assaults into the Firebase Ripcord area by elements of the 101st Airborne's 3rd Brigade supported by the 1st Regiment of the ARVN 1st Infantry Division were delayed by the last of the northern monsoon weather until the middle of March 1970. The 'Currahees' of the 2nd Battalion, 506th Infantry (2-506) and the 4th Battalion, ARVN 1st Infantry Regiment (4-1) were ordered to conduct airmobile combat assaults into the area. The original firebase on Hill 927 had been opened by the 1st Cavalry Division in 1968 to support their assault into the A Shau Valley. When the hill was re-occupied by the 101st in 1969, it was named Fire Support Base (FSB) Ripcord.

Colonel William Bradley, who commanded 3rd Brigade at the time, thought that Hill 927 was an indefensible position because it was dominated by the two peaks of Hill 1000 only 1 klick to the west (see map above). Colonel Bradley believed that Hill 902 was a more easily defended place to open the new Firebase Ripcord and ordered an air assault to occupy that hill. Colonel Bradley, who had thoroughly studied reports of enemy activity in the area, advised Brigadier General Hennessey, the 101st Assistant Division Commander, that any attacks into the Ripcord area would more than likely meet with very heavy resistance. Bradley told Hennessey that if a single US battalion was sent into the area, the operation would not succeed unless more troops were made available. General Hennessey did not agree and the operation was ordered to proceed as planned with no additional troops allocated to the operation.

    A slight break in the monsoon weather occurred on March 12. Taking advantage of this, Captain Carmelito Arkangel, commanding Company B 2-506 landed on a ridge leading off to the southeast from the peak of Hill 902. After B/2-506 was safely down, two ARVN companies were inserted to the west of Hill 902 onto the 1,500-meter-long ridge leading up to Hill 1298, Coc Muen Mountain.

As Company A 2-506, commanded by Captain Albert Burkhart approached the peak of Hill 902, Burkhart saw that the jungle growth on the planned LZ was too thick to allow a helicopter to set down. This came as a surprise; not wanting to reveal the location of the landing, no detailed recon of the proposed LZ had been conducted prior to the mission's beginning. The battalion commander, LTC Andre Lucas and COL Bradley conferred and decided to divert the combat assault (CA) onto Hill 927, old FSB Ripcord. The 'slicks' (unarmed troop transports) carrying A/2-506 orbited in the area while the new LZ was prepped with rocket fire from supporting Cobra gunships. Finally, the ships carrying Company A approached the hilltop and, after the first few helicopters landed and the troops dispersed around the LZ, the following slicks began receiving heavy small arms fire from the west.

Captain Burkhart remembers that Alpha One got down onto the LZ without incident. As the following platoon began to land, heavy fire from NVA positions on the side of the hill came into the LZ, wounding one man. One of the helicopters dropping off troops was shot down, wounding the door gunner. Fortunately, the LZ was not blocked by the downed slick and the helicopters following it got down and dropped off their troops. The downed Huey was lifted out later by a CH-47 Chinook cargo helicopter.

Burkhart brought in his last platoon and, shortly after the last slick landed, dropped its troops and lifted off, the NVA fired about twelve 60mm mortar rounds that were off target by about 25 meters (about 80 feet) to the north. Burkhart then moved Alpha Four onto a small knoll to the north to try and spot where the mortar fire was coming from and to counter any movement by the NVA toward the LZ from that direction. About a half-hour later, 15 more mortar rounds came in on Alpha Four's position, killing LT Davis, Alpha Four's platoon leader and wounding four other men.

Captain Burkhart had ordered the last platoon of Company A to land on Hill 927 so that he would have his whole company on the ground. Burkhart then moved Alpha One off the LZ to a position about 400 meters to the west. Every slick that had come in to the LZ had been taking small arms fire from the north and west. When it began to get dark, he moved Alpha Four back up to the LZ and Company A, minus Alpha One, began to dig in for the night. Shortly afterward, another 10 rounds of 60mm mortar fire impacted on the LZ, wounding one man.

From their night defensive position (NDP) 400 meters to the west, several men from Alpha One spotted the muzzle flashes as the mortar was fired. Burkhart called in aerial rocket artillery (ARA) 'Cobra' gunships that thoroughly blasted the area with 2.75-inch rocket fire. No more mortar fire was received but the company, expecting a ground attack, remained on alert through-out the night and got very little sleep.

The next day, which happened to be Friday the 13th, Burkhart moved Alpha Three off Hill 927 toward a hill about 600 meters to the west. Alpha One moved back to the LZ on Hill 927 to secure it; then Burkhart and Alpha Two moved to join Alpha Three on their hill between Hill 927 and Hill 1000. Late that afternoon Alpha One, up on Hill 927, spotted an NVA mortar team setting up down in the valley to the west of Hill 927. Again, ARA was called in to blast the area with rocket fire. No mortar fire was received from that location, but as a precaution, Burkhart kept H and I (harassing and interdicting) fire from tube artillery coming in all night.

Just at dusk, a near-tragedy occurred. An ARVN 155mm battery, firing from near-by FSB O'Reilly got their coordinates mixed up and dropped four artillery rounds onto Burkhart's NDP site. Luckily, even though it was Friday the 13th, the big artillery rounds did no damage and the only casualties were a badly bruised leg and some sprained ankles incurred as everyone dove for cover.

The morning of March 14 Major Herbert Koenigsbauer, the 2-506 operations officer (S-3) called Burkhart on the voice-encrypted radio and told him that the ARVN had captured an NVA document on the 13th stating that an NVA battalion CP (command post) was in the jungle about 1,300 meters west of Company A's current location. The S-3 had planned to CA the entire company into the area to try and capture the enemy CP, but the monsoon weather returned and Burkhart's location was covered by low-hanging clouds and fog all that day. Low on rations, Burkhart asked for a re-supply. The 'log bird' (supply helicopter) managed to reach Company A by flying at tree-top level under the clouds. As the log bird hovered over Burkhart's position kicking out the supplies, a lone NVA fired an AK-47 at it, but did no damage.

On March 15, LTC Andre Lucas (call sign 'Black Spade') decided to withdraw Company A from the Hill 927/Ripcord area. While waiting for the extraction helicopters to arrive, Captain Burkhart decided to disband his 4th Platoon by integrating its few remaining men into the other three platoons. Most line companies in the 101st Airborne at that time had only three platoons; the fourth platoon's personnel were moved into an a 'heavy weapons/recon' company usually called Company E. This company operated the battalions' 81mm mortars, 90mm recoilless rifles and .50 caliber machine guns. They were usually stationed on the firebase supporting the parent battalions' operations. One platoon of Company E was customarily designated as the 'Recon Platoon' which regularly operated by itself, not attached to any of the line companies, A through D. Captain Burkhart's A/2-506 was unusual in that it still had a 4th Platoon.

Even with a 4th Platoon, Company A's field strength was only about 75 men and Black Spade had informed Burkhart that an entire enemy regiment (in this case, the 6th Infantry Regiment of the Independent Thua Thien Province Viet Cong Force) was operating in the area. Black Spade had decided to extract Company A and bring in 'Arc Light' (B-52 heavy bomber) missions to blanket the area with 1,000-pound bombs. So, after three days of fighting had failed to secure Hill 927, the troopers of A/2-506 were lifted off the hill. Further south, B/2-506 and the two ARVN companies were left in position to continue their patrol and ambush operations around Hill 902 and Coc Muen Mountain.

Heavy bombing by B-52 bombers, numerous tactical air strikes and artillery raids directing their fire at specific areas continued to pound the jungle around Hill 927. This was a necessary tactic and had a purpose; to keep the enemy off-balance and prevent him from consolidating his positions around the proposed site of the firebase. However, the tactic had a drawback; all that fire power concentrated in such a small area also told the NVA that the 101st Airborne would probably be coming back.

The 101st did come back; on Sunday March 29 C/2-506 made an air assault onto Hill 316 about seven klicks northeast of Hill 927 at YD416211. When the hill was secure, B Battery 2-319 Field Artillery, commanded by Captain David Rich, airlifted six 105mm howitzers onto the hill. In a very short time, Hill 316 was transformed into FSB Gladiator, ready to support operations in the Hill 927/FSB Ripcord area to the southwest.

Three days later, on Wednesday April 1, the official start date of Operation Texas Star, B/2-506, now commanded by Captain Bill Williams, made a combat assault onto Hill 927. As soon as the slicks carrying B Company came in to the LZ to land, enemy gunners began pummeling the hilltop with mortar, recoilless rifle and small arms fire. The fire came in from areas all around the hill and was intense, continuous and accurate. The NVA gunners had taken advantage of the lull in the fighting since March 15 to register their weapons on every foot of Hill 927. The NVA mortar crews 'walked' the

CH-47 Chinook heavy lift helicopters move 105mm howitzers and a basic load of ammunition onto a hill top in I Corps in March of 1970. First an infantry unit secured the hill, then the guns were brought in; instant firebase. Authors collection © 1970 and 2017 shells back and forth across the hilltop as the men of B/2-506 frantically dug in and tried to return the fire.

Lucas decided to re-enforce B Company, still under intense fire on Hill 927, with the 2-506 Recon Platoon, commanded by 1LT John Wilson. Wilson was a veteran of five months in-country but had only been in command of the Recon Platoon one day when they got the call to CA from Camp Evans onto Hill 927. As the slicks carrying the Recon Platoon approached the LZ on Hill 927, the NVA gunners increased the rate of fire coming into the blasted hilltop. The fire was so heavy that the helicopters could not land or even hover over the LZ. LT Wilson and 10 of his men managed to jump from low-flying Huey's as they slowly glided across the LZ. The other slicks, carrying the remainder of the Recon Platoon, had to return to Camp Evans to re-fuel.

Attempting to suppress some of the mortar fire, LTC Lucas airlifted Captain Rembert Rollison's D/2-506, into an LZ northeast of Hill 927. Lucas also moved Burkhart's A/2-506 onto a rocky hill about 700 meters east of B/2-506. Company A was mortared as soon as they came in but a Cobra gunship flying overhead spotted the NVA mortar out in the open on near-by Hill 805. The Cobra gunner fired his entire load of rockets at Hill 805 and obliterated the mortar position, causing several secondary explosions.

As dusk approached, the mortar fire petered out. Company B had suffered seven dead and twenty-one wounded, too many casualties for the company to hold the hill. Lucas ordered Company B, the officers from the battalion forward command post and the few men from the Recon Platoon to link up with Company A. As Williams, Company B and the others prepared to move, Williams called Captain Burkhart and asked him to send a detail from Company A up the ridge to guide them into Burkhart's positions, reducing the risk of a friendly fire incident. Burkhart refused.

LT Wilson and his Recon troops led the others on a halting, seven-hundred-meter march through the black night to Company A's hill. Artillery illumination flares were burning overhead and the men, hanging onto each other's rucksacks to stay in contact, moved slowly down the ridgeline, moving only in the dark when the overhead flares burned out.

The next day, the situation went from bad to worse. Thunderstorms moved in and the scheduled extraction of the battered Company B was cancelled. When the rain slowed to a drizzle, Wilson's 10-man recon team, covered by a heavy fog, moved up onto Hill 927 and recovered the dead left behind the night before, transferring them to a squad from Company A waiting on the ridge below Hill 927. As soon as Recon completed the gruesome task of retrieving the dead, Lucas ordered them back onto Hill 927. Wilson and five men were to remain on Hill 927 while the remaining five, covered by the fog, were to move onto Hill 1000 and mark the NVA mortar positions there for counter-battery fire. They tried, but when they got to the small knoll in the saddle between Hill 927 and Hill 1000 they ran into several AK-47's and an RPD machine gun. When they returned fire, their muzzle flashes in the fog revealed their positions to an NVA with an RPG. The high-powered rockets wounded two men and kept the small force from moving any further.

LT Wilson and his five men joined them and they broke contact, just vanishing into the fog. The wounded could not be evacuated because of the fog and, as they moved back, Wilson discovered that he had lost his SOI (signal operating instructions) book somewhere on Hill 927. Wilson wanted to go back to Hill 927 and look for the book, but the men balked. They were only a squad-sized unit and two of them were wounded. Wilson was adamant; he did not want to be the cause of the entire 101st Airborne having to change their radio codes. Reluctantly, the men agreed to follow Wilson back up the hill to look for the book.

As they moved through the fog, the point man found two NVA soldiers asleep in an old bunker. Wilson ran up and shot them with his silenced M-16. Even with the silenced M-16, they drew AK-47 fire and began to withdraw. An RPG came in and landed directly in front of Wilson and the point man, seriously wounding Wilson in the chest and head. Dragging him down the hill, they called for a Dust-off (medical evacuation helicopter) from Camp Evans. The pilot managed to get into the area but could not find them in the fog. The Recon team could not see the Huey but could hear him circling around them. They tried to direct him by sound but several attempts failed. Finally, the Dust-off, low on fuel, had to return to Camp Evans. When Wilson, desperately fighting for life, learned that the medevac had gone, he gave up and died.

Bad weather continued to dog the operation. Stranded in the fog, the three companies around Hill 927 began to run out of food and water. The troops shared what rations they had and cut bamboo stalks to get the water stored in the stalks. The weather cleared for a time on April 4, long enough for a Dust-off to evacuate the wounded recon troops. The log bird that came in to back-haul the dead drew mortar fire as the bodies were loaded aboard.

Inclement weather moved in again before Company B could be extracted or any supplies brought in. Company B moved off the rocky hill and linked up with Company D at the northern base of the ridge on which Hill 927 sat. The Air Force then tried dropping supplies into the area by parachute but the pallets were lost in the fog. Company D shared what rations they had with Company B.

■ ■ ■

The situation in the mountains just east of the A Shau Valley had been forced into a stalemate by the lingering monsoon weather. During the interval, BG John Hennessey, the assistant division commander for operations flew into Camp Evans for a strategy session with the 3rd Brigade commander, Colonel Bill Bradley and his staff. From the start, Bradley knew there would be a third assault. For that matter, there would be as many assaults as needed so that Ripcord would be open and ready to support the attack into the 'Warehouse Area' around Co Pung Mountain when the dry season finally came. Bradley later said that it wasn't just the 3rd Brigade, but the entire 101st and the 1st ARVN that were committed to cutting the NVA supply lines that ran through the deep jungle and mountains along the Laotian border. Hill 927/Ripcord was, literally, the only feasible place to build a firebase to support the coming operation, code named 'Operation Chicago Peak.'

The proposed site for the new FSB Ripcord was, indeed, strategically placed: 38 kilometers (24 miles) west of Hue; 12 klicks northwest of FSB Maureen; 12 klicks southeast of FSB O'Reilly; 5 klicks northwest of FSB Granite and 9 klicks north of Co Pung Mountain and the Warehouse Area. COL Bradley emphasized that the further west from Hue you went, the more dangerous it became and the more troops you needed. Bradley had three maneuver battalions on paper but only LTC Lucas' 2-506 'Currahee' Battalion was available for an attack into the Hill 927/Ripcord area of operations. The 1-506 was totally involved in protecting the string of firebases in the foothills above the populated areas and the 3-187 'Rakkasans' were completely committed to the pacification program in the villages along the coast since the battalion was almost destroyed on Dong Ap Bia (Hamburger Hill) in May 1969.

BG Hennessey committed LTC Bobby Brashear's 2-501 Geronimo Battalion, considered a very tough outfit, to the capture of Hill 927/Ripcord. The 2-501 was currently the division 'swing battalion'; it was always ready to move where it was most needed. COL Bradley was careful to point out to BG Hennessey that the division should move on Hill 927/Ripcord in strength or not go at all. Hennessey listened because Bradley was a thoroughly professional officer and some considered him the best brigade commander in the 101st.

The brain-storming session continued with a briefing from the 3rd Brigade intelligence officer who gave a detailed analysis of the enemy troop strength in the A Shau Valley and in the mountains around Hill 927/Ripcord. The facts were clear; the NVA was advancing from Laos into the A Shau in battalion and regimental-sized units and if the 101st did not respond with equal force, Hill 927 was going to become untenable.

The final recommendations made to BG Hennessey were that the 101st use its airmobile capabilities to hit the NVA where they were the weakest, at the points where they were trying to infiltrate through the foothills into the populated lowlands. There, the NVA was operating at the end of a long supply line and, since the division already had a string of occupied firebases in place, it was easy to support operations against the enemy. The last recommendation made was that the 101st go back in and re-occupy Hill 927/Ripcord and hit the enemy in this vital area.

When the briefing was finally finished, all BG Hennessey said was, "Well, you're going back to Ripcord."

Left: Brigadier General John Hennessey, Assistant Division Commander. **Right:** Colonel William Bradley, 3rd Brigade Commander. Photos from 101st Airborne Yearbook for 1969, authors collection.

Chapter 4
__BUILDING RIPCORD__

"There be no sandbagged bunkers on this firebase. That is the way the Army does it, but when you see a sandbagged bunker, you're looking at a death trap. On my firebase, we have fighting positions – we don't have no sandbags stacked up so the gooks know where to shoot." Captain Isabelino Vazquez-Rodriguez, C/2-506 Infantry 101st Airborne

Even though the 2-506 had been prevented from occupying Hill 927 and building FSB Ripcord by enemy action and the foul monsoon weather, they continued to patrol the mountains and jungle around the hill. The 101st was determined to open a firebase in the heart of the NVA's 'Warehouse Area' for several reasons. The very existence of the base would draw the NVA like ants to a picnic, giving the division a chance to bring its considerable firepower to bear on concentrations of enemy troops as they gathered to attack the firebase.

Ripcord would act as a forward logistics base and as fire support for assaults into the A Shau Valley and Co Pung Mountain areas. Any enemy troops destroyed or dispersed by the 101st around Ripcord would lessen the threat to the populated areas in the lowlands and along the coast.

To prepare for the coming third assault onto Hill 927/Ripcord, LTC Lucas spread out his companies and ordered them to find and destroy the NVA mortar positions around the site of Ripcord. On April 6, two platoons from Company C walked into a large bunker complex in the saddle between Hill 927/Ripcord and Hill 1000. A heavy fire fight developed and, pinned down, they had to dig in where they were as night fell. 1Lt Hawkins, as acting company commander, took charge and blasted the enemy positions with carefully placed artillery fire. When Hawkins called in a Dust-off for his wounded the next morning, they came under fire from NVA positions on Hill 927/Ripcord itself.

The enemy troops the 2-506 were encountering were well equipped. Company D, moving toward Hill 805, killed a lone NVA who had tossed a grenade at them and tried to run. The soldier was carrying an AK-47, extra magazines, grenades, web gear and pack, an extra uniform and a rain poncho. He had a map of the area and documents identifying him as the leader of a 7-man squad equipped with RPG launchers.

A break in the monsoon weather allowed the 2-501, the division reserve, to be moved into the area. Company D from the 2-501 landed on a hot LZ on the summit of Hill 902. After securing the LZ, Captain Christopher Straub immediately sent Delta One on a RIF (recon in force) up the ridge leading to Hill 1298 (Coc Muen) where they found an un-occupied NVA camp. As they were setting up security, an NVA squad walked unaware into the American unit. Their point man killed, the rest of the enemy squad fled back up the ridgeline toward Hill 1298. Delta One chased them for 6 hours before finding another base camp.

Passing through the camp, they moved on up the ridge to a small knoll. The platoon leader, 1Lt Terry Palm sensed an ambush and ordered his men to take cover. No sooner had they done so when the NVA blew a large claymore mine and pelted them with satchel charges. Palm's quick thinking had saved a lot of casualties. Delta One put out a very heavy return fire and withdraw back down the ridge to an NDP position with all personnel and equipment accounted for.

Small, quick contacts with enemy troops continued all over the area for the next two days. During this time, likely mortar positions and base camp sites were blasted with tactical air strikes, artillery and ARA. Enemy resistance tapered off. With American units spread all around the area on high ground on the look-out for mortar sites, it was time to take Ripcord.

LTC Lucas picked 1Lt Hawkins and Company C for the third assault on the hill. Company C was already perfectly positioned for the assault with their NDP about halfway up the south slope of Hill 927. They would be supported by Rollison's Company D. Hawkins began moving his men into their assault positions while it was still dark. After a quick pre-assault artillery bombardment at first light on April 11, the attack began. No enemy fire greeted them as they moved into the open and advanced into the heart of the firebase. Hawkins men nervously checked the area for booby traps and found none. 1LT Michael Anderson and his pathfinders were airlifted in to control the numerous helicopter sorties needed to lift in the equipment necessary to open a firebase.

The troops on the hilltop anxiously watched as the first big Chinook hovered over the LZ with an engineer bulldozer slung underneath. No mortar rounds or ground fire came in at all; the NVA did not contest the third attack in any way. The pathfinder team set up their base of operations next to the huge boulder at the top of the hill because it offered the best view for controlling the hundreds of helicopter flights that would be coming in and out of Ripcord.

That afternoon, the hard work of opening a firebase began. Major Sidney Davis, the 2-506 executive officer (second-in-command) flew out to Ripcord to begin the work of opening the battalion CP (command post). On his second tour in Vietnam, Davis knew what he was doing when he ordered Hawkins and Company C to get a concertina (barbed wire) barrier in place around the perimeter of Ripcord before nightfall. Hawkins protested that he did not have the proper equipment (hammers, shovels and gloves) needed to string concertina wire. Davis jumped all over him, telling him that there were NVA all over the area and he should have his men wrap their hands in sand bags and use the flat side of axes as hammers. Davis wanted the wire in place and would accept no excuse. Chastened, Hawkins and his men labored furiously and, by dusk, had one row of concertina wire in place and had started on another.

Bad weather moved in again, shrouding the hill in clouds and fog for the next five days, preventing the insertion of the 105 mm howitzers of Battery B/2-319th Artillery. The battalions' 81 mm mortar battery had been emplaced and were constantly firing. The battalion chaplain, Captain Leroy Fox managed to get into Ripcord and found the morale at a low ebb. The base was socked in until nearly noon every day and there was incoming. The days were spent digging holes, filling sandbags and stringing concertina then pulling guard duty all night. When the fog burned off, the heat was merciless and the men were exhausted. 1Lt James Campbell, Company C's second platoon leader, had men coming to him begging to be sent off the hill on the next combat patrol. They were willing to do almost anything to get away from the endless labor involved in setting up a major firebase. Chaplain Fox reported all this to LTC Lucas but there was not a lot Lucas could do about it. Ripcord had to be built and properly secured; the work went on.

Captain Vasquez-Rodriguez, CO of Company C, returned from his R&R and assumed responsibility for the construction of Ripcords' perimeter defenses. Vasquez, a tough, no nonsense soldier, had served several tours with the Green Berets in their border outposts. His idea of a perimeter bunker was radically different from standard US Army practice. Most army base camps and firebases used huge bunkers constructed of timber and sand bags piled up above ground level, an inviting target for an NVA soldier armed with an RPG. Vasquez told his men that those types of bunkers were death traps and he would not allow them on 'his' firebase.

Instead, Vasquez had his men dig L-shaped trenches hidden among the tree stumps scattered around the perimeter. The bottom of the 'L' was large enough to hold three men abreast and was used as a fighting position. The perpendicular leg of the 'L' was used as a sleeping position, large enough for two men to lie down with the third man on guard duty at the bottom of the 'L'. The fighting leg was open but the sleeping position had overhead cover made of PSP (pierced steel planking) covered with sand bags and a layer of earth. There were no sand bags piled up above ground level, so the whole thing blended in with the bare ground of the hillside.

They continued to string concertina wire around the perimeter, the second-most hated job on a firebase; the first being burning the contents of the latrine barrels. They laid two rolls of concertina wire side-by-side with a third stacked on top. All of it was tied down so sappers could not crawl underneath. Other rolls of concertina were mashed down into the gullies and ravines on the hillside, tied down to keep it in place. When finally finished, the wire barrier was 50 meters (164 feet) wide and nearly 3 meters (10 feet) high. The wire had hundreds of trip flares and claymore mines scattered through it, the detonating wires leading back to the fighting positions carefully covered with dirt.

Another special forces innovation used by Vasquez was a fifty-five-gallon fuel barrel placed in front of every fighting position full of a thickened fuel mixture called 'Phou gas', like napalm. The barrels, buried at a 45° angle with the open end pointed downhill toward the wire, were ignited by a claymore mine placed at the bottom of the barrel. Setting one off blew a spectacular display of burning fuel out into the wire.

The main area of FSB Ripcord was about the size of four football fields and shaped like a rough figure eight. The base had two levels, an upper and a lower. The 105mm battery was emplaced on the higher, southeastern level about the size of a football field. The main logistics LZ was at the far end of this level next to the ammunition supply point for the l05's. This LZ was used for the many daily flights of helicopters bringing in beans, bullets and bandages as well as personnel.

There was a saddle between the southeastern level and the lower, smaller northeastern tier. This area, once occupied by an ARVN 105mm battery, was taken over by the 155mm howitzers of A Battery 2-11 Field Artillery when the ARVN battery moved to FSB O'Reilly.

The saddle rose to a small knoll with a huge boulder at the top that could be seen from all over the firebase. It was called 'Impact Rock' because of the shrapnel scars on its side. The NVA gunners were apparently using the boulder as an aiming point for their incoming mortar rounds. Adjacent to Impact Rock, an M55 four-barreled 'Quad-50' anti-aircraft machine gun had been emplaced. Nearby, a second LZ had been prepared with sand bagged blivets containing JP4 aviation fuel for emergency refueling of helicopters.

By the end of April, the once-bare hilltop had become a formidable position which would have cost the NVA heavy casualties had they chosen to attack with a ground assault They never attempted such an assault, choosing instead to bombard Ripcord with a steadily increasing barrage of RPG's, 82mm and 120mm heavy mortars and 57 and 75mm recoilless rifle fire. It took about two months for the NVA to marshal and move the weapons into place for the bombardment, but when they did, Ripcord quickly became an untenable position.

155mm howitzers of A Battery 2-11 Field Artillery in place on Ripcord with 'Impact Rock' visible in the background. The red and white pole is an 'aiming stake' used to aid gunners in quickly lining up a gun on a target that was frequently fired at. Photo from alphaavengers.com/Anthony Critchlow.

M55 Quad 50 'Blood, Sweat and Tears' on Firebase Ripcord, 1970. Photo by Jack Wilhite 2-506, 3rd Brigade, 101st Airborne Division.

Chapter 5
THE FIGHT ON 'RE-UP' HILL

"I learned perhaps the most valuable lesson of my life as a soldier that night [on 'Re-Up' Hill] and that is American soldiers, above all else, fight for each other"
Then-Captain Ed Mitchell, commanding A/2-501 Infantry, 101st Airborne Division

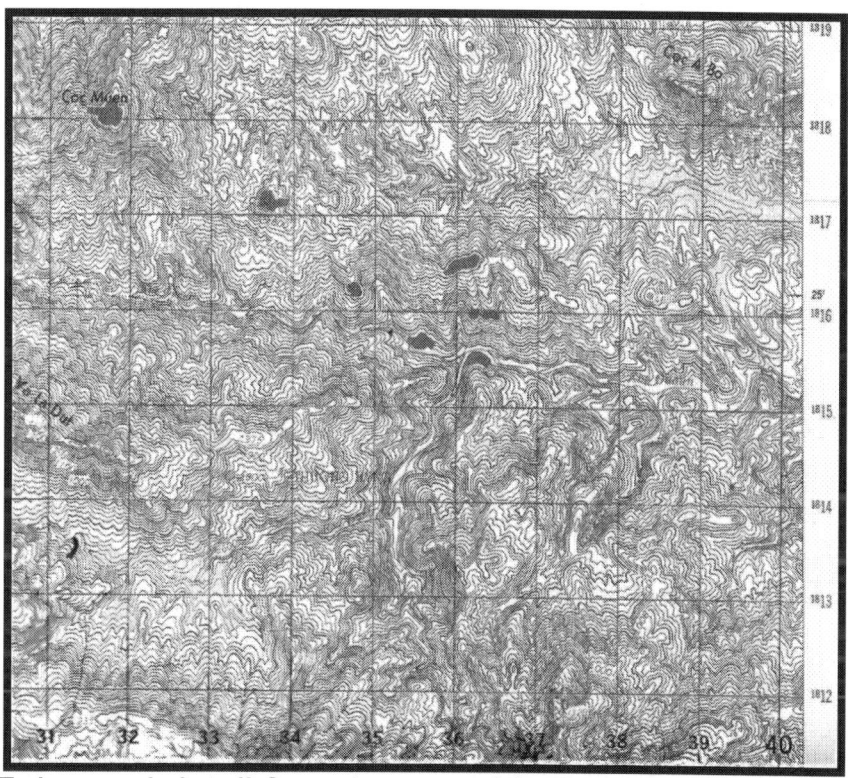

Enhanced detail from topographical map sheet 6441-4, series L7014 A Luoi District of Thua Thien Province showing A 2-501 positions highlighted in blue. Trails and suspected NVA positions highlighted in red. Map from author's collection. Enhanced map © 2017.

The build-up of US forces in the jungle-covered hills surrounding FSB Ripcord continued into April. Around noon on 8 April, A/2-501 received a movement order and a new mission. They were to be moved by air into a new area of operations code-named Pear. Company A's new mission was to "locate and destroy enemy forces, base camps and cache sites."

Accordingly, Company A clambered aboard the lift ships at a PZ (pick-up zone) at YD498282 near FSB Jack in Quang Tri Province. The flight of slicks, each carrying five heavily loaded infantrymen and a four-man crew, circled over the low lands as they gained altitude. Taking a westerly heading, they moved toward the high chain of mountains forming the eastern side of the A Shau Valley.

Captain James Edwin 'Ed' Mitchell had been in command of Company A only since February. As the flight of Huey's flew over the towering jungle-clad mountains, Captain Mitchell recalls admiring the beauty of the scene passing below. Heading toward their new LZ at YD337172 on the peak of Hill 902, the men savored the cool air rushing into the cabin through the open doors of the aircraft.

The LZ ahead was already secured by the 2-501 Recon Platoon, who had combat assaulted onto Hill 902 earlier that day. The lift ships slowed from their 80-knot cruising speed and began the slow, careful approach to the LZ. The slicks headed directly for the hill top, not having to loiter while they waited for the LZ to be prepped with artillery shells and aerial rocket artillery from the escorting Cobra gunships.

Company A hit the LZ without incident, formed up and quickly began their move to the east-southeast along a wide, well-used trail running along the ridgetop. The ridge was only 10 to 15 meters wide at its widest part and fell steeply away on both its north and south sides. The Khe Ouaun River flowed through a deep gorge at the bottom of the southern slope of the ridge. The slopes of the ridge were covered with primary jungle growth, characterized by tall trees and underbrush.

The company objective for the day was a trail junction at YD362165 on top of a low hill almost three klicks from the LZ on Hill 902. Surrounded by high ground on all sides, Captain Mitchell did not consider the trail junction to be a good place for his overnight position, but he had his orders. Mitchell told the point platoon to move cautiously, sweeping the sides of the ridge as they went because Mitchell wanted the way thoroughly checked out in case the company had to move back to the LZ on Hill 902 in a hurry. His intention was to set up the company NDP right at the trail junction before sunset that evening.

About one klick below the LZ, the company's movement down the trail suddenly stopped. When they didn't begin to move right away, Captain Mitchell went forward from his position in the middle of the column to check things out. At the point of the column, Mitchell found that his senior 'Kit Carson Scout', called Ki, had balked and refused to go any further. There was a small trail leading south down the side of the steep ridge. The frightened scout pointed to a sign on a tree at the trail junction. Written in Vietnamese, the sign read," this way to the mess hall."

Because of the wide, well-used trail and the sign so conspicuously posted, it was determined that a large NVA unit probably had its headquarters in the area. In his pidgin English, KCS Ki kept repeating "beau coup VC! Beau coup VC!" meaning a lot of enemy troops were in the area. He refused to go any further.

After fifteen or twenty minutes of discussion with Ki through Mitchell's interpreter SGT Tui, Ki was finally persuaded to go on with the mission. Ki was adamant in his belief that they were moving into an area unlike anyplace they had previously operated in. It was an AO that the NVA felt they owned and they would vigorously defend it.

When they got underway again, several of the men noticed old-fashioned porcelain electrical insulators fastened to trees along the trail. There was no wire attached to them but it was clear they had been put in place so the NVA headquarters could have land line communications with its subordinate units.

Company A arrived at the trail junction late in the afternoon of 8 April without contacting the enemy or even finding fresh signs of NVA activity. The three platoons immediately formed a perimeter around the small hill where the two trails branched off. The main trail angled northeast and downhill to a small river flowing through a valley below Hill 805 and Coc A Bo mountain. The other trail headed south down the precipitous side of the ridge into the steep-walled valley where the Khe Ouaun river ran.

The area Company A chose to defend was covered with many old fighting positions, most of which were partially filled in. The holes appeared to have been dug by the ARVN or the NVA because they were far too small for a GI to use and were useless for Company A's purposes. Captain Mitchell adjusted the perimeter to fit the terrain and they dug in as quietly as possible. Right at dusk, trip flares and claymore mines were put in place around the perimeter and Company A's first day in the new AO ended uneventfully.

That changed at around 2200 hours when one of the company CP radio operators told Captain Mitchell that the S-3 (battalion operations officer) wanted to talk to him. This officer, Major O'Connell, was at the tactical CP up on Hill 902. O'Connell asked Mitchell how long it would take Company A to move back to Hill 902? Mitchell was startled for it meant trying to quietly break down Company A-sized NDP in total darkness, then moving back up the steep trail to link up with the tactical CP and Recon on Hill 902.

After a long pause, Mitchell jokingly told the S-3 "About two days, Sir". With no comment on the joke, Major O'Connell told Mitchell to break down his NDP and move as quickly as possible to the LZ on Hill 902.

The platoon leaders and platoon sergeants did not question Mitchell's order to break down the CP. The soldiers silently stowed their personal gear in their ruck sacks, gathered their ammo and retrieved the trip flares and claymore mines. They were ready to move in less than an hour.

They began their move back up the ridge about midnight and made the march without detection by the NVA. As they neared Recon's position on Hill 902, Mitchell asked for a two-man team from Recon to meet them on the trail and guide them through Recon's positions on the hill to the west side of the LZ. The linkup was made with no undue confusion or 'friendly fire' incidents.

At first light on 9 April, Company A began moving northwest up the long ridgeline toward the summit of Coc Muen mountain at YD317181 and their new AO. Their mission remained the same: locate and destroy enemy forces, base camps and cache sites along the ridge leading to the top of Coc Muen, also known as Hill 1298. After moving less than a klick from the LZ on Hill 902, Captain Mitchell halted his exhausted company and formed a hasty defense perimeter so they could get some rest. The two-kilometer climb to the top of Coc Muen would be a grueling tactical assault for the grunts, each man carrying 80 to 100 pounds of equipment. Mitchell wanted to rest his men as much as possible before they began the ascent because he did not want to risk running into the NVA near Coc Muen's summit with Company A exhausted from the steep climb and lack of sleep.

Company A moved out of their hasty perimeter in the early morning of 10 April. They moved slowly up the ridge, clearing the trail and their flanks as they went. They met no NVA and closed on the top of Hill 1298 in the late afternoon. Rain and fog moved in, making the last few hundred meters of steep trail a muddy, slippery mess for the heavily-laden infantrymen.

They were surprised at how small the actual summit of Coc Muen was. Mitchell had expected to find an LZ on the summit; instead he found the top covered with thick underbrush. There were old, shallow fighting positions scattered around the top of Coc Muen. In a pouring rain, they formed a perimeter around the military crest and prepared positions for what would turn into a lengthy stay on Hill 1298.

For the next six days, it was impossible to reach Company A's position on Coc Muen by helicopter. When the atmosphere cooled at night, the clouds dropped down into the valleys and they could see stars. As the atmosphere heated up after sunrise, the clouds and fog rose out of the valleys and completely covered the peak of Coc Muen. They could hear helicopters down in the valley, but they were totally isolated by fog and an incessant, drizzling rain. They began to run out of food, but caught enough rain in their ponchos to keep their canteens filled. Company A just sat there, soaking wet, cold and hungry. They sent out occasional recon patrols to maintain security but saw no sign of the NVA.

Finally, on 15 April, a break in the miserable weather occurred and a very welcome 'log bird' full of C rations, radio batteries and other necessary supplies got through to the rain-soaked hilltop. Captain Mitchell expected another change of mission as the weather rapidly improved. Sure enough, late on the 15th, Mitchell received word that Company A would be air assaulted from Coc Muen the next day to a small LZ at YD362187 on the southern slope of Hill 805. The actual LZ turned out to be at YD361175 about 1 klick southwest of Hill 805. This LZ was on a small, narrow hill surrounded by higher terrain and only partially cleared of debris. The LZ itself was surrounded by tall thick jungle growth with barely enough clearance for a Huey's 44-foot rotor span.

Thankfully, the LZ was cold and they completed the assault without incident. Their new mission was to move quickly south about a kilometer to the trail junction at YD 362165 they had last occupied on 8 April. As soon as all his troops were on the ground, Mitchell began to move the company south. Because the LZ was so small, it was crowded with troops and made an inviting target for NVA mortar fire. The plan was to move the company by platoon in column down the south slope of the ridge the LZ was on and across the intermittent stream running through the valley before nightfall. Mitchell wanted to conceal the company for the night on the north slope of the ridge holding the trail junction. Company B was in position at the trail junction at that time but they would move east early on the morning of 17 April. Company A would then move up the ridge to the trail junction and the old LZ close by. Mitchel coordinated his move with the commander of Company B; he wanted to make sure B Company knew his exact position to avoid any chance of B Company defensive fires hitting Company A.

It was a quiet night for Company A but right at first light on 17 April, Company B came under attack. From their NDP 600 meters north of Company B, Company A could hear M-16 and M-60 fire as well as sharp explosions from grenades and claymore mines. They also heard what seemed to be NVA mortar rounds falling on Company B. Mitchell raised the Company B commander, Captain Bob Stanton, on the radio to ask if they needed help; Stanton replied "No."

The sudden attack ended in about an hour with the NVA withdrawing south. Tactical air strikes and ARA were brought in on suspected NVA withdrawal routes and medevacs called in. The probe had been short but violent. B Company had several wounded and CPL Norman D. Peery was killed.

Company A moved up the steep slope of the ridge and briefly linked up with Company B. Captain Stanton was still busy directing air strikes onto a small hill southeast of the trail junction near YD368163. As Company B began moving off the trail junction to the east, Company A moved in and set up a hasty defensive perimeter.

After setting up a rough perimeter, Captain Mitchell sent out security patrols to probe south in the direction the NVA had withdrawn. The platoon leaders and platoon NCO's moved about assessing how best to distribute the 130 men of Company A around the perimeter to afford the best coverage of the terrain. Moving the men into position, they established platoon boundaries and selected sectors of fire for each fighting position and for the crew served weapons.

Captain Mitchell was studying his map to try and determine the mostly likely places the NVA would use to establish their base camps. He had no specific knowledge of the enemy forces he was facing. He knew the NVA did not have that problem; they knew right where Company A was and their exact strength. Mitchell knew his one big advantage was Company A's ability to maneuver and the enormous firepower he had available only a radio-call away. The key terrain for Mitchell was the trail junction and the LZ nearby. From his position, he had a clear view of the valleys and ridges to the south and east. He knew the NVA needed access to water just as he did and determined that their positions would be near the Khe Ouaun river in the valley to the south. Mitchell did not know this, but division intelligence had determined that the 803rd NVA Regiment had its headquarters right in that same area Mitchell thought was likely to be occupied by enemy troops.

Later that day, Company A came under a sudden 60mm mortar attack. Their foxholes were completed for the most part and the men scrambled for cover. The mortar was so close that they could hear the 'BANG' as the rounds left the tube. Captain Mitchell gathered all the M-79 grenadiers on the south side of their perimeter and fired several volleys of 40mm grenades toward the sound of the mortar tube; the mortar stopped firing quickly. (B and C Companies, 2-502, would use this technique on 29 April while attacking a large bunker complex on Hill 714).

Because of the attack on B Company's perimeter that morning, Captain Mitchell and the artillery FO (forward observer) 1LT Russ Cook, spent a lot of time adjusting 105mm defensive fire to 'danger close' around their perimeter. They also plotted pre-planned 155mm fire on the south slope of the ridge to fall between their perimeter and the Khe Ouaun river in the valley below.

On the morning of 18 April, Alpha Two began a RIF (reconnaissance in force) down the south slope of the ridge, following the suspected route of withdrawal used by the NVA force that had attacked B Company the morning before. Alpha Two had the point, followed by Alpha One. Captain Mitchell traveled with Alpha One. The terrain was rough and steep and the point team angled to the east trying to find an easier route. When they came to a very steep ravine, the point man halted, telling his squad leader that he felt the NVA had set up an ambush at the ravine. Ordered to cross, the point man made it across the ravine before the NVA opened fire. It was a short, violent fight and Alpha Two lost two wounded but SGT Michael J. Vagnone and SP4 Robert L. Dangberg were killed.

Mitchell sent Alpha One toward the ambush with orders to find the NVA and destroy them. The point man for Alpha One spotted the NVA and opened fire, killing one NVA soldier. A 'pink team' (a Cobra and a LOH) was orbiting overhead and they were called in for 'danger close' rocket attacks on the NVA positions. The Cobras also engaged likely NVA positions south of where Alpha Two first made contact.

Captain Mitchell ordered both platoons to join up and form a perimeter so they could evacuate their wounded. They accomplished this as darkness fell and the Dust-off helicopters had to find them in the dark. They marked their position with strobe lights set in up-turned helmets and one man was evacuated. A second Dust-off arrived and began to hover, dropping the jungle penetrator down through the canopy. The remaining wounded man, who was unconscious, was strapped onto the penetrator and hoisted up. Mitchell got a radio call from one of the pilots who said they were taking fire and had to break station. The cable was cut and the wounded man plummeted to the ground still strapped to the jungle penetrator. The medics rushed to the fallen man, expecting to find him dead, killed by the fall. To their surprise, he was still alive! Another medevac helicopter was called and this time the wounded man was evacuated safely.

It was now pitch black and the two platoons were faced with a difficult climb back up the ridge carrying the two dead men. Captain Mitchell decided to remain on the slope with Alpha One and Two because of the difficulty of moving up the steep, thickly forested slope in the dark. They waited tensely for an NVA attack that never came. Mitchell and Cook kept both 105 and 155mm artillery falling south of their position all during the night. Big 155mm illumination flares were called in, but they were on the 'gun-target line' and the big aluminum canisters that had held the illumination rounds kept falling on their position.

On Sunday 19 April, Company A's Alpha Two and Three moved south down the ridge to attack the NVA and attempt to destroy their base camp and cache sites. Alpha One remained at the NDP site to secure Company A's base and act as a reserve if needed. Because of the difficult terrain, the two platoons moved down the slope in column, one behind the other. Mitchell told the lead platoon to advance until contact, then they were to maneuver their squads to place the maximum fire on the enemy. The platoon leader was directed to use indirect fire (artillery) to help fix the NVA in place and prevent the enemy from withdrawing.

The move south was slow and cautious, sometimes using the NVA trail or moving parallel to it. During one of the frequent halts, the point team squad leader SSGT Dean L. Frey came to confer with Captain Mitchell about the terrain ahead. During this conference, Frey's point team made contact and a stiff fire fight began. SSGT Frey left at a run to rejoin his squad but was killed on his way back down.

Alpha Three had discovered at least a platoon-sized bunker complex and Mitchell knew they would not be able to fight through the complex and destroy it before darkness came. Reports came in that the enemy was fighting from large 'A-frame' bunkers with numerous 'spider hole' fighting positions from which they could pop up and fire on Alpha Three's troopers as they tried to advance.

A-frame bunkers were very strong and were made by lashing logs together in an upside down 'V' shape. These were then lowered into a previously dug hole and covered over with earth and camouflaging vegetation. Once completed, these bunkers were very hard to spot and difficult to destroy.

During the fight, one of Company A's soldiers crawled close to enough to spot an enemy soldier fighting from one of the bunkers. The NVA would pop out of the bunker, fire a burst from his automatic weapon and drop down again. The GI, one of Mitchell's RTO's (radio-telephone operator), managed to toss two grenades into the bunker. He then crawled forward into the bunkers. When he came back out, he was dragging the dead NVA with him.

Right after that, the NVA withdrew and Mitchell decided to withdraw from the bunkers, evacuate his wounded and call in massive amounts of indirect fire onto the well-fortified bunker complex. They would then move back to the NDP site on the ridge for resupply and plan how to destroy the well dug in base camp. Back at the NDP, Mitchell decided not to order another ground attack until he had hit the base camp with artillery, aerial rocket artillery and tactical air strikes. He would then move back down the slope and kill any NVA left and destroy the bunkers completely.

All that night Mitchell or the artillery FO (pronounced 'foe') called in big 155mm high explosive shells on the bunkers. They asked for 'fuse delay' artillery rounds which did not explode until burrowing into the ground. However, it seemed that most of the fuse-delay rounds were duds which did not explode at all. Disappointed, they kept the 'fuse instant' high explosive rounds raining down on the NVA position all night.

Company A received an emergency re-supply of C rations, water and ammo on 20 April. LTC Livingston, the battalion commander, stopped by to check on his troops and two chaplains also dropped into the LZ. While this was going on, Mitchell and the FO kept busy directing artillery fire into and all around the bunker complex. They were given priority for air strikes and several F-4 Phantom sorties dropped 250 pound high-drag bombs on suspected NVA positions to the south of the trail junction.

It was around 20 April that rumors began to circulate around Company A that all you needed to do to get away from the miserable conditions on the hill was volunteer to re-enlist, or to 're-up' in GI slang, and you would be pulled out of the field. It was said that if you re-enlisted, you could get an MOS (military occupational specialty) other than 11B10 (light weapons infantry) and you wouldn't have to go back out in the field. Six to eight (possibly more) of the men from Company A decided to take that option so they could get away from combat.

Almost from the moment those 're-up" men left the field, the former no-name hill became known as 'Re-Up Hill.' Soon, within twenty-four hours, a crude sign made from an ammo crate appeared nailed to one of the trees in the perimeter: 'RE-UP HILL A CO/2-501 ASSASSINS.' A little later, a cardboard sign was added, nailed to the tree above the original sign: 'Gone to Eagle Beach, Will Return, Alpha Assassins, 2-501 Infantry.'

All through the night of the 20th, Company A remained fully alert, expecting an attack at any moment. Helicopters had been coming and going all day long, and Mitchell knew the NVA had pinpointed their exact location. They all knew that the longer they remained in position at the trail junction, the more likely they would be attacked. Defensive 105mm artillery fire was kept falling around the perimeter while the larger 155mm fire continued to drop on the bunker complex. Periodically, illumination shells were called in to light up the area around the perimeter.

On 21 April, part of Company A cautiously moved down hill to the NVA bunker complex with enough explosives to destroy it completely. The area had been turned into a wasteland by almost two days of continuous artillery fire, but some of the bunkers had survived. The bunkers were searched and their contents either destroyed or sent back to the 3rd Brigade base at Camp Evans. The Company A men found numerous blood trails leading away from the bunkers and blood spatters on trees around the bunkers. No bodies were found but the NVA had paid a heavy price by remaining in or near their bunkers.

The night of 21 April was a repeat of the night before. Artillery fell all night with occasional illumination rounds causing eerie shadows to flicker through the jungle. The illumination rounds were rationed due to a division-wide shortage. On alert the whole night, fatigue began to be a factor in the morale of Company A.

On 22 April, a few replacements came out to join the company and a resupply of food, water and ammo was delivered. Squad-sized security patrols were sent out around the perimeter but no contact with the NVA was made. The three platoon leaders spent the day adjusting the perimeter due to losses from NVA mortar fire hitting the NDP. They were hit sporadically every day by very accurate NVA mortar fire. They had no fatalities, but a steady stream of wounded left the company increasingly short-handed. The men stayed close to a hole they could dive into as soon as they heard the 'BANG' of a mortar round leaving its tube. Adjustments in defensive artillery fire had to be made to compensate for the shrinking perimeter.

The longer they remained in position at the trail junction, the more certain it was that they would be hit by a ground attack. About an hour before sunset each day, the men prepared their positions to defend against an attack. They ate a quick meal, laid out grenades and extra ammo, checked trip flares and claymore mines. Platoon leaders and squad leaders checked to ensure that each position knew their sector of fire and that the fighting holes were deep enough to protect the men from incoming RPG's or mortar fire.

Finally, at about 0345 hours on 23 April, the attack came. A trip flare popped into bright light followed almost immediately by several others only fifteen or twenty meters in front of the perimeter. In the bright light of the trip flares, NVA soldiers should be seen crouching down with their AK-47's in their hands. The attack seemed to be centered on the trail running west up the ridge toward Hill 902 and Coc Muen. Instantly, the men on Company A's perimeter opened fire with M-16's, M-79's, grenades and claymore. The NVA disappeared in a cloud of dust and smoke. At about the same instant, the perimeter was hit by RPG's and satchel charges. Captain Mitchell was hit by a piece of shrapnel just above his left ear. Mitchell's RTO shouted into his radio "Six is hit! Six is hit!" but it was not a serious wound.

The fight continued and, during a lull in the firing, someone was heard yelling "Get down...I'm gonna blow the big one!" There was a huge explosion between the perimeter and the attacking NVA; one of the men had set off an improvised explosive device. The men had loaded several ammo cans with two pounds of C-4 each and packed them full of M-60 ammo linkage and spent brass cartridges and fused it with an electrically detonated blasting cap. These big mines were tied to the front of large trees facing outward from the perimeter. Within seconds of the huge blast, the NVA ceased firing. It was strangely quiet around the perimeter, the silence broken only by an occasional grenade thrown out to 'clear the area.'

Shortly after 0600, the NVA launched another sudden attack, again centered on the trail leading up to Hill 902. Most of the fire coming against Company A was AK-47 fire, RPG's, satchel charges and 60mm mortars. A large explosion occurred on the perimeter, wounding several men and killing PFC Garry Worley. Worley's squad was down to five people at the time of the attack on the perimeter, as were many of the squads manning the perimeter.

Almost as soon as it began, the NVA attack petered out and the NVA withdrew to the southwest. Company A waited tensely for a third attack that never came. Pushing out from their perimeter, they found seven dead NVA within fifteen meters of the perimeter. Another dead NVA soldier had been blown up into a tree. The area was littered with discarded weapons and equipment with too many blood trails to count.

Within a few hours of the end of the fight on Re-up Hill, Company A received a 'change of mission' radio message. They were told that they would be moved to FSB Granite on 26 April to take over responsibility for perimeter defense on the firebase. They were lifted off Re-up Hill late on 23 April and flown to Eagle Beach for well-deserved 3-day stand down.

Chapter 6
HILL 714

From a message found on a dead NVA soldier:" *If you make contact with the airborne, get out fast; they will surround you and kill you."*

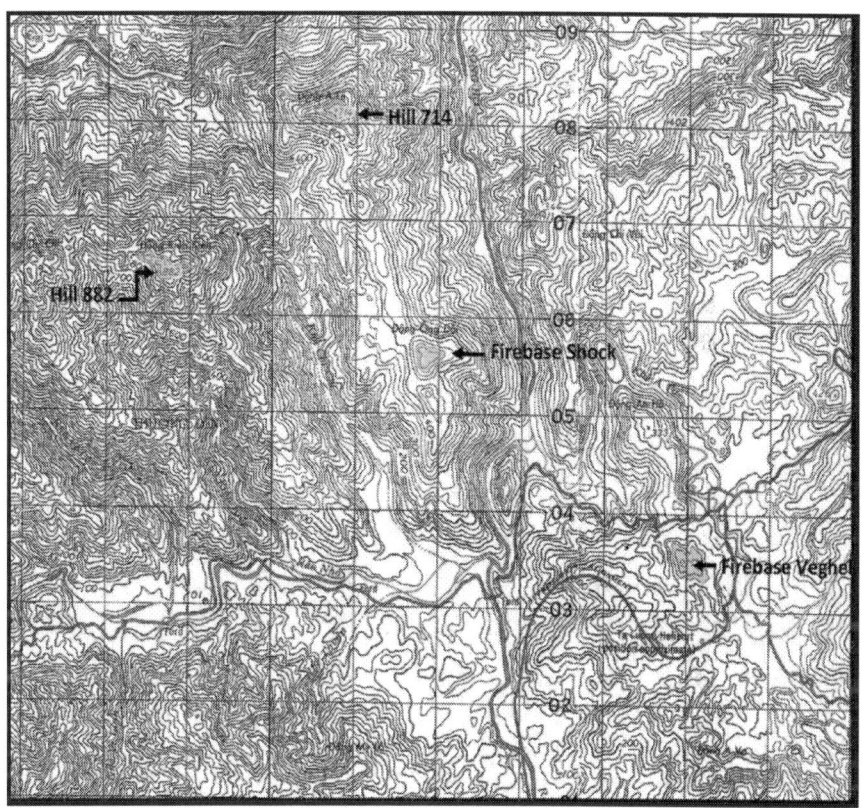

Color-enhanced detail from topographical map sheet 6441-1, series L7014, Ap La Bang District of Thua Thien Province showing 2-502 positions highlighted in yellow. Original map from authors collection. Color-enhanced map © 2017.

The first week of Operation Texas Star got off to a slow start for the men of the 1st Brigade, 101st Airborne Division. In the southern portion of Thua Thien Province, the 2/502 opened FSB Falcon at YC 567988, a new firebase out in the triple canopy four klicks east of the Rao Nai River. No contact was made and four days later, on 8 April 1970, FSB Falcon was closed and Companies B and D became OPCON (operational control) to the 2nd Brigade, Company A OPCON to the 3rd Brigade and C Company was under the OPCON of the 2/327, engaged in patrol/ambush operations along Highway 1 in the Phu Loc District.

While under the OPCON of 2nd Brigade, Companies B and D operated around FSB Arsenal at ZD 118014. Contact with the enemy was light. Company D made a CA (combat assault) onto an LZ at YC 165942 and encountered several old booby traps, wounding one man. A sniper team operating with the Recon Platoon encountered 5 NVA and killed one. Contact with the enemy was light and on 13 April, Companies B and D were released from the OPCON of 2nd Brigade and joined Company A under the OPCON of 3rd Brigade. C Company was brought up from Phu Loc and the 2/502 began operating as a battalion once again around FSB Jack at YD 498282. The battalion patrolled the foothills west of 3rd Brigade Headquarters, interdicting enemy forces moving against Camp Evans

At dawn on 16 April, an NVA force attacked the 2nd Platoon of D Company. The enemy engaged the platoon while they were still in their NDP with RPG's and AK-47 fire, killing SP4 James Tyner before they were driven off. On 17 April, the 2nd Platoon turned the tables and ambushed a small NVA patrol, killing one and wounding several others.

On 19 April, the 2/502 returned to the OPCON of its parent 1st Brigade and opened FSB Strike at YD 577171. The battalion was to work the jungled hills north of Highway 547 and around the Song Bo River. Division intelligence indicated heavy enemy activity in this area, but the battalion found little resistance east of the Song Bo. So, on 22 April, the battalion moved to FSB Veghel at YD 549036 and opened its TOC (tactical operations center).

At first the new AO remained quiet. Company A was acting as security on FSB Veghel and the other three companies and the Recon Platoon searched the single and double-canopied hills around FSB Veghel for the enemy with no results.

The situation changed on 25 April when the Recon Platoon, led by 1LT James T. Hill (retired in 2004 as a four-star general), made a CA onto the summit of Hill 714 at YD 508082. As the slicks carrying the platoon approached the LZ they drew small arms fire from a ridge running south from the summit of Hill 714. The platoon landed safely and after scouting the area around the summit with no contact, they were extracted. Once again, the lift ships drew small arms fire from the ridge as they picked up the Recon Platoon.

The hill, known to the Vietnamese as Dong A La and designated Hill 714 on US military maps, was 2342 feet above sea level. It was about 6 kilometers long from north to south and nearly three kilometers wide from east to west. Its north side plunged steeply down into the gorge cut by the Rao La River. The eastern slope dropped steeply down to the Song Bo River; the western side angled down into a deep saddle at the bottom of which ran a stream called the Khe Chi Chi. A long, narrow ridge ran southeast from the summit to a smaller hill named Dong Ong Doi. This ridge continued southeast to slant steeply into a valley where the Rao Nho and Rao Nai rivers met to form the Song Bo. Hill 714 was covered with dense bamboo thickets and double and triple-canopy jungle. It was perfect terrain for an NVA base camp and that, as it turned out, was what the NVA had done.

Based on the enemy activity of 25 April and additional information from an intelligence source, the Recon Platoon was sent back to Hill 714 on 26 April. The platoon came under fire as soon as they hit the LZ. A platoon from B Company, already alerted, was lifted to Hill 714 in support of the Recon Platoon. The platoon from B Company and Recon began moving down the ridge, following a well-defined trail. A few hundred meters from the LZ, the point man of the B Company platoon made contact and a sharp firefight developed. Recon, following behind the B Company platoon, paused on a small knoll from which they could see the muzzle flashes from the NVA weapons as they fired at the B Company platoon.

In his book *West of Hue: Down the Yellow Brick Road*, author Jim Brinker, a member of Recon, says that they fired over the heads of the B Company men, aiming at the muzzle flashes from the NVA weapons. At that point, the NVA noticed Recon up on the knoll and began firing at them as well as the B Company platoon. Soon after that the NVA stopped firing and fled down the ridge. PFC Charles R. King from B Company was killed and there were several wounded.

A 'white team' (two Cobra gunships) had been called to assist the troops as they moved cautiously down the ridge. One of the Cobra's was fired on by several NVA and damaged enough that it had to make an emergency landing.

Continuing their sweep south down the ridge, Recon found five abandoned bunkers. As they searched these bunkers, Recon was fired on by two NVA soldiers, who quickly broke contact and ran down the ridge. Recon, returning fire, quickly followed the fleeing NVA. Recon found and followed a heavy blood trail but could not locate the wounded enemy soldiers.

In the early evening hours of 26 April, 15–20 82mm mortar rounds were dropped on FSB Veghel. Quite a few of the rounds fell outside the wire perimeter, but others detonated inside the wire and several men were wounded. All the wounded had been wearing flak jackets so no one was killed.

On 27 April, Alpha One from Company A located a large NVA mortar position at YD 539028 about 1200 meters to the southwest of FSB Veghel. Troopers found three bunkers for personnel, two ammo bunkers and two mortar pits large enough to accommodate 82mm mortar tubes and their base plates. Also found was a forward observer position with a view of FSB Veghel; the FO position had communications wire leading back to each mortar pit. Fresh boot prints in and around the position led the Company A men to the conclusion that the mortar attack against FSB Veghel the night before had come from this position.

Troopers from C/2-502 gather on an LZ for movement by air to the FSB Veghel area on 22 April. Photo from authors collection. © 1970 and 2017

C/2-502 troopers scramble off the Huey slicks as they land at an LZ near FSB Veghel on 22 April. Photo from authors collection. © 1970 and 2017

Up on Hill 714, while moving south down the trail from their NDP site, Recon walked into an ambush by 4 to 5 NVA at YD 509079. Returning fire at the enemy, who were only 20 meters away, Recon and part of B Company drove the NVA off. Killed in the ambush was PFC Steve Sandlin; four other men were wounded.

About ninety minutes later, Recon and B Company were fired on by a single enemy soldier who was killed by return fire. Captured was an AK-47, three satchel charges, three loaded magazines, two Chinese-made grenades, 100 loose rounds of 7.62x39 ammunition, a bag of rice, medical supplies and a new NVA uniform.

Because of the ever-increasing contact with the NVA on Hill 714, LTC Young, the battalion commander of the 2-502, decided to reinforce Recon and B Company. C Company was tapped to make the combat assault onto Hill 714. Young chose an LZ on Dong Ong Doi, the hill in the middle of the long ridge leading from the top of Hill 714. Once on the ground, C Company was to attack to the northwest, up the ridge toward Recon and B Company.

C Company's Charlie One was chosen to lead the assault and they were picked up from an LZ north of Firebase Veghel. As the slicks carrying Charlie One approached the LZ on Dong Ong Doi at YD 518056, they came under heavy small arms fire and the lead helicopter was shot down, crashing directly on the LZ, preventing the other helicopters from landing. Tactical air strikes were called in to protect the 4-man crew of the downed Huey and its load of six grunts.

The other incoming helicopters pulled away and began to circle, waiting for another LZ to be selected and prepped with artillery fire. Aboard one of those circling Hueys was the author, at that time a 22-year old 'Shake n Bake' sergeant with Company C's Charley One. The slicks circled for ten or fifteen minutes before beginning to approach the LZ on the summit of Hill 714. The LZ was cold and all of Charlie One, followed by Charlie Two got down safely.

Back on Dong Ong Doi, the air strikes had driven off the NVA around the LZ. The 3rd Platoon of D/2-502 was brought in to secure the LZ and protect the downed Huey until it could be extracted. The crew of the downed Huey and the six troopers from Charlie One were taken out by the slicks that brought in D Company's Delta Three.

Recon and B Company continued to move down the ridge and at YD 508077, they made contact with an unknown number of NVA at a range of 20 to 30 meters. The enemy appeared to be in bunkers, firing RPG's, machine guns and AK-47's at the attacking troopers. Recon and B Company formed a line and, firing as they went, moved toward the NVA positions. The enemy fled, leaving behind one dead soldier, three AK-47's and one RPD machine gun. Also recovered were 88 TNT satchel charges, NVA uniforms and nine Russian-made grenades. The O-Deuce troopers searched the area and found that the NVA had been defending a large bunker complex, largely unoccupied, made up of 55 bunkers. SP 4 Delbert E. Hall was killed and seven more troopers were wounded.

Documents recovered from the enemy dead showed that they were members of C-6 Company, 8th Battalion, 29th NVA Regiment. Intelligence developed later showed that the 29th Regiment, along with the 803rd and 812th Regiments, were part of the NVA's 324B Division. The troops from the 29th Regiment had been moving into place to join in the attack on FSB Ripcord when they ran into the 2-502 Infantry on Hill 714 and later, on Hill 882.

At about 0500 hours 28 April, an unknown number of NVA attacked Bravo Two and Three of B Company at YD 510072 while they were still in their NDP. The enemy began the attack with a barrage of RPG fire followed by automatic weapons fire. B Company had sensor devices in place and had been alerted to the NVA's approach. They responded by detonating their claymore mines, followed by M-60 and M-16 fire. The contact lasted about 15 minutes before the enemy was driven away. Patrols pushed out from the NDP perimeter found 12 dead NVA with several blood trails leading away from the area. B Company lost 19 wounded but PFC Michael T. Sears was killed. Only 6 of the wounded required evacuation; the others remained in the field.

B Company pushed on down the ridge and about three hours later discovered a bunker complex at YD 5090779. This complex contained a large heavily reinforced bunker fitted out as a command center surrounded by 36 smaller bunkers. Hidden in some of the bunkers, B Company found 14 recently killed NVA.

B Company found another bunker complex nearby at YD 509077, this one made up of 35 fighting bunkers of various sizes. Again, the NVA had hidden 16 recently killed soldiers in this group. They appeared to have been killed by small arms fire and artillery.

About a hundred meters further down the ridge at YD 508076, B Company found a third bunker complex consisting of a large command bunker and 35 smaller fighting bunkers. The NVA had hidden 20 dead soldiers in these bunkers, killed by small arms fire and artillery. B Company troopers recovered an AK-47 and an RPD light machine gun.

Numerous documents were recovered from the enemy dead. Some of these documents were a commendation issued to Dinh Van Dua by his commanding officer. Also awarded to Dinh Van Dua was a 'Certificate of American Killer' dated 28 November 1969. Apparently Dinh Van Dua had been quite an accomplished soldier; several other documents were found awarding him medals. A transfer order and letter of introduction transferring him from the C-8 Company to an unknown new command was found as well as Dinh's notebook containing several Communist Party slogans.

After a quiet night, the action continued 29 April when the 3rd Platoon of D Company was attacked in their NDP at YD 519056. The platoon was still securing the downed Huey left on the LZ on 27 April. An unknown number of NVA assaulted Delta Three with automatic weapons fire and grenades. Cobra gunships were called in support of 3rd Platoon and their rocket fire set off secondary explosions. The enemy withdrew after that. 3rd platoon suffered three lightly wounded.

The NVA was on the move all around the area. A patrol from B Company's Bravo Two spotted a single NVA soldier. When fired upon, the soldier ran east. Shortly after that, B Company's Bravo Three saw another single NVA moving south. He was brought under fire but escaped into a bamboo thicket.

Shortly after this, the patrol from B Company's Bravo Two set off a booby trap with no injuries. Apparently the NVA had set the booby trap as a warning device. Almost immediately, Bravo Two came under automatic weapons fire and received several 60mm mortar rounds. Several men were wounded and Bravo Two called for help. They were joined by Bravo Three and they launched an attack on the bunker complex from where the enemy fire was coming.

B Company discovered additional bunkers at which time they came under heavy machine gun fire. They called for help and Charley One and Two of C Company joined in the attack. All the M-79 grenadiers available were placed in a line and they began firing over the heads of the advancing skirmish lines of B and C Companies to try and suppress the enemy fire. Enemy fire was heavy but by late afternoon, the two bunkers complexes were captured.

B and C Companies lost 26 wounded including the Battalion Executive Officer Major Jerrell Hamby and an artillery forward observer. The enemy lost 15 killed, seven of which had been wounded previously; they were found with older, bandaged wounds Several American weapons were recovered including an M-79 grenade launcher and an M-60 machine gun. An American PRC 25 radio with a long antennae and extra batteries was found along with several enemy weapons.

Because of the heavy contact with numerous enemy, D Company's Delta One was moved up into a blocking position south of B and C Companies. An OP at D Company's position fired on a single NVA seen approaching their perimeter. The enemy fled and a patrol was sent to chase him. The patrol was ambushed with heavy small arms fire from 6 NVA, The D Company patrol lost two wounded and PFC William J. Stieve was killed.

At about 2200 hours, B Company's NDP received twenty 82mm mortar rounds. The rounds were off-target and they could hear the mortar firing from about 500 meters to the southwest of their NDP. Artillery fire was called in and the mortar stopped firing.

All the action on 27 April through 29 April had taken place within 500 meters of the summit of Hill 714. Over a hundred bunkers had been discovered and 85 NVA had been killed by actual body count. The O-Deuce losses had been heavy, especially in Recon and B Company. C Company, having suffered only three wounded, was ordered to pass through B Company and take the lead the next day as the advance down the ridge continued.

On 30 April, C Company assumed the point position and began sweeping southeast down the long ridgeline from the top of Hill 714. Expecting contact with the enemy at any moment, the point squad from C Company's Charlie One checked everything thoroughly. At about 1400 hours, the point team found an apparently abandoned NVA rucksack lying beside the trail. After checking for booby traps, the pack was searched. It contained a PRC 25 radio with antennae, a handset, rain gear, medical supplies, AK-47 ammunition and a 100cc can of Albumin serum. While checking the area around the rucksack, the point team found, at YD 512076, two carefully camouflaged bunkers in which numerous weapons and ammunition were hidden.

Charlie One immediately went into a defensive perimeter around the two bunkers. After checking the bunkers for booby traps, men were assigned to begin removing the weapons cache from the two dugouts. 1LT Gerald F. Dillon, the platoon leader, reported the find to CPT James Schoonover, the company commander, who called battalion and described the large weapons cache that had been found.

An inventory of the captured weapons was taken which included: 17 French MAT-49 9mm submachine guns, 17 Russian-made rifles, 3 heavy machine guns, 1 RPD light machine gun, a Czech-made SKS assault rifle with a folding bayonet and four complete 60mm mortars (tube, tripod, baseplate and aiming device). Also found

were eight 57mm recoilless rifle rounds, hundreds of rounds of belted machine gun ammo and thousands of rounds of rifle ammo in boxes and crates.,

The weapons cache discovered by C/2-502 on Hill 714, 30 April 1970. The eastern slope of Hill 882 can be seen in the background. US Army photo courtesy Colonel (ret.) James F. Schoonover.

Not all the action was confined to Hill 714 itself. At about 1630 hours on 30 April, Alpha One of A/2-502 was moving along Highway 547 near FSB Veghel when one of the men stepped on a pressure-detonated mine placed on the roadway. The explosion killed SP4 Donnie Horton and wounded 4 other men all of whom went out by medevac helicopter. Company A continued to secure FSB Veghel; their trial by fire would come later, on Hill 882

D Company's Delta Three continued to secure Dong Ong Doi at YD 518056 which had been chosen as the site of a new fire base to be named FSB Shock. Two engineer bulldozers would be airlifted to the site and construction would begin on 1 May

On the night of 1 May while B Company was in their NDP at YD 509079, an unknown number of NVA probed their perimeter and fired three rounds into the position from a captured M-79 grenade launcher. B Company returned the fire with their own M-79's and the enemy fled the area. There were no casualties.

Early in the morning of 2 May, B Company moved out from their perimeter and had moved about 300 meters to YD 508076 when they hit an ambush. The enemy used a claymore mine, RPG's, small arms fire and a command detonated mine at a range of 30 meters to inflict five casualties on B Company. They returned fire with small arms and M-79's and the NVA broke and ran to the west. ARA was called in to chase the fleeing NVA. SGT Leo J. Ludvigsen was killed and SP4 Harold G. Graft later died of his wounds.

Two Troopers examine the ammunition cache captured by C/2-502 on Hill 714, 30 April 1970. US Army photo courtesy Colonel (ret.) James F. Schoonover

Late on the afternoon of 2 May, a squad from the D Company's Delta Three was patrolling around the new FSB Shock, still under construction, when they ran into an enemy unit which opened fire on their flank, wounding one man. They returned fire with M-16's and an M-60 machine gun. They were joined by another squad from Delta Three and they too came under fire from RPG's, satchel charges and AK-47's. The action was reinforced by D Company's Delta Two and their added firepower caused the NVA to break contact. Searching the area, the unit found two newly-constructed L-shaped bunkers. They found one dead NVA soldier with an AK-47 wearing a new green uniform.

Early on 3 May, D Company's Delta Three received nine incoming mortar rounds just outside their perimeter. Delta Three pinpointed the mortar fire as having come from the vicinity of YD 514063, so ARA was requested. When the Cobra gunship arrived on station and began to maneuver into firing position, several NVA fired at the gunship with automatic weapons. The Cobra was damaged and withdrew after calling for additional gunships to respond.

Later in the morning of 3 May, a squad from C Company's Charlie One conducted a RIF (reconnaissance in force) into an area about 1 klick northwest of FSB Shock near YD 513063. The squad found a well-used trail along a small stream, noticing that numerous trees had been cut and that the stream had been dammed to form a pool. Squad members detected the smell of wood smoke and the point team found a latrine site and two hooch's.

As the point team started up a small rise, a sniper fired one shot, wounding the patrol leader, SSG Phillip Gibbons. The squad moved into line and returned fire. The NVA responded with RPG rounds and automatic weapons fire. The fire was so heavy that the squad withdrew back down the trail and called for assistance.

While waiting for the rest of Charlie One to join them, the squad detected NVA moving into position around them and began to fire at the movement. The movement stopped and they received no return fire. Then the platoon leader, 1LT Gerald Dillon, arrived and called for a medevac for SSG Gibbons. The Dust-off came on station and began to hover, lowering a jungle penetrator for the wounded man. As the wounded sergeant was hoisted above the trees, the NVA fired at the medevac with an AK-47 on full automatic. Neither SSG Gibbons or the Dust-off was hit.

1LT Dillon called for ARA and the area at the top of the small knoll was blasted with 2.75-inch rocket fire. As soon as the Cobra's finished their attack, Charlie One moved into a skirmish line and began to move up the hill. After advancing only a few meters, the NVA opened fire with RPG's, machine guns, AK-47 fire, grenades and satchel charges. Several men were wounded and the Charlie One had to withdraw down the hill, dragging their wounded.

The platoon leader called in artillery fire and asked for Charlie Two to reinforce Charlie One while the area was being pounded with artillery. When Charlie Two arrived, led by 1LT David Simpson, the artillery fire stopped and both platoons started to advance from different directions up the hill. The advance was pushed back with the NVA firing .51 caliber machine guns and dropping satchel charges down onto the advancing infantry from overhead platforms in the trees. The NVA seemed to be hidden in bunkers which were not clearly visible due to the heavy under brush.

More artillery was called in and another advance was attempted. This advance was pushed back also, with more .51 caliber fire and satchel charges thrown from the trees. During this advance, SGT Glen Witycyak was killed and several other troopers were wounded.

SP4 Bruce Scott was with Charlie Two. He remembers, *"I was in Glen Witycyak's squad. He was a Shake n Bake who came to the company in early January 1970 and he somehow got the nick-name of 'Psychedelic. . .someone, I assume it was the LT called to Glen and we got up and followed him. . .The next thing I know there was AK fire and explosions, either grenades or RPG fire. . .all of a sudden, my position was fired up. The bullets were coming so close I actually thought I could see them. . .There was a call for a medic and a call for help to come up to the front of the line. I moved up and learned that the sergeant [Witycyak had been hit. Doc Kenneth Fuller had gone to help him and was also hit."* Mighty Men of Valor – page 91.

By that time, C Company had thirteen wounded, including Charlie Two's platoon leader and Charlie Two's medic. When the Dust-offs came in and began to hover, the NVA fired at them, using AK's on full automatic. Artillery was called in and under cover from the exploding artillery rounds, the wounded were successfully evacuated.

While this was going on, troopers from both Charlie One and Two were maneuvering, trying to pinpoint the bunkers. They could not locate the bunkers but spotted several snipers in the trees and brought them down. As it began to grow dark, C Company began to withdraw, counting 27 dead NVA scattered around the hillside.

On 4 May, C Company remained in a defensive position while artillery and tactical air strikes pounded the hill holding the bunker complex. Battery A/2-320 Artillery (105mm) had been moved from FSB Bastogne to the newly-built FSB Shock and they added their firepower to the bombardment of the enemy positions. This was in line with the 101st Airborne's policy of reducing casualties by using firepower to destroy enemy positions instead of attacking with infantry. The NVA took no offensive action against C Company, and RIF's sent out around C Company's perimeter found no sign of enemy activity.

D Company's Delta One received a re-supply and when they moved off the LZ they were ambushed by five NVA with AK's at 20-meter range. D Company returned fire with M-16's and frag grenades, killing one NVA. While checking the area, they found 3 bunkers with log-and-earth overhead cover. They captured an AK-47, ammunition, clothing and medical supplies. The dead NVA wore a new uniform and had a fresh haircut.

D Company's Delta Two and Three found several un-occupied bunkers with overhead cover and connected by trenches. In the center of the bunkers, they found a recently used mortar pit. All the bunkers were destroyed with explosives.

FSB Veghel was closed and the battalion TOC, mortars and artillery were moved by CH-47 to the newly constructed FSB Shock on Dong Ong Doi at YD 518056. The enemy did not contest the move in any way. By this time, the action on Hill 714 had resulted in 115 NVA killed while the O-Deuce had lost 10 killed and 118 wounded, 110 of them medically evacuated.

View of Hill 714 and Hill 882 as seen from FSB Veghel. The Recon Platoon, B Company and C Company landed on the peak of Hill 714 and fought down the ridge toward Dong Ong Doi, which later became FSB Shock. D Company landed on Dong Ong Doi. Photo courtesy alphaavengers.com, A/2-501 Infantry, 101st Airborne.

Early on 5 May, after tactical air strikes had hit the bunkers with bombs and napalm one last time, Charlie One and Two again attacked the bunker complex. The artillery and bombing had blasted away a lot of the covering vegetation, so it was easier to spot the bunkers. The NVA fired at the advancing troopers with RPG's and small arms. Hiding in bunkers and 'spider holes', the enemy had to be rooted out one bunker at a time, using grenades and small arms fire. The fight lasted several hours with the bunkers finally captured at 1300 hours. C Company lost 16 wounded; SFC William E. Malcolm, SP4 Gerald A Kulm, PFC Vernon L. Okland and SGT Francisco Carvajal were killed. SFC Malcolm's body was not recovered until 7 May. C Company captured two SKS assault rifles and an AK-47. Five enemy bodies were found in the bunkers and several enemy soldiers were seen fleeing down into a draw leading to the saddle between Hill 714 and Hill 882 to the west.

PFC Robert Noffsinger remembers the fight on 5 May. *"We were almost to the top when we heard grenades and fire behind [us] and one of the guys cry for help. I was almost to them and crawling over a log when I felt an AK round hit the side of my helmet. I dropped back behind the log and sprayed the area where the round came from, although I did not see whoever had shot at me."*

Noffsinger was helping the medic treat a badly wounded SGT Frank Carvajal when the medic asked for a canteen. Noffsinger gave him one of his. *"He threw it back to me and, as soon as I caught it, I knew it was empty, it was so light; then I saw the hole in it and looked back at my hip and the canteen cover on my web belt. My hip and butt cheek were a bloody mess. It did not hurt at all, I guess the adrenaline was overpowering it." Mighty Men of Valor* – page 102.

In the late afternoon of 5 May, a Medevac came on station and began to hover over C Company's position. A 'jungle penetrator' was lowered and two wounded troopers were hoisted up toward the helicopter. As the men on the hoist cleared the tree tops, an NVA fired a full magazine at the men and the helicopter. No one was hit and the Dust-off flew safely away. The enemy then sprayed the perimeter of C Company's position with AK-47 fire; again, no one was hit.

At day break on 6 May, an unknown number of NVA attacked C Company's NDP at YD 510063 with RPG's and AK-47 fire. C Company returned fire with M-16's and grenades. Some of the enemy charged to within 15 meters of the perimeter and claymore mines were discharged with unknown results. The enemy withdrew after only a few minutes. C Company lost 5 wounded and PFC Phillip R. Warfield was killed by an RPG.

The author remembers what happened that morning" . . .*I sat on the edge of my hole and wrapped myself in my poncho liner against the morning chill. The NVA chose that moment to spray the perimeter with AK-47 fire, RPG's and satchel charges. I grabbed my M-16 as I rolled into my fighting hole. I heard the scream of an RPG coming in. Looking up from the bottom of my hole, I saw the rocket dart overhead with a whooshing, sound trailing sparks and then explode with a bright flash in the tree above me. Most of the shrapnel blew the other way but some of it whined past my head, but I wasn't hit.*

Grabbing a grenade, I pulled the pin and heaved it into the brush in front of my hole. Other men were throwing grenades, detonating claymores, and firing into the brush around the edges of our perimeter. Someone was screaming for a medic, so I knew there were wounded." Mighty Men OF Valor – page 105.

A mortar barrage was fired from FSB Shock into the area where the NVA was seen withdrawing and C Company sent out combat patrols to follow the enemy. No further contact was made but one patrol found two dead NVA killed by small arms fire left behind by the withdrawing enemy. Shortly after this, C Company was reinforced by D Company and both companies moved out to search the remaining bunkers of the complex. During the search, the body of SFC William Malcolm was recovered by C Company's Charlie Two.

In the late afternoon of 6 May, B Company's Bravo Three found a small hooch and several unoccupied bunkers. While searching the area, Bravo Three was attacked by 8 NVA from 20 meters away with RPD machine gun and AK-47 fire. Bravo Three returned fire and the enemy fled to the south. One man was wounded and SSG Kenneth L. Foutz was killed.

In the afternoon of 7 May, C Company moved to the west down into the saddle between Hill 714 and Hill 882. At YD 508066, C Company found an unoccupied bunker complex. In one of the bunkers, searchers discovered 8 NVA rucksacks, uniforms, food and cooking implements, ammunition, tools, medical supplies and some captured US steel helmets. A bundle of US Chieu Hoi pamphlets and assorted NVA documents were also recovered. These documents included individual soldiers' diaries, propaganda pamphlets, pay records and food consumption records.

As of 7 May, the intense fighting on Hill 714 had cost the O-Deuce 17 killed and 144 wounded. Recon Platoon had been airlifted to Camp Eagle for a much-needed stand down; they had received 50% casualties since 27 April. The NVA had lost 123 known killed with an unknown number of wounded. Several NVA weapon and supply caches had been captured or destroyed.

On 9 May, the O-Deuce closed FSB Shock, a temporary firebase, and moved back to FSB Veghel. Each battalion of the 1st Brigade was directed to organize 30-man work details for movement to FSB Veghel to assist the engineers in clearing fields of fire, laying concertina wire, and building bunkers and fighting positions. FSB Veghel was being improved because 1st Brigade anticipated operating around the firebase for more than 60 days.

The construction of FSB Veghel continued with six 155mm guns from Battery A 2-320 Artillery moving on to Veghel. Ammo for this battery was moved from FSB Bastogne to Veghel in a 37-truck convoy secured by B/1-327 Infantry. Four 8" self-propelled guns were also moved from Bastogne to Veghel in anticipation of further fighting on Hill 714 and to support other battalions from the 1st Brigade operating in the AO west of the Song Bo River.

On 12 May both B and C Companies found unoccupied bunker and tunnel complexes. Some of the bunkers had log and earth-covered roofs and log floors. D Company found two dead NVA killed by air strikes. Scattered around the dead enemy soldiers were more than 25 loaded M-16 magazines. The 2-502 was ordered to secure an LZ at YD 558029 for movement of the 3rd Battalion 3rd ARVN Regiment by CH-47 from Camp Sally. The ARVN's were to work the area around FSB Veghel to add to the security of the greatly expanded firebase.

C Company had been scheduled to make a CA on 14 May but the move was cancelled and C Company began to move down into the deep saddle between Hill 714 and Hill 882. They received orders to build an LZ to receive a re-supply, so Charley Two sent out a squad to check the area while the LZ was being cleared. This patrol found a trail leading down into the saddle and began to follow it. At about 0900 at YD 504071, this patrol ran into 10 to 15 NVA and fired on them. The NVA responded with AK-47 fire, RPG's and 60mm mortar fire. The fire fight was sharp and quick and four NVA were killed. The NVA broke contact and ran southwest, deeper into the saddle. The patrol had received five wounded and were not able to pursue the enemy as they ran.

During the confusion of the withdrawal, one man became separated from the rest of the patrol and was left behind. After they had returned to the C Company perimeter carrying their wounded, the lost man began to yell and curse and could be heard crashing through the brush outside the perimeter. Until that point, no one had noticed that he was missing. The author was one of the men who went out to find the lost man and guide him back to the 'safety' of the perimeter. He was extremely angry and accused the men from Charlie Two of running away and leaving him.

A Dust-off was called to evacuate the wounded, but SGT Ronald E. Schmidt died of his wounds before he could be flown to the hospital.

The re-supply LZ was completed at YD 504072 and late that afternoon, the 'log bird' arrived and began his approach to the LZ. About 100 meters out from the perimeter, the NVA began to fire at the slowly moving helicopter. The men on the perimeter facing the area where the NVA fire was coming from began to return fire. Vinh, the Kit Carson Scout for Charlie Two was injured during the exchange of fire. The log bird circled around and came in from another direction with the door gunners firing cover fire. The helicopter landed safely and delivered the supplies. Vinh was flown out by a Dust-off.

On FSB Veghel, a tragic accident occurred late that morning. Two men were carrying a wooden ammo box containing frag grenades, claymore mines and trip flares when it suddenly exploded for unknown reasons. Six men were wounded and SP 4 James E Mirement was killed.

After receiving the re-supply and evacuating the wounded, C Company began to move back up the western slope of Hill 714. A heavy thunder storm moved into the area and, with visibility reduced to a few meters, C Company was forced to stop for the night.

Early on the morning of 15 May, The NVA fired 10 rounds of 60mm mortar fire at C Company's NDP. The rounds fell short and no casualties occurred. D Company in their NDP nearby heard the mortar firing from down in the saddle between Hill 714 and Hill 882 1,200 meters northwest of C Company's NDP. Artillery was called in and the mortar stopped firing.

1st Brigade headquarters received an intelligence report that indicated units in the field and on firebases should expect attacks on their perimeters by NVA troops armed with flame throwers. This intelligence resulted from the capture of an NVA flame thrower team near FSB Henderson in Quang Tri Province. The flame thrower was of Soviet manufacture and had a range of from 30 to 50 meters.

Action was quiet on Hill 714 for the next three days. On 18 May, word came down from division headquarters that a 24-hour cease fire would go into effect from 1200 on 18 May until 1200 on 19 May to mark the birth of the Buddha. The companies of the 2-502 were directed to find a good defensive position and remain there until the afternoon of 19 May. Offensive operations were not to be undertaken, but both ambush and recon patrols were authorized to prevent the NVA from using the cease fire to move into position to attack US units.

As the end of the 24-hour cease fire approached on 19 May, C Company was directed to move back into the area of the contact on 14 May. Charlie One took the point and began to move north back down into the saddle between 714 and 882. At about 1120 hours, the point team for Charlie One found an enemy unit of unknown size moving south on the same trail. During the exchange of fire, the point man SP4 Billy R. Lucas was killed with two others wounded. The enemy withdrew to the north and air strikes were called in on their path of retreat with unknown results.

C Company continued to move down into the saddle and on the afternoon of 20 May found 6 newly constructed bunkers with two feet of log and earth overhead cover. There no NVA occupying the bunkers but C Company found 60mm mortar rounds and ammunition for AK-47's and some clothing. Everything was destroyed in place.

C Company crossed the saddle and climbed the steep eastern face of Hill 882. Late on the afternoon of 21 May, C Company linked up with the Recon Platoon and Company A on a narrow ridge finger at YD 494069 about a klick to the northeast of the summit of Hill 882.

Three days later, on 24 May, the 2-502 was relieved by the 1-327 who immediately began offensive operation on Hill 882. The intense fighting on Hill 714 had cost the O-Deuce heavily; 30 men killed in action and 206 wounded, 194 of these men had to be medically evacuated by helicopter. The NVA had lost 184 men killed in action with an unknown number of wounded. The O-Deuce had captured or destroyed several tons of weapons, ammunition, food and clothing and had forced elements of the 29th NVA Regiment to abandon their positions on Hill 714. The 2-502 was moved into a quieter AO around FSB Bastogne to allow replacements to be trained and integrated into the under-strength companies. The next major operation for the 2-502 would begin in August around FSB Barnett in Quang Tri Province.

Chapter 7
FIREBASE GRANITE - PART ONE:

"I have often compared my experience in Vietnam to eating very hot, spicy food for a long time. . .returning to the 'world' was like taking all the spice away making everything very bland. . .I don't think I have completely gotten over that feeling, even today."
Mark Hendrickson, C Company 1-506 Infantry, 101st

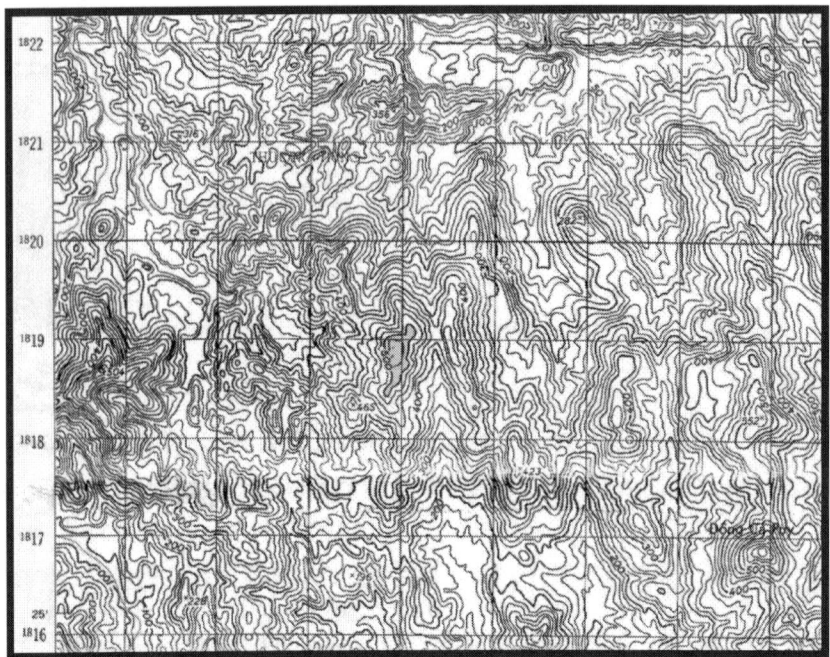

Airborne Division.

Color-enhanced detail from topographical map sheet 6441-1, series L7014, Ap La Bang District, Thua Thien Province showing positions of A 2-501 Infantry and C 1-506 Infantry on FSB Granite highlighted in yellow. Original map from author's collection. Color-enhanced map © 2017.

During the first part of March 1970, in anticipation of the start of Operation Texas Star on April 1st, the 3rd Brigade decided to open a new firebase to support infantry operations around what was to be FSB Ripcord. The first location chosen for the new firebase was at YD 445195, a long, narrow hill mass about 1,500 meters long and running almost due north and south. The base was dubbed FSB Mooney.

Construction began in early March but it was soon discovered that the site would be dominated by the top of the hill on which the base was being built. Infantry security patrols around the construction site discovered several NVA log-and-earth bunkers on the top of the hill, only 200 meters from the base.

It was decided to move the new firebase and another location was chosen at YD 439188, only 900 meters to the southwest of the site of Mooney. The new base was named Granite and construction began on March 12. The site chosen was on a hill a little over 500 meters high. The top of the hill was about 300 meters from north to south and about 100 meters wide at the widest point. At the time construction began, 3rd Brigade intended to keep Granite open for about ten days to support an operation.

FSB Granite as seen from the air looking east. The firebase was dominated by higher terrain to the south. Image from B2501airborne.com.

An infantry unit leaves FSB Granite as part of a security patrol to check for NVA activity around the base. Image from B2501infantry.com.

The area that was occupied inside the barbed wire barrier was an oval about 150 meters from northeast to southwest and about 75 meters wide; it was a small firebase. There were gradual slopes to the north and south but the sides were somewhat steeper. The 105mm howitzers of Battery A 2-319th Field Artillery occupied the center of the hill and an 81mm mortar battery from E Company, 1-506 Infantry was just north of the howitzers. The single LZ was at the south end of the hill with the ammo storage area right next to it.

Company C/1-506 was charged with firebase security and their company CP was near the center of the position. Company C's Charlie Three defended the west side of the base, Charlie Two the south and Charley One defended the northeast sector. Most of the fighting positions were foxholes only, without overhead cover. There had not been time to construct sand-bagged bunkers with reinforced roofs.

Granite had been built in an area where contacts with the NVA by 1-506 Infantry companies patrolling in the surrounding hills were on the increase. On March 14, Company A/1-506 had a sharp encounter with the NVA only three klicks southeast of FSB Granite. A security patrol from C/1-506 found a tunnel complex near Granite on March 15 and D Company 1-506 had several contacts with the NVA all within a few klicks of the new base. Later intelligence showed that FSB Granite had been placed in an area claimed by elements of the 29th NVA Regiment. One of these elements was the 7th Sapper Battalion.

Infantry companies assigned to firebase security often looked on this duty as a nice break from humping the boonies carrying an 80 to 100-pound rucksack in 100° heat and 85 to 90% humidity, punctuated by drenching rain storms. If construction on the firebase had been completed, then the duty was routine and could be restful, even boring. However, if the base was still under construction, the infantry grunts were expected to pitch in and help. They strung barbed wire, set out trip flares and claymore mines, dug fighting positions, filled sandbags, built bunkers and sent out security patrols. Then, after working all day in the scorching sun, they pulled guard duty around the perimeter all night. After a week or so of this 24-hour work-and-vigilance routine, the men began suffering from exhaustion and, at best, performed at only 70% of the mental alertness needed. This was the case with C Company, 1-506 Infantry when the sapper attack hit them on FSB Granite.

Ralph "Doc" Matkin, a medic assigned to A Battery 2-319 Field Artillery on Granite describes finding bare footprints in the mud around the gun emplacements on 19 March in his article *Reflections on the 1st Battle at FSB Granite*. Since no GI ever went bare foot on a firebase, Matkin and others reasoned that the foot prints could only have been made by an NVA sapper who had infiltrated the firebase on a reconnaissance mission.

William Higgins, the platoon leader for 1st Platoon C 1-506, recalls that the attack began about 0200 on 20 March. In his internet article *Charlie Company, 1st Battalion 506 Infantry May 1969 to October 1970,* Higgins says that there was no moon that night and the sky was heavily overcast. Captain Moore, C Company's commanding officer, was checking positions on the perimeter when he saw a sapper in the wire and killed him. The gunfire put the firebase on alert and kept the sappers from infiltrating through the wire undetected.

"Doc" Matkin remembers the fight starting at about 0130 when the first explosions woke him up and he looked at his watch by lighter flame. Matkin's quarters were located on the southwestern slope of Granite, ten feet below the artillery FDC. He shared the shelter with four other men and he was the last out the door as he stopped to put his boots on and grab his medical aid bag.

Matkin checked with the gun crews up on the main level of the base and found they had no casualties yet. Someone told him that the mortar pit at the northern end of the hill had taken a direct hit and someone had yelled for a medic. When he reached the mortar pit, he found an infantryman there firing his M-16 into the wire. This man told him there were wounded inside the mortar pit.

Crawling inside the position, Matkin found it was pitch black; he literally could not see his hand in front of his face. Fumbling around, he touched the body of a man lying on his back who was mumbling incoherently and gurgling as he tried to breathe. Matkin rested the mans' head on his thigh and his breathing improved. Checking for wounds entirely by touch, Doc found the man had severe head wounds and his right leg had been blown off above the knee. He had begun putting a tourniquet on the man's leg when the mortar pit was hit by two explosions, possibly mortar rounds. The second blast blew Matkin up and out of the pit and sprayed his right side and butt with shrapnel.

Dazed by the concussion, it took him several seconds to recover. He started to crawl back to the mortar pit when he was stopped by the infantryman he had spoken to earlier. The grunt asked him where he was going and Matkin told him he had to retrieve his aid bag. At that moment, two more explosions shook the mortar pit. Thinking that the wounded man was now dead for sure and his aid bag destroyed, Matkin began to crawl toward the 105mm battery to get more medical supplies. As he crawled, he saw red (US) and green (NVA) tracers zipping overhead. The firebase was a cacophony of sound; yells, screams, booming artillery, explosions and gunfire.

Each of the three infantry platoons had sent 4-man listening post (LP's) teams 75 to 100 meters outside the wire to give early warning in case of attack. Each team carried a PRC-25 radio and the men took turns standing watch and monitoring their platoon's radio frequency.

The four-man team from Charlie One was Carroll Shiltz, Gary Tarpein, Lloyd Bryant and 'Gus' Mack. Gary Tarpein was asleep when the first shots from the perimeter jolted him awake. The volume of fire coming out from the perimeter increased to dangerous levels so the four men crawled down the slope several meters to get away from the 'friendly fire' buzzing overhead and all around them.

As artillery or mortar rounds started falling around them, all four got up and ran toward the wire, a very dangerous move. They forgot to bring the radio and Tarpein had to go back and get it. As they got close to the wire, they found a huge tree that had been knocked over with all the roots still attached. Calling the Charlie One CP on the radio, they asked permission to come through the wire. They were told to stay where they were and dig in. Having no entrenching tool, they were forced to crawl in among the exposed tree roots to find shelter from the artillery and small arms fire. Everyone found a spot but Tarpein who lay flat about ten feet out from the felled tree, trying to see what was going on.

Artillery, possibly from another firebase, began to land around them and one round landed about 8 to 10 feet from them and wounded all but Lloyd Bryant. Tarpein managed to get to the radio and yelled for them to call off the artillery fire because it was hitting the LP. The artillery battery got the message for no more rounds fell near them.

They bandaged each other's wounds and stayed hidden during the rest of the battle which started slacking off about four of five AM. When the firing died down, Tarpein called the CP on the radio and a patrol was sent to bring them inside the wire barrier.

As they came in through the wire, Tarpein noticed the engineer's bulldozer parked right next to the wire with four or five dead NVA lying around it. There were satchel charges and equipment lying scattered all over the ground and they had to walk carefully to avoid stepping on them. They were taken to the LZ with the other wounded to wait for a medevac to find its way through the fog. Tarpein remembers seeing many US dead and wounded lying around the LZ; it was a horrible sight he has never forgotten.

Lloyd Bryant remembers that the LP did not see or hear any NVA before the attack started. Bryant believes the enemy may have seen the LP and went around it or just decided to ignore it. He remembers Tarpein calling the CP and telling them to stop the artillery, but they were told to take cover because the artillery fire could not be stopped.

Carroll 'Turp' Turpin said that Granite had been "socked in" for four days and they were running out of food and water. Turp's position was in Charlie One's sector which was hit hard. Most of the men were either wounded or killed. He threw eight grenades, all he had, at the attacking NVA and killed five of them. Turp, who was an M-60 gunner, had been firing the machine gun until he saw the NVA had gotten inside the firebase perimeter and he was surrounded. He stopped firing because he knew the NVA would take him out with a shower of satchel charges or an RPG. The NVA got so close to him that he had to play dead for a long time. The sappers were all around him and everyone else near him had been killed.

David Causey said he was sent outside the southern side of the perimeter with another man, acting as a forward observer. When the attack started on the northern side of the base, "all hell broke loose." They decided to make a run for it, trying to get back inside the wire. They dodged friendly small arms fire, exploding claymores and got tangled in the wire. Causey made it unhurt but the man with him lost an eye.

Back on Granite, Doc Matkin picked up more medical supplies. He was told about a badly wounded engineer who had been carried inside one of the shelters the gun crews had built. Matkin found the man and saw he had too many wounds to count. They hung a tarp over the doorway to conceal the light and used crude candles made by twisting the wax-covered paper wrappings taken from ammo crates. By this flickering light, Doc managed to cover the largest wounds with field dressings and bandaged the other wounds using strips torn from the mans' t-shirt.

Matkin then made his way to the LZ which the medics had decided would be their triage site. He saw at least ten wounded being treated at the LZ by other medics when he arrived. He helped one infantry medic treat a soldier whose legs had been blown off. They ran out of medical supplies and Matkin went to his shelter to try and find more. All he could find were some IV kits and two bottles of D5W but no field dressings.

Matkin was called to the artillery position where the battery commander CPT Phillip Michaud had received a head wound. The injury was bleeding heavily as head wounds tend to do but Matkin saw it was not serious. He used a pressure bandage to help stop the bleeding and Michaud went back to work. Michaud remained in command of A Battery 2-319 Artillery until July when he was transferred to FSB Ripcord to command B Battery 2-319 Artillery after CPT David Rich was seriously wounded.

Matkin had begun to make his way back to the LZ when he saw a man silhouetted by an explosion moving south in a crouched position. He was wearing what looked like a GI 'steel pot' a pair of shorts and nothing else. Matkin realized that the man was an NVA sapper.

Many medics carried .45 caliber Colt pistols and Doc Matkin had his. He pulled out the big pistol, chambered a round and aimed at where he thought the man would be. When another explosion back lit the man, Matkin fired one shot and the next explosion showed no one. Thinking he had missed, Matkin went back to the LZ to help.

Very early the next morning, he went back to check and found a dead NVA sapper and the GI helmet lying near him with a single bullet hole in the right side. Matkin thought the dead NVA looked as if he were sleeping but his entire brain lay in the mud 2-3 feet away from the body.

Doc then heard the artillery crew men yelling for everybody to get down. He saw that the two northern-most guns had been cranked down so that their barrels were horizontal. They were getting ready to fire 'bee hive' and white phosphorous rounds out into the wire to stop any further penetration onto Granite from the north. He flopped down and then felt the concussion of several salvos boom over his head.

A few minutes later, more yells came from the artillery battery to get down and take cover. Soon, artillery shells began to burst inside Granite's barbed wire barriers, called in by CPT Michaud. They must have come from a nearby firebase, probably Rakkasan or Gladiator. The barrage lasted for some time and Matkin remembers the ground shaking under him and the loud whooshing sound the big rounds made pushing through the air just before impact.

Matkin moved around the base looking for wounded to treat. He came across a badly wounded infantryman who had taken a round in the elbow, badly mangling his arm. The wound was bleeding badly and the man was in shock. Matkin used his belt to fashion a tourniquet, then tried to find a vein to start an IV using his last bottle of D5W. The grunt had no field dressing. So Matkin tipped up his shirt to make one.

The IV bottle began to run dry, so Matkin sent an artilleryman to get another from the triage location on the LZ. When the bottle ran dry, he made the mistake of pulling out the needle. When the cannoneer returned with more D5W, he tried to start a new IV but couldn't find a usable vein. He had to do a 'cut-down' procedure on the man's wrist, using the Swiss Army knife he always carried in his pocket. He found a vein and started a new IV.

By this time, it was beginning to grow light and the firing died away. It was very foggy with visibility reduced to 75 yards or so. At around 0730, a Huey managed to get through the fog, landed and loaded aboard seven of the worst wounded men. As it lifted off, the helicopter quickly disappeared into the fog. A CH-47 Chinook landed next. They had found the firebase by flying to the bases coordinates above the fog. Then the pilot had slowly dropped down until they were below the fog and right at tree top level. Then they had slowly flown up the side of the hill, staying just above the trees until they saw the firebase. The big Chinook took more than 20 wounded from Granite.

Later that day, when the survivors had been policing up the NVA bodies, they found a sketch map of Granite carried by a dead sapper. The map, though crudely drawn, showed every position on the firebase. The map must have been drawn by the sapper whose bare foot prints they had found on 19 March.

An NVA prisoner, taken the next morning, told them the supporting artillery fire coming in from other firebases killed the enemy assault commander and dispersed and killed many of the two NVA infantry battalions waiting to overrun Granite after the Sappers had cleared the way.

US losses during the attack were 11 KIA and more than 20 wounded. Killed were SGT James L Davis; SP4 Harold R Harris; SP4 James P Kurth; SP4 Ronald F Leonard, a medic; SP4 Gary R Stacy; Sp4 Tinsley J Wells; SP4 Willie Walker; PFC Michael J McGuire and PFC Dale A Blake. Also killed were Dennis Morrill and Robert Thompson from B Company, 326th Engineer Battalion.

The exact number of NVA losses is unknown but at least seven NVA were found on the firebase with numerous blood trails leading through the wire and down the hill. NVA equipment losses were heavy with many rifles and explosive charges left behind.

Reinforcements were flown out to FSB Granite quickly; repairs and new construction were begun immediately. The firebase remained open and manned.

Chapter 8
THE BATTLE OF FIREBASE GRANITE: PART TWO

". . .I fought for and with them; I led them off the hill when so ordered. They were (and are) common Americans of uncommon patriotism, valor and fidelity. They fought for me and I fought for them. . ." Captain (Brigadier General, Ret.) James E. Mitchell

A little over a month had passed since the first battle on FSB Granite when, on 26 April, A/2-501 Infantry was airlifted onto FSB Granite directly from Eagle Beach, the 101st Airborne's in-country R&R center on the South China Sea. Company A had been rewarded with a two-day stay at the beach after their 8-day ordeal on Re-Up Hill. During their short stay at the beach, Company A had received a few badly needed replacements. Several Company A men had minor shrapnel wounds that needed attention. Clean uniforms and a chance to swim and bathe their jungle sores in the warm waters of the South China Sea did wonders for morale.

But their visit ended all too quickly and they were loaded aboard Huey slicks bound for the single-ship LZ at the north end of FSB Granite. The 2-501 Infantry's Tactical Operations Center (TOC) was already up and running on Granite under the guidance of LTC Otis Livingston, the battalion commander. A battery of 105mm howitzers from the 2-319 Field Artillery was in place along with the 81mm mortar platoon from E Company 2-501. Company A's mission was to provide security and a relatively stable platform from which the 105's and 81's could deliver fire support for the other infantry companies from the 2-501 operating in the jungle-covered hills surrounding the firebase.

The 2-501 Infantry Battalion had been assigned to the 3rd Brigade the first week of April. Since then, Company A had made four combat air assaults, fought for over a week on Re-Up Hill, Hill 902 and Coc Muen Mountain. The 2-501 TOC was now set up on its third firebase (Jack, Gladiator and now Granite) since Operation Texas Star began on 1 April,

The first task Captain Mitchell set for himself on his arrival on FSB Granite was to walk the perimeter of the firebase and get an idea of where all the various units were emplaced on top of the hill. Mitchell saw that the base was quite small compared to other firebases he had been on and all the various units were packed tightly together on the hilltop. Granite, like many of the hills in that area, was very rocky around the summit which made digging bunkers and infantry fighting positions very difficult The west-facing slope of the hill was very steep, reducing the effectiveness of grazing fire from the defensive positions on that side of the base. The eastern slope was more gradual but many big boulders provided good cover for any enemy troops attacking the firebase from that direction. Because of these scattered clumps of granite outcrops, attackers would have cover until they were only 10 to 15 meters from defense positions.

Mitchell's inspection tour revealed that the slope on the eastern side of the hill and the finger ridge to the north on which the LZ sat were the most likely avenues of approach for an attacking force. The perimeter, following the contours of the hill, was irregularly shaped and Company A did not have enough men to properly man the existing fighting positions. There was a division-wide shortage of infantry replacements and it was not likely that Company A would receive enough replacements to bring it to full strength.

Company A's first three days on Granite passed uneventfully with no contact by the NVA. Men on night guard duty on Granite's perimeter reported seeing lights moving around on near-by hills. Artillery was called in on these lights, but no direct attacks on the firebase itself occurred. Things remained very, almost unusually, quiet and the grunts of Company A spent their days laboring over the defenses and their nights nervously on guard.

As darkness began to fall on Wednesday, 29 April, the defenders of Granite went about the business of preparing for the night. While some remained on guard, others moved out into the wire to check the placement of trip flares, claymores and early warning devices fixed to the barbed wire. In the fighting holes, extra M-16 magazines were laid out along with frag grenades and hand flares where they would be within easy reach in the dark. Checks were made to verify that no friendly units were in position near the bases defensive positions. As full darkness descended on FSB Granite, the defenders went on full, 100% alert. Mitchell and the three platoon leaders walked the perimeter checking each fighting position and giving final instruction for each sectors' night defense. They had received no intelligence warning of an imminent attack, but at that moment the 7th NVA Sapper Battalion, supported by two battalions of the 29th NVA Regiment, were moving into their final attack positions in front of the east and northeast sectors of FSB Granite.

Inside the Company A command post, a 10-foot by 10-foot hole covered with a roof of pierced steel planking and sand bags, CPT Mitchell and his artillery FO went over artillery defensive fire target lists, ensured they were in good radio contact with individual platoons, the artillery FDC and mortar platoon and made plans for the next days' work on the firebase defenses. RTO's were busy relaying daily supply requests and personnel information to 3rd Brigade Headquarters at Camp Evans. It was business as usual in the crowded CP with no hint of enemy activity.

At about 2140 hours, all along the eastern and northeastern sectors of Granite's perimeter, trip flares suddenly and without warning blazed into light. Instantly, small arms fire began coming against Company A's defensive positions, followed rapidly by a series of explosions from satchel charges and RPG's. Hand flares zoomed skyward, providing immediate illumination as the hill shook from large explosions all along the eastern bunker line and near the 81mm mortar pit. More hand flares streaked into the sky as the tempo of explosions built into a continuous roar.

From the way the attack began, CPT Mitchell immediately knew Granite was being attacked by a large, well-armed NVA force that had already penetrated the outer defensive wire barrier in several locations. All the fighting position on the east and northeast sides of the firebase were pelted with a steady rain of satchel charges of varying sizes, some as large as 10 pounds of TNT. RPG's left their trail of sparks as they streaked toward perimeter bunkers and the artillery battery.

The mortar position, manned by troops from E/2-501, was hit by a barrage of satchel charges and RPG's. The mortar was destroyed and the crew killed without having fired a single shot. It was obvious the Sappers knew the position of every crew-served weapon on the firebase and was systematically taking them out.

The infantrymen on that side of the base, already 100% alert, immediately responded to the attack with M-60, M-16 and M-79 fire as well as hand grenades thrown out into the wire. Within the first 15 or 20 minutes of the fight, the Phou gas barrels were detonated all along the eastern perimeter, illuminating the area with a bright glow beneath intensely burning flares hanging in the sky.

The sheer volume of fire coming so quickly from the bunker line speedily stopped the Sappers' mass attack. Several men whose positions had overlooked the Phou gas barrels later said they had seen scores of NVA soldiers on fire, running back into the jungle. Even though the attacking force had been driven back with massive losses, the attack was not over. It continued for several more hours as a determined NVA force, in groups of two or three, attacked specific positions along the perimeter and the interior of the firebase.

The NVA Sapper teams were fanatical and they very clearly had assigned targets. They were well trained and appeared desperate to accomplish their mission no matter what the cost. All through the remainder of the night, there were sudden, violent engagements with surviving Sapper teams as they tried to destroy their assigned targets.

While the battled raged, other supporting assets began to make their presence felt. Cobra gunships arrived to bombard NVA routes of approach and retreat with aerial rocket artillery. Artillery from supporting firebases around Granite blasted the surrounding hills and an Air Force AC-119 gunship equipped with 20mm mini-guns strafed possible concentrations of NVA troops.

In the first few minutes of the battle, the NVA managed to destroy several fighting positions in front of the company CP. As a result, the CP, which was several meters to the rear of the perimeter bunker line, became part of the perimeter defense overlooking the northern LZ. During the most intense part of the fight, members of the CP group joined in firing at enemy soldiers who suddenly appeared only 15 to 20 meters in front of the CP. As the NVA tried to advance, they were met with intense small arms fire and a shower of grenades. It was very difficult to tell US soldiers from the NVA in the flickering light of the flares hanging overhead.

The men shouted back and forth from position to position as they spotted advancing NVA soldiers. Quick, sharp firefights occurred as the Sappers were spotted and identified as the enemy. Soldiers in CPT Mitchell's CP killed several NVA Sappers as they tried to throw satchel charges into the CP from the area of the LZ. An M-72 LAW (light anti-tank weapon) was used to blast a group of determined NVA from a clump of boulders near the CP.

NVA Sappers used these boulders as cover when they launched their assault on FSB Granite on 29 April 1970 against defenders from A/2-501 Infantry. Photo from alphaavengers.com.

As dawn finally broke over the battered firebase on 30 April, the engagements with small groups of sappers died away and Company A began to reconsolidate the perimeter. Ammunition was resupplied and sweeps checking for NVA stragglers were made a short distance into the wire checking for NVA stragglers. The priority shifted to locating and evacuating the wounded and those killed in action.

On one of the security sweeps into the wire, CPT Mitchell found an NVA soldier who was still alive, though badly wounded. Wanting to get the man to the rear as a POW, they began carrying him to the aid station. As they struggled up the side of the hill, a very accurate mortar barrage began to fall on Granite. Dropping the POW, they dove into the nearest foxholes to wait out the attack. When the fusillade lifted, they managed to get the man to the aid station where he was treated before being evacuated to Camp Evans later that day.

During another security sweep of the eastern sector of the perimeter, troopers found a group of dead NVA Sappers lying scattered among the boulders. They were shirtless, wearing only shorts and they were barefoot. Their bodies were painted black and some of them had shoulder bags full of satchel charges and spare AK magazines. Lying among the bodies were several AK-50 folding-stock assault rifles, RPG launchers, high explosive war heads and propellant boosters for the rockets. All the weapons were collected for shipment to the rear.

Although Company A expected more ground attacks against Granite that day, there were none. The priority shifted to accounting for all the men who had been wounded or killed, reorganizing the perimeter defense to account for the losses in personnel and evacuating the wounded. The mortar attacks, which began around 1000 hours, continued throughout the day. There were at least five mortar attacks on Granite and Company A received about 30 more wounded from the extremely accurate NVA mortar fire. The mortar attacks came without warning as they were unable to hear the rounds being fired over the noise of helicopters and almost continuous air strikes on the surrounding hills.

An NVA prisoner, taken the next morning, told interrogators the supporting artillery fire coming in from other firebases killed the enemy assault commander and dispersed or killed many the two NVA infantry battalions waiting to overrun Granite after the Sappers had cleared the way.

Company A was extracted from FSB Granite late on the afternoon of 30 April. They left with the whereabouts of one of their soldiers unknown; PFC Edward J. Bishop, Jr. They knew that his assigned position had been along the eastern side of the firebase, near the 81mm mortar pit. When it was determined that Bishop was missing, an all-day search was organized. They thoroughly searched the firebase and the ground immediately around the base, but they could find no sign of PFC Bishop. The men at Bishop's assigned fighting position had faced some of the heaviest fighting with a veritable shower of satchel charges coming at them. It appeared the main thrust of the NVA's effort to overrun Granite had come against Bishops position. No one knows to this day what happened to PFC Bishop.

The After-Action Report for the battle of FSB Granite lists 41 wounded, 8 killed in action and one missing in action. Those killed from Company A are: Dennis W. Hunter; Roy H. Snyder; Frederick D. Wortman and Robert J. Shannon.

Company E lost two men from its mortar platoon: Larry N. Jones and Carl E. Patten. Robert S. Boggs from Company B and Linwood A. Walker from Company C were also killed.

Chapter 9
HILL 882

"These guys are going to get us all killed anyway. It might as well be today." From *West of Hue-Down the Yellow Brick Road;* James P. Brinker - page 186.

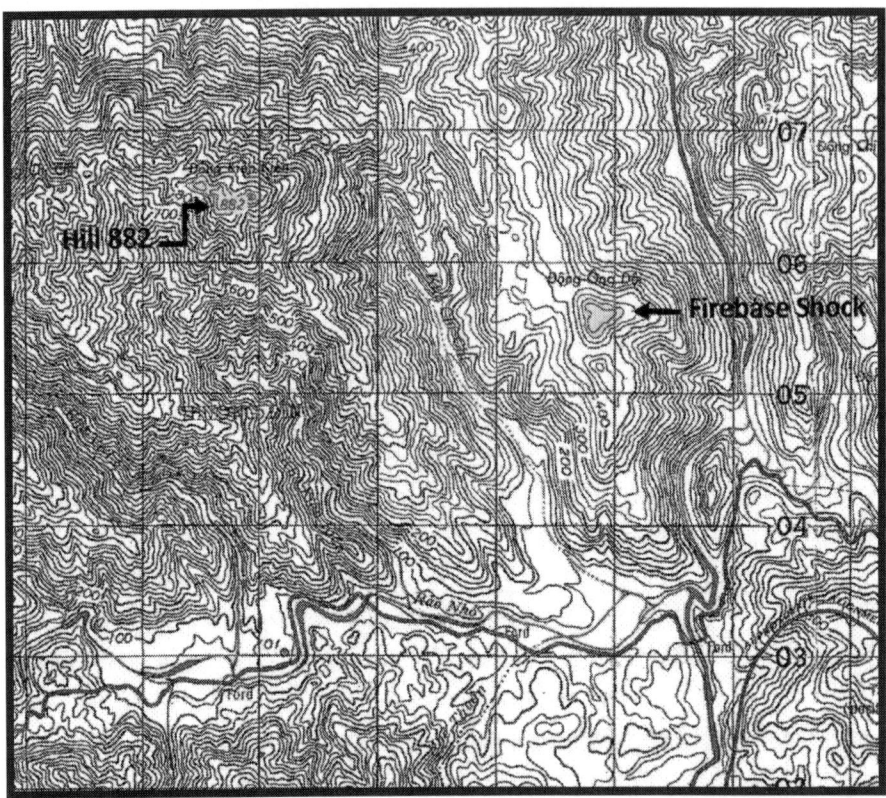

Color-enhanced detail from topographical map sheet 6441-1, Series L7014, Ap La Bang District, Thua Thien Province showing 2-502 Infantry and 1-327 Infantry positions highlighted in yellow. The red line is Highway 547 running from Hue west to the A Shau Valley. Original map from author's collection. Color-enhanced map © 2017.

On 4 May, Company A was moved by air from the vicinity of FSB Veghel to an LZ on a finger ridge leading west from the summit of Hill 714 at YD 507082. Company A remained overnight at that location and prepared to be moved by air on 5 May from Hill 714 to a new AO on Hill 882. The planned landing site was to be an LZ on a narrow ridge running southeast from the summit of Hill 882 at YD 498048.

Hill 882 is a large hill mass with the main peak located about 2 klicks southwest of the summit of Hill 714. Hill 882 was some 500 feet higher than the surrounding hilltops with very steep slopes covered with double and triple canopy jungle. The hill was about 5 kilometers long from north to south and about 6 kilometers wide from east to west. Hill 882 has two main ridges; one runs from the summit due west for almost 4 klicks before dropping down into a narrow saddle. The other ridge leads southeast from the peak of Hill 882 about 4 klicks before dropping sharply down into the Rao Nho River valley. The northern slope drops steeply down into a narrow canyon cut by the Rao La River; 882 shares a saddle on the east side with the western slope of Hill 714 cut by a small stream called the Khe Chi Chi. Hill 882 was largely un-explored with very few landing zones available to insert troops. The NVA was believed to be present on Hill 882 in battalion strength.

At about 0900 on 5 May, twenty-four UH-1H slicks dropped one by one into the LZ on the slope of Hill 714 and the troops of Company A /2-502 climbed aboard for the short flight to the LZ on the ridge some 2,000 meters southeast of the crest of Hill 882. On the LZ, the troops formed into a file and, led by Alpha One, moved slowly up the steep trail toward the summit of Hill 882.

After moving 200-300 meters up the ridge from the LZ, they were met by RPG and AK-47 fire at a range of only twenty meters. Two Cobra gunships had been covering Alpha One's advance; as they moved in to fire on the NVA positions, they, too, received heavy fire. After only a few minutes, the NVA broke contact and ran northwest up the ridgeline. Calling in artillery fire to fall in front of them as they advanced, Alpha One moved after the fleeing NVA. Three dead NVA were found and one AK-47 was captured. Company A lost 4 men wounded and squad leader SGT Green E. Miller and his point man, PFC Ivory L. McKinney, were killed in the initial burst of fire.

The next day, Company A's Alpha Three conducted a patrol and at YD 496052, found piles of bloody bandages, a fully-loaded AK-47 magazine and a gas mask. Apparently the NVA had stopped at this spot to treat their wounded while withdrawing from the fight near the LZ the day before. Another Company A patrol found a heavily travelled trail on a ridge southwest of Hill 714. It appeared that the NVA had used this trail as an infiltration/exfiltration route for the bunker complex recently attacked by C Company on 3-5 May. Judging by the number of bunker complexes and enemy troops being encountered, it appeared that there was probably an NVA battalion or regimental headquarters located somewhere in the Hill 714/882 area.

On 8 May, Company A's Alpha One resumed its push up the long ridgeline toward the summit of Hill 882. At about 1000, Alpha One walked into what appeared to be an L-shaped ambush. The NVA opened the fight with AK-47's firing on full automatic and a shower of Chicom grenades. The fire was heavy and Alpha One called for help. Company A's Alpha Two arrived at 1045 and both platoons tried maneuvering against the NVA positions, Several RPD light machine guns opened fire on the Company A troopers and they were forced to pull back and call for ARA from Cobra gunships, One of the Cobra's was hit several times as it dove in for a strafing run.

After consolidating their positions, both platoons tried another assault at about 1100 but they were driven back by a shower of RPG's and captured M-79 fire. They pulled back while the ARA pummeled the NVA with 2.75-inch rocket fire. They tried another assault but were again driven back by heavy RPG and machine gun fire. One of the Cobra's was hit by small arms fire and both pilots were wounded. The damaged Cobra managed to fly about 4,000 meters southeast to abandoned FSB Blaze where it landed. Both pilots were medevacked to the 85th Evacuation Hospital at Phu Bai near Camp Eagle.

Both Company A platoons pulled back while the NVA ambush positions were pounded with artillery. The NVA did not wait for the GI's, but attacked their perimeter at about 1300 with a barrage of satchel charges. Company A began to cautiously advance and spotted one of their casualties lying near an RPD machine gun position. They were unable to recover the casualty, so they backed off and called in a heavy artillery barrage. After the barrage, a LOH was sent to try and accurately locate NVA positions. The LOH was hit by 10 to 15 rounds and had to withdraw.

Late that afternoon, the NVA withdrew and both Company A platoons moved up through the ambush positions. They recovered 7 AK-47's, numerous documents and a compass of Chinese manufacture. They found 6 dead NVA and SGT Mike Lucky of Alpha Two remembers that, *"Some of the dead NVA were still clutching grenades (US-made 'baseball frags), which they hadn't got a chance to use, and there was a huge Chicom-type mine set up right beside the trail, which hadn't gone off."* Echoes of a Distant Past – front cover. The fight had cost Company A 7 wounded and SGT Dave D. Stansfield and SP4 Wayne K. Smith were killed.

All that day, during the fight, eight combat engineer troops had worked to improve the LZ being used by Company A Utilizing chain saws and C-4 plastic explosives, they cleared some of the double and triple canopy trees and underbrush from around the LZ.

The NVA continued to harass Company A with hit-and-run attacks. In the early morning of 9 May, an unknown number of NVA approached Company A in their NDP and sprayed the perimeter with AK-47 fire. There were no casualties. Later that same morning, Alpha One conducted a sweep of the area looking for the NVA who had attacked their NDP. Suddenly they were attacked by 10-12 NVA using AK's, RPG's, frag grenades and satchel charges. Alpha One took several casualties in the initial burst of fire and had to withdraw.

Alpha Two moved up to reinforce Alpha One and artillery, ARA and tactical air strikes were called in on the enemy positions. Both platoons then tried to advance, using recon by fire. The NVA eventually withdrew but not before Company A lost 10 men wounded and 1LT Roy L. Richardson was killed. Company A troopers searched the abandoned positions and found more than 20 log-and-earth reinforced bunkers. They also found many spent M-16 and M-60 machine gun cartridges, indicating that the NVA had been using captured US or ARVN weapons against Company A. Counting the number of fighting positions and bunkers with spent cartridges around them, it was estimated that at least 40 NVA had been using the bunkers. Company A counted 27 dead NVA left behind when the enemy withdrew.

On the morning of 10 May, Company A was moved by air from the ridge southeast of the summit of Hill 882 into the lowlands south of FSB Veghel. They remained in that area for two days for a rest and re-supply. Battalion headquarters was planning another assault on Hill 882 and wanted to be sure that Company A was ready.

Former Recon Sgt. James Brinker, in his book *West of Hue-Down the Yellow Brick Road,* explains what battalion planned." *The new mission was simple. Recon was to rappel out of Hueys onto the top of Hill 882 and secure the top while engineers rappelled down. They [the engineers] were going to blow an LZ on this previously unexplored hill. The guys immediately balked and started arguing with LT Hill. These were experienced, battle-hardened grunts who had risked their lives many times before and this seemed like a suicide mission. . .This went on for ten minutes with LT Hill trying to convince us to go."* (*West of Hue;* page 185)

Finally, one of the 'old-timers' stepped forward and said *"These guys are going to get us all killed anyway. It might as well be today."* With that, the Recondo's gathered their gear and climbed the hill to the 2-502 LZ to await what came next.

The top of Hill 882 had been heavily blasted by artillery that had cleared the immediate area of enemy soldiers. However, it also told the NVA that an assault was soon to take place. The Recon team rappelled down with only one minor injury. They hurriedly set up a perimeter to provide cover for the soon-to-arrive engineer troops.

Soon, the Huey carrying the team from Company A 326th Engineer Battalion, arrived and began to hover over the hilltop. Several NVA began to fire on the hovering slick from further down the hillside. All the engineer troops got down safely but the helicopter was damaged and had to leave. The crippled bird made it to FSB Shock where it landed. One of the pilots had been wounded and later died. Another slick arrived and kicked out the supplies the engineers needed and they set to work.

As soon as the LZ was completed, Company A was moved by air onto the top of Hill 882. The Recon Platoon was ordered to scout the well-used trail leading down the ridge from the peak of 882. The trail was very wide and it was obvious that large enemy forces were in the area. Recon and Company A set up a combined perimeter right on the top of Hill 882 at YD 487065.

Bad weather moved into the Hill 882/Hill 714 area with thunderstorms and high winds slowing down the pace of combat operations for three days. On 15 May, Company A formed their NDP on the peak of Hill 882 with Recon setting up their NDP about 300 meters northeast and down slope from Company A. A steady, cold rain began to fall that lasted all night.

Eraldo Lucero, in his book *Echoes of a Distant Past-Screaming Eagles,* describes what happened in the early morning hours of 16 May. *"We had been up on Hill 882 for four days and had utilized the same defensive perimeter throughout this time. This gave the NVA way too much time to probe both our defenses and our perimeter."*

Lucero woke up at about 0400 that morning, needing to relieve himself. Finding it was still raining, he decided to wait until everyone else got up at about 0600. *"Just as I was beginning to pull my poncho liner [back] over my head, I witnessed the first huge, fire-burning flash of an NVA RPG round hitting one of the machine-gun perimeter positions. I heard the screams of the wounded. I also heard a burst of AK-47 automatic weapons fire, but only a single shot from an M-16 rifle. . .I grabbed my M-16 and ammo bandolier and jumped into the night-guard position foxhole, which was located directly in front of our sleeping area. . . It had been raining for days and the foxholes were three-fourths full of rainwater. . . Immediately upon jumping into the foxhole, I opened up with a full magazine of M-16 automatic rifle fire, sweeping the area in front of my foxhole.*

As I reloaded another magazine of ammo into my M-16, I came under an intensive barrage of NVA satchel charges. . . These consisted of huge fire-burning explosions that occurred within feet of my foxhole and head. In my rush to seek cover in the foxhole, I had forgotten to grab my helmet. I realized that I had given my position away with the [M-16] rifle muzzle flashes. Even worse, I knew that the NVA were not in front of my foxhole. They had already penetrated our perimeter, and I had no idea where they were as they lobbed their satchel charges at me."

Lucero's graphic description of the beginning of the Sapper attack on Company A's NDP illustrates the danger of using the same NDP position for more than a couple of days. Any longer than that lets the enemy thoroughly scout the location, mapping the exact positions of each foxhole, as well as the placement of automatic weapons. Lucero says ". . . *As was typical of an NVA Sapper attack, they hit your position with the surgical precision of a well-trained, well-disciplined commando unit in the dead of night and without warning. They would inflict maximum casualties and slip away under the cover of [the] chaos and darkness." Echoes of a Distant Past, pages 113-118*

    The attack ended as suddenly as it had begun. Artillery rounds from FSB Veghel began to fall around Company A's beleaguered perimeter. As it began to grow light, Lucero and others on his side of the perimeter thought they could see NVA moving around outside the perimeter. They fired their M-16's on full auto; the M-60's firing in long, sustained bursts.

    Henry "Hank" Trickey, one of the M-60 gunners, saw a lone NVA Sapper break through the perimeter and run toward the center of the position. Trickey couldn't fire because he would have hit the company CP, set up in the middle of the NDP. He says that the image still haunts him.

The Recon Platoon, in position down the ridge from Company A, listened to the fight. SGT Jim Brinker, on the PRC-25 radio, monitored the progress of the fight, whispering "sit reps" to the platoon leader, 1LT James Hill who passed the news to the rest of the platoon. As Brinker listened, an NVA soldier interrupted Company A's transmissions and, in broken English, started bragging about the damage they had done to Company A. Brinker pressed the transmit key and growled into the handset *"Fuck you, gook!"* When he received a warning look from LT Hill, Brinker went back to listening.

At about that time, they were startled by a thunderous explosion; one of the perimeter guards had blown a claymore mine at an approaching NVA soldier, blowing him completely in half. A few minutes later, a second NVA walked into the Recon position and was quickly dispatched. Shortly after that, a third NVA came along and was also killed. All three had been eliminated by a hyper-alert "short-timer" who had only a few days to go before he rotated back to "the World." All three of the enemy soldiers had been carrying RPG rocket launchers and AK-47's.

Company A began to sweep the area around their perimeter looking for dead or wounded NVA. They found several blood trails, an AK-47 magazine, a B-40 rocket and about 25 un-used satchel charges. Two dead NVA were found. The surprise attack had cost Company A 22 wounded. SSGT David Jones, SP4 Billy McCullough, SP4 David Christopherson and PFC John R. Mariani from 2-502 Headquarters Company were killed. Recon took no casualties.

The weather continued to be a factor. Scattered thunderstorms limited air activity and the KIA's from Company A were not air lifted out until 17 May. The next day, the 24-hour cease fire honoring the Buddha went into effect and Company A moved to a new location about 500 meters down the north slope of Hill 882 and remained there during the cease fire.

At mid-morning on 19 May, Company A's Alpha Three and the Recon Platoon walked into a 6-man ambush. The NVA, using AK's, RPD machine guns and RPG's, fired from a range of 10 meters. No casualties were incurred and the enemy ran away after the first burst of fire. When Alpha Three followed the fleeing NVA, they triggered a second ambush. The enemy used AK's and an RPD machine gun again at a 20-meter range. After about 5 minutes, the NVA broke contact and Company A was left with 5 wounded.

Following the enemy after the second ambush, Alpha Three discovered three fresh graves. The dead enemy were dug up for intelligence purposes and Alpha Three found the enemy were dressed in khaki shirts and shorts and had been killed by small arms fire. Each grave was marked by a C-ration can split down the side with both ends cut out and then flattened. The cans were marked S-21, S-22 and S-23. At the foot of the graves was a tree with "T", "S" and "2" carved into the bark.

While moving east from YD 496069, Company A, with the Recon Platoon leading, walked into an ambush by 20 to 25 NVA. The ambush had been carefully set; 6 RPG's were fired from the south from a range of only 15 meters. AK-47 fire was received from the north; RPD machine gun fire from the east and claymores and grenades came from all around. A squad of enemy troops attempted to maneuver between Company A and Recon, trying to cut Recon off from Company A. This squad was driven off with heavy M-16 fire. Two men were wounded in the first burst of fire. Seeing they were in danger of being surrounded and chopped up, Company A and Recon charged the enemy positions, firing on full automatic. Twenty or more enemy soldiers broke contact and ran east.

Searching the enemy positions, the troopers found one dead enemy with "K-7" on his shirt, an AK, an RPD machine gun, gas masks and ammunition. Company A lost 1 wounded while Recon lost 7 wounded. SP4 Gary W. Gear, PFC John A. Claggett and PFC Robert E. Cain from Recon were killed.

Tragically, Gear and Cain were not killed outright. A Dust-off had been called but bad weather had moved in and the top of Hill 882 was completely shrouded in heavy fog. Recon Platoon medics Mike Ackerman and Dennis Moreau worked frantically to keep the two badly wounded men alive, but they could not stop the bleeding and the two men slowly bled to death. The Dust-off could be heard circling above the fog-covered trees but the pilot could not find a way through the fog. The helicopter ran low on fuel and had to go off station. Shortly after the Dust-off flew away, Gear and Cain died.

Early on the morning of 21 May, the weather cleared enough for all the casualties from Company A and Recon to be evacuated from Hill 882. At about 1140, a re-supply bird coming into the Company A LZ on the top of 882 was fired on by a single AK-47 with negative hits. About 4 hours later, two LOH's (a 'white team') were hovering over enemy positions and throwing grenades into bunkers when they were fired on by several enemy soldiers. One of the LOH's was hit so badly the pilot was forced to land on Company A's LZ at YD 496069. Two of the LOH's four rotor blades had taken hits. The crew chief checked out the bird and judged it safe to fly back to Camp Eagle. Before they left, the helicopter crewmen reported finding a lot of enemy troops and bunkers. Late that afternoon, A Cobra and a LOH (a 'pink team') were working over an area about 150 meters east of the Company A LZ. The LOH took enemy fire and was hit in the transmission. It was forced to land on Company A's LZ. The crew checked the bird and found it was un-flyable. Just before dark, a Huey came in and lifted the disabled LOH back to Camp Eagle.

Late that afternoon C Company, who had moved across the deep saddle from Hill 714, linked up with Recon and Company A. All three units formed a single NDP along a narrow finger ridge about 800 meters below the top of Hill 882 at YD 494069.

On 22 May, short patrols were conducted around the three-unit position with no contact by any of the patrols. Company A had captured some enemy documents on 20 May and a preliminary interpretation was sent out. The documents showed that Company A and Recon had been fighting the 8th Battalion of the 29th NVA Regiment. One of the documents contained instructions for taking POW's. It also listed rice distributions for the 5th, 6th, 7th, 8th, 9th and 11th NVA Companies, all attached to the 29th Regiment.

On 23 May, Company A and Recon left the large NDP site. After moving about 200 meters down the ridge, they discovered a huge bunker complex at YD 499069. 20 bunkers were found, some of them partially destroyed by artillery. Twelve above-ground hooch's were discovered containing 12 dead NVA. 60mm mortar rounds, RPG war heads, launchers and boosters, AK-47 and RPD machine gun ammunition were found along with fuses, powder charges and grenades. Surgical equipment was recovered along with medication. NVA uniforms were found along with several mess kits and an English-language Bible. Most of the items were destroyed in place.

* * *

On 24 May, the word came down that the 2-502 Infantry would be relieved in place by the 1-327 Infantry who would assume responsibility for operations in AO Tango (the Hill 714/Hill 882) area of operations. The 2-502 would be moved to AO Uniform (FSB Bastogne) to assume responsibility for operations in that area. As the helicopters came into the various LZ's, the men from the 1-327 got off and men from the 2-502 got on. Unknown to them, the 1-327 Infantry had landed in a very hot AO.

When the 1-327 Infantry moved into their new AO, Company B was given the mission to combat assault onto the peak of Hill 882. At about 1407 hours on Sunday, 24 May, Bravo one landed near the summit, an area previously blasted by bombs, napalm and artillery. Their mission, once safely on the ground, was to move down the long northern slope of Hill 882, locating and destroying the enemy as they advanced. Under the command of CPT Terry "Terrible Terry" Mills, Company B had an assigned strength of one hundred-five men. The company's three platoons had been issued extra M-16 ammo and extra barrels and ammo for their M-60's. Each squad was given an 90mm recoilless rifle for use against bunkers.

Quickly moving off the LZ to avoid a mortar attack, CPT Mills split the company into its three platoons, putting two platoons forward and holding one platoon plus the company CP in reserve. The forward platoons moved down the long northern slope of the hill for three days without contact with the NVA.

On Tuesday 26 May, Company B was due for a resupply. Bravo One was not near an LZ, so the Huey log bird was to hover overhead and 'kick out' the supplies. When the log bird approached, the pilot asked for green smoke to help him locate the platoon. The RTO popped a green smoke and waited but the Huey did not appear overhead.

After waiting for some time, LT Schultz, the Bravo One platoon leader, asked the log bird where they were. The pilot told Schultz that they had already delivered the supplies. Schultz told the pilot that he had not kicked out the supplies to Bravo One. Confused, the pilot replied that he had identified and hovered over a green smoke and had kicked out the supplies to men he had observed on the ground. Puzzled, LT Schultz again told the log bird that it was not his unit who had received the supplies and that they needed a food and water resupply ASAP.

It appeared that the NVA had been following Bravo One and monitoring their radio frequency. When the pilot had asked for a green smoke, the NVA had complied and had received Bravo One's resupply. Pilots were not supposed to specify a smoke color when they asked for smoke. The unit on the ground would pop a smoke and then ask the pilot to identify the color that he saw. The ground unit would then confirm that the pilot had identified the correct color of smoke. By specifying green smoke, the pilot had tipped off the enemy. The log bird crew had then been tricked into kicking out Bravo One's badly needed supplies to the NVA. The Huey pilot was fortunate he had not been shot down after delivering the supplies to the enemy.

That afternoon, Bravo One heard the unmistakable sound of an M-60 machine gun being fired somewhere down in the valley between Hill 882 and Hill 714. The RTO tried several times to make radio contact with the unit firing the gun, but no one replied to their queries.

A scout dog team had been assigned to Bravo One and was moving with them down the long hillside. On Wednesday 27 May, a small recon patrol went out, led by the scout dog and his handler. Suddenly, the jungle silence was shattered by the **'clack-clack-clack'** of an AK-47 on full automatic, answered by the bark of an M-16, also on full auto. The firing stopped and it was quiet until several grenades or RPG's exploded, then more rifle fire. The men on Bravo One's perimeter got ready for an attack, but the firing gradually died down. The patrol came back shortly afterward and they learned that the scout dog had set off an ambush the NVA had laid for the patrol and the dog was killed by an RPG. The NVA hated and feared scout dogs and would kill them every chance they got.

Bravo One moved cautiously down the trail to the ambush site, but the NVA were long gone. After burying the remains of the scout dog, Bravo One waited for dark before moving to an NDP site for the night. By moving into their NDP after darkness fell, Bravo One made it more difficult for the NVA to locate them and launch an attack.

Unknown to Bravo One at that time, they had set up their NDP within fifty meters of an NVA bunker complex and base camp. The NVA were not sure where they were and so did not attack that night.

Early on the morning of Thursday 28 May, a six-man recon patrol went out from Bravo One's NDP. Moving back up the existing trail, the small patrol began cutting a new trail leading to the west. Cutting a new trail is slow, strenuous and noisy work with much starting and stopping to look, listen and take compass bearings to keep on track.

Despite their caution, the NVA detected the patrol and sent out a decoy to try and lead them into an ambush. The decoy, possibly dressed in US jungle fatigues, made noise, rattled the bushes and allowed the point man brief glimpses as he led them toward an "L-shaped" ambush they had set for the patrol. The confused point man, never sure of his target, held his fire.

The patrol took a break to consider their options. The NVA chose that moment to launch the ambush by firing three RPG's, one from the right and two from the front of the L-shaped ambush. RPD machine gun and AK fire poured into the kill zone. Frozen in surprise, the patrol was pinned down and in a serious situation. Because the patrol was not firing back, the enemy small arms fire increased, the bullets buzzing all around them.

1LT Schultz, leading the patrol, yelled for the Law's to be brought forward. In his internet article *Hill 882,* Ted McCormick, carrying the LAW's, describes what happened next: *"Frozen with shock and fear, I somehow managed* [to find] *enough courage to move. Under fire, I ran to the front of the column. When I got to the front, I found LT Schultz dazed and crouched over the point man behind a fallen tree. He was barking orders into the radio receiver but was unable to hear; his right hear was bleeding, indicating a blown ear drum from the concussions. He was in shock and had a possible head concussion. The point man, covered in blood, lay in a fetal position and was unconscious; he had suffered multiple wounds and was losing a lot of blood. He looked ashen and close to death."*

Yelling for everyone to keep their heads down, McCormick quickly fired all five of the LAW's he was carrying. He began firing his M-16 in short bursts, the only one from the patrol firing back at the NVA.

Unable to hear, Schultz handed McCormick the PRC-25 radio handset and told him to try and adjust artillery fire onto the enemy positions. A battery of 105's and a battery of 155's responded to McCormick's call but the first rounds fell several hundred meters away. McCormick tried to adjust the fall of the artillery, but because of the incredible noise transmitted over the radio from the small arms fire, the artillery FDC on FSB Veghel could not understand his adjustments, so the rounds continued to fall harmlessly into the jungle.

Schultz and McCormick threw all the grenades they had, so McCormick told Schultz he would go back to Bravo One's NDP site and bring back help. McCormick ran, under fire, back up the freshly-cut trail to Bravo One only to find them under attack also. The NVA were probing the area, trying to find Bravo One's exact position.

Bringing reinforcements, McCormick returned to the ambush site to find the patrol still pinned down by heavy small arms fire. McCormick and the reinforcements began to return fire and they started to bring out their wounded. The point man was critical, barely clinging to life. The NVA ambushers were now on both flanks, firing into their position.

They managed to get back to the NDP site with no further casualties. A medevac was called and, as it hovered overhead lowering a basket for Schultz and the point man, the whole platoon put out heavy covering fire to try and keep the NVA from firing on the medevac. Both men were successfully evacuated. After the Medevac left, Bravo One began to withdraw back up the hill. The NVA probed their flanks but did not attack.

D/1-327 was operating where the northeast slope of Hill 882 met the northwest slope of Hill 714 above the Rao La River. At about 1425 hours on 28 May, Delta Three was moving on a trail along the Rao La near YD 496088 when the point man triggered a booby trap made from an RPG warhead with a fish line trip wire strung across the trail. Not realizing they had triggered a booby trap, Delta Three began firing their M-16's and M-72 LAW's into the brush around the ambush site. The NVA watching the booby trap site returned fire but Delta Three took no more casualties. During the exchange of fire, a single NVA soldier was seen dragging two bodies into the brush, away from the area of the contact.

The explosion killed the platoon leader, 1LT William Reynolds and the point man Timoteo Romero and wounded two others. When a medevac was called to evacuate the wounded, the NVA fired on it with AK's as it made its approach. After several attempts, the dust off had to break away to refuel. After refueling, the dust off tried again and the wounded men were lifted out about 1745 hours and flown to the 85th Evacuation Hospital at Phu Bai.

On the morning of Friday, 29 May, Bravo One was resupplied at the LZ near the summit of Hill 882. During the resupply, Bravo One received orders to move back down the north slope of Hill 882 and attack the bunker complex they had found in the saddle between 882 and Hill 714. Bravo One moved in column down the slope until they neared the area of the bunkers, where the platoon moved into a squads-on-line formation and slowly moved forward. The men were about ten feet apart, close enough to see the man on either side in the heavy brush.

The NVA waited until Bravo One was almost inside the bunker complex before opening fire at about 1100 hours, 29 May. The fire was heavy, coming at Bravo One from both sides. After a short but heavy exchange of small arms fire, Bravo One pulled back about one hundred fifty meters as planned, crossing to the opposite side of a small finger ridge. Cobra gun ships were called in and made several passes, firing 2.75-inch rockets and 7.62mm miniguns. When the Cobras pulled away to refuel and rearm, 105's and 155's from FSB Veghel blasted the area of the NVA camp.

Early that afternoon, after the artillery had finished, two F-4 Phantoms from Da Nang Air Force Base were called in. The jets began dropping 500-pound bombs, dangerous because Bravo One was only one hundred fifty meters from the impact area. They were so close to the target that the explosions sent bomb fragments ripping through the trees with chunks of earth and trees falling all around them. The NVA fired at the diving Phantoms with every weapon they had, waiting until the last second before diving into their bunkers.

After expending their bomb load, the jets began dropping napalm canisters. The first pass was right on the money, engulfing many of the bunkers in flames. The next pass was off-target, the bursting canisters splashing flames into Bravo One's positions. Screams sounded as the napalm engulfed Bravo One, burning the triple-canopy jungle away. Ted McCormick recounts what happened next: *"The second we were hit, I looked to my left and saw Greg Kuehl, a fellow soldier who was the assistant gunner on the M-60. He ran towards me; his fatigues had been burned away, and he held his arms outstretched. He ran towards my position, in shock and fear, stumbling up the hill.*

I stuck my foot out and tripped him, trying to avoid touching his burning skin. I held Greg down to prevent him from getting up and running off into the jungle and certain death. I called for the medic, who was busy attending other burned victims." Hill 882-page 6.

All around Bravo One, what had been double-and-triple canopy jungle had been burned away. A thick, viscous white substance, still burning, dripped down from the blackened trees. The strong smell of high explosives and burned plastic permeated the air. A check revealed that of Bravo One's five casualties, three were from napalm and two from small arms fire.

After the Phantoms left, the platoon got orders to assault the bunker complex. Moving cautiously through the burned and blasted area, Bravo one entered the NVA camp. The bunkers were so well camouflaged, even after the air strikes, that Bravo One found themselves among the bunkers before they were aware they had entered the complex. They found two dead NVA soldiers, partially buried in their destroyed bunker. A search found some twenty-five bunkers, fifteen of them destroyed; all were hit by napalm. Burned uniforms and equipment were strewn throughout the camp.

Eric Miller, in his internet article *A Hill to Remember,* describes what he found inside the big camp. *"I pulled a John Wayne (entry before throwing grenade) in one large bunker that was; 1. Empty, thank God and 2. A hospital. I had hoped to take a prisoner or just shoot some of the bastards that were trying to kill us. I threw a grenade in one small bunker and crawled in only to see that after I had blown the linings of the walls out, a mother rat with babies clinging to her had survived and ran past me. I wouldn't believe this either, but I saw it. Nothing but a daisy cutter (a 15,000-pound, parachute-dropped bomb used to blow LZ's) works on rats."*

The NVA had constructed a trail as wide as a city street through the camp, concealing it from the air by pulling the tops of the trees together and tying them in place. The camp had been occupied by sappers; rows of concertina wire were still in place, clearly a training area for the sappers.

While Bravo One was searching the camp, the scout dog (a replacement for the one killed) suddenly alerted and movement was heard in the brush to Bravo One's front. The platoon quickly found defensive positions within the camp. Because the sun was going down, the decision was made to set up an NDP in the sapper's camp. The NVA had apparently decided not to attack their own camp, for the night passed quietly.

On Saturday, 30 May, Bravo One was notified that Bravo Two had been ambushed and had taken several casualties. The NVA had also succeeded in shooting down a LOH from the 2-17 Cavalry, a scout unit attached to the 101st Airborne. Bravo One was told to move as quickly as they could to Bravo Two's position and from there conduct a search and rescue mission for the downed LOH and the two-man crew.

After marching over one kilometer through double-and-triple canopy jungle, a move that took them all morning, Bravo One linked up with Bravo Two and the Company B CP. CPT Mills briefed 1LT Schultz and Bravo One on their new mission.

There was no radio contact with the downed LOH, but the 2-17 Cavalry had monitored radio signals from the aircraft ELT (emergency landing transmitter), so it was possible that at least one of the aircrew had survived the crash. Even if there were no survivors, it was important to recover the 7.62mm minigun and the crews' personal weapons from the LOH to keep them out of NVA hands.

CPT Mills took charge of the recovery team and Ted McCormick walked point carrying an M-60 with three hundred linked rounds over his shoulder. CPT Mills walked slack behind McCormick. The pace was slow; McCormick had to watch the trail for any trip wires from booby traps while at the same time, look for NVA on the trail or in ambush positions.

The trip took the remainder of that day. By late afternoon, McCormick spotted a lot of fired AK-47 shell casings littering the trail. They continued for another hundred meters and began to see burned foliage, Suddenly, they were right on top of the crash site.

McCormick describes what they found: *"All that was identifiable that this was a helicopter was a piece of the tail rotor fuselage. The torso of a man hung hideously from a tree. In the middle of the trail lay what I first thought was a log but on closer inspection [I] realized it was a dead American soldier. He was intact and charred black from being burned from the explosion and frozen in position as if he was still seated in the cockpit. . .. We secured the minigun and other components of the aircraft and set up a defensive perimeter for the night."* Hill 882 – page 7.

B/1-327 gradually worked their way down the south slope of Hill 882 and into the valley of the Rao Nho River near inactive FSB Cannon at YD473029. McCormick remembers being on guard duty at night down in the valley and seeing red-filtered flashlights dotting the slopes of Hill 882 as NVA units moved into position to attack FSB Ripcord over twenty kilometers (12 miles) to the northwest.

Ted McCormick recalls his thoughts as Bravo One worked its way down the long southern slope of Hill 882: *"I thought of these dead pilot's families as their bodies lay in pieces, burned beyond recognition. I was prepared to give my life, but not for country and cause. I was ready to die for 'esprit de corps' and my fellow soldiers. I had become adept at fighting guerilla warfare. I was nineteen."* Hill 882 – page 7.

Chapter 10
'HARD LUCK ALPHA' at FIREBASE HENDERSON

". . .most of us saw our senior leadership as stark aliens helicoptering in from their stuffed chairs and elaborate headquarters, freshly showered/shaved and well-fed... adorned in starched jungle fatigues and spit-shined boots. . .ready to shake a few hands and ask a few mundane questions before disappearing [back] into the sky in a matter of a few moments." Captain (Brigadier General, ret.) James E. Mitchel

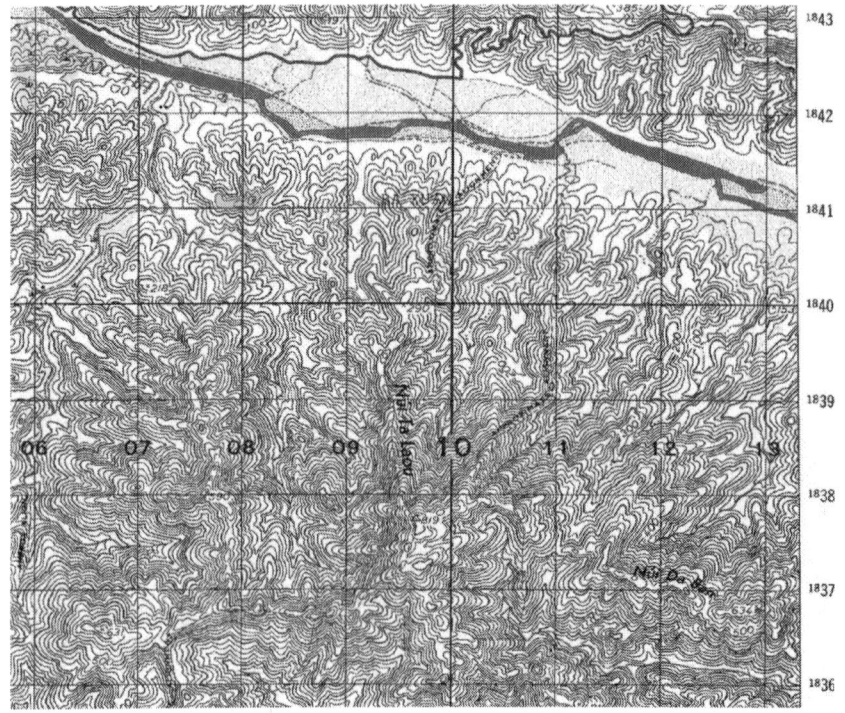

Color-enhanced detail from topographical map sheet 6342-2, Series L-7014, Thon Doc Kinh District, Quang Tri Province showing A/2-501 Infantry positions on FSB Henderson highlighted in yellow. Map from author's collection. Color-enhanced map © 2017.

Fire Support Base Henderson was an older firebase first built by the US Marine Corps. It was used by the 2nd Battalion, 9th Marine Regiment in June 1969 to support Operation Apache Snow, the incursion into the A Shau Valley. Henderson was re-opened by the 3rd Brigade, 101st Airborne Division in late April 1970 to support Operation Texas Star. In re-opening Henderson, the 3rd Brigade assumed responsibility to provide base defense and security for both the US and ARVN artillery batteries firing in support of ARVN infantry units operating in the area.

Henderson was opened during the last week of April. B Battery 2-11 Field Artillery 155mm (US) and B Battery 12th Field Artillery 105mm (ARVN) were the initial artillery units to occupy the base. The 54th ARVN TOC was opened on the base to support and control the 1st and 2nd Battalions of the 54th ARVN Regiment operating to the west and south of the base.

The site of FSB Henderson was at YD 081411 on a hill overlooking the Song (river) Quang Tri, the name now changed to the Song Thach Han by the current communist government of Vietnam. The dominant terrain feature in the area is Nui Ta Laou or Hill 819 located at YD 097377. At 2686 feet, it is the highest hill within several kilometers of the firebase. A long, gradually sloping ridge nearly 4 klicks long runs northwest from the summit of Hill 819, ending in the valley cut by the Song Quang Tri. FSB Henderson sat on a hill rising out of that ridge some 800 meters south of the river, dominated on the west, south and east by higher terrain. The hilltop itself is small, about 200 meters long by 50 to 75 meters wide.

A/2-501 (now known by some as 'Hard Luck Alpha') arrived by air on FSB Henderson about midday on 5 May 1970. The base had recently been reopened on 30 April. It had been secured initially by D/1-501 Infantry. As was his usual practice, CPT Mitchell walked the perimeter to get an idea of what needed to be done to improve the hill's defenses. Mitchell, in his internet article *The Battle of FSB Henderson,* remembers his reaction. *"In absolute shock, I instantly recognized that defensive preparations on Henderson were next to non-existent compared to any other firebase I'd ever seen."*

After almost six days of occupation by D/1-501, it seemed almost nothing had been done to fortify the hilltop. The fighting positions along the perimeter line were nothing more than waist-deep holes; very few were sand bagged and none had any overhead cover. Only a single coil of concertina wire had been put in place with no 'tangle-foot' barrier under the concertina at all. Protective fields of fire had been cut less than 15 to 20 meters forward of the fighting positions. Dense jungle growth, offering the NVA perfect cover and concealment, was left standing very close to the perimeter. The only positions that had been sand bagged with overhead cover were the ARVN TOC, the ARVN medical aid station and the CP for the defending infantry company commander.

As Company A continued to land, CPT Mitchell climbed to the top of the hill to get an overall view of the positions and to get a better understanding of the ground Company A had to defend. He was surprised to see five to eight pallets of artillery projectiles sitting out in the open; they had not been moved to covered revetments after delivery by CH-47 helicopter. He saw one or two bladders or 'blivets' containing fuel inside the artillery positions. This was a dangerous situation and would prove to be a deadly mistake some twelve hours later.

Mitchell made his way to the ARVN TOC to introduce himself. While there, he met an ARVN captain who had attended the US Army Infantry School at Fort Benning, Georgia. Through casual conversation, Mitchell learned that after nearly a week, no one had bothered to set up a combined force defensive plan, no direct or indirect (artillery) fire plans, no plans for a counter-attack, no surveillance plans, no defensive obstacle plans and that no land lines had been laid for direct communication between Mitchell's CP and the other positions on Henderson. CPT Mitchell left the ARVN TOC confused and angry but determined to fix what he could in the remaining hours before night fell.

When he returned to his CP, Mitchell contacted his platoon leaders by radio and told them to concentrate on improving the fighting positions around the perimeter; deepening the holes and erecting adequate overhead cover. Company A by itself had 80 men present for duty, less than 60% of the authorized strength for an infantry company. It was not enough to adequately man all the defensive positions along the firebase perimeter. 1LT Jim Knight led Alpha One; 1LT Lyn Hargrove Alpha Two and SSGT Bob Nichol Alpha Three. These men were all experienced leaders but experience would not be enough if the firebase was attacked before they could get ready.

1LT Rick Hawley and 17 men of the 2-501 Recon Platoon had been attached to Company A at the last minute to bolster their 'foxhole strength.' Around mid-day, a few more infantry replacements were flown out to the firebase. This brought their strength to 120 men, but many of them were inexperienced replacements. It was still not enough men to adequately defend Henderson's irregularly shaped perimeter but it was all they were going to get. In total, there were 162 US soldiers to defend FSB Henderson. This included Company A, Recon and a few men from C Company 2-501 Infantry.

Included in the figure of 162 men were gunners from B Battery 2-11 Artillery, a squad from B Company 326th Engineer Battalion, a small detachment from the 501st Signal Battalion and a small mortar platoon from E Company 2-501 Infantry. The remainder of the 311 men on Henderson belonged to the ARVN artillery battery and the ARVN TOC.

Another problem developed when they found they had no reliable radio communication with 3rd Brigade Headquarters, nearly thirty miles to the southeast at Camp Evans. They only had one radio and one antenna capable of reaching Camp Evans and then only through a 're-transmission site' or 'booster' on a distant hill somewhere. After the fight, CPT Mitchell learned that the ARVN TOC, only 20 yards distant, had a multi-channel radio system and a trained operator provided by the 101st Airborne Division. Company A was forced to relay all their communications through other units who had reliable radio contact with 3rd Brigade Headquarters. Both Division and 3rd Brigade had been aware of the communications problem on FSB Henderson for over a week but they took no action even though they had provided the ARVN TOC with up-to-date radio equipment.

Late that afternoon a CH-47 Chinook arrived over Henderson, hovered and set down a sling load of 105mm ammunition near the ARVN 105 battery. It was growing dark quickly, so no one bothered to move the howitzer shells, fuses and powder bags into secure revetments. They were left sitting in the open and that failure to follow procedure would turn out to be a fatal error.

All through the afternoon and into the evening of 5 May, the men of Company A labored to improve the inadequate defenses of FSB Henderson. They had been told that duty on Henderson was to be "*a quiet and welcomed break to give the company some time to rest and reconstitute itself and integrate the many replacements*" that had been sent out after Company A's heavy losses on 'Re-Up Hill' and FSB Granite. CPT Mitchell and the veterans of Company A knew better; they were very vulnerable. They had done their best in the short time available to them and, as darkness fell, they hoped they could get through the night ahead and be able to start work in earnest on firebase defenses the next day. By 2100 hours, FSB Henderson was quiet and fog had moved up from the Song Quang Tri valley, making the night even darker.

Mitchell and his team of RTO's from the company CP were up most of the night trying to resolve the communication problems with the rear area at Camp Evans. By 0430 hours on 6 May, the artillery FO and Mitchell had climbed to the roof of the CP dug out and were working out last minute changes to a series of pre-planned artillery strikes on the hills and ridges some 700 meters to Henderson's east. It was SOP in Company A when they were defending a firebase to hit targets in the terrain surrounding the firebase with artillery barrages hoping to deter or break up any early morning attack. They did not know that the 8th and 33rd NVA Sapper Battalions, 66th NVA Regiment from the 304B Division was already in their assault positions between the firebase perimeter and pre-planned targets on the surrounding hills.

At about 0505 hours, a single burst of fire from an automatic weapon shattered the pre-dawn silence on FSB Henderson. This burst of fire was apparently a signal, for it was immediately followed by a barrage of RPG's, satchel charges and AK-47 fire, answered by exploding claymores, grenades and M-16, M-60 and M-79 fire from Henderson's defenders. By the way the attack began, Mitchell knew the NVA were already in or through the single line of concertina wire and eyeball-to-eyeball fighting had already begun. Within a few minutes, the tempo of the ground attack against the eastern side of the base had increased noticeably. Hand flares fired by the defenders zoomed skyward and their flickering light revealed NVA Sappers in front of the CP, between the bunker line and Mitchell's position. The appearance of Sappers so close to his CP told CPT Mitchell that the defenders in the foxhole line to his front were already wounded or dead.

Members of the CP fired at the elusive Sappers as they ran crouched over, some crawling, throwing satchel charges as they came. One NVA soldier appeared out of nowhere, firing a single RPG round before anyone could get a shot off. The rocket hit the tall AN/GRC 292 aluminum radio antenna on top of the CP bunker and exploded with a terrible concussion, showering Mitchell and his RTO with bits of aluminum and warhead shrapnel. Later, Mitchell realized that the NVA had probably been aiming at the ARVN TOC some twenty yards to the rear of his CP and had hit the antenna by accident. For several more seemingly endless minutes, the CP personnel shot at anyone moving around them who was not showing the familiar silhouette of a US Army 'steel pot' (steel helmet).

The NVA Sappers had penetrated the perimeter between 1LT Jim Knight's Alpha One and 1LT Richard Hawley's Recon Platoon, cutting off one of Alpha One's forward positions. The sappers concentrated their efforts against the ARVN TOC and the 155mm howitzers of B Battery 2-11 Artillery at the top of the hill.

Medical SP4 Dennis Hughes, attached to the 155 battery, was asleep beside the wheel of one of the big guns when an explosion blew him into the air. Hughes' remembers: *"When I came to my senses, I crawled over to help two guys, one of whom was on fire."* Even though he was wounded, Hughes treated others, moving through a series of trenches on the hill. He had lost his medical aid bag in the first explosion, so he cut strips from his uniform to bandage wounds. Several times Hughes rushed, under fire, to pull wounded men to safety and treat them. He saved several lives and was awarded the Silver Star for his conspicuous bravery after the battle.

Back at the Company A CP, CPT Mitchell saw by the volume of fire directed at the top of the hill that the Sappers main attack was directed specifically at the 155's of B Battery and the ARVN TOC. The firing was so intense that it blended into one continuous roar. The fire was so heavy from both US and NVA that no one could move out of their fighting positions without being hit.

About a half hour into the fight, Mitchell heard several long hissing sounds which he recognized as the sound made by a flamethrower. There was a report that one of Company A's infantryman had been set on fire by the flamethrower and had run, engulfed in flames, off the hill. He was never seen again. The sound came from his right rear near the 155 battery. Mitchell had heard that characteristic hissing sound in training and he had a hard time believing the NVA were using the weapon in actual combat.

CPT Mitchell could see fires beginning to grow and spread near the artillery ammo pallets, still out in the open. As the fires grew larger and hotter, individual artillery rounds began to 'cook off' from the heat. For about 10 minutes, rounds exploded one or two at a time, blowing unexploded rounds into the air to fall all over the hilltop. Suddenly, a huge explosion rocked Henderson; the whole firebase shuddered as if struck by an earthquake. The giant detonation killed both US and NVA soldiers and ruptured and ignited one or more of the unprotected fuel blivets. A river of burning fuel poured down Henderson's east slope and into several fighting holes manned by Rick Hawley's Recon Platoon.

Trapped between the exploding 155 rounds and the NVA inside the wire, the Recon men were consumed in the massive conflagration. Their fighting holes were death traps and many of Hawley's men died in their foxholes or tried to fight their way through the NVA, preferring to take their chances against NVA gunfire rather than burn.

As the sky began to grow light, exposing a scene from hell, Cobra gunships arrived on station above FSB Henderson. The low cloud ceiling, ground fog and smoke from the massive fires on the eastern perimeter prevented the Cobra's from diving down on attack runs. The Cobra's made pass after pass over the flaming hilltop but could not fire because it was impossible to tell friend from foe. However, their mere presence over the battlefield was a strong deterrent and the NVA began to withdraw.

1LT Jim Knight had so far survived the fight. As the firing began to die away and the Cobra's roared overhead, Knight spotted several NVA soldiers casually walking away from the hill. Knight remembers: *"They were illuminated by flares and were at sling arms, uncaring, as if we were all dead."* Backlit by the flares, they were easy targets and Knight and his 1st Platoon men cut them down.

As the sappers fled the firebase in the growing light, The Cobra's unleashed volleys of 2.75-inch rockets and long bursts of 7.62mm mini-gun fire onto the ridges and draws leading away from Henderson. The ARVN 105mm battery cranked their guns down into direct fire position and fired salvo after salvo of high explosive rounds almost point blank at the ridges only 6 or 7 hundred meters east of the firebase.

As the firing died away, the survivors began a frantic search to find and treat the many wounded and to rescue others trapped in collapsed fighting positions. Sporadic rifle fire and occasional RPG rounds still fell on Henderson but most attackers were fleeing from the Cobras and ARVN artillery fire toward the hills to the east.

In the early morning twilight, Company A's surviving leaders moved from position to position in their sectors, searching for missing infantrymen and establishing a new line of defense around the destroyed hilltop. There were many soldiers and some leaders missing as full daylight came and the fog began to burn away. Survivors of the battle who had previously had no leadership position found themselves suddenly pushed into that role regardless of rank.

CPT Mitchell moved to the top of the hill and through what was left of B Battery's 155's. The position was nearly unrecognizable and all the howitzers had been damaged or destroyed; some of the barrels on the big guns had been peeled back like bananas. The infantry fighting positions on the far side of the battery in the eastern sector of the perimeter were hard to find due to fires that were still burning and the damage done by the tremendous blast that had shaken the hill only an hour before. Most of the area around B Battery's position was now scorched, still smoldering wreckage.1LT Rick Hawley's position was a pile of rubble, still burning and too hot to approach. Hours later, Mitchell came back to search the wreckage for Hawley's body but found no trace of him.

When it was safe to do so, medevac helicopters began coming in to the LZ just below Company A's CP. This LZ became the triage and treatment point for the wounded; the medics who had survived the attack worked feverishly to prepare the wounded for the flight to the 18th MASH near Camp Evans. The edges of the LZ were lined with the seriously wounded and the ground soon turned to bloody mud.

About 0730 hours, CPT Mitchell got a call from COL Bill Bradley, 3rd Brigade Commander. Bradley told Mitchell he was in-bound in his C&C helicopter and wanted to land on the LZ next to Mitchell's CP. Mitchell told the colonel it was too dangerous to land and that the colonel should just relay any orders he had by radio. Mitchell was concerned because of the NVA's habit of dropping mortar rounds onto an LZ when a helicopter tried to land, especially just after an attack. Mitchell told Bradley of his concern that, if he did land, he should wait in the Company A CP to see if the NVA were going to drop any mortar rounds onto the LZ. Bradley said he was going to land anyway and would then walk up to the ARVN TOC, more than 30 meters from the LZ.

The C&C helicopter landed and the pilot, wise in the ways of NVA mortar crews, immediately took off. COL Bradley, MAJ 'Tex' Turner and the Brigade CSM, Ray Long, began to walk deliberately up the hill toward the ARVN TOC. Mitchell motioned for them to come to his CP but they continued to walk toward the TOC. COL Bradley had just entered the TOC doorway when a mortar round landed about 15 feet behind Maj Turner and CSM Long. Major Turner was seriously wounded and CSM Long was killed instantly.

Seeing what had happened, CPT Mitchell and his CP medic ran to the ARVN TOC. Long was already dead so the medic began to treat MAJ Turner. COL Bradley ordered Mitchell to call in a medevac to extract the dead CSM. Mitchell pointed out to the colonel that it was against policy to call a medevac to an LZ still under fire to evacuate a dead man, but Bradley ordered him to do it anyway. The medevac was called in and when it lifted off, Mitchell got an irate radio call from the pilot who chewed him out for risking his helicopter and crew by calling him in to a 'hot' LZ to carry out a dead man. One of Company A's wounded had been bumped from the flight to accommodate the dead CSM. COL Bradley's bad decision had resulted in the unnecessary loss of a valuable member of the brigade staff and Bradley's and Mitchell's relationship suffered because of the incident.

The remainder of the day was spent evacuating what seemed an endless stream of wounded and, finally, the dead. Between medevac flights, log birds brought in a re-supply of food, ammo and water. Tube artillery from supporting firebases and ARA from Cobra gunships continued to pound possible NVA targets on the higher ridges that overlooked FSB Henderson on three sides. Between sporadic NVA mortar barrages, the survivors of Company A continued to search for several men who were still missing. That afternoon, they were harassed by recoilless rifle fire from the northwest but many of the rounds were duds and they caused little damage.

Despite their thorough search, often under fire, CPT Mitchell and the remaining men of Company A could not locate 1LT Rick Hawley, SGT Larry Kier or SGT Refugio Teran. What was left of Company A, about 40 men, was airlifted off FSB Henderson in the late afternoon of 6 May and flown to Camp Evans. Many of these men, including CPT Mitchell, had minor wounds that were treated at an aid station near the Camp Evans main LZ. As soon as they were stitched up or had shrapnel removed, they slowly walked back to the LZ to find those men who had not needed medical attention fast asleep lying around the edges of the LZ.

Shortly after he got back to the LZ, Mitchell received a summons to report to COL Bradley. When he arrived at Bradley's office, the colonel lost no time in ordering Mitchell not to talk about or discuss the FSB Henderson battle with anyone. COL Bradley made it very clear that Mitchell was not to talk to the press about the battle unless ordered to do so by a senior officer from Headquarters, 101st Airborne. Bradley then offered Mitchell the use of the brigade 'VIP Hooch' for the night, but Mitchell declined. Mitchell was contacted later by LTC Bobby Brashears, Mitchell's former battalion commander, and asked to give a detailed statement regarding what happened at FSB Henderson.

The exact number of US casualties incurred on Henderson has been debated from the time the battle ended until now. 101st Airborne official records show that 32 men were killed on Henderson but CPT Mitchell's personal records can account for 'only' 27 men that can be listed as 'killed or likely killed' on Henderson.

Since the NVA had ample time to carry away their wounded and killed, only 29 dead NVA were found in the area around and on FSB Henderson itself.

An accurate count on the number of men wounded on Henderson also remains elusive. The total wounded may never be known, but Mitchell is certain that at least 70 men were treated for wounds received on 6 May 1970.

The following is a list of known killed in action or missing in action on FSB Henderson, listed by assigned company and rank at time of death:

Company A 2-501 Infantry
SGT Larry G. Kier; PFC George W. Bennett, Jr.; PFC Lawrence L. Gordon; SP4 Frank F. Lewis; SGT John J Willey; SGT Frederick P. Ziegenfelder; SP4 Michael L. Angle; and PFC Tommy I. Hindman.

B Company 2-501 Infantry
SGT Robert A. Denton

E Company 2-501 Infantry
SP4 Gregory A. Chavez; PFC Douglas W. Day; SGT Refugio T. Teran; PFC Ronald D. VanBeukering; SSGT Gary F. Snyder; SP4 John G. Widen; 1LT Richard A. Hawley; SGT David E. Ogden; SP4 Dickey W. Regan and SP4 Edward Veser.

Headquarters Company 2-501 Infantry
SP4 Melvin Bowman and SP4 Jay T. Diller.

Company A 501st Signal Battalion
SP4 James D. Jennings

Headquarters 3rd Brigade
CSM Ray L. Long and CPT Billy J. Williams (attached from the Military
Assistance Command, Vietnam)

B Battery 2-11 Field Artillery
SGT Michael F. Brown; PFC John E. Granath, Jr. and PFC David Yeldell.

During a training session at Camp Eagle just before the start of Operation Texas Star, a captured NVA sapper demonstrates to troopers from C/2-502 Infantry the methods used to penetrate wire barriers and disarm claymore mines. Photo from author's collection. ©2017

Chapter 11
THE NVA QUICKEN THE PACE

"...we were seriously disrupting the enemy's ability to resupply their units in the coastal plains. We were definitely an obstacle to their plans...a thorn, in hindsight, that they were going to remove at any cost." MAJ Herbert E. Koenigsbauer, 2-506 Infantry *Ripcord-Screaming Eagles Under Siege,* Keith W. Nolan page 96.

The NVA did not relent in their attacks against the US units and bases scattered around northern I Corps. The next major contact involved D/1-506 Infantry under the command of 1LT Donald R. Workman. D Company combat assaulted onto the summit of Hill 980 at YD 429122, the site of an old firebase named Maureen. D Company's three platoons moved quickly off the hill in three different directions.

Late on the afternoon of 5 May, D Company's Delta Two led by 1LT Lawrence E. Fletcher returned to the hilltop at YD 429122 to set up their NDP. Earlier that day, Delta Two had been in contact with the NVA below the top of Hill 980, so they were probably followed back to their NDP on the bare summit of Hill 980.

On 6 May, Fletcher led the platoon on a long patrol around Hill 980. It began to grow dark before Fletcher could find a good NDP site, so he decided to again return to old FSB Maureen to spend the night, a serious tactical error because the NVA now knew exactly where they were.

There was no moon that night so NVA sappers crept, un-detected, past the perimeter defenses. When the attack started at about 0445 hours with a barrage of satchel charges from inside the perimeter, LT Fletcher, his RTO and the platoon sergeant were the first men killed. With the senior leaders' dead, the platoon was left on its own.

Delta Two had a brand-new medic: a unique soldier named PFC Kenneth M. Kays. When the Selective Service System had sent Kays his Order to Report for Induction, he had immediately applied for conscientious objector status. When the application was denied, Kays promptly fled to Canada. He agreed to return and allow himself to be drafted only after the army promised he could serve as a medic.

Once the attack began, several men were hit immediately and began screaming for help. Grabbing his aid bag, Kays began running across the perimeter. He hadn't gotten very far before a satchel charge blew off his left leg below the knee. In shock, Kays did not realize he had lost a leg. He jumped back up, but when he tried to run, he fell headlong because his left foot was gone. Realizing the situation, he grabbed a tourniquet, tied off the stump and began crawling from man to man, treating them while shielding them with his own body.

Delta Two began receiving AK-47 fire and some 60mm mortar rounds which landed east of their position, causing no damage. The attack had initially come from the north and northwest but the enemy now swung around to attack from the south. Delta Three, in their NDP about 500 meters to the northeast at YD 432123 began to move toward the embattled Delta Two. Before they could reach Delta Two, they ran into an ambush and received AK-47 fire and satchel charges. They took no casualties but were delayed in their movement toward Delta Two.

During the sudden attack, Delta Two had lost 6 men killed and 12 wounded almost right away. There were only a half-dozen uninjured men left to hold off the advancing NVA. They managed to stop the sappers coming up the slope with a shower of grenades, firing at those sappers inside the perimeter with their M-16's.

The NVA withdrew, leaving four of their dead behind as it grew light and the ARA Cobra's came on station. 1LT Workman arrived shortly afterward with the 3rd Platoon and took over. They found PFC Kays, weakened by blood loss, huddled beside a wounded man he had been treating after the man had been blown down the hill by a satchel charge. Kays survived and was later awarded the Medal of Honor for his actions on Hill 980.

The names of those killed on Hill 980 are not noted in the battalion Daily Staff Journal for that date; they are listed only by their line or 'pack' numbers.

■ ■ ■

The NVA relentlessly tried to find an 'easy' way to penetrate the wire defenses around FSB Ripcord. On many otherwise quiet nights, noises were heard in the wire or the ground radar would detect movement and B/2-506, then responsible for firebase security, would throw fragmentation grenades and M-79 gunners would lob HE (high explosive) rounds down-slope into the wire while the 81mm mortar crews dropped in their own HE rounds. At different times during the night, even if it was quiet, a so-called 'Mad Minute' would be called when every rifleman, machine gunner and grenadier available would fire for 60 seconds to deter any sappers trying to penetrate the wire.

SGT Thomas P. Tolson wrote in a letter home that *"there are beaucoup gooks all around. Three days in a row now we found tracks just outside our wire. . .Last night the guy in the hole next to mine was looking through his 'starlight scope'. . .and he saw a gook on his stomach right at the wire."* At that moment, the 81's fired some illumination rounds which make a popping sound just before they ignite. Tolson continues *"As soon as the round popped, the gook got up and ran behind a big rock. About the time he got up to run, the guy next to me opened up for all he was worth, guys were shooting and throwing hand grenades, but this morning when they went down and checked it out it was the same old story, just tracks. . ."* Ripcord, page 95.

All the shooting, grenade throwing and artillery fire was not entirely wasted. Captured NVA documents revealed that numerous sappers were killed trying to get through the in-depth defenses of FSB Ripcord. Two NVA, captured in a firefight with another company from the 2-506, said they (the NVA) had been sending people up to the wire to try and find a way through the wire but so far, an easy way had not been found. The prisoners said their company had their camp at the bottom of the Ripcord hill and that 20 of their number had been killed by close-in mortar and artillery rounds constantly fired to keep them (the NVA) away.

The NVA and Viet Cong could be, and often were, extremely ruthless in the way they fought the war. Many of the NVA regulars had been living, working and fighting in the jungles of I Corps for several years. They knew they would not be leaving the mountains around the A Shau Valley unless they were killed, seriously wounded or won the war. They were often fanatical in the way they prosecuted an attack against the ARVN or an American unit, preferring to be killed rather than give up.

An American soldier or airman, on the other hand, could look forward to going home after a 12-month tour, the exception being the hard-luck Marines who endured a 13-month tour. Unlike the NVA, US servicemen would board the "Freedom Bird' at Da Nang, Cam Ranh Bay or Tan Son Nhut airports and ride in luxury back to 'The World' or, as it was sometimes called 'The Land of the Big PX.' For most of the infantrymen fighting in the jungles of I Corps, the promise of that flight home kept them going through some very difficult situations.

An excellent example of NVA ruthlessness was experienced by a recon squad from E/2-506 Infantry on 28 May. Several recon teams from the Recon Platoon had been inserted into the Triple Hill area near YD 331203 about 1,500 meters northwest of FSB Ripcord. One of the recon squads made contact with an unknown size enemy force and Cobra gunships were called in. Two of the recon men were wounded by shrapnel from a Cobra firing rockets in close support. A medevac from the 326th Medical Battalion, known as Eagle Dust-off, was called to extract the men. The medevac helicopter, clearly marked with large red crosses on the doors and nose, came to a hover over the team and a jungle penetrator was lowered through the trees. After the wounded were strapped to the seats on the penetrator, the crew chief began to pull them up.

An NVA fired an RPG at the medevac, scoring a direct hit in the helicopters' fuel cell. The crew chief remembered to cut the hoist cable and the jungle penetrator, with the two wounded men stilled strapped on, fell like a rock down through the trees to the ground. This saved their lives because a few seconds later the medevac smashed into the hillside and exploded in a ball of fire, killing the four helpless crewmen.

Two other recon squads, after monitoring radio reports that a medevac had been shot down, had linked up and were rushing to the aid of the embattled team. SP4 John Mihalko, a member of one of the squads moving to the aid of the single team wrote: *"We were all numbed by the reality of what had just happened. Saving the other team was of the utmost importance, but we also wanted to exact a measure of revenge." Ripcord* -page 117.

The loss of the unarmed medevac had sent a lot of furious and very determined Screaming Eagles into action. Heavy traffic filled the radio frequencies and a line unit was being readied for immediate insertion onto Triple Hill.

The recon teams, who were the closest, got there first. Ralph Motta was point man and Mihalko was walking slack (second man) as they followed an NVA high-speed trail up the hill. Mihalko remembers: *"There was a huge boulder just off the side of the trail. Just as we reached it, we both saw the NVA gunner with an RPG pointed right at us." Ripcord* – page 117. Both men dived for cover behind the boulder just as the rocket hit the rock. The NVA fired a second rocket and the medic, 'Doc' Speed, rushed up the trail to treat any wounded. Finding no wounded, Speed risked a quick peek around the boulder, then tossed several frag grenades up into the rocks where the RPG gunner was hiding. The firing stopped.

Behind them, D/2-506 Infantry was landing at the bottom of the hill. They quickly assaulted up the hill past the recon men. Mihalko cautiously checked the RPG gunners' position and found him dead, killed by the grenades. Says Mihalko: *"I took a very long look at the face of the man who had calmly and deliberately destroyed an unarmed medevac." Ripcord* – page 117.

The grunts from D Company found a second dead NVA at the top of the hill and had taken a POW. Mihalko describes what happened next: *". . .a very terrified NVA prisoner. He looked almost pitiful, standing there stripped down to his underwear, pondering his fate. There was talk of blowing him away for what had happened to the medevac, but cooler heads prevailed. A bird flew in with an interpreter. He was questioned for a while and then whisked away, much to his relief." Ripcord* – page 117

In mid-June, LTC Lucas received intelligence reports of enemy forces moving into the Triple Hill area so, on June 14, Lucas moved B/2-506, commanded by CPT William J. Williams onto the hill. B Company worked the area for six days with no results, but on June 21, they found twenty unoccupied bunkers which they destroyed.

On June 22, Bravo One, led by 1LT Joe Delgado (a pseudonym), moved onto a knoll where they found a well-used trail. SGT Thomas Tolson and his squad were sent to check it out. One of the men noticed a trail marker cut into the bark of a tree, identical to one they had found at the bunker complex two days before. Checking the area, they found a pile of mortar rounds hidden between the roots of a large tree. A little thatched roof built over the top of the rounds kept out the rain and they rested on a small platform of woven twigs. What looked like a seat was on top of the little shelter so a trial watcher would have a place to sit while he guarded the cache.

Tolson left his squad at the cache site and started back up the hill to report to LT Delgado when he saw the bushes begin to move on his left rear. Quickly ducking off the trail, he moved back to his squad as rapidly as he could. The squad had also seen the movement and had taken cover; Tolson and his men braced for a firefight.

Unknown to Sgt. Tolson, LT Delgado was also moving down the hill to re-fill canteens from a small stream close by. Delgado was startled to see a file of men walking quickly through the jungle – two Vietnamese, wearing American steel pots with M-16's, were leading with a shirtless, blond-headed man carrying an M-60 bringing up the rear.

A man from Tolson's squad gave a shrill whistle and Delgado, thinking the whistle was for him, shouted *'Currahee!'*, the battalions' recognition signal. SGT Tolson immediately thought the shout had come from the men in the bushes and was puzzled when the *'Currahee'* shout was answered with an *'Okay!'* Confused, Tolson waited a bit before asking *"Who are you?"*, but there was no answer. Delgado, thinking the *'Okay'* was Tolson acknowledging that they had identified him, hurried back up the hill, glad he had not been mistakenly shot by his own men.

Tolson's squad whistled again but got no answer. From their position, they could see the bushes shaking as the strange group moved down the hill, then up and over another hill and out of sight.

SGT Robert Judd also saw the strange procession. He counted five uniformed NVA wearing their characteristic pith helmets, with a light-skinned blonde man carrying an M-60 bringing up the rear. Judd started to fire but was confused because of the blonde-haired man, who stood head-and-shoulders over the Vietnamese. When LT Delgado shouted *'Currahee'*, instead of answering with the correct, profane response of *'Currahee, motherfucker!'*, the group instantly started running and quickly disappeared.

LT Delgado called CPT Williams to report the strange incident and was told there were no other friendly units in the area. Delgado, Tolson and some men from Tolson's squad began chasing the men and, after crossing a little creek, entered an area where the NVA had cut trees to build bunkers. Finding a trail with fresh tracks, they took off down the path at a trot. The trail led past a bunker and Delgado, leaving Tolson to check the bunker, went on up the trail alone. Shortly, Delgado came running back shouting that the 'gooks' were coming back.

The small patrol waited for several minutes, holding their breath as the enemy passed by all around them. They could hear, but not see, the NVA who obviously did not see them. When it appeared safe, they moved quickly back to join the rest of the platoon. Delgado then led the entire platoon back to the bunkers but there was no sign of the enemy.

CPT Williams brought the three platoons of B Company together and on June 24, they cautiously moved out under the triple canopy jungle, on the look-out for the blonde NVA. They found twenty-five un-occupied bunkers but saw no enemy. Word was passed down that the 'brass' wanted the man taken prisoner if possible. This prompted one of the men in Bravo Three to write in a letter home: *"Our Capt. said if we see him not to shoot to kill but I've got news for him. . ." Ripcord* – page 120.

B Company continued to work the area, finding bunker after bunker. After running out of daylight, they dug in on a hill near some bunkers they had checked that afternoon. After moving out of their NDP the next morning, they again checked those bunkers and found fresh, leafy branches in some of the bunkers. The NVA used these branches to sleep on, so enemy soldiers had crept back and slept in the bunkers just below B Company's NDP.

Sometime that afternoon, the NVA snuck into the NDP B Company had used the night before and dug up the foxholes, looking for discarded food and ammo. They found nothing because CPT Williams enforced a strict policy of policing up NDP's, requiring his men to cut up C-ration cans to keep the NVA from using them to manufacture booby traps. (See *Mighty Men of Valor – With Charley Company on Hill 714*, page 223 for a description of how the NVA used C-ration cans to make a booby trap.)

They decided to leave a surprise for the NVA scroungers in case they came back. SGT Judd helped set up a big mechanical ambush, using six claymore mines daisy-chained together and placed at the top of the hill where two trails intersected. They moved into a new NDP site and waited.

Late that night, B Company troopers heard the **'BOOM'** as the claymores detonated. Cautiously returning to the ambush site the next morning, they found shredded flesh and bits of uniform cloth blasted into the trees, but found no bodies or equipment. The NVA had removed the bodies and the big pieces but couldn't get all the flesh scattered into the trees.

Some three days later, B Company observed another enemy patrol wearing US combat gear. It was an eerie, spooky area; every morning when patrols were sent out to check the area around the NDP before they moved out, they found signs that the NVA had scouted their NDP's. They spotted numerous NVA, but the cagey enemy would disappear into the brush before frustrated B Company men could get off a shot.

They found a huge bunker complex of more than 75 bunkers, big enough to get lost in. SGT Tolson wrote: ". . .*I know because I was lost for 3 hours yesterday. We have uncovered small quantities of rice and marijuana. . .The people in the know seem to think that there is a Bn. of gooks heading this way from the south and there is just a small party up here trying to fix things up before the Bn. arrives. If this is true I certainly don't want to be around when they get here. . ." Ripcord* – page 120.

At the beginning of July, an NVA mortar team began dropping rounds onto FSB Ripcord from a position on the reverse slope (east side) of Hill 805 as seen from the firebase. LTC Lucas ordered CPT Williams and B/2-506 to assault Hill 805, silence the mortar and occupy the hill to prevent its use by the NVA.

Williams and Bravo One and Two were in position on Hill 797 about four klicks northwest of Ripcord when they received the order; Bravo Three was on an adjacent ridge. Moving to a near-by one-ship LZ, the men formed into six-man teams, ready to board the slicks as they came in to the small LZ, one at a time. The men could see their objective, six klicks to their southeast, the hill smoking from artillery and air strikes. Gunships wheeled and dove, firing rockets at the hilltop.

The flight to the objective was short but rough due to the gusty mountain winds. The LZ was about two hundred meters west and some ten meters lower than the boulder-strewn peak of Hill 805. As the slicks started their run into the LZ, a pair of Cobra's zoomed ahead, firing volleys of rockets to keep the enemy's heads down until the last possible moment. This did not stop the single NVA who popped up and began to fire at the slow-moving slicks as the Cobra's pulled away.

The slick pilots couldn't risk a landing; they came to a hover 3-4 foot above the LZ and the troops jumped from the skids, landing hard under the weight of their rucks. The first men down scrambled into a line of old foxholes around the LZ's perimeter and put out suppressive fire, trying to cover the approach of the next helicopter.

As SGT Judd's slick made its' approach, Judd saw somebody hiding among the rocks on the summit of Hill 805. *"He was firing at us as we went by and the door gunner was firing back at him,"* remembered Judd. When the Huey came to a hover, *"we un-assed it as fast as we could."* Ripcord – page 26.

While the slicks came in, CPT Williams determined that only one NVA was in position on top of Hill 805 with two or three more firing from the thick jungle to the west of the LZ. The single-ship LZ was in a bad spot; anyone could fire right down into them from the hilltop, almost a hundred feet higher than the LZ. They were starting to take casualties; one of 1st Platoon's machine gunners was hit in the back by fire from the hilltop.

When all of Bravo One was on the ground, SSGT Thomas Rubsam, who was platoon leader because of a shortage of officers, formed them into a line and started an attack up the slope. The men moved slowly up the hillside, firing as they went. Rubsam was so caught up in the action that he did not realize he had taken an AK round through his left biceps. It was a clean wound, the bullet passing through the muscle without striking the bone. He was also hit in the face by a bullet fragment but he did not notice either wound. Rubsam continued firing, ducking from boulder to boulder until the platoon's medic caught up with him and told him he was bleeding.

CPT Williams halted the assault as two more Cobras zoomed in on the hilltop, plastering the rocky peak of Hill 805 with 7.62 mini-gun fire, grenades and 2.75-inch rockets, finally killing the single (and very brave) NVA soldier who had held them up.

B Company's Bravo Three arrived last on the LZ because they'd had to move to the LZ on Hill 797 from a near-by ridge. Led by 1LT Stephen C. Wallace, Bravo Three operated with an alertness not normally seen in the average line platoon. Nicknamed 'Whispering Wallace' by LTC Lucas, Wallace insisted on, and strictly enforced, noise and light discipline, even when talking on the radio, when they were out in the bush.

As the slick dropping off the last of Bravo Three's troops lifted off, the NVA down in the brush to the west of the LZ cut loose with AK-47's. The small LZ was a very crowded place with all three platoons occupying it, so CPT Williams ordered Wallace and Bravo Three to assault, capture and occupy the summit of 805.

Leaving their rucks on the LZ, Bravo Three moved into the thick jungle between the LZ and the bare top of 805. Bravo Three's point man Rodger D. 'Chip" Collins recalls: *"We had to climb over and around and through stuff, and we were all bogged down."* It was a nerve-wracking movement as the platoon leapfrogged forward over the last open ground just below the top of the hill. The men knew that if anyone were still up there, he'd get some of them with his first burst of fire. Said Collins of the move: *". . .hiding behind a tree stump or whatever, and then climbing and scuffling to the next little place of cover. There wasn't any fire, but many of us, me included, just threw up when we reached the top from the heat and the anxiety and the physical exertion."* Ripcord – page 30.

Scouting the top of the hill, they found a small bunker hollowed out under a boulder. Collins tossed in a frag grenade and, after the explosion, another trooper went in and dragged out a dead NVA through one of the small openings.

The other two platoons moved up to the top of the hill and Williams placed his company CP in among the boulders. There was not enough room on top for a three-platoon perimeter so Bravo Three moved back down the hill and set up its' NDP on the LZ. They immediately began digging in and setting out trip flares and claymores. Each platoon sent out three-man LP's (listening posts) to monitor the most likely avenues of approach to the NDP's.

About 2,000 meters northwest of Hill 805, FSB Ripcord began receiving mortar rounds and some inaccurate fire from a 75mm recoilless rifle. By following the smoke trail left by the 75mm rounds as they flashed toward the firebase, the rifle was seen to be firing from a position on Triple Hill. Artillery was called in to try and silence the fire from the recoilless rifle.

Big CH-47 Chinook's began delivering sling loads of artillery rounds to replace those fired during the day. About twenty-five of the huge helicopters were assigned to the mission and late that afternoon, one of them took enough hits to force it down on Ripcord where it had to shut down. The NVA immediately began mortaring Ripcord, trying to destroy the Chinook.

Just before dark, another big Chinook was hit by fire from a 12.7mm (.51 caliber) machine gun and forced down on the logistics LZ on Ripcord. Swarming over the helicopter, the crew repaired the Chinook well enough for it to take off for a firebase closer to the lowlands along the coast where it could be safely repaired.

Up on Hill 805, B/2-506 received a probe of their perimeter from an unknown sized NVA force. Using hand grenades and M-79 grenade launchers to fire at the enemy who were firing AK's and RPG's at them, troopers kept the enemy at bay. The GI's did not fire their M-16's and M-60's because the muzzle blasts would have invited a shot from an RPG. Down on the LZ, LT Wallace located the RPG gunner by following the trail of sparks left by the rockets as they zoomed in on the target. He used an M-72 LAW to silence the RPG gunner. Wallace later said: *"after I fired the LAW at the guy with the RPG launcher, he shut up right quick." Ripcord* - page 33.

Chapter 12
HILL 902 – A NIGHT OF TERROR

"There's too many people in here. . .They know this is the goddamn CP. We're all going to get killed with one grenade. I'm outta here!" PFC Gerald A. Cafferty, C/2-506 Infantry. *Ripcord-Screaming Eagles Under Siege* page 51.

On 15 June, C/2-506 was combat assaulted onto the long ridge running southeast from Hill 902. They were replacing Company A from the 1-506 Infantry who went out on the same slicks that had ferried in C Company.

The 2-506 was returning to the field after a week-long battalion stand-down at Camp Evans. During the stand-down, leadership of Company C had passed from CPT Isabelino Vazquez-Rodriguez to CPT Thomas T. Hewitt who had received his commission from an ROTC program. Company C was Hewitt's first combat command. The two men were exact opposites in their leadership styles. Vazquez-Rodriguez was tough as nails and made sure his men followed procedure and stayed alert while in the boonies. Hewitt had previously served as an advisor to an ARVN battalion and had extended his tour for the opportunity to command a US company in combat. His experiences with the ARVN had not prepared him for combat in the triple-canopied mountains of I Corps against an increasingly aggressive enemy around FSB Ripcord.

1LT James H. Campbell's Charlie Two had been chosen to lead C Company's assault onto Hill 902. Campbell, his point man, RTO and his best M-60 team were on the first slick into the LZ already secured by the 1-506. Immediately on landing, Campbell and his men started down the trail running along the narrow crest of the ridge. Taking slack behind his point man, they moved rapidly down trail for about 150 meters to a small knoll. As they came over the top of the knoll, they were amazed to find themselves facing two very startled NVA.

The NVA had been setting up a claymore mine for an ambush when the Huey's began landing C Company. They had begun taking apart their ambush when they were confronted by Campbell and his men. Says Campbell of the encounter: *"They were standing in the middle of the trail and, suddenly, we were right there on top of them. The closest gook [to Campbell] was rolling the claymore in his hands, wrapping the detonating wires back around it. When he saw us, he just looked at the AK-47 he had leaning up against a tree. He knew he was screwed. He didn't have any place to go. We killed him and his buddy just like that. We just shot the shit out of them. . .."* Ripcord – page 37.

Not knowing what they had run into, the M-60 gunner ran up and began blasting the area, laying down covering fire. As Campbell was reloading, he saw a third NVA to one side of the trail. Campbell fired but the man disappeared into the brush. No one fired back, so they dragged the two dead NVA back to the LZ.

When all three platoons were safely on the ground, they moved down the ridge, setting up separate NDP's each night. They worked down the ridge for the next four days. Under CPT Vazquez-Rodriguez, the company had avoided using trails, but CPT Hewitt wanted to save time and cover more ground by traveling on established trails despite the danger of encountering booby traps or an ambush. This drastic change in tactics made the men nervous, but that wasn't the only thing making the grunts uneasy. The ridge, covered with double and triple-canopy, was sprinkled with newly constructed, well-camouflaged bunkers.

A squad from Charlie One found a thick cable about five feet off the ground attached to the trees with old-fashioned green glass insulators. New guy PFC Michael Womack wanted to cut the wire, but the 'old-timers' in the squad wouldn't let him. They explained that the NVA would send a repair party who might discover their presence. Discouraged, Womack told them he thought that was why they were there.

When they reached the southeastern end of the four-klick-long ridge on 20 June, they were airlifted back to their original LZ. The plan was for the company to push uphill this time to the top of Hill 902. Hewitt planned to begin the move after a squad from Charlie One had retrieved a mechanical ambush that had been set on the trail running through the NDP site they had used on 15 June. The single squad from Charlie One spent the night with Charlie Two.

The next morning LT Campbell called the mortar section on Ripcord and asked for some 81mm mortar H&I (harassing and interdicting) fire along the route the squad would use. The mortar section sergeant on Ripcord said they were busy and, probably because it wasn't a unit-in-contact fire mission, it would be sometime before he could fire any rounds.

Unwilling to wait, the squad moved out without waiting for prep fire. Following the trail, but moving cautiously, the patrol reached the site of the first mechanical ambush only to find that the NVA had moved it. Hidden in a 'spider hole' alongside the trail, an NVA soldier waited for the point man to pass before he detonated the mine, wounding the next three men in line. The point man, not knowing the mine had been command detonated, rushed back to the three wounded men, apologizing profusely. He thought he had blundered into a trip wire.

LTC Lucas, in the area in his C & C Huey, landed before the medevac arrived. He began to chew out LT Campbell for not using mortars to prep the area before the patrol moved out. Campbell, defending himself, told Lucas what had happened. Lucas was skeptical, so Campbell told Lucas to ask for a fire mission using Campbell's radio call sign. Lucas did and received the same excuses that Campbell had. Furious, Lucas called Ripcord using his own call sign of 'Black Spade' and ordered the mortar section leader to be 'standing tall' in the TOC when Lucas arrived. The battalion commander, without apology, stomped off to his waiting helicopter and took off.

On 21 June, Charlie One accompanied by CPT Hewitt and his CP group, moved up onto Hill 902. LT Campbell and Charlie Two were to join them by the end of the day. As evening approached, Campbell and his point man carefully moved toward the top of 902. Worried about being fired on by a nervous Charlie One, Campbell radioed ahead several times to make sure that Charlie One knew they were coming up the trail. When they reached the top of Hill 902, Campbell was shocked to find that Charlie One had occupied only the eastern half of the bald hill top, leaving the western side of the perimeter undefended. If Campbell and his Charlie Two had been the NVA, they could have walked right into C Company's NDP.

As it grew fully dark, Campbell noticed a GI, sitting out in the open in the center of the perimeter, using a heat tab in a C-ration can stove to boil water. Heat tabs burn with a bright blue, highly visible flame. Angry, Campbell kicked over the stove and can of water. He cursed at the man for lighting a heat tab after dark but the man defended himself, telling Campbell *"L.T.* (pronounced ell-tee), I *was just cooking a cup of coffee for the captain." Ripcord* – page 40.

LT Campbell's six months in the field were over, but as the most experienced officer in C Company, LTC Lucas had left him in the field for another month to help CPT Hewitt transition into the company commander slot. Trying not to insult Hewitt, Campbell called him aside and told him that it was dangerous to light a fire or cigarettes after dark because The NVA could see the flame from a long distance and pinpoint the company's position.

Campbell then asked Hewitt about the lack of security on the western half of the perimeter. Hewitt said he knew Charlie Two was joining them so he hadn't put anyone into position on that side of the NDP. Campbell next asked if there any LP's posted along the trails running by the perimeter and learned there were not. LT Campbell knew that the men hated pulling OP duty; the small three-man outposts were extremely vulnerable during an attack. Campbell tried to explain the need for posting LP's every night because the NVA were very aggressive in the Ripcord AO and LP's could give warning of a pending attack.

Hewitt defended himself by telling Campbell how the ARVN had operated. They went into the field in battalion-sized units and carried live chickens and ducks with them to supplement their rations. They built big cooking fires every night; they were noisy and lax in posting perimeter guards and almost never sent out LP's. The ARVN thought that security was related to the size of the unit; the larger the unit the safer they were. Campbell cautioned Hewitt about his relaxed attitude toward security, saying they were inviting an attack.

Campbell later said of the draftee infantrymen who were the majority in Company C: *"In a firefight, they were hellacious soldiers. They'd do whatever you told 'em. But there's no sorrier bastard in the world, soldiering wise, than a US soldier who's not scared, and that's the never-ending problem of being a commander – trying to keep the men combat ready when they decide there's nothing to worry about and get complacent." Ripcord* – pages 41-42.

Company C continued to patrol and on 24 June they again reached the southeastern end of the long ridge. CPT Hewitt called in a report that he had spotted fifty NVA moving across an open area on the side of a mountain about 1,300 meters to the south. Every bit of firepower that could be marshalled was brought to bear on the mountain slope – artillery, gunships, mortars and tactical air. When it was over, Company C humped over to the mountain to check the results of the massive strike and found nothing – not one body, body part, weapon or shred of clothing lay on the cratered slope.

An alert Charlie One spotted two NVA on 27 June and fired on them, driving them toward Charlie Two, who blew a claymore on them at 25-meter range. The platoon then opened fire and killed them both.

LTC Lucas had established a morale-boosting program where line companies out in the jungle were flown to FSB Ripcord, one platoon at a time, for a mini-vacation. On 28 June it was Charlie One's turn, so they were lifted to Ripcord for a night off and a BBQ over sawed-in-half 50-gallon oil drums. Charlie Two went in the next day for their turn and Hewitt went with them. A poker game began in one of the bunkers and Hewitt, who loved the game, won a lot of money.

In the meantime, Charlie One had moved up to the summit of Hill 902 where Hewitt and Charlie Two joined them late on 30 June. Charlie Three then went to Ripcord for their night off.

At about 0700 hours on 1 July, the NVA began heavily shelling FSB Ripcord. By nightfall, the enemy had managed to shoot down a CH-47 Chinook and 15 artillerymen from B Battery, 2-319 Field Artillery had been wounded.

Up on Hill 902, CPT Hewitt and others spotted a mortar firing on Ripcord from the eastern slope of Hill 805. Mortar fire and then gunships were called in on this difficult target. As the Cobra's zoomed skyward after a rocket run, green tracers were seen flashing past them. Men from Company C also spotted another mortar position firing from the reverse slope of a hill near YD 343186, less than a kilometer from FSB Ripcord. Gunships, tactical air strikes, mortar and artillery fire was directed onto these NVA firing positions by Hewitt and his team from their vantage point on 902. It took time to vector in all the aerial assets onto the targets and Hewitt's men, while they waited, began firing several M-60 machine guns at the position, even though it was at the maximum range for an M-60 at 1,100 meters.

Late in the day, someone in Company C saw another mortar firing on Ripcord through a small hole in the jungle canopy. Each time the mortar fired, a perfect smoke ring puffed up through the trees. This mortar was located at the base of Hill 902 on a line between Hewitt's position and Ripcord. Some men on that side of the perimeter used LAW's to fire at the mortar. The first LAW rocket fell short but the second, aimed a little upward to give it extra range, hit the target. There were no secondary explosions but no more fire came from that mortar position.

Unknown to LTC Lucas or any of his company commanders in the field, a special unit had taken up residence on FSB Ripcord. Known as an SSI (special signal-intercept) team, they worked in a sandbag-covered, underground Conex a few feet from Lucas' TOC. Their job was to intercept, translate and interpret NVA radio transmissions. They intercepted and translated an NVA plan for a sapper attack against CPT Hewitt's position on Hill 902 in response to Company C's directing counter battery fire and then firing machine guns and LAW's at their mortar positions. Company C had proved to be a definite thorn in the enemy's side and the NVA had decided to do something about them.

For security purposes, signal intercepts by the SSI team were routed directly to 101st Airborne Headquarters at Camp Eagle. Someone there decided what, if any, intelligence would be sent back down to the line battalions. Division did prepare a warning about the coming attack, but for unknown reasons the information was not received by Lucas until after the attack on Company C.

CPT Hewitt asked permission from LTC Lucas to move his NDP but Lucas, probably because Hewitt had been useful in spotting and directing fire against NVA mortar positions on 1 July, told him to remain in place on Hill 902. Company C began to prepare the NDP for another night on Hill 902. Their preparations were half-hearted; Hewitt did not send out LP's and did not insist that everyone dig in and camouflage their positions. This was not entirely Hewitt's fault He was an inexperienced commander and so had a false sense of security. C Company, like most other line companies at this stage of the war, suffered from a lack of experienced platoon leaders and sergeants.

Many of the lieutenants who led platoons were graduates of the US Army Infantry School's OCS program at Fort Benning, Georgia. Others received their commission after completing an ROTC course at a college or university. These young officers had little or no combat experience. The army's policy of rotating officers from a field position to a staff job in the rear after six months, while maximizing the number of officers exposed to combat, ensured that an officer left the field just as he began to understand how to lead a unit in combat.

Because there were not enough professional NCO's (non-commissioned officers-sergeants) at the platoon, squad and fire-team level, the army had filled the NCO ranks with graduates of the NCOCS (non-commissioned officers' candidate school) from the Infantry School at Fort Benning, often called 'shake-n-bakes.' These young men were intelligent and motivated, but did not have the experience to go with the stripes; they tended to be buddies with the men instead of leading them. The honor graduate from each class was given the rank of staff sergeant - E6; all others graduated with the rank of (buck) sergeant – E5. Quite a few of the E6 graduates served as platoon sergeants and, in a few cases, as platoon leaders when there were no lieutenants to fill that slot. *

For these and other reasons, the men went about preparing for nightfall with a relaxed and casual attitude. Gerald Cafferty, the senior medic and the senior RTO, SGT Jack Dreher, dug in near CPT Hewitt, who slung a hammock between two bare trees near the LZ that had been cleared at the top of the hill. The summit of the hill was bare after several air strikes had blown away the vegetation. SP4 Robert Smoker, in charge of company re-supply, thought the CP area was too crowded for safety and he dug a hole off by himself.

The author is a graduate of NCOC Class 47-69 US Army Infantry School, Fort Benning, Georgia and served with C Company, 2-502 Infantry 101st Airborne from January through December 1970 as an E-5.

Charlie One and Two together could muster only about 40 men to cover the perimeter. Charlie One, with 15 men, held the eastern side and Charlie Two covered the opposite slope with 25 men. There were 13 three-man positions, each about ten yards apart; in all the perimeter covered an area about the size of a baseball diamond with CPT Hewitt and the CP in the center.

Some of the troops did dig foxholes but the majority did not. Of the ones who did, most simply dug out the loose dirt from the old, shallow holes dug by the first unit to occupy Hill 902 years before. When SSGT Paul Burkey, leading Charlie Three, came to the relief of Charlie One and Two the next day, he was disgusted when he saw they had used the old fighting positions. By the time C/2-506 occupied Hill 902, the NVA had ample opportunity to scout the hill and plot the exact location of every foxhole.

In the CP area, SGT's Herndon, Mayer and Steele had not bothered to dig in. Instead, they had erected a small poncho shelter about two feet high. Such shelters, called a hooch, offered shade during the day and some warmth at night. They were also highly visible, reflecting moonlight and starlight, an easy target for an RPG or hand grenade. Other hooch's dotted the perimeter, equally as easy to see even on a moonless night. SP4 Stephen Manthei, a veteran of ten months in the jungle with C Company, remembers: *"I thought putting up a pup tent was really stupid. I spoke to 'em about it, but they outranked me and nothing was done. You looked up the hill and the CP was sticking out like a sore thumb, too. It was ridiculous to set up like that after we had ticked off the enemy by firing down at them that morning." Ripcord* – page 44.

Manthei said that neither he, Bob Tarbuck or Don Holthausen, all manning the same position facing south, thought it was a good idea to put up any kind of shelter. *"We dug our holes deep as we were expecting totally to get messed with,"* recalled Manthei. At least one man was supposed to be awake at each position and Manthei took the first watch. He recollected. . ."*it was a beautiful night, starlit, with some mortar and artillery shows you could see off in the distance. We pulled our guard shifts with a little more intensity that night – at least at our position." Ripcord* – page 44.

Example of 'poncho hooch' used as a sunshade or rain shelter. In C/2-502 Infantry poncho hooch's were taken down at nightfall. Photo from author's collection. ©2017

The NVA launched probes on both FSB Ripcord and B/2-506 occupying Hill 805, perhaps as a diversion to draw attention away from their primary target on Hill 902, The attack on C Company did not come until nearly four in the morning. It was an ideal time for an attack, when the sleepy sentry's let down their guard and begin to nod off. The last two hours before dawn was always the most dangerous time and Stephen Manthei remembers: *"It was really quiet on the hill, almost an eerie quiet."* Manthei was pulling his final shift on guard when someone whispered that they had seen movement in front of their position. Manthei silently woke up Tarbuck and Holthausen and gestured for them to get in their holes. A radio message ordered the perimeter guards to open fire and, said Manthei *"all hell broke loose. I saw an RPG flash across the hill into the command post and the radio went dead from that position. The explosion knocked me backwards against the inside of my foxhole, and then in the next instant numerous grenades and satchel charges started going off, gunfire erupted from everywhere, and there was a lot of hollering and screaming in the dark, both by us and the Vietnamese." Ripcord – page 44-45.*

In the CP on top of the hill, SGT Thomas Herndon woke SGT Jerry Moyer for his turn at guard duty. Moyer crawled to the downed tree in front of their hooch they were using as a guard position carrying his M-16. Grenades, extra magazines and the little detonators for the claymore mines were laid out within easy reach. Almost right away, Moyer heard something moving on the hillside below him. He didn't report it because it might be a big jungle rat or a monkey but he became fully alert.

When the noise continued, Moyer contacted SGT Jack Dreher who had the radio listening watch in the CP. Moyer told Dreher that he had steady movement down in the brush below the perimeter and he thought the company should go on fifty percent alert, at least until daybreak. Dreher told him to wait as he apparently woke up CPT Hewitt for instructions. A minute later, Dreher told him to start waking people up.

Moyer was not the only sentry who reported sounds and movement. PFC Michael Mueller, on duty two holes to Moyer's left, heard something moving in the low brush several meters below his foxhole. Then Mueller clearly saw the dark silhouette of an enemy soldier outlined against the lighter brush, but the shadow quickly disappeared. Mueller got Dreher on the radio and was told that the next time he saw the man he was to open fire. Mueller instantly dropped the radio handset and sprayed an entire magazine of M-16 bullets into the brush. It was too little, too late; the NVA were ready to attack. An RPG whooshed out of the night and exploded in the CP. Someone blew a claymore and satchel charges began exploding all over the hill. Mueller tried to blow the claymore in front of his hole but it didn't go off; sappers had apparently disabled it.

Up in the CP, the new artillery FO was knocked senseless by the exploding RPG. CPT Hewitt, suspended above the ground in his hammock, was killed instantly, one arm and both legs blown off.

In the CP foxhole, Jack Dreher was wounded by the same RPG that killed Hewitt. The company medic, PFC Gerald Cafferty, was sprayed with rocket fragments and his left arm ripped open from wrist to elbow. Cafferty remembered that he was so frightened he did not know he had been wounded. Cafferty frantically searched for his aid bag but could not find it, the bag apparently blown away by the explosion.

Dreher was frantically muttering into the radio handset, asking for illumination rounds and gunships. Crouching in the hole, "Doc" Cafferty felt something land on his back. Twisting around to look, he saw it was a satchel charge. The NVA were using one-pound blocks of C-4 plastic explosive that caused huge blasts. If the C-4 blocks were impregnated with enough metal pieces, they could rip an arm or leg off. The satchel charge tossed into the CP foxhole was wedged between Cafferty's back and the side of the hole. Cafferty remembers, "*I said to myself, this is it, I'm gone. I'm going to blow all over Dreher – he won't get hurt because it's behind my back – but the thing never went off. The blasting cap didn't work, which was very common, thank God." Ripcord*-page 47.

SGT Moyer had started to crawl back to the CP to wake up Herndon and SP4 Gary Steele when the first RPG hit. Both rolled from under the hooch and stood up. Steele saw a man wearing a floppy 'boonie hat' at the top of the hill pointing an RPG launcher at them. Steele was shocked that a sapper could get to the top of the hill so quickly. The sight persuaded him that sappers had already penetrated the perimeter before the attack started. Steele raised his M-16 to shoot the man, but when he squeezed the trigger, nothing happened. In his fear and excitement, he had forgotten to move the little lever from safe to auto.

The sapper fired and the rocket exploded just behind the poncho hooch. Blown off his feet by the blast, Steele lay where he landed unable to move, hoping the NVA would think he was dead. Blood trickled from his ears, mouth and rectum and he struggled to breathe. Later, at the hospital, he was told that a big chunk of rocket fragment had penetrated his back, fracturing several ribs and puncturing a lung.

SGT Herndon was in very bad shape. He was screaming in fear and pain, so the sappers on the hill top began tossing satchel charges down at him. One of them wounded Herndon again and sprayed Steele with shrapnel in his legs and buttocks, blowing him further down the hill.

The first parachute flare fired by the mortar platoon on Ripcord popped into light and the sappers dove for cover. As soon as the flare burned out, they were up again, tossing more satchel charges at Herndon and Steele. Another flare lit up and the enemy fire died down again. When darkness returned, satchel charges exploded in a staccato **BOOM! BOOM-BOOM!** across the hillside.

Herndon was crying out in a delirium of pain and a lot of the satchel charges were thrown at him. Steele whispered loudly to his badly wounded friend, *"Shut up, Tom. Shut up!" Ripcord*-page 48.

Every time Herndon cried out PFC Richard Conrardy, huddled behind the log with Moyer, tried to get up and go get him. Conrardy, the new platoon medic, was in his first firefight. Moyer grabbed him and told him to wait until the firing died down. But Conrardy, a nineteen-year old conscientious objector, couldn't wait and jumped up, saying he had to go get him (Herndon).

Conrardy rose to his knees but was shot before he could make another move. He fell back against Moyer, who knew he was dead when he felt his lifeless weight. Moyer had trouble realizing that the shot that killed the medic had come from the top of the hill, that there were sappers behind him. Seconds later, another satchel charge went off, suddenly cutting off Herndon's screams of pain. For his attempt to get to Herndon, medic Conrardy was given a posthumous Silver Star.

On the southwestern side of the perimeter, SGT Lee Lenz was in a foxhole next to an M-60 team covering the trail that entered the perimeter from that direction. The machine gun position was destroyed by a satchel charge during the first few seconds of the attack. Lenz clambered up the hill looking for cover. His machine gunner, SP4 Roger Sumrall had been killed by the blast. The next morning, while searching for dead and wounded, they realized Sumrall's assistant gunner, PFC Stephen Harber, was missing. All that could be found of Harber was a jungle boot with his foot still inside and Harber's dog tag secured to the laces.

In the photo above, one of the author's dog tags can be seen in the laces of his jungle boot. The tags were worn this way instead of around the neck to prevent them clinking together and making noise while moving through the jungle. Photo from author's collection. ©2017

SP4 Stephen Manthei saw a trooper who looked like Harber get out of the machine gun position and start to run up the hill. *"There was a hell of an explosion at that moment,"* recalled Manthei, *"and he was gone. He was blown away. There were pieces of human everywhere. It was terrible. Harber had a lucky dollar bill that he carried with him all the time, and right after the explosion a ripped half of that dollar bill floated down next to my foxhole. I still have it . . ."* Ripcord- page 49.

Gary Steele painfully crawled up to the shredded poncho hooch looking for his M-16. Fumbling around in the flickering shadows, he found the weapon but it was too damaged to use. He located the grenades he had laid out, ready for use, pulled the pins and threw them at the sappers on top of the hill. He was so dazed that he forgot to remove the safety clips on the 'spoons' before he threw them. Horrified, Steele thought, *"Oh, you dumb son of a bitch, now they're gonna take them clips off and throw 'em back."*

In the brief times between illumination rounds burning overhead, sappers fired RPG's and threw what seemed like hundreds of satchel charges. There was very little AK fire; most of the rifle fire came from US M-16's and M-60 machine guns.

Three klicks to the northeast, the men of B/2-506 on Hill 805 watched, fascinated and horrified, as the summit of Hill 902 literally glowed and sparkled under the parachute flares and exploding satchel charges. Because their perimeter had been probed earlier that night, B Company was on one hundred percent alert, waiting in the pre-dawn darkness for an attack that never came.

Sgt. Jerry Moyer and several others could hear the NVA infantry supporting the sappers moving around in the brush down the slope. Moyer thought that all the satchel charges coming at them were being thrown by them. He looked for targets as the flares cast distorted, moving shadows through the bare trees. He heard a satchel charge hit the ground behind him and roll downhill, stopping next to his boot. Instantly he scrambled over the log he was hiding behind and waited for the blast. *"It never did go off,"* remembers Moyer. *" I scooted back to my position, but it still hadn't registered that we had been overrun. I couldn't comprehend that they were behind me. You know, they don't get behind you. That just didn't happen."* Ripcord-page 50.

As PFC Mike Mueller opened fire. SGT Mendez, Mueller's team leader, instantly came awake and rolled into the foxhole with him, closely followed by the ammo bearer, a youngster nicknamed 'Shaky.' Mendez manned the M-60 but held his fire, unwilling to expose his position until the NVA made a rush. Mueller fired a few shots from his rifle down slope until he happened to look back up the hill. He saw the silhouettes of men who were obviously not GI's darting across the top of the hill and realized sappers were already inside the perimeter. Before Mueller could aim his rifle at the dark figures, he saw a satchel charge rolling down the hill toward them. He ducked down below the rim of the foxhole. One explosion came immediately, followed by three or four others. One of the satchel charges rolled into the hole with them. All three of them popped out of the hole, falling face down in the dirt. The charge went off and they rolled back into the hole.

As soon as they got back in the hole, another satchel charge plopped in with them and they scrambled back out. Another explosion and they jumped back in. The first flares burst into light overhead and they saw two sappers in black uniforms behind a log on the slope above them, systematically tossing satchel charges at their foxhole A third satchel charge rolled in and Mueller flopped up hill, tripped, lost his footing and slid back down so that his left leg was across the foxhole just as the charge went off. His leg bleeding badly, Mueller slipped back into the hole, grabbed his M-16 and, popping up, blasted away at the sappers behind the log.

It was utter chaos on the hill with many small fights happening at the same time. Jack Dreher and 'Doc' Cafferty were still in their hole when SP4 Robert Radcliffe and another man Cafferty didn't recognize (it was SGT Lee Lenz) fell into their hole, frantically looking for cover. The hole was too small for four men and Cafferty crawled away. He did not know until later that almost as soon as he left the hole, an RPG exploded on the edge. Dreher survived, but Lenz and Radcliffe were killed instantly.

Cafferty finally noticed that his left arm was sliced open, but he didn't care. Seeing the artillery recon sergeant by himself in a little foxhole, Doc fell in on top of him. The foxhole was so small that Cafferty could not get all the way in. As he lay there, his upper body out of the hole, something hit his helmet. Doc recalled: *"I got hit in the helmet with a goddamn grenade. It bounced off and was lying there in front of my face. It was a US baseball grenade. I might have been able to reach it, but I just froze. I said to myself, that's it, I'm gone. I thought of my mother and my fiancé. . ." Ripcord*-page 51.

The grenade did not explode. Cafferty came back and examined it after the battle. He saw that the pin had been pulled but the safety clip was still in place, holding the spoon down. Cafferty figured that a sapper had grabbed the grenade and pulled the pin, not knowing about the safety clip. The grenade may have been one of the two thrown in such a hurry by Gary Steele that he forgot to remove the clips.

Cafferty then saw that the artillery FO was hiding in the bottom of the hole under the recon sergeant. The FO, a lieutenant, was next in rank on the hill to Hewitt and, when Hewitt was killed, should have taken command. Cafferty remembers that all he did was hide in the bottom of the hole during the battle.

Angry at the frightened lieutenant, Doc climbed out of the hole, grabbed his rifle and opened fire. Says Cafferty: *"I finally got my shit together and started shooting. I finally got some balls. . ."* The sapper was about thirty feet from Cafferty getting ready to toss another satchel charge at them when Cafferty put most of an eighteen-round magazine into him. He went down in a heap.

Only then did Cafferty see a second sniper beside the one he had shot. Cafferty frantically pulled at the empty magazine, but it jammed in the weapon. He did not notice that the magazine had been hit by a bullet until the next day. Cafferty was so focused on shooting the first sapper that he had not seen the second sniper firing back at him with an AK. Feeling completely helpless, he wrestled with the jammed weapon until the damaged magazine suddenly came free. Pushing in a fresh magazine, he opened fire. He blew away the second sapper and put down several more who appeared out of the shifting flare light and shadows. "*I can still picture those guys lined up,*" Cafferty recalled, still haunted after thirty years. "*I just shot. I put it on semi-automatic, and just started firing 'em up as fast as I could. If they stopped shooting, I figured I got 'em. I was scared to death. . .but somebody had to do something. Everybody else on that side of the hill was dead or fucked up. There weren't a lot of other guys firing, and I figured I was already dead. I should have been killed by that satchel charge. I should have been killed by that grenade. I had already said my prayers and said goodbye to my girlfriend and my mother and father. . .I didn't have anything to lose. . .*" Gerald 'Doc' Cafferty from West Haven, Connecticut, was awarded the Silver Star for his actions that morning on Hill 902. *Ripcord*-page 52.

In his foxhole, SP4 Bob Smoker heard a noise behind him. He turned to look and saw a man standing about ten feet uphill from his hole. The figure was so small Smoker knew he wasn't an American and, at first, he thought the man must be one of the company's Kit Carson Scouts. Then he suddenly remembered that CPT Hewitt hadn't trusted the scouts and all of them had been left on Ripcord. The intruder hadn't noticed Smoker in the darkness and he slowly raised his M-16 and cranked off a single shot at the figure outlined against the starry sky. The NVA collapsed in a heap, shot through the forehead. Some other sappers Smoker couldn't see began frantically whispering loudly to each other. He threw two frag grenades in the direction of the whisperers and the whispering stopped.

After the last satchel charge exploded in their foxhole, Mike Mueller saw Shaky scuttle down the hill and SGT Mendez also disappeared. Mueller finally found his missing bandoliers which gave him fourteen magazines. In the light of the overhead flares, he found his web gear with several frags attached. Now fully armed and able to fight back, Mueller blasted away at the sappers who had been tossing satchel charges down on him from behind the log.

Mueller ducked down to change magazines, but when he popped up to fire again, one of the sappers popped up at the same time with his AK-47 at the ready. The sapper got his shots off first. Mueller heard rounds crack past his head and then something slammed into his left shoulder. Stunned, Mueller dropped back down into the foxhole. Both sappers jumped over their log and started downhill to finish him off. Knowing he was about to die, Mueller pulled himself together, raised up and was just about to pull the trigger when SGT Mendez suddenly darted out of a hole in front of Mueller, bellowing "Don't shoot, don't shoot."

Mendez dove to the left out of the line of fire but Mueller was so shaken up from nearly shooting Mendez that he dropped back down into the hole. The two sappers, also shaken and confused by the commotion, scurried back behind their log and threw another satchel charge at Miller. As soon as the charge went off, they charged down the hill, one of them armed with an AK-50, the folding-stock version of the AK-47, favored by sappers because of its compact size.

Mueller shot the sapper armed with the AK-50, then turned his fire on the sapper carrying a bag of satchel charges. Hit, the man went down and rolled away, screaming. Mueller fired off two more magazines trying to shut off the horrible screams. The screaming got to Mueller, so he climbed out of his hole to put the man out of his misery and was immediately shot in his left thigh. The round entered his upper thigh and, shattering a compass in his pocket, ricocheted down his thigh and exited just above his knee.

The small, intense battles between the sappers and GI's continued. Steve Manthei, Don Holthausen and Bob Tarbuck heard something moving in the low brush in front of their hole, so Manthei blew their claymore. Most of the enemy were over on Charlie Two's side of the hill, but the sappers did attack the position manned by SGT Dan Smith, the platoon sergeant for Charlie One. SP4 Robert Zoller was killed and Smith was wounded along with one other man.

Smith, badly wounded, kept yelling for Manthei to come and help him, but there was no way for him to get to Smith without getting hit himself. Instead, the three men threw grenades out in front of Smith's hole to keep the sappers away. During this time, the action began to slow down, most of the sappers having been killed during the first half-hour of the attack.

Cobra gunships made it out to Hill 902 at last, so Manthei threw a trip flare south of his position and another as far as he could to the southwest. Getting on his radio, Manthei told the Cobra pilots to put everything they had on a straight line between the two burning flares.

As the Cobras made their passes, the fighting on the hill died away to an occasional gunshot or explosion. SGT Jerry Moyer, still lying behind his log, hadn't seen a single attacker during the entire battle. Then, without warning, a satchel charge landed next to him and went off. Amazingly, he was not badly hurt; his rucksack absorbed much of the blast but his buttocks took a load of shrapnel and he was blown down the hill where he landed in a pile of brush. When he could function again, he reached down to check his numb legs and saw that the back of his trousers was on fire. He quickly swatted out the flames, afraid the sappers would see the fire and come after him.

As he lay in the brush, Moyer's heart was pounding with fear. The explosion had blown off his helmet and ammo bandoliers and he had no grenades but he did have his rifle with a full magazine. He was afraid to try and crawl back to his log because SP4 Layne Hammons was in the hole next to Moyer's log with an M-60 and Hammons would fire if he saw Moyer crawling toward the perimeter, thinking he was a sapper. He couldn't call for help for fear of attracting the enemy. So, Moyer decided, the hell with it, I'm just gonna stay right here till day break and hope for the best.

The best was another parachute flare popping into light above Moyer, revealing an NVA creeping up the hill with an AK-47 ready to fire. The NVA was about twenty feet away when Moyer opened up on semi-automatic, hitting the man at least four times. Remembering he only had one magazine, Moyer stopped firing. Afraid to move or make noise by checking his magazine, Moyer lay still, waiting for daylight.

    The sky started to turn grey and a hush fell over the hill. In the odd silence, SP4 Gary Steele heard voices loudly speaking Vietnamese. They were uphill from where he lay, only about twenty feet away. Steele thought *"those sappers must think we're all dead,"* so loudly were they talking. Steele found a grenade, pulled the pin and safety clip and began to painfully crawl toward the sappers. He had to do something; he was afraid the sappers would find him still alive and kill him. He quietly let the spoon fly off the grenade and held on to it for two or three seconds – letting it cook-off. He tossed it into the group of surprised sappers and scuttled back down the hill as fast as he could go.

    Steele hid until it got light then spotted three men in a hole to his right. No firing had come from that hole during the fight, so Steele had assumed they had all been killed. They had not. They were 'Cherries' – new guys – too frightened to do anything but huddle in the bottom of their hole. When it was light enough for them to recognize him, Steele called out that he was wounded and was coming over.

Not sure if the enemy had captured the hill or not, Steele pulled the pin on his last grenade and began crawling, holding the spoon down tightly. If the NVA got him, they'd get a big surprise when they checked his body.

To reach the foxhole and help, Steele had to get past a big log. He couldn't crawl under it, so he tried to dive over it. As he did, a single shot rang out from behind him, the bullet going straight up his anus, severely damaging his rectum. The pain and shock was so awful, he was astonished he didn't drop the frag and blow himself away. Another shot rang out and this time the bullet grazed his right knee.

Steele eventually reached his goal and pulled himself into the hole, forcing one of the terrified cherries to get out and find another place to hide. Fading into unconsciousness, Steele let the frag slip and the spoon flew off. One of the cherries grabbed the grenade and flung it down the hill. Steele asked for a cigarette and, just before he blacked out, said "*I quit.*"

As the eastern horizon grew pink, four sappers tried to slip off the hill. They had waited too long, however, and they were spotted by Mike Mueller, outlined against the sky as they moved down from the top of the hill. Mueller rose out of his hole and shot two of them with his M-16. The remaining two threw themselves behind some debris and Mueller threw two frags at them. They did not move again. They were discovered later that morning during a sweep of the hill, one of them lying on a loaded RPG launcher pointed right at Mueller's foxhole.

It was so quiet on the hill just before sunrise that Jerry Moyer began to imagine he was the only one left alive. When the sun finally came over the horizon and it was light enough to see, Moyer made eye contact with Layne Hammons, still manning his M-60. Holding up two fingers, Moyer pointed to the brush in front of him. The assistant gunner, Chuck Damron, grabbed two grenades and joined Moyer, still lying in the brush pile. Damron asked what he had and Moyer told him he had last seen two 'gooks' in the brush right in front of him. Damron pulled the pins and threw the two grenades where Moyer pointed then stayed with him until the relief force began landing. Damron then helped Moyer limp up the hill and, as they passed the bodies of sappers wearing only shorts, Moyer realized for the first time that the sappers had been inside their perimeter all night.

The very top of the hill had been secured by 'Doc' Cafferty just before the relief force arrived. Cafferty could hear the shouts and screams of the many wounded coming from Charlie Two's side of the perimeter. He found two men from Charlie One, who reluctantly got out of their foxhole to help with the wounded and act as Cafferty's security while he searched the hill. One of the men screaming in pain was the sapper shot by Mike Mueller just before daylight. One shot sounded and the enemy soldier's cries abruptly went silent. Mueller, still lying wounded, heard Cafferty shout *"Currahee"*, the old 506th Regimental motto and now their recognition signal. Mueller answered with the profane reply, *"Currahee, motherfucker"* in his unique stutter. Surprised to hear anyone reply, Cafferty shouted, *"Alaska, is that you?"* Hearing his nickname, Mueller answered that it was him and Cafferty shouted, *"Get up here and help me clear this hill!"* Mueller replied that he was wounded but Cafferty said, *"We all are, man. Get up here!"* *Ripcord* – page 59.

Mueller managed to get up the slope and he and Cafferty walked over the hill, carefully shooting each NVA they came upon in the back of his head. Of this gruesome task, Cafferty later said, *"To this day I regret having to do that, but what was I going to do? I didn't want to walk by one who wasn't really dead and have him shoot me in the back."*

Bob Smoker started picking up and then throwing the unexploded satchel charges off the hill. There were heaps of the one-pound charges lying all over the hill, but Smoker didn't realize at the time that any one of them could have exploded when he picked it up. In the meantime, mostly because no one else was either willing or able to take charge, 'Doc' Cafferty realized he was the one calling the shots for C Company. He was in a rush to help the wounded, but first he had to establish a perimeter again. Moving the survivors into foxholes around the hilltop, he then gathered all the battle dressings he could find amid the wreckage and did what he could for the wounded. He organized teams to carry them up the hill to the LZ on make-shift litters where they could be treated.

Gary Steele, in terrible pain, came to long enough to realize he was being carried up the hill by six men. 'Doc' Cafferty came by, gave him a dose of morphine and slapped a big bandage on his ripped open anus. As his pain faded away, he asked how many sappers they had killed and was told "*a lot, man.*" There were fifteen dead sappers on the hill, but that did not include the ones who had crawled off the hill to die, leaving blood trails behind them. Weighed against the enemy casualties, C Company had lost seven killed in action with six others wounded and one missing. Those killed were CPT Thomas Hewitt; SGT Thomas Herndon; SGT Lee Lenz; SP4 Roger Sumrall; SP4 Robert Radcliffe, Jr; SP4 Robert Zoller II; PFC Richard Conrardy and PFC Stephen Harber, listed as missing in action.

Sickened by the death all around them, Cafferty and his teams located the dead from C Company and prepared them for removal from Hill 902. They found CPT Hewitt's blown apart body still tangled in his shredded hammock. Doc was surprised and saddened to find the decapitated bodies of Lenz and Radcliffe still in the hole Doc had crawled away from because it was too crowded. Stephen Manthei remembers the scene on the LZ as the worst he had ever seen. A young black soldier totally lost control, grabbed an M-60 and blasted several hundred rounds into the pile of NVA bodies before they stopped him. They consoled him as best they could.

Charlie Three, led by SSGT Paul Burkey, left Ripcord under mortar fire and, as they landed on hill 902, began receiving small arms fire. Charlie Three quickly fanned out around the hill, ready to repel a ground attack if it came. They were shocked at what had happened to the other two platoons of C Company.

As the medevacs began to come in, Burkey tried to persuade Cafferty to get aboard one, but he refused, saying he would not leave until every other casualty had been evacuated. Cafferty placed Hewitt's remains, wrapped in a poncho, aboard one of the medevacs himself. When Steve Harber's jungle boot was found with his foot still in it, men from Charlie Three searched the mountain below Harber's foxhole for his body but no trace of him was ever found. There was a sense of urgency about their actions; they knew the longer they stayed on the hill, the more likely they would be mortared. They knew the NVA had Hill 902 zeroed in.

When the first rounds came in, tactical air strikes were called in to hit likely mortar firing sites on surrounding hills. Red smoke was popped on the LZ, warning incoming Huey crews that the LZ was under fire. After all the casualties went out, what was left of Charlie One and Charlie Two were flown to Ripcord. Charlie Three was lifted out, under mortar fire, around noon. SGT Rodney Moore, with four other men, waited for the last Huey to come in. Mortar rounds were landing all over the hilltop, so the Huey could not sit down but had to come to hover three or four feet off the ground. The other four clambered aboard ahead of Moore, but the pilot started to lift off just as Moore got one foot onto the skid. With supreme effort, SGT Moore hauled himself aboard, landing on his butt facing out the door. A mortar round burst on the LZ as the Huey rose from the dangerous hill. SGT Moore, the last man off Hill 902, watched several more rounds explode on the hill as the Huey, engine screaming, banked away.

Chapter 13
RIPCORD UNDER SIEGE
PART ONE

"The North Vietnamese had pretty good intelligence. Much of it came from our US radio nets. Major Ho Van Thuoc, Operations Officer of the 6th Tri Thien Regiment at the time of the Ripcord Battle, told me in an interview with him in Hue in June 2001, that they listened to our radio nets. The CIA confirmed that the enemy had over 200 radio listening posts in South Vietnam with English speaking operatives." Major General (ret.) Benjamin L. Harrison, *Hell On A Hill Top* – page 89.

The siege of FSB Ripcord began when the first five 82mm mortar rounds hit the hill at about 0703 hours on Wednesday, July 1. They fell without warning; the mortar tubes were too far away to be heard when they fired and the whistle of the rounds as they fell toward the hilltop was masked by the perpetual winds blowing across the firebase.

One of the rounds impacted on a corner of the heavily sand bagged 2-506 TOC but caused no significant damage except for the ringing ears of the radio men and staff officers inside the bunker. The other four rounds hit the helicopter LZ immediately adjacent to the TOC, barely denting its concrete-like surface. LTC Lucas, impressed by the accuracy of that first salvo, remarked that the NVA must have pinpointed all the major targets on Ripcord. It was later determined that NVA gunners were using the big, bright red wheeled fire extinguisher setting at the edge of the LZ as an aiming point.

Seconds later, CPT Rembert Rollison, commanding D/2-506, the infantry company securing the base, reported by radio that Ripcord was receiving automatic weapons fire and RPG's, coming from a rocky hill at YD 349194, only seven hundred meters east of Ripcord. This hill was part of the same jungle-covered ridge as Ripcord, separated from the base by a shallow saddle. The grunts from Company D reacted quickly, surprised the NVA would attack them during daylight. Diving into their foxholes, the men were soon returning fire with their M-16's, M-79's, M-60 machine guns and an M-2 tripod-mounted .50 caliber heavy machine gun.

The 105mm howitzers of Battery B 2-319 Field Artillery, commanded by CPT David Rich, speedily joined the 155's of Battery A, 2-11 Field Artillery, commanded by CPT Gordon Baxendale, in answering the NVA's fire. The artillery fired on pre-plotted targets of likely NVA firing positions all around the firebase. Ripcord's perimeter was shaped like a figure eight, with the 105's positioned on the higher, wider southeastern level. The larger 155's held the lower and narrower level that sloped up to a boulder-covered knoll at the northwestern end of the base.

The enemy gunners received much more fire than they could deliver. Along with the big howitzers, six 81mm mortars from E/2-506 were putting out rounds from the mortar pits positioned just below the TOC. Some fifteen minutes after the first rounds fell, air support began to appear over Ripcord. The first air unit to arrive was a Pink Team from the 2-17th Cavalry, the 101st Airborne's air cavalry squadron. The so-called Pink Teams consisted of an OH-6 Cayuse LOH from the White Platoon and a deadly AH-1G Cobra gunship from the squadron's Red Platoon.

The Pink Team went after a mortar tube firing from the eastern slope of Hill 805 near YD 362187. The LOH dove down and marked the position with colored smoke grenades for the Cobra. The enemy mortar position had been spotted and called in by CPT Thomas Hewitt, commanding C/2-506, two platoons of which were in position on the summit of Hill 902 about 2,500 meters to the southwest of Ripcord.

At about 0728 hours, an incoming salvo wounded one of CPT Rich's gunners, the first casualty of the siege on the firebase. CPT Hewitt quickly spotted this new mortar, firing from the south side of a knoll in the valley below Ripcord at YD 345183, less than a klick from the base.

A team pf rocket-armed Cobras from the 4-77th Aerial Rocket Artillery (ARA) followed the Pink Team. The ARA battalion was used to attack dug-in targets such as mortar pits and bunkers; the minigun-armed Cobras from the 2-17th were most often used against NVA troops in the open. The LOH from the Pink Team spotted another mortar tube in a gully one klick southeast of Hill 805. The little ship pulled up sharply as green tracers zipped past from Hill 805.

By then an Air Force FAC in a small O-1 Bird Dog was circling high overhead. The FAC spotted still another mortar firing from a small knoll at the northern base of Hill 902 near YD 348176. The FAC marked the targets with brilliant white smoke from white phosphorous rockets. F-4 Phantoms, dropping a deadly combination of bombs and napalm, dove on Hill 805 and the ridge seven hundred meters east of Ripcord. The 'snake 'n nape' were right on target, but as the jets pulled away, NVA gunners lobbed a few more mortar rounds onto Ripcord. When the LOH's went down for a closer look, they were chased away by heavy automatic weapons fire.

It was the same old story; the 101st Airborne had the firepower, but the mountains and jungle favored the NVA. They remained hidden under the jungle canopy, alternating their fire from several locations. The main terrain features surrounding FSB Ripcord were Hill 805 about two kilometers to the southeast and Hill 1000, one klick to the west. Five hundred meters west of Ripcord, a small knoll sits on the ridge between Hill 1000 and the firebase, often used by NVA lobbing RPG's at the base. Coc Muen mountain, rising to 1,298 meters, is the dominate terrain feature to Ripcord's southwest. A long ridge runs east from Coc Muen to Hill 902 about two and a half klicks south of Ripcord. This ridge continues east to Re-Up Hill, about two klicks south of Hill 805. All these ridges, hills and valleys were cloaked in thirty square kilometers of double-and-triple canopy jungle.

The 2-506 was stretched too thinly to be able to occupy all this high ground and, before the siege began, had no reason to be tied down in defensive positions. On the morning of 1 July, D/2-506 was defending Ripcord. A/2-506 was securing FSB O'Reilly, a US-ARVN firebase seven kilometers northwest of Ripcord. Two Platoons of C/2-506 were in position on top of Hill 902. The third platoon was on Ripcord for a brief rest. LTC Lucas had received an intelligence briefing predicting the movement of an NVA battalion into the hills between O'Reilly and Ripcord. Lucas' remaining units – a Recon Team from E/2-506, B/2-506 and D/2-501 (OPCON to the 2-506) – had been moved to meet that threat.

The NVA mortar fire seemed to be concentrated against CPT Rich's 105mm battery on the highest tier of the firebase. During the day, a dozen gunners were wounded, as was 1LT Tore Hewlett, the executive officer and SFC Frank Rankins, the battery firing chief. Most of the wounds were minor but three men required a medevac.

Artillery officers are trained to check the crater left by each incoming round as it exploded to determine where it came from by the angle of impact. Cpt Rich was hit twice by mortar fragments while performing this crater analysis. In combination with Rich's crater analysis and trajectories measured by Ripcord's counter mortar radar, the 105's from Battery B were able to deliver very accurate counter battery fire onto the NVA mortar positions around the firebase. In three and a half hours of shelling, NVA gunners managed to put only about thirty rounds into the air, fifteen of which overshot Ripcord.

Mortar fire was reported coming from a long ridgeline with three peaks along it known as Triple Hill. An air strike was called in on Triple Hill and the FAC who went down for a closer look reported that the mortar tube had been destroyed and an NVA gunner killed.

The lull in the bombardment lasted until about 1335 hours when a single mortar round impacted on Ripcord. About fifteen minutes later, a 75mm recoilless rifle began firing from Triple Hill. Some of the rounds missed Ripcord, but others did not. B/2-506, who had been moved by air to Hill 805 to deny its use by the NVA, had a clear view of Triple Hill over three kilometers away. According to SGT Robert Judd of Bravo One, *"You could see where the recoilless rifle was firing from, and you could see the smoke trails zipping toward Ripcord."* Judd watched as Company B's artillery FO, 2LT Aaron Andrasson called in artillery on the firing site. *"He called in one marker round, then adjusted and fired for effect – and got secondary explosions. We let out a cheer."* Ripcord – page 31.

LTC Lucas asked for a resupply of the depleted mortar and artillery ammunition, and late that afternoon CH-47's from the 159th Aviation Battalion began arriving in groups of two or three at a time. Twenty-five of the big helicopters replaced the more than one thousand artillery rounds fired that day. Each Chinook took its turn hovering over the log pad and, guided by a pathfinder, set down its sling-load of shells and powder charges. The large numbers of CH-47's arriving over the firebase attracted heavy anti-aircraft fire. As the escorting Cobras dove in on one muzzle flash, other guns would begin to fire from adjacent hill sides. At about 1550 hours, one Chinook from B/159th took enough hits for it to make a forced landing on the firebase.

At the same time as the resupply was underway on Ripcord, an 'aero rifle' platoon from the 2-17th Cavalry was inserted into a hot LZ on Triple Hill. They were looking for the reportedly destroyed mortar tube and recoilless rifle but they could not be found. The NVA who had fired on the platoon as they landed withdrew when gunships arrived over the ridge. By the time the platoon was lifted out the next day, they had found bunkers all over the hilltop and several trails heavily marked with fresh sandal prints.

Other mortar positions around Ripcord began dropping rounds onto the base attempting to destroy the disabled Chinook. At about 1921 hours a second CH-47, this time from A/159th, was shot down on the log pad by a 12.7mm (.51 caliber) heavy machine gun. The crew quickly repaired the damage enough for the Chinook to fly to a nearby lowland firebase where it could be completely repaired.

The 12.7mm was spotted firing from a knoll down in the valley between Ripcord and Hill 805 near YD 341186. CPT Rich had one of his 105 crews roll their gun to the edge of the hill so they could fire directly down on the little hill. However, the 12.7mm was emplaced in a cave dug out of the hillside. When a helicopter arrived over Ripcord, the machine gun crew would roll it forward and open fire. Up on Hill 805, SGT Judd watched it all ". . .*when the artillery zeroed in on them, they'd just wheel it back inside. The fast-movers* [jets] *came in and napalmed the whole area, and we thought, boy, nothing can be alive down there—but after the air strike the little bastards wheeled that gun back up to the opening and popped off a few more rounds just to let us know they were still there." Ripcord* – page 32.

The battalion and brigade leadership believed that the NVA would pull back during the night after causing some damage to the firebase. The big concern as darkness fell was that the NVA would launch a sapper attack against Ripcord as a follow-up to the day-long shelling. No one really anticipated the all-out offensive that was about to take place.

Throughout the night, the 105's and 155's fired periodically at likely avenues of attack around the firebase. When a trip flare ignited on the knoll between Hill 1000 and Ripcord, the 81's blasted the spot. On perimeter security, Company D troops reported brush breaking about seventy-five meters down the slope from their fighting positions on the southern side of the hill. A grunt from Company C, watching from Hill 902, later said, *"When the flares went up, you could see the NVA moving around outside the wire. They were really getting bold."* Ripcord – page 32.

There was a ground attack that night but not against the firebase. At about 2230 hours on 1 July, the NVA launched the anticipated attack on B/2-506 in position on the rocky peak of Hill 805. The NVA opened fire with AK's and RPG's from the heavy brush around the top of the hill. However, the NVA action against the troops of 805 turned out to be only a probe, perhaps to divert attention away from their real objective—Hill 902.

At about 0346 hours on the morning of 2 July, the two platoons of C/2-506 on Hill 902 were attacked in their NDP and overrun by sappers and NVA infantry. Company C beat off the attack but with heavy losses, including one man missing in action and never located.

As the fighting on Hill 902 died away in the early morning light, The NVA again attacked Company B on Hill 805. Artillery, mortars and Cobra gunships were called in and the enemy withdrew as it became full daylight.

Up on Ripcord, a rigger team from Camp Eagle prepared to extract the downed CH-47 left on the firebase overnight. When a sister ship from A/159th tried to hook up the disabled helicopter it, too, was hit by 12.7mm fire and crashed next to the helicopter it had come to recover. The crew worked on the downed aircraft all day, using parts from the first Chinook so the second ship could safely take off late that afternoon.

NVA gunners continued their shelling of the firebase during the second day of the battle. Several men were wounded and evacuated during heavy counter-battery fire. Steady 12.7mm fire came in against the resupply Chinooks. One such gunner set up his big machine gun in a small clearing only a hundred meters northeast of the B Company troops on Hill 805. An amazed SGT Judd wrote, *"I don't know if he didn't realize we could see him through the trees or what his problem was, but he didn't pay any attention to us. He was totally focused on Ripcord."*

PFC Ramon Santiago quickly brought the man under fire with his M-60. *"He took off running, but I know he was hit at least three times,"* remembered Judd. *"You could see his body take the hits."*

SGT Judd led his squad to check the firing position. They found a blood trail but not a body. Three NVA rucksacks had been left behind along with the big tripod-mounted gun. A helicopter picked up the gun and carried it to Camp Eagle where it was put on display at division headquarters. *Ripcord* – page 124.

A 12.7mm/.51 caliber heavy machine gun like the gun captured by B/2-506 Infantry near Hill 805 on 2 July 1970. This weapon could also fire captured .50 caliber US ammo but US guns could not fire .51 caliber ammo because it was one millimeter too large for the bore of US-made weapons.

B/2-506 received mortar fire at sundown, fired from the slope of its own hill. A patrol went out but the tube and gunners were long gone. Another security patrol found several more freshly-built bunkers on another slope of the hill.

Company B endured another rough night of intermittent mortar and RPG fire. More patrols went out the next morning and one of them found a large ammo cache. On the same morning C/159th Aviation, escorted by several gunships and smoke ships, made a concerted effort to recover the downed Chinook still on Ripcord. Cobras suppressed 12.7mm sites around Ripcord while two CH-47's flew off with the downed helicopter's two rotor systems. A third Chinook lifted out the stripped-down aircraft itself and flew it to Camp Evans, then ran out of fuel on its way to the POL (petrol, oil, lubrication) pad and crashed. Both Chinooks were then flown by huge Sikorsky CH-54 Sky Trains to the main repair depot at Phu Bai.

The NVA were most active after dark, with lights blinking on the hillsides all around Ripcord and sounds in the wire barriers around the perimeter. Because of all the after dark activity, the firebase defenders developed an aggressive plan of defensive fire that was put into effect every night. The six mortar crews based on Ripcord fired over five hundred rounds a night, a nearly constant rain of 81mm rounds falling around the firebase.

At the beginning of the battle, casualties on the firebase were light. LTC Lucas was lightly wounded when a mortar round exploded near him and MAJ Koenigsbauer, standing on the steps that lead into the TOC and scanning the hillsides for enemy mortar positions.

Several of the rounds that came in on 4 July were CS tear gas and not high explosives. The troops on Ripcord had been issued light weight, largely ineffective M-28 gas masks that provided only partial protection, the eye pieces quickly fogging up. LTC Lucas had the battalion XO, MAJ Sidney Davis, commandeer an emergency issue of the bulkier M-17 gas masks in storage at Camp Evans. These more reliable masks were shipped out to Ripcord by the end of the day. Everyone on the hill carried them all the time until the end of the battle. In response to the NVA's use of chemical weapons, 3rd Brigade authorized the use of CS artillery rounds in the defense of Ripcord.

CPT Rich of B/2-319th FA, although wounded several times while performing crater analysis, closely supervised his 105's as they fired on a new NVA mortar team firing from atop Coc A Bo mountain, nearly five kilometers to the east. The quickly delivered counterbattery fire caused several secondary explosions on the summit of Coc A Bo.

Soon after they silenced the mortar on Coc A Bo, MAJ Koenigsbauer was scanning the hills from a position near the highest point of Ripcord when he saw a puff of smoke as a recoilless rifle fired a round from a spot high on the eastern slope of Hill 1000. The major hurried to notify CPT Rich, reaching him just as the NVA gunner fired a second round which Rich also saw. The NVA fired two more shots as Rich ordered two 105's lowered for point-blank fire. They fired a half-dozen rounds at the spot, either destroying the weapon or driving the crew to take shelter in one of the many bunkers dotting the slopes of Hill 1000.

1LT Fred Edwards commanded the combat engineer platoon attached to Lucas' 2-506 Infantry on Ripcord. Edwards kept a journal detailing all the major activities on the firebase. His notes at the beginning of the battle related a feeling in general that the situation on the base was serious but not yet critical and that it would end soon. Edwards wrote that he was surprised that the enemy could keep up their harassing fire in the face of all the firepower being used against them. On 9 July, Edwards wrote *"They've been averaging about 20-30 rounds a day in 5 or 6 volleys."* He added that he had *"talked to some NBC correspondents out here . . . and they said Ripcord was being played up pretty big back home [and] even called it a siege—it's not that but it is very unpleasant [and] unhealthy." Ripcord* - page 281.

So far there had been numerous injuries but no one had been killed. Edwards kept the engineer bulldozer busy cutting new LZ's, supply pads and revetments for fuel bladders. The engineers often worked under fire and were congratulated by LTC Lucas for their good work under combat conditions. LT Edwards noted that the high winds constantly blowing in the Ripcord AO had kept any helicopters from landing for two days, putting them in danger of running out of food and ammo.

On 10 July, SSGT Thomas Rubsam, who had recovered from his arm wound, returned to B/2-506, still securing Ripcord. CPT Williams, in the rear on an admin run, had picked up Rubsam in a LOH for the trip out to Ripcord. The small helicopter was spun around 360° by the high winds several times on the flight out to the firebase.

On arriving at Ripcord, SSGT Rubsam was told he had been transferred from Bravo Two to Bravo One and that he would soon be taking over as Bravo One's platoon leader from LT Delgado. After he had reported to his new platoon, Rubsam climbed on top of the nearby mess bunker to check the layout of Bravo One's positions on the perimeter. He was about to climb down when a 75mm recoilless rifle shell flew right into the door of the mess bunker. Rubsam believes that was an accident; that the round was aimed at him as he stood on the bunker's roof.

Accident or not, the round killed PFC Victor De Foor of Bravo Three who had just entered the bunker to get some coffee and wounded several other men Rubsam did not know. He ran to the Company B CP for help and men from De Foor's squad went to pick up his body. PFC Rodger 'Chip' Collins later wrote, *"When the guys came back with tears in their eyes, telling how they had tried to pick Vic's scalp up, we got with other units and agreed to take care of their bad KIA's if they would take care of ours."* Ripcord – page 282.

The other troops in the mess bunker were from D/2-506 having just walked onto the firebase for a resupply after their ordeal on Hill 1000. Mortar rounds began falling on the base as Company D came in through the wire barrier. Four of the infantrymen found shelter in the mess bunker. Standing near the doorway, they waited for the shelling to stop. De Foor came in to get two cups of coffee and had started back out the door when the shell exploded while he was framed in the doorway. De Foor took the full force of the explosion and was blown onto the serving counter, killed instantly. The four Company D men were blown across the bunker, landing in a heap against the far wall. One of the four, PFC Bruce McCorkle, remembers running out the back door and up to the aid station, where he was told that he had been hit in his right lung by shrapnel and that his war was over.

Day ten (10 July) marked the first day in which men were killed by incoming mortar and recoilless rifle fire. The attack lasted a half hour during which NVA gunners dropped twenty-five 82mm rounds, fired from several positions, onto the base. Fourteen of the firebases defenders were hit badly enough to be medevacked. One of those men, PFC Larry Plett, an artilleryman with B/2-319 Field Artillery 105's), died of his wounds at the 85th Evacuation Hospital in Phu Bai.

Two more men were killed instantly in addition to PFC De Foor. SP4 Frederick Raymond of A/2-11 Field Artillery (155's) was killed when he left his bunker to carry a case of C-rations to the FDC. He had not put on his flak jacket or steel helmet because it was a short trip to the FDC and the shelling appeared to have stopped. PFC Patrick Bohan, a pathfinder busy guiding in the Dust-off helicopters for the wounded, died when he left his covered position to get a replacement for his malfunctioning radio.

During all the incoming, CPT David Rich commanding Battery B/2-319, kept his 105's firing. He had been wounded for the fifth time that morning as he directed a 105 to be lowered for direct fire at a recoilless rifle firing on the medevac helicopters from the top of Hill 805. CPT Rich, who had begun his career as an enlisted man, had won a direct commission during the second of his four tours in Vietnam. Rich, short and thin in stature, had a cocky, abrasive personality and often said he wanted to stay in Vietnam until the war was over.

Rich's CO, LTC William Walker, said about him, *"He wasn't a paperwork guy but he was the perfect kind of high-energy combat officer to have out in a situation like Ripcord. He set the example not only for his own people but for everybody on the base."* Ripcord - page 283-284.

Walker described how Rich would run to the craters of each new mortar salvo, carrying a radio with him. When he had determined the back-azimuth, he quickly called them in to the FDC. The azimuths were used to determine which of the pre-selected enemy firing positions were being used and the new firing data was quickly sent to the gun crews who put out a heavy counter mortar fire.

■ ■ ■

*CPT David F Rich (**L**) supervises a fire mission by Battery B 2-319 Field Artillery (105mm) on FSB Ripcord. The 1st Air Cavalry patch is from a previous tour. US Army photo by SP5 Chris W. Jensen.*

As the battle grew in intensity and the number of mortar rounds dropped on the base increased steadily, the location of the nearest bunker took on an added importance. For the most part, the bunkers on Ripcord were strong enough to protect the occupants even from a direct hit. The base defenders only went outside when necessary; either on work parties or checking the perimeter wire every morning for evidence of tampering or infiltration. The infantry performed this task early each morning, often under sniper fire from the lower slopes of the hill. At the first sign of incoming, everyone ran to the nearest shelter and the base took on the aspect of an abandoned village with no movement except for the everlasting wind. There were many near misses because the sound of an incoming round was often masked by the wind.

The battalion S-3, CPT William J. Williams was blown down the steps leading into the battalion TOC by the concussion from a near miss, landing in a heap at LTC Lucas' feet, unhurt except for his dignity.

LTC Lucas exposed himself to enemy fire routinely, every day. Lucas took his role as base commander – 'King of the Hill' in 101st slang – very seriously and made it a point to be highly visible to his troops, knowing that men under fire day after day needed an extra morale boost. When shells were falling, Lucas would be out checking positions, letting his men know he was there with them.

During a mortar barrage, CPT Rich was directing one of his 105's as it fired on an NVA mortar position on the ridge just east of Ripcord. An enemy 12.7mm opened fire on the gun and a bullet passed right between CPT Rich and LTC Lucas, burying itself in a bunker right behind them.

Another example of how Lucas exposed himself to enemy fire occurred when he was checking a perimeter position manned by a squad from Company B. The squad leader for the position, SGT Christopher Hinman, began firing an M-60 to provide cover fire for the helicopters coming in on a resupply mission. Hinman and SP4 Thomas Searson, each with an M-60 were firing steadily at an NVA mortar crew who were dropping rounds on the base as the log birds landed. In return, Searson and Hinman drew fire from a 12.7mm machine gun and a ricochet hit Hinman's helmet, knocking him senseless to the ground. Lucas rushed forward and, picking up the M-60, joined Searson in blasting away at the enemy mortar until the resupply was completed and the Huey's roared away at top speed.

The medics assigned to the aid station on Ripcord also took chances with their lives. Everybody else would be undercover during incoming, but if the cry for a 'medic' was heard, they would respond immediately, dashing into the incoming with no thought for their own safety. CPT James Harris, the battalion surgeon on Ripcord, said of his medics, "*I was really proud of my medics. A lot of them hated that war, but they all did their job. They weren't going to let their buddies down. Ripcord* – page 286.

Doctor Harris himself was a hawk about the war. He had been conditioned by his service in a MASH unit near Saigon where he had treated many civilian victims of communist terrorism. Harris took his job more seriously than most draftee doctors and was thought of a as a hero by many of the men on FSB Ripcord. Harris often went with his medics into harm's way during an attack, helping load wounded men aboard medevacs under fire. Harris said of his transfer to the 101st, *"It was a real eye opener. I just didn't think it was fair to use my position as an officer and a doctor to send my medics out there if I wasn't willing to do it myself."* Doctor Harris was awarded the Silver Star for his actions on Ripcord.

Harris made light of his own bravery. He explained that because the NVA did not know which LZ to mortar until the medevac actually landed and because it took some twenty to thirty seconds for a mortar round to travel from the tube to impact on the base, *"you had a window of opportunity there to get your wounded aboard. If everyone had their shit together, the medevac would be airborne again and we would all be back inside the aid station before the first shell hit the LZ." Ripcord* – page 286.

■ ■ ■

On 9 July, a group of three US Army combat photographers showed up unexpectedly on Ripcord, led by SP5 Chris Jensen. The three-man team had just returned from documenting the US-led incursion into Cambodia beginning in May 1970. Word had filtered down to Jensen's unit at Long Binh, near Saigon, about a big fight in the 101st Airborne's AO at a place called Ripcord. Jensen and his team decided to head north to I Corps to see what was going on.

They flew to Camp Eagle and reported to the 101st's PIO (public information office) where they were told in no uncertain terms that no media, civilian or military, was allowed on Ripcord. Only a few journalists had ventured out to the firebase and, as the situation worsened, a news blackout was imposed by division headquarters. Headquarters was probably concerned that Ripcord would become a public relations nightmare as had 'Hamburger Hill' (Dong Ap Bia Mountain) the year before.

The refusal only made Jensen and his people more determined to find out what was going on out in the western mountains of Thua Thien Province. They managed to hitch a ride on an in-bound medevac and surprised LTC Lucas when they showed up at his TOC festooned with cameras and wearing clean fatigues and soft-brimmed 'boonie hats.' Jensen told Lucas he wanted to get out into the canopy with a line company but Lucas absolutely refused, telling Jensen it was just too dangerous. Lucas offered to let the photo team stay on Ripcord and gave them steel helmets, flak jackets and a bunker to live in.

Jensen and his crew freely roamed the base for several days, photographing and filming the 105's in action and they had some near-misses of their own. One time, a mortar round exploded right where Jensen had noticed one of his crew, SP4 James Saller, standing to try and line up a shot. Jensen remembers, "*The blast sprayed all this hot, wet stuff on my shoulders and the back of my neck. I thought, 'oh shit, that's Saller', and I reached back to wipe the crap off my neck—and it was Spanish rice. The round hit a mermite can full of hot food. Saller had moved from the area right before the explosion, and was perfectly okay, but lunch was ruined.*" Ripcord – page 287.

SP4 Saller's luck ran out two days later when he was hit in the side by recoilless rifle shrapnel. The third member of the team decided to get out while the getting was good and flew out on the same medevac with Saller, but Jensen decided to stay on the base for a few more days. Jensen had noticed that, "*There was no feeling of impending doom on Ripcord. There was a reasonable amount of incoming, and nobody was happy about that, but everyone was well dug in. People were in good spirits. Morale was solid.*" Ripcord – page 288.

SSGT Thomas Rubsam, now the platoon leader for Company B's Bravo One, had a squad leader whose eccentric behavior under fire was a great morale booster. According to Rubsam. *"It was hard to get people out of their holes once they'd taken cover. Everybody would be hunkered down, but then all of a sudden, you'd see skinny, pimple-faced Phil [Thomas P.] Tolson prancing back and forth, wielding an old trash-can lid like it was Captain America's shield, cursing and taunting the NVA. It was hilarious, especially to guys who were scared shitless, and it was a great motivator. It let people know that the shelling's weren't the end of the world." Ripcord* – page 288.

To the men on Ripcord the only thing more enjoyable than cursing the NVA was shooting back. SSGT Rubsam got that chance one day when a Huey landed on the refueling pad in Bravo One's sector of the perimeter. The slick came under AK-47 fire from a bunker dug under a huge boulder on the hill just east of Ripcord. A passenger sitting in the door of the Huey was wounded before the ship could get back off the ground. Rubsam could see the sniper in the firing aperture of the bunker through his binoculars. The return fire against the bunker seemed to have no effect, situated as it was under the overhanging boulder.

After much delay, Rubsam managed to get the outgoing artillery fire from Ripcord stopped so a Cobra could fly directly over the base on its rocket firing runs. The gunship made several rocket firing runs until the pilot informed Rubsam he almost run out of rockets and fuel, but the rockets seemed to have no effect. Apparently, the Cobra gunner was having difficulty seeing the small firing aperture under the shadow of the boulder.

Desperate to silence the sniper, SSGT Rubsam gathered several M-72 LAW rockets and tried to mark the target for the Cobra gunner, using a dead tree above the bunker as an aiming point. The first two LAW's missed but were surprisingly accurate. Thinking he might be able to destroy the bunker himself, Rubsam readied the third rocket and fired. The third LAW rocket sailed right through the small opening and exploded with a satisfying **'THUMP'**. Rubsam remembers ". . .*It tickled everybody in the platoon. The guys were just bored, watching the show, and when the rocket exploded inside the bunker it was standing-ovation time. I don't know if the enemy soldier was still in there, or if he had an escape tunnel, but we never took fire from that position again." Ripcord* – page 288-289.

Chapter 14
HILL 1000 – AN EXERCISE IN FUTILITY

We're up against it. We're not getting anywhere. We're just expending ammunition." 1LT John Flaherty to CPT R.G. Rollison on Hill 1000, 7 July 1970.

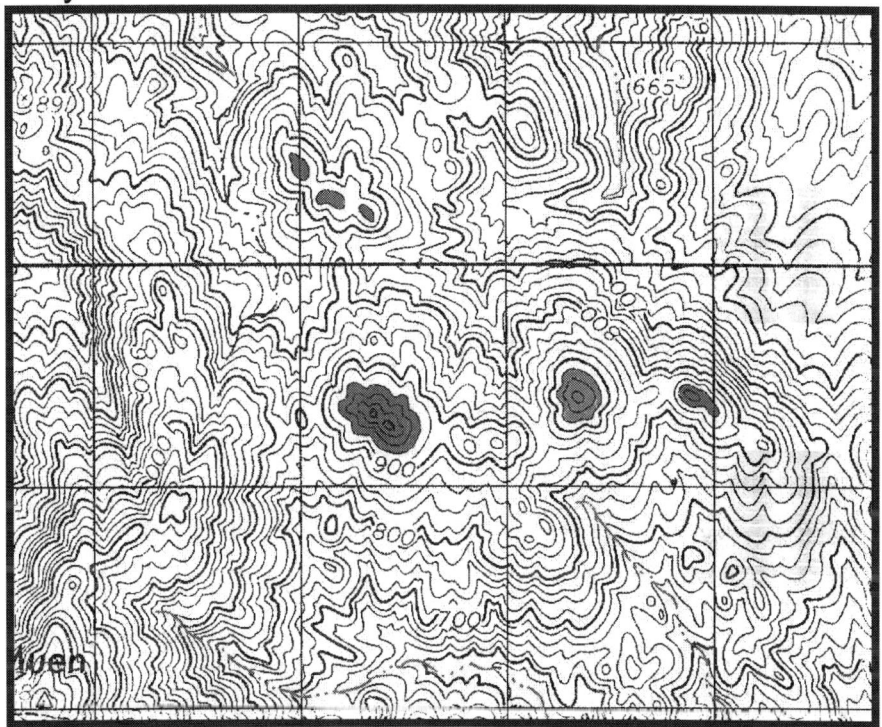

Color-enhanced detail from topographical map sheet 6441-4 Series L-7014 A Luoi District of Thua Thien Province. Firebase Ripcord outlined in blue; NVA firing positions on Hill 1000, Triple Hill and ridge east of Ripcord outlined in red. Map from Authors collection. Color-enhanced map © 2017.

By the first week of July, the 2-506 Infantry Currahees had taken so many casualties that it became increasingly obvious that the battered battalion could not continue to face alone the increasingly aggressive NVA units operating around FSB Ripcord. On 2 July, the 2-501 Infantry (Geronimo Battalion), commanded by LTC Otis W. Livingston, combated assaulted onto LZ's along the ridge running southeast from Hill 902. Livingston and his CP then moved onto FSB Ripcord, temporarily sharing the TOC with LTC Lucas and his staff.

A/2-501 landed atop Hill 902 after the battered remnants of C/2-506 were lifted off. Company A landed in the middle of an 82mm mortar barrage and two men were slightly wounded. Further down the ridge, a Cobra gunship wounded three men from C Company 2-501 when the supporting fires came too close to their position.

The rain of mortar and recoilless rifle rounds onto FSB Ripcord continued. LTC Lucas had inserted a recon patrol to check the buildup of NVA forces north of the firebase. On 29 June the team, led by SGT Robert O. Granberry, Jr., found a black commo wire fastened to the trees in a gully the recon team was following. The team's Kit Carson Scout discovered the wire. He urged them to get out of the area because he knew the enemy would be patrolling the commo wire. The scout, whose name was Hai, was adamant about the danger. "*Beaucoup NVA. Di di mau, di di mau. Beaucoup NVA, beaucoup NBA,*" Hai stuttered, a look of terror on his face.

Granberry reported what they had found to the TOC on Ripcord. He expected the small recon team to be withdrawn and replaced by a full line company. The TOC radioed that a slick was inbound with a tape recorder and clips that could be used to tap the line. Cautiously they moved back to their insertion LZ to wait for the Huey, a dangerous move. When the equipment was delivered, the team found a secluded spot and tapped the line. They took turns listening with a pair of headphones sent with the tape recorder but they heard no voices, only static. After a while they moved to a position on the slope overlooking the draw so they could observe the tape recorder. Their presence had been announced by the helicopter so they were very anxious about an attack by the NVA bent on protecting their communications link.

Another slick came in the next morning to pick up the tapes and deliver a replacement set. The very nervous recon team monitored their wiretap for most of four days, leaving their concealed position only to change tapes on the recorder. The mission was not recon's usual method of operation. Said team member John Mihalko, *"Line companies were too big and loud, but our little recon teams could cruise and bruise right in the enemy's backyard. We initiated most contacts because the NVA didn't even know we were there. We walked right into one of their little camps once and fired 'em up as they sat there cooking rice. They didn't have guards out because they felt safe."* To troops accustomed to operating in such secrecy, staying in one place for nearly four days was absolutely crazy. A lot of resentment began to build up against LTC Lucas. *Ripcord* – page 126.

The rain of 82mm mortar and recoilless rifle rounds falling onto Ripcord was becoming a definite health hazard. Work details on the base began to look for ways to remain near bunkers, trenches and foxholes that could be ducked into when there was incoming.

Commanders at the brigade and battalion levels began to look for methods to better defend the firebase from the incoming rounds. A plan was developed to augment the fire from the bases 81mm mortars and 105mm howitzers by using the Quad-50 in position at the northeast corner of the firebase. Most of the NVA firing positions were sited on the back side or reverse slopes of the hills as seen from Ripcord. A method was developed where the Quad-50 was fired at an extreme angle, the stream of half-inch bullets traveling in a high arc and falling on the back sides of the hills. The rain of fire blasting down through the trees must have cost NVA gun crews heavy casualties because the enemy made a concerted effort to destroy the big four-barreled gun. Enemy gunners would walk mortar rounds across the firebase trying for a direct hit. There were some casualties among the crew and the gun was damaged several times but never put out of action for long.

LTC Lucas was so pleased with the weapons' performance that he ordered a second Quad-50 to be delivered to Ripcord. MAJ Koenigsbauer, the battalion S-3, ordered the battalion's transportation section to send out as many .50 caliber machine guns as could be spared from the rear area at Camp Evans. Koenigsbauer had been trained initially as an armor officer and was familiar with the firing characteristics of the big .50's. He set up the guns, mounted on tripods, at strategic spots around the perimeter and test fired them himself.

The big CH-47 Chinook's from the 159th Aviation Battalion, on their daily supply runs, were primary targets for the enemy gunners manning the big 12.7mm machine guns. Careful notice was taken of the firing positions for these guns. The Chinooks were sent out in groups of two or three and, when the huge helicopters were two minutes out from the firebase, the Quad-50's, ground-mounted .50's, mortars, recoilless rifles and the 105's all would fire on known or suspected anti-aircraft guns sites around Ripcord. These suppressive fires were kept up as long as the Chinooks were over the firebase. In-bound and out-bound routes for the big helicopters were carefully planned to avoid, as much as possible, over-flying known NVA firing positions.

LTC Lucas was aware that a great deal of mortar and recoilless rifle fire was coming against FSB Ripcord from the area of Hill 1000. Nearly two hundred fifty feet higher than Ripcord, Hill 1000 overlooked the firebase from a kilometer to the west. The firebase was connected to the big hill by a narrow ridge which rose to a hill some five hundred meters west of Ripcord, then fell into a saddle before rising again to the double peak of Hill 1000.

So, on 6 July, LTC Lucas conceived a new mission for the recon team from E/2-506. Calling SGT Robert Granberry, known as 'Junior', and his assistant team leader, SP4 John Schnarr, to the 506 Infantry TOC on Ripcord, Lucas outlined the simple plan. Granberry listened in disbelief as Lucas explained the details of his plan–the recon team was to move on foot from Ripcord along the ridge connecting the firebase to Hill 1000. Neither tactical air strikes or artillery barrages had destroyed the mortars dug in around the top of the hill, so Lucas needed Granberry's team to find the exact location of the mortars.

When they were dismissed, Schnarr and Granberry decided they were going to take their time climbing that hill and if they could not locate the mortars without being detected, well, that was too bad.

That afternoon, SGT Granberry led his team, following a patrol trail through the wire, off Ripcord onto the ridge. By early evening, they had moved about six hundred meters and set up their NDP in the saddle just below Hill 1000.

When the mortars began firing the next morning as a CH-47 with a sling load of 105 ammo hovered over Ripcord, the recon team could hear a mortar firing about four hundred meters west of them near one of the small knolls on the top of hill 1000. As each round left the tube, Granberry would alert the TOC on Ripcord that they would be receiving an incoming round. Granberry gave the TOC an estimated distance from the team's location and an azimuth for counterbattery fire. As far as Granberry and his team were concerned, they had done the job they had been sent to do.

However, the duty officer in the TOC ordered the team to move further up the hill to get an exact location and, if feasible for such a small team, to destroy the mortar. The team was irate when they heard the new mission. They told Granberry to tell the TOC they were not going. Granberry told them they had to go, but they would move with extreme caution.

SP4 Doug Jacoway, their most experienced point man, led the way. As they approached the top of the hill, they saw that the last fifty to seventy-five meters before the actual summit had been blown clear of trees by artillery and air strikes, so there was little or no cover. The team managed to sneak into a bomb crater right at the edge of the undamaged trees. Speaking in whispers, they talked about their next move as the NVA fired another round. Granberry dutifully told the TOC another round was on the way and the team watched the shell explode over on Ripcord.

Granberry told the TOC that the mortar team was just above them; they could hear the gunners talking. Granberry gave the grid coordinates and told the duty officer he could adjust artillery or mortar fire onto the NVA position. Told to wait, the duty officer then told him that they wanted the team to assault the mortar position. Incredulous, Granberry again told the TOC that they were only a small team and offered a second time to adjust artillery fire onto the NVA mortar position.

The duty officer told him again to assault the position and Granberry, disregarding radio procedure, replied. "That's not a good idea." But the duty officer, for a third time, told Granberry their mission was to launch an assault on the NVA position. Granberry and Schnarr formed the impression that Lucas himself was prompting the duty officer.

Earlier, Lucas had flown over the team's position in his personal helicopter and he must have been excited that a recon team had managed to creep within attack distance of a known target. Lucas knew the team would have the advantage of surprise and, the duty officer explained, a platoon from D/2-506 was moving to support them.

CPT Rembert Rollison, commanding D Company, was at that moment moving over the small hill between Ripcord and Hill 1000. Even with reinforcements on the way, Granberry thought the order to assault the mortar was so foolish that he was ready to risk a court-martial for refusing to make the attack.

Point man Doug Jacoway, who was sometimes reckless, said they should give it a try and see what happened. Granberry's assistant, John Schnarr said he would take one other man and try to move closer to see if an attack was feasible instead of risking the whole team.

Granberry agreed and Schnarr moved out with PFC Gaskins, a black kid from the deep south with the improbable nickname of 'Dixie.' The two worked their way into some cover and they, moving on hands and knees, then low crawling, made their way toward the eastern-most knoll atop Hill 1000. The only cover available was not much over two feet high, so they could only move a few feet at a time, stopping often to look and listen before crawling another few feet.

Staying in the low brush, Schnarr managed to reach a spot near the top, stopping when he heard people speaking Vietnamese. Looking through the brush, he saw a face underneath a green pith helmet. Schnarr thought he could kill the man and moved his M-16 into firing position. Before pulling the trigger, he noticed his target was talking to a second NVA. Then he saw at least six more enemy soldiers, all wearing the distinctive pith helmet of the North Vietnamese Army, moving around in trenches dug among the downed trees along the military crest of Hill 1000.

Recon team leader SGT Robert Granberry, Jr. holding a captured AK-50 folding stock assault rifle. Granberry's team tried to destroy an NVA mortar tube on Hill 1000 on 6 July 1970. Photo by SP4 John Mihalko, E/2-506.

*SP4 John Mihalko (**L**) and SP4 John Schnarr, recon platoon E/2-506 Infantry after the Battle of FSB Ripcord. Photo by SP4 John Mihalko, E/2-506.*

Knowing they were completely exposed, Schnarr motion to Gaskins to move back before they were discovered and killed. Schnarr whispered that they had to get out of there because there were too many NVA for them to handle. In a hurry to get back to the crater, they crawled straight down the nearly bare slope instead of to the right, the way they had come. The tops of their heads were exposed for only a few moments but it was enough for the sharp-eyed NVA to spot them.

They reached the crater concealing the rest of the team and Schnarr began briefing Granberry on what he had discovered. At that instant, the NVA fired three RPG's down at the team. Two of them impacted at the upward edge of the crater and all seven team members were wounded in the huge blast.

Schnarr, regaining his senses, discovered he had been wounded in his chest, back and neck. Gaskins had several large wounds on his legs. The RTO, PFC James Neff, not aware he had been hit in the face and leg, scrambled to his feet and took off running for the tree line. Neff heard someone yelling for help which stopped his headlong rush down the hill. Turning, Neff saw the team medic stumbling toward him with blood gushing from a severed jugular vein. Grabbing the medic, Neff pulled him back into the crater. Schnarr told Neff to call D Company and get them up there in a hurry. Turning to the PRC-25 radio he had been wearing on his back, Neff saw it had been destroyed by a big chunk of shrapnel.

Seeing the ruined radio, Granberry jumped up and began to run down the hill. Schnarr screamed, "*Junior, where the hell are you going?*" Granberry yelled, "*I'm gonna get Delta.*" Schnarr told Granberry that Delta would come up when they heard the firing, but Granberry, feeling the need to do something, anything, to help his team kept up his headlong rush down the hill.

The medic tried to follow Granberry but Schnarr stopped him. Neff secured a field dressing around the medic's neck that almost choked him, trying to control the bleeding neck wound. As it was, the medic had lost so much blood that he kept passing out while he treated the other wounded.

In the meantime, 'Junior' Granberry reached D Company's lead platoon. While the grunts from Delta were organizing a patrol to bring back the recon team, Delta's medic took one look at Granberry and told him to sit down and take his shirt off. Still dazed, Granberry wanted to know why. The medic told him again to take off his shirt and sit down. Confused, Granberry did as he was told and was shaken when he saw the blood soaking the back and sleeves of his shirt. Despite his wounds, Granberry wanted to lead the patrol when it went up the hill to bring back his men because he knew their exact position. The Delta Company medic refused to let him go, saying a dust off had been called and was on the way. Granberry's protests were ignored and he was evacuated right away.

Up on the side of Hill 1000, Schnarr and Jacoway, who was wounded in the hand, took cover at the uphill edge of the crater, ready to fire on anyone who tried to come down the hill after them. Worried about being flanked, Schnarr had Neff use the teams 'thump gun' to lob 40mm grenades into the brush to their right and along the crest of the hill, but the NVA made no move. Schnarr wanted to wait for D Company, but Jacoway and Neff urged him to get down the hill before the NVA tried to cut them off.

Schnarr asked the medic if 'Dixie' Gaskins, the most seriously wounded, could be moved. The medic told Schnarr that Gaskins had to be gotten off the hill but wasn't sure how to safely move him. Schnarr decided to carry him and, hoisting Gaskins onto his back, staggered down the hill. Shouting "*Currahee, Currahee*" every few steps, Schnarr stumbled down the hill toward Delta Company's answering shouts.

The author at Camp Eagle with an M-203. An experimental weapon in 1970, the weapon, with improvements, is now standard issue. Photo from author's collection. ©1970 and 2017.

The rest of the team followed as Schnarr met the point man for the D Company patrol as he reached the saddle below the summit of Hill 1000. Jacoway, who was walking 'drag' (last man), stopped at the edge of the un-damaged trees to fire his M-203 (combined M-16 and M-79) back up the hill to discourage anyone from following them. Neff asked Jacoway what the hell he was doing and Jacoway replied that he just wanted to make sure they weren't followed. Exasperated, Neff grabbed him and pulled him into the trees saying, *"C'mon, let's just get the hell outta here!" Ripcord* – page 152.

CPT Rollison and D Company formed a hasty perimeter down in the saddle and then sent SSGT Gary Radford back up the hill with a patrol to bring back the weapons, radio and rucksacks left behind by the recon team. One of the weapons they had left behind was a sniper rifle with a top secret telescopic sight. Not wanting that weapon to fall into NVA hands, the patrol started out as it began to grow dark. When they left, Rollison told Radford who, unusual for a shake n' bake E-6, was both Ranger and Airborne qualified, not to get into any firefights. Rollison told him he was to recover the equipment and they would deal with the NVA in the morning.

When the patrol reached the crater, SSGT George Strasburg crawled forward to retrieve some of the gear. As he reached for a rucksack, an RPG exploded against a tree stump close by. The concussion so startled Strasburg that he turned and bolted back to cover. Before Radford could make a move, several AK's opened fire on them. When Radford heard a mortar round leave the tube, he ordered a retreat and the patrol scrambled back down the hill without any of the equipment they had come to recover.

When Radford returned to the temporary NDP, Rollison saddled up the company and moved out of the saddle onto the small hill between Ripcord and Hill 1000. From their new NDP, Rollison plastered the top of Hill 1000 with 81mm mortar fire and bursts of Quad-50 counterbattery fire.

A medevac was called for the four most seriously wounded recon troopers, but the pilot had to abort when the flare marking the LZ destroyed his night vision. He tried again and this time he landed and loaded the wounded, leaving Schnarr and Jacoway to wait for another Huey.

'Junior' Granberry, evacuated earlier, had been met on the LZ by the anxious first sergeant from E Company. An enraged Granberry told the startled first sergeant, *"There's an officer up on Ripcord who's gonna die. If I ever find out who he is, I'm blowing his fucking brains out." Ripcord* - page 153.

■ ■ ■

During the night of 6–7 July, CPT Rollison organized D Company for the coming assault on Hill 1000 the next morning. Artillery from FSB Ripcord fired on the hill throughout the night and a heavy barrage began falling on the eastern-most of the two knolls as the platoons moved into their assault positions. Rollison's plan was simple; Delta Two would come up the hill from the southeast while Delta Three would attack from the northeast. Rollison and his CP would travel with the reserve platoon, the shorthanded Delta One. The plan called for the two assault platoons to begin their move up the hill as the artillery was still falling on the knoll. The fire would shift as the troops moved up the slope with the attack coming in behind a moving curtain of artillery fire. The men hoped to be inside the enemy positions before the dazed enemy could recover.

Before D Company left Ripcord, every man had been issued a full load of M-16 ammo with each man carrying at least eight high explosive fragmentation grenades. The men were confident after the all-night artillery barrage. They knew CPT Rollison was an experienced combat commander who had proved he knew what he was doing.

The assault platoons moved slowly and cautiously into their jump-off locations. The morning was clear and hot. They had left their cumbersome rucksacks back at the NDP position on the hill between Ripcord and Hill 1000 to give them more freedom of movement when the assault began. It was about three hundred meters from the NDP to the top of the easternmost knoll with the last seventy-five meters covered with a tangle of branches and tree trunks blown down by artillery and airstrikes.

The artillery lifted as Delta Three, led by 1LT Jack Flaherty, started across the tangle of downed trees. The point man, PFC Michael Grimm, was about twenty-five meters from the top of the knoll when a single shot sounded and Grimm fell forward onto his face. Delta Three quickly sought cover and returned fire. The NVA fired back and their fire was so heavy that Delta Three could not move forward.

At about the same time, The NVA fired on Delta Two, led by 1LT James McCall. That morning, several men had refused to walk point and SSGT Gary Radford thought he was going to have to do it when several other men volunteered to draw straws. SP4 Lewis Howard, Jr., drew the short one. Howard and Radford were close friends and Radford suddenly had the bad feeling that Howard was not going to make it. Howard had been Radford's RTO for six months before asking to be assigned to a rifle squad.

LT McCall led Delta Two past the crater where Granberry and his recon team had left their equipment and saw it was no longer there. McCall briefly stopped the platoon at a rock formation, spoke on the radio, then gave the word to move out. Howard and his slack man, SGT George McIntosh, moved up the hill about fifty meters when they heard firing start on Delta Three's side of the hill. Suddenly, several RPG's came zipping in on them, one of which hit a tree next to SP4 Howard, who dropped to the ground. SGT McIntosh, badly wounded, crawled away. As he did he heard Howard scream for a medic and then nothing else.

The lead troops returned fire at the unseen enemy and SSGT Radford crawled forward to see what was going on. Radford, who had extended his year-long tour another six months to remain with his men, remembers he had a case of 'short-timers fever', having only a few weeks to go before he went back to the 'world.' He had placed himself at the rear of the column, unconsciously trying to avoid coming under fire until the last moment. When the firing started, he felt guilty and crawled forward. Learning about Howard, he led a few men up to try and drag Howard back but they were driven back by heavy fire.

The NVA began firing RPG's into the tallest tree stumps, trying to shower Delta Two with rocket fragments. Radford then led a squad to the left, trying to outflank the NVA, but it didn't work. As soon as they saw any movement, the NVA threw satchel charges down on the squad.

On the northeast side of the hill, Delta Three was in the same bind. When the troops went to ground under the withering fire, they could not see the enemy from behind all the downed trees, so they were firing blindly. LT Flaherty saw that the NVA, looking downhill, had a good view of Delta Three when they tried to maneuver; they could fire at specific men. Flaherty spread the men to his left over a fifty-meter front and they started to maneuver forward, firing and throwing frags as they went. The move bogged down when they began taking fire from hidden positions that had waited until they were in range before opening fire.

They could not crawl under the downed trees so they began to throw grenades over the logs and, as soon as the frag exploded, scurry over the log. Flaherty and his RTO, using this technique, started over a downed tree when the RTO, SP4 Thomas Gaut, was shot and fell back onto Flaherty who pushed him back over the log into a crater then fell in on top of him. The NVA who had shot Gaut was in a bunker only ten feet above them, one they had not seen until he shot Gaut. Huddling in the crater, Flaherty and Gaut were reasonably safe because the enemy soldier in the bunker above them could not depress his machine gun barrel low enough to shoot them. The round that had shattered Gaut's hand and forearm had also destroyed the radio handset. Flaherty shouted to some nearby troopers that Gaut was hit and he needed a replacement handset. A trooper crawled back and got one and, crawling to within five or six feet of the crater, tossed it to Flaherty. Gaut, who was going into shock, insisted on operating the radio, saying, *"Give me that radio. I'll just use my other hand." Ripcord* – page 162.

Flaherty managed to throw several grenades into the bunkers' firing aperture but after each explosion, it was only a few minutes before the gun began firing again. Apparently, the bunker was connected to a tunnel system and the NVA simply sent a new man through the tunnel to replace the wounded and dead gunners.

Shake-n-Bake SSGT George Strasburg rose to fire a burst at a bunker when he was hit in the head by fire from a bunker that he had not seen. Says Strasburg, *"My helmet flew up, landed on the ground and was sitting there, rocking [back and forth], with a hole in it. I thought, this is it, this is that split second between life and death, the moment before you leave your body. . . It was the strangest sensation." Ripcord* – page 162.

LT McCall with Delta Three was also thinking that the enemy bunkers were linked by tunnels. They located one bunker and destroyed it by throwing grenades through the opening; the blasts blew the body of an NVA soldier out through the opening. They moved on toward the next position and were surprised when they began receiving fire again from the 'destroyed' bunker.

The side of the hill was so zeroed in that anyone who moved drew fire and the assault bogged down. The troops at the front, lying among the logs, could not do anything but toss grenades and keep their heads down. CPT Rollison and his RTO, SP4 Rick Rearick, began to move up toward LT Flaherty when a machine gun that had not fired before opened up on them. The NVA gunner thoroughly blasted the area but did not hit either Rollison or Rearick. Rollison let two grenades, one in each hand, cook off for two seconds then threw them at the bunker. As soon as the frags went off, he jumped to his feet and blasted the area with his shotgun, killing the NVA gunner.

Rollison crawled to within a few feet of Flaherty who was out of grenades. Then LTC Lucas arrived overhead in a LOH (pronounced loach) and using a radio, told Rollison, who couldn't see the targets, where to throw his grenades. One of them landed too close to Flaherty who took shrapnel across his entire back. The next two grenades hit the target and Flaherty, who could still function, jumped up and blasted the position with double-00 buckshot from his twelve-gauge shotgun.

Before the NVA could move more men forward, Flaherty grabbed Gaut and started down the hill. After dragging Gaut fifteen or twenty yards, Flaherty was met by a couple of medics who took Gaut to an area where they had set up an aid station out of the line of direct fire.

LT Flaherty took the radio back up the hill and joined CPT Rollison sheltering behind a log. Rollison told Flaherty to keep up the volume of fire on the NVA positions while he tried to move around their right flank with some of the men from Delta One. As Rollison began his move to the right, an RPD began to fire on them from a well-hidden bunker no one had noticed, kicking up dust from the muzzle blast. Rollison grabbed a LAW and fired the rocket right through the firing aperture. With that gun silenced, the men from Delta One began to move again.

Not more than three minutes later, another RPD began firing from the same bunker. Rollison used another LAW to take out the gun a second time, but by then the volume of NVA fire had become too heavy for the flanking movement to continue.

LTC Lucas was in a LOH circling about fifty feet overhead, trying to direct accurate fire onto the NVA positions. Late that morning, a White Team (two LOH's equipped with 7.62mm miniguns) came on station, delivering bursts of fire when they identified a target among the jumble of logs on the hilltop. The NVA tried to shoot down the little helicopters using AK's and RPD's. One NVA fired an RPG at Lucas' LOH but missed.

After that, LTC Lucas had to return to Ripcord to refuel and pick up more frag and smoke grenades to drop to Company D. Major Koenigsbauer offered to relieve Lucas who appeared exhausted, but he refused saying it was his responsibility to help lead the attack.

Back over Hill 1000, the pilot dropped the LOH down to about fifteen feet above the battle line and Lucas kicked out several cases of fragmentation and smoke grenades to Rollison's men. By then, the little helicopter had taken several hits from small arms fire. The pilot told Lucas they were losing oil pressure and had to return to Ripcord before the engine failed.

A Hughes Aircraft Model 500C Light Observation Helicopter (LOH/OH-6) from Company A, 101st Assault Helicopter Battalion (Comancheros) on an abandoned firebase during an 'artillery raid' somewhere in Thua Thien Province in March 1970. Author's collection, ©1970 and ©2017.

McCall threw the last of the grenades that had been dropped to him. Delta Two and Delta Three could not move up the hill against the heavy volume of fire, so Rollison popped smoke at one end of the D Company line and had Flaherty mark the other end. Rollison asked the White Team if they could make a strafing run between the two smokes. The pilot was reluctant because the fire would hit dangerously close to the Company D men at the front of the attack. Finally, the pilot agreed to try and the two LOH's zipped along, miniguns blasting. A few of the bullets hit within a foot of Rollison, but the NVA fire immediately diminished.

One of the little scout ships buzzing around the hill dropped a bag full of grenades to LT McCall, who had marked his position with a smoke grenade. McCall had thrown all his grenades attempting to knock out a bunker directly above; he could not get a grenade through the firing aperture. McCall radioed the LOH pilot and explained his problem. The pilot told McCall to mark the bunkers position with smoke and that the LOH would hover over the bunker and draw the NVA soldier outside where McCall could get a shot at him.

The LOH pilot moved the ship over the bunker and the NVA popped out and began to fire at the hovering helicopter. McCall heaved a grenade and, able to see the NVA from the chest up, shot him several times.

SSGT George Strasburg was ordered to make one last try at getting close to the enemy. Telling the two nearest men, troops he did not know from Delta One, to follow him the sergeant crawled to the top of the knoll where he found a trail he would have to cross to flank the bunkers. Strasburg rolled across the trail in a flash and found himself on the elephant grass-covered reverse slope of the eastern knoll. Strasburg slipped into the elephant grass, suddenly realizing the two men from Delta One had not followed him across the trail. He could hear the LOH's buzzing around, firing off bursts from their miniguns. Strasburg, worried that he could be mistaken for an NVA and get blasted, pushed down the elephant grass around him so the pilots could see he was an American and waved at a pilot as he zipped past.

Working his way through the razor-edged grass, he came out in a clear area and saw the bare earth of a bunker about thirty feet to his front. Laying his M-16 on the ground next to him, he reached into a cargo pocket on his fatigue trousers for a grenade and found nothing. He had not realized that he had already thrown all his frags.

Suddenly, an NVA soldier wearing a pith helmet stuck his head out of the bunker and looked in Strasburg's direction. Thinking he was about to be shot, Strasburg slowly reached for his M-16 and just as slowly brought it up to firing position. Aiming at the man's head, he squeezed off three rounds and the NVA dropped straight down. Strasburg scurried away through the elephant grass, looking for the two men from Delta One but they were nowhere in sight. He crawled back the way he had come and ended up in the same crater where he had spent most of the battle.

By then, it was apparent that D Company could not advance any further. After a quick radio conversation with LTC Lucas, CPT Rollison received permission to withdraw. Lucas planned to hit Hill 1000with more artillery and air strikes after D Company had pulled back. He ordered a platoon from B Company to move from FSB Ripcord and secure an LZ on the hill between Ripcord and Hill 1000. D Company needed a secure LZ to bring in medevacs and they would set up their NDP on the same hill.

SSGT Strasburg dragged the body of PFC Mike Grimm partway down the hill and then went back up to help LT Flaherty bring the rest of Delta Three down. CPT Rollison crawled up to where Strasburg had left Grimm to bring him the rest of the way down when an enemy soldier suddenly stood up from a bunker only ten feet from him. The man was bigger than a Vietnamese, so tall and husky that Rollison felt he might be a Chinese advisor. He was wearing an unusual bush hat with a large red star pinned to it and held an RPD machine gun in one hand and a satchel charge in the other. He tossed the satchel charge at Rollison and, before the charge hit the ground, Rollison shot the man twice in the chest and then in the face with his shotgun as the man fell to his knees. The satchel charge went off and blew Rollison about twenty feet down the hill. He was deafened and lost his shotgun which he did not recover. *"I got distracted by something,"* says Rollison, *"Got turned around and never turned back around. I loved that shotgun. That ol' Winchester was a sweet-shootin' gun." Ripcord* – page 169.

As Delta Three continued to withdraw, PFC Bruce McCorkle, an RTO with the D Company CP, grabbed a can of M-60 ammo and took it up the hill to one of Delta Three's forward deployed machine guns. The gunner was screaming for ammo and his assistant gunner was nowhere to be seen.

McCorkle was joined by SGT Stanley Diehl and, passing their M-16's to other soldiers on their way down, they went up to get PFC Grimm's body. They picked up Grimm and started down the hill as a machine gun fired at them, the bullets passing so close it seemed they could see them. Hitting the ground, they looked for the NVA gunner, but saw no one. McCorkle saw a LOH zip past and realized the small helicopter had probably been caught in a downdraft as it was firing. It was a miracle no one had been hit, but McCorkle saw a bullet hole in Grimm's wrist that had not been there before.

Over on the southeast side of Hill 1000, Delta Two, led by LT James McCall, began the difficult task of withdrawing while under fire. McCall threw the last of the grenades that had been dropped to him by LTC Lucas in his LOH while SSGT Gary Radford controlled the move. Radford was grieving because they had not been able to recover the body of his friend, Lewis Howard. The platoon had moved to the left of the spot where Howard lay and there was too much fire for anyone to get to the body.

When they got to the relative safety of the tree line and Radford took stock of his men, he realized that PFC Charles Beals, an assistant gunner on an M-60, was also missing. Someone told Radford that Beals had been hit, so Radford went back up the hill to get him. He found Beals lying face down, not moving, with the irreparably damaged M-60 lying close by. Radford grabbed Beals but, as he did, a satchel charge went off so close to him that he was knocked unconscious and both eardrums were ruptured. He came to as his RTO, SP4 Joe Gibson, dragged him behind a downed tree. Says Radford, *"Had Joe Gibson not followed me to find Beals, I may have also been left behind on Hill 1000." Ripcord* – page 171.

When LT McCall ran out of frags, he radioed CPT Rollison and told him he needed help. Rollison gave McCall control of the Red Team (two Cobras) from the 4-77th Aerial Rocket Artillery that had replaced the White Team shortly after mid-day. McCall popped one of his last two smoke grenades to mark the bunker closest to him and told the Red Team leader to put his rockets on the smoke.

The Cobra pilot asked how close he was to the bunker and McCall told him "fifteen feet." The team leader told McCall he was too close to the target, so McCall tried to move back to give the Cobras room to work. As soon as he jumped up, AK rounds zipped past him. He made it to a fallen log and told the team leader that he could move no further.

The Cobras fired a rocket salvo and McCall scrambled to his feet and sprinted down the hill, leaping over obstacles. He reached the safety of the trees and only then did he realize that he had been hit in both elbows by rocket fragments.

LT McCall and SSGT Radford were probably the last Americans off Hill 1000. Radford had also run downhill when the Cobras fired the rocket salvo and he was hit in one arm and leg by shrapnel. The Cobras left shortly after that to make room for a FAC (forward air controller) and a flight of F-4 Phantom fighter-bombers. Rollison told the FAC that they were taking AK-47 and RPG fire from a clump of boulders near the saddle through which D Company was withdrawing. LTC Lucas also spotted enemy movement to the south and southeast of the LZ on the hill between Ripcord and Hill 1000, already occupied by Bravo Three. To prevent the NVA from cutting off Rollison from the LZ and, thinking that the thick jungle would absorb a lot of the bomb blast, Lucas told the FAC to put the airstrikes within three hundred feet of D Company.

Rollison linked up with Bravo Three on the LZ and they were released to move back onto FSB Ripcord. D Company began the task of evacuating the wounded and receiving a resupply of food, water and ammo. The cost of the assault had been heavy. PFC Michael Grimm was killed outright. SP4 Lewis Howard, Jr. and PFC Charles Beals were missing in action and presumed to have been killed. There were thirteen seriously wounded and numerous lightly wounded troopers to be taken care off. The company had killed nine NVA, confirmed by the LOH pilots.

LTC Lucas dropped out of the sky to have a talk with CPT Rollison. Lucas was very upset that D Company had failed to capture Hill 1000. It was likely that only a company or less was occupying the bunkers on the hill. PFC Bruce McCorkle, an RTO with the D Company CP group, remembers," *We were in a position to take the hill. It was like we were on third base, and when push came to shove the order was never given to assault the bunkers with the standard fire-team rushes we had been taught in Basic* [training] *and AIT* [advanced infantry training]." McCorkle went on to say, *"The reason we did not take the hill was very simple. The NVA were willing to die for what they were fighting for. We were not." Ripcord* – page 174.

Lucas ordered Rollison to attack the hill again as soon as he could. Rollison argued, saying he didn't think they could do it so late in the day. His troops were exhausted and they needed supplies and a chance to recover from their ordeal. Rollison told Lucas that he understood that capturing Hill 1000 was necessary to ensure the security of Ripcord and they would try again the next day. CPT Rollison wanted Lucas to order a heavy bombardment of the hilltop throughout the night. The enemy bunkers were well built and heavy artillery or air strikes would be needed to take them out. LTC Lucas finally agreed, saying he would bring in C/2-506 to reinforce the attack the next morning

After firing sporadically throughout the night, the artillery prep began to steadily pound Hill 1000 at about eight in the morning of 8 July. CPT Jeffrey Wilcox and what was left of Company C were air lifted to the LZ on the hill between Ripcord and Hill 1000. LTC Lucas flew in and held a conference on the LZ with Captain's Rollison and Wilcox plus Lieutenant's Campbell from C Company and McCall from D Company's Delta Three. LT Flaherty was still at Camp Evans being treated for his wounds. Lucas described his simple plan: C Company would move along the northern base of Hill 1000 to a position below the western knoll while D Company moved into place below the eastern knoll. They were to launch a simultaneous attack on the two knolls.

LT Campbell, leading Charlie Three, asked LTC Lucas why they were assigned to attack the NVA positions furthest from the LZ. C Company was still recovering from their ordeal on Hill 902 six days earlier and could field only about 30 men. Campbell was concerned that with so few men, they could not take care of heavy casualties or prevent the NVA from cutting them off from the LZ. Lucas told LT Campbell that D Company wanted to go back to the eastern knoll to try and recover the bodies of PFC's Howard and Beals.

After dropping their cumbersome rucksacks at the LZ, the two understrength companies moved out along a trail following the northern slope of Hill 1000. Artillery fire roared overhead as they moved. LTC Lucas was going all out: he had called in fires from 105mm, 155mm, 175mm and 8-inch guns on FSB's Rakkasan, Barbara, O'Reilly and Ripcord. The target was so close to Ripcord that the 105mm battery there had the tubes lowered for direct line-of-sight fire onto Hill 1000.

Major Koenigsbauer, on Ripcord, coordinated artillery fire with the Air Force FAC circling overhead, stopping the artillery when a flight of F-4's arrived to bomb the hill. The Phantom's dropped 250- and 500-pound high-drag bombs as well as napalm. The heat from the napalm was so extreme that it could be felt on Ripcord, a kilometer away.

D Company reached their assault positions first with C Company reporting in a short time later. Lucas ordered the assault at 1030 hours as Koenigsbauer fired the last artillery salvo of CS gas shells into the enemy emplacements.

Brigadier General Sidney Berry, the Assistant Division Commander, was on Ripcord watching the attack unfold. Berry asked Koenigsbauer why he had not shifted the artillery fires to the reverse slope of Hill 1000 to prevent the NVA from reinforcing the bunkers on top of the hill. Major Koenigsbauer told the general that the intense bombardment of Hill 1000 had diminished the stock of 105mm shells on Ripcord and Ripcord and the major wanted to hold the remaining ammo for observed fire missions. Berry ordered Koenigsbauer to use the artillery from the other firebases as well as the big guns from XXIV Corps. Major Koenigsbauer told General Berry he hadn't wanted to use the big 175mm and 8-inch guns at Corps level because he was unsure of their accuracy at such long range. General Berry assured him of their accuracy and Koenigsbauer soon had the big shells falling on the back side of the hill.

When the fire shifted away from the bunkers, the NVA left their cover and were waiting for the assault troops as they started up the hill. The troops from the 2-506 were not aware of the true extent of the NVA log-and-earth bunker complex and that it was likely the heavy artillery preparation had done very little damage.

CPT Wilcox and LT Campbell of Company C looked at the debris-covered, 150-meter wide slope and realized they didn't have enough men to effectively assault the hill. The company was so understrength that they did not have platoons any longer. They divided what troops they had into a maneuver element and a supporting fires element. LT Campbell would lead off with Charley Three and the few men left from Charley Two. Wilcox would stay back with Charley One and coordinate supporting fires.

SSGT Paul Burkey led C Company's assault on the western-most of the two knolls. They moved through the debris field to the top of that knoll without being fired on. Burkey led his men to the left, trying to get into position to bring the eastern knoll, nearly one hundred meters away across a saddle, under fire. As they reached the edge of the western knoll before it dropped down into the saddle, they came under fire from an RPD and several AK-47's and everyone dropped flat.

The rest of the assault element was still scattered along the side of the hill when the RPD fired and they all hit the dirt. The assault element began firing as the support element moved past. It was difficult to move up the slope; the hillside had been bombed and blasted with so much artillery that the earth had taken on the consistency of fine sand. Slipping and sliding, the troopers finally reached the top of the hill.

CPT Wilcox and LT Campbell found themselves sheltering in the same bomb crater at the very top of the hill. They moved up two M-60 teams and placed one to the right and the other to their left to anchor the ends of the line. Burkey's men were throwing frags and firing quick bursts from their M-16's at the eastern knoll. The RPD gunner returned the fire with un-nerving accuracy. The two M-60 teams had found perfect positions from which they could put direct fire on the NVA positions. By the end of the fight, one of the gun teams had burned out the barrel of their gun and fired every round they had.

They could not pinpoint the location of the RPD. SGT Frank Bort had a general idea of where the gun was but could not put it out of action no matter how many 40mm HE shells he fired from his M-203. There was no muzzle flash, no dust or smoke and the gun was not firing tracers. SSGT Burkey remembers, *"That gun emplacement was perfect. I mean the fuckers were in the side of the hill. Their line of fire was straight across the saddle into the top of our hill, and we simply could not see the hole the fire was coming from. The man behind that RPD wasn't some guy that went to the Ho Chi Minh School of Machine Gunnery-it was the fuckin' guy that taught the class."* Ripcord – page 187.

The NVA could see the C Company men clearly. The RPD ginner wounded the M-60 gunner on the right and a bullet set off a smoke grenade on his web belt. Disregarding his bullet wound, the man kept firing while the assistant gunner got rid of the burning smoke grenade.

Besides the RPD and AK fire, the NVA were firing a captured M-79 at them. Wilcox could hear the distinctive **'thump'** as the M-79 fired and then the **'clunk'** of the round bouncing down through the bare trees. None of the M-79 rounds exploded; They were duds or had not traveled far enough to arm themselves. At first, Wilcox thought they were receiving long rounds from D Company, but a radio check revealed it was not friendly fire. All they could do was hope that the next round would not be the one that exploded.

LT Campbell was amazed at how D Company seemed to be dragging their feet. He could see five or six men just past the tree line at the bottom of the eastern knoll with another man out in front, throwing grenades as fast as he could. The rest of D Company had not yet left the cover of the tree line.

LTC Lucas, circling overhead in his C & C bird wanted to bring in a Red Team. CPT Wilcox told him that no matter which way the Cobras approached, they could not make their rocket-firing runs without endangering both C and D Companies. Lucas called in a white team from the 2-17 Cavalry. The two LOH's zipped over the enemy-held hill, firing their miniguns with great accuracy until one of the little gunships took a hit in the engine and had to make an emergency landing on Ripcord.

Frustrated, Lucas then ordered Wilcox to advance across the open saddle and capture the eastern knoll. LT Campbell told LTC Lucas via radio that there was no cover down in the saddle and that the NVA could fire down on them as they tried to advance. Campbell urged Lucas to get D Company moving up the eastern knoll while C Company laid down a heavy base of fire to keep the NVA's heads down. Lucas cut Campbell off and, getting CPT Wilcox back on the radio, gave him a direct order to attack across the saddle.

Campbell was horrified and urged Wilcox to call Lucas and explain the situation more fully. He did not think Lucas fully understand what they were up against. Campbell reminded Wilcox that they had two M-60's, several M-79's and M-203's and they could lay down a heavy covering fire if only D Company would move out of the trees and attack the eastern knoll.

Wilcox made the call and tried to explain the situation to Lucas but Lucas cut him off, harshly criticizing him for resisting a dangerous order while under fire. Wilcox, turning to Campbell, reluctantly told him that they had to carry out the order. Campbell, realizing they had no choice, tried to lay out a plan of attack to Wilcox, but the captain interrupted him and said he was going to lead the attack. Wilcox explained to Campbell that he had to set the example and show his men that he was not afraid to lead them in combat.

The RPD had them zeroed in and Wilcox wanted to try one more time to locate it before the assault pushed off. He had SGT Bort put his helmet on the end of a stick and move it along the edge of the crater where he had taken cover. The old trick worked; the RPD fired but Wilcox, ready to take the gun out with a LAW, still could not spot the bunker the gun was firing from. Frustrated, they fired several LAW's at likely positions but could not tell if they had gotten the gun.

CPT Wilcox loaded himself down with canteens, frags, smoke grenades, two bandoliers of M-16 ammo and slung several LAW's over his shoulder. Wilcox thought that if he could get close enough, he could take out key NVA firing positions with the 66mm LAW rockets.

Wilcox signaled the M-60's and the gunners put out a covering fire in three to six round bursts. CPT Wilcox stood up and moved out, followed by a group of troopers from Charlie Two and Charlie Three but the attack lasted less than thirty seconds. During that brief time, SP4 James Hupp was killed by a burst of fire from the RPD and three other men were wounded. CPT Wilcox explained, *"The fire on us was just withering. We got up, went down, then immediately came scrambling back."* Ripcord – page 189.

When SP4 Hupp was hit, SGT Bort yelled for a medic. PFC Rickey Scott, the medic and a conscientious objector, had been in the field with C Company only two days before the attack on Hill 1000. Scott instantly started forward, but because he was so new, he walked upright, out in the open, when he should have crawled. Bort screamed at him to get down but it was too late. The RPD gunner shot him through the head, killing him instantly.

The sporadic firefight went on with Wilcox's men beginning to run out of ammo as well as water. One of the little gunships still circling the hill radioed CPT Wilcox that he had spotted a large enemy force moving through the jungle toward Hill 1000 from the west. LTC Lucas, who had overheard the urgent radio call, ordered Rollison and Wilcox to break contact and immediately pull back. LT Campbell reacted angrily to the pull-back order. He told Wilcox that if they left now, they would have to do it all over again the next day. Campbell felt that they were in a good position on the western knoll and if D Company would only get moving and take the eastern knoll, they could get resupplied and hold on to the hill. Wilcox disagreed, telling Campbell they had to pull back to keep the NVA from getting between them and the LZ on the hill next to Ripcord.

Resigning himself to the pull-back order, Campbell threw several smoke grenades into the saddle to mask their withdrawal. SSGT Burkey dragged Hupp back while Campbell and another trooper brought in Scott's body. When they reached cover, Campbell was surprised to see that D Company was gone, already on the LZ.

D Company had barely been involved in the second attack on Hill 1000. Only a handful of men, led by LT McCall had moved up the hill and come under fire. The remainder of the company had stayed under cover among the boulders and still-standing trees below the eastern knoll. PFC Bruce McCorkle remembers *"a prolonged shoot-out between our machine gunners and theirs. Most of us were back down the hill among the trees and boulders. We didn't move forward and weren't asked to. The second day was nothing like the first." Ripcord* – page 191.

Concerned that his small force would run into the NVA unit coming in from the west, Wilcox led C Company at an angle down the northern slope of the hill, keeping below the line of sight of the enemy bunkers on the military crest of Hill 1000. Campbell moved along with them, but stayed above them, throwing more smoke grenades to shield the move. LT Campbell stayed alone on the knoll, firing his M-16 at the bunkers and throwing smoke until he was joined by SSGT Burkey. As soon as C Company reached the cover of the trees, Wilcox called in artillery on the two knolls. As artillery shrapnel buzzed overhead, Campbell and Burkey crawled down the dusty slope to re-join the company.

LT Campbell carried the body of PFC Scott across his shoulders up to the LZ, while Burkey struggled in the suffocating heat with the much heavier SP4 Hupp. No one came to help them so by the time Burkey and Campbell reached the LZ, they were completely exhausted.

Before Burkey and Campbell even got back to the LZ, LTC Lucas landed in his C & C bird. Walking confidently over to Rollison and Wilcox, he abruptly asked them when they could be ready to mount another assault Caught completely by surprise, Wilcox blurted out that they would be crazy to try another attack in the condition they were in. LT McCall joined the conference and listened in amazement as an angry Wilcox told Lucas that another attack would be futile and would only produce more casualties for no good reason. Wilcox explained that he only had twenty-two men left in his entire company and that they were exhausted and dehydrated from the heat. He strongly urged Lucas to let them rest overnight while artillery and air strikes were called in on the hill.

LTC Lucas' order to mount another attack quickly spread through what was left of C Company. An angry squad leader ran breathlessly up to an exhausted Campbell and told him *"that stupid goddamned colonel, they're talking about us re-assaulting the hill right now." Ripcord* – page 195. Campbell did not believe what he heard and went to join the conference up on the LZ.

When he joined the small group of officers, Campbell immediately saw that something was wrong. He was astonished when Lucas confirmed that he had ordered an attack to begin as soon as possible that afternoon. Campbell then asked Lucas to take a good look around him at the exhausted men he was ordering to launch another attack. Campbell asked the colonel to let the men rest through the night and they would go back up the next day. Wilcox added that if his men had a chance to rest, they would have a better chance of taking the hill the next day.

Lucas told Wilcox that he understood that they'd had a very rough time but it was essential that they keep the pressure on because pushing the NVA off Hill 1000 was vital to the security of Ripcord. Lucas then asked Rollison for his opinion. CPT Rollison told Lucas he realized the importance of pushing the enemy off the hill and he was ready to lead another assault whenever the colonel gave the order. 1LT Campbell, still angry over D Company's lack of participation in the attack that morning, sarcastically asked Rollison if his attack was going to be like the one that morning. Lucas ignored Campbell's implied criticism of D Company's behavior and did not ask Rollison why his company had held back during the earlier attack. The colonel did not seem to realize the difference between the exhausted condition of C Company and the relative freshness of D Company.

(L to R) SSGT Paul E. Burkey, SGT Frank Bort and 1LT James H. Campbell of C/2-506 pose at Camp Evans several months before the Battle of Firebase Ripcord and Hill 1000. Photo courtesy of Paul Burkey.

Black Spade (Lucas' radio call sign) was in such a rush to get the attack moving that he did not offer to bring in reinforcements nor did he take the time to work out a plan of attack where one company could call in gunships for close support without endangering the other. The attack would succeed only if both companies attacked forcefully and with close support from the Cobras.

Campbell lost his temper and swore, "Goddamnit, we've only got a few hours till dusk. It's going to take an hour and a half just to get resupplied and get back into position to attack from the tree line, and then what, are we just going to make the same assault from the same direction? It didn't work the first time with a twelve-hour artillery prep and all those air strikes. What if we're still trying to fight our way up the side of the hill when the sun goes down? We'll never be able to get into a strong defensive position for the night and get our dead and wounded out. It's not worth the risk. We can take that damn hill tomorrow morning." Ripcord – page 196.

Lucas, though visibly angry, restrained his temper at Campbell's outburst and ordered him back to his men to get his temper under control. Wilcox stepped in and, grabbing Campbell's arm, walked with him part way down the hill from the LZ. Wilcox told Campbell not to worry that he would take care of the situation.

When he returned to the platoon, the squad leader who had protested earlier came over to Campbell and asked if the order for a second attack had been canceled. When told it had not, the young NCO burst out: *"We ain't going up that goddamned hill again today!"* At that outburst, Campbell turned on the man. *"Let me tell you something, you mother fucker! If I tell you to go up that goddamned hill again, you're going up that goddamned hill, you understand? What are you gonna do, let me and the captain and Sergeant Burkey go by ourselves?"* Suddenly ashamed, the squad leader stammered, *"Hell, L.T., we wouldn't let that happen. If you say go, we'll go, but we ain't going just cause that stupid fuckin' colonel says to go."* Ripcord - page 197.

The squad leader, along with a few others who felt the same, had been trying to organize a full-scale combat refusal to attack the hill a second time. Most of the men ignored them, and it is not likely that the protesters themselves would have refused to attack if given a direct order. Their actions were a symptom of their exhaustion and frustration, not cowardice. SSGT Burkey said, *"Going back up was fuckin' crazy. It didn't make sense. We didn't have anything left in us and the guys were grumbling, but there's no question that [if] push comes to shove every one of us would have gone back up there and done what we had to do."* Ripcord – page 197.

CPT Wilcox did not let it come to that. He spoke up and told Lucas that he didn't think Hill 1000 was worth the death of another of his men. Wilcox said that in fact, he thought the whole war was a waste of soldiers' lives. He told the colonel that his conscience would not let him order his men back up the hill.

SGT Bort, who had been called into the huddle regarding the placement of the RPD machine gun, remembers Wilcox saying, *"Sir, if you want to send me back up there, fine, I'll go alone, but I will not ask my men to go back up there. They are simply in no shape for another assault"* Bort was awestruck that his captain had stood up for the company against what they all thought was a foolish order. Bort believes Wilcox's standing up to the colonel literally saved their lives.

LTC Lucas was the opposite of impressed. In a sarcastic manner, he ordered CPT Wilcox to go stand by his C & C helicopter and wait for him.

Lucas then turned to CPT Rollison of D Company and asked his opinion. Rollison replied that he was willing and ready to lead another attack up Hill 1000 if LTC Lucas told him to go. Rollison then back-peddled a little and told Lucas that though he was ready to go, he thought it was not practical to attack again that afternoon. He told his colonel that it would probably be better to hammer the hill all night with artillery and they would go up as far as they could under the umbrella of artillery fire and attack at first light.

*LTC Andre C. Lucas **(L)** commanding 2-506 Infantry and MAJ Herbert E. Koenigsbauer, battalion operations officer shortly before the siege began. Photo from Herbert E. Koenigsbauer.*

1LT James McCall, the youngest officer there, was amazed when Lucas turned to him and asked what he thought. Lieutenant colonels do not normally ask the opinion of first lieutenants, and McCall hesitated. After a moment, he told Lucas that he worked for CPT Rollison and would follow him but that he was not sure they could take the hill because the NVA were dug in deeply. He explained that he felt the hill should be neutralized by heavy artillery bombardment and hit by tactical air strikes every day. McCall ended by saying, *"If we can get the firepower we need to reduce Hill 1000 down to Hill 997, that should take care of it." Ripcord* – page 198.

LTC Lucas said he would think the situation over and get back to them in a few minutes and the meeting broke up. 'Black Spade' walked off by himself and sat down on a fallen log on the edge of the LZ. CPT Rollison thought something might be wrong with the colonel and walked over to check on him. Rollison hesitated, not sure if he should bother Lucas but then he noticed that Lucas was crying, tears rolling down his face. Trying to reassure Lucas, Rollison sat down beside him and told Lucas that if another attack was ordered, Lucas could count on him. Lucas looked at Rollison for a moment and then said that he had decided not to lose any more people and that he was going to attempt to destroy the enemy positions on Hill 1000 with firepower alone.

CPT Rollison summed it up, *"Lucas hadn't asked for that sonofabitch objective and that's why I didn't fight him. I knew that what he had to do as a battalion commander was unpopular. He was my boss and there was a job that had to be done, but he was incredibly compassionate. He had a tough veneer, and he had to have it, but he cared about every single man there. There was never any doubt in my mind about that." Ripcord* – page 199.

Major General John J. Hennessey, the 101st division commander, had been forced to delay the attack on the Co Pung Mountain/Warehouse Area, code-named Operation Chicago Peak because of the difficulty of securing the terrain around FSB Ripcord. The firebase had been opened specifically to support Chicago Peak but the discovery of an NVA regiment near Khe Sanh had drawn off a significant number of the forces needed for Chicago Peak. The continued heavy resistance of the NVA around FSB Ripcord also drew down the number of battalions available to mount the new operation and the pressure from XXIV Corps and above was considerable. The attack on Co Pung and the Warehouse Area needed to begin soon so that as much damage as possible could be done to the enemy before the onset of the monsoon forced the 101st out of the mountains surrounding the A Shau valley.

The new operation could not begin until the NVA forces around Ripcord had been defeated. The assaults on Hill 805 by A/2-506 and D/2-501 was part of the plan as was the increased use of airpower and other supporting arms around Ripcord.

■ ■ ■

The division's plan next called for LTC Otis Livingston's 2-501(-) Infantry, the division swing battalion, to assault, take and hold Hill 1000. This hill had been pummeled by numerous air strikes since the two failed attacks by the 2-506 had shown the extent of the NVA bunker complex atop Hill 1000. COL Benjamin Harrison, the 3rd Brigade commander, knew that air strikes alone could not push the NVA from the hill. The only definite solution would be infantry taking and holding the ground.

To prepare them for the coming assault, the 2-501 minus Company D, was lifted from the field to Camp Evans on 11 July. LTC Livingston flew to Evans from the TOC on Ripcord he shared with LTC Lucas to brief his company commanders. Livingston described an attack that would use a rolling artillery barrage, behind which Companies A, B and C plus the 2-501 recon platoon would attack from different angles and push the NVA off the hill.

On the afternoon of 12 July, the recon platoon combat assaulted into a hot LZ on the top of Coc Muen mountain near YD 317181. Companies B and C landed on the same LZ later that day. CPT Donald Goates, leading Company A, CA'd onto Triple Hill into an LZ already secured by CPT Rollison's D/2-506.

D/2-506 had moved on foot off Ripcord on 10 July, receiving 82mm mortar fire as they passed through the base's perimeter wire. The mortar fire caused no casualties, but the company's already thin ranks had been further depleted by the wounding of several men from recoilless-rifle fire during their stay on FSB Ripcord.

On 11 July, Company D battled its way to the top of Triple Hill, defended by a squad of NVA. They had seen a Caucasian with the enemy squad, possibly the same one spotted in the area by B/2-506 about three weeks earlier. CPT Rollison wrote, *"I personally saw him at the top of the hill while we were still at the bottom. He was wearing a bush hat and aviator shades. I assumed he was a Russian advisor. Without taking my eyes off him for fear I would lose sight of him in the vegetation, I borrowed an M-16 from one of my RTO's, sighted in, aiming uphill, and squeezed off a single shot. When we took the hill, we found a large blood stain where he had been* [standing]." *Ripcord* – page 249.

LTC Livingston and his field CP had come in with Company A. They moved off the LZ and set up their NDP on another knoll of the three composing the top of Triple Hill. 1LT James Kwiecien was amazed that a battalion commander had put on a rucksack and joined his men in the field. The grunts loved him for it. It impressed them that a forty-year-old lieutenant colonel would give up his starched fatigues and spit shined boots to struggle up a hill alongside them.

When they had dug in for the night Livingston, who was ranger qualified, told Goates that he wanted to make a night recon of Hill 1000, but only with volunteers. Goates tried to organize the mission but could only come up with ten volunteers. Livingston, who was going to accompany the recon, decided not to go with such a small team. It would have meant a two-thousand-meter round trip; down into the deep saddle between the two hills and up the slope of Hill 1000, then back again.

14 July was spent prepping the objective with massive artillery and air strikes. Early on 14 July 1LT Victor Arndt, leading his recon platoon, approached the hill from the southwest, a two-klick march down the ridge from the top of Coc Muen. Company A would come at Hill 1000 from the north. They were still a thousand meters from their objective when LT Arndt's point man stopped the column and told Arndt that he had spotted NVA off to their right front. Looking in the direction the Recondo pointed, LT Arndt also saw an NVA soldier, only about forty meters away, walking between one position and another in what appeared to be a big bunker complex. Asked what to do, Arndt told the point man to shoot, then quickly brought the rest of the platoon into line.

When the point man fired, the enemy immediately fired back. LT Arndt was rushing back up to the front when a volley of RPG's began bursting in the treetops. Arndt was blown backwards over a log with a little shrapnel in his right shoulder but a lot in his left leg. The shower of RPG's into the trees wounded a total of nine Recondo's.

The worst wounded was winched out by jungle penetrator and Arndt brought in Cobra gunships after the dust-off left. All the platoon's attempts to move against the bunkers from different directions was met with a hail of enemy fire. Another medevac, hovering over a clearing one hundred meters back from the bunker complex where the rest of the wounded had been taken, took a burst of fire in its fuel cell and tail boom. Crippled, it managed to fly the fifteen hundred meters to Ripcord for an emergency landing.

Four hours later, two more medevacs landed on the LZ on the peak of Coc Muen. LT Arndt wrote later that *"Those of us who were wounded had to crawl away from the bunker complex. You couldn't stand up and expect not to get shot."* When the medevacs came in on top of Coc Muen, the enemy brought them under fire as they approached. The dust-offs *"stopped just long enough for us to jump in, then took off again as fast as those Huey's could go."* Ripcord – page 250.

LTC Livingston had told B/2-501, commanded by CPT Robert Stanton, to move around Arndt's recon platoon and attack the enemy from the flank. Six and a half hours after Recon had started the action, Company B was three hundred meters north of Recon's position. There, the lead platoon found still more NVA bunkers on the northeast slope of Coc Muen, close to the draw separating the 4,257-foot high mountain from Hill 1000. Company B's point man was less than fifty meters from the carefully camouflaged bunkers when the NVA opened fire. 1LT Robert Worrall, the platoon leader, was hit right away as was the platoon's medic. One of the platoon's RTO's grabbed the medic's aid bag and began treating the wounded until he, too, was hit. The medic from the following platoon ran forward and became a casualty almost as soon as he got there. In just a few hectic moments, SP4 Dennis Huffine was killed and eleven others were wounded.

Coordinating with the wounded platoon leader, CPT Stanton called in a Red Team of two Cobras from C/4-77th ARA to blast the bunker complex so the lead platoon could break contact and pull back. The first Red Team was replaced by a second when they had to leave to refuel and rearm. The forward elements of Company B popped smoke grenades to mark their positions and the rocket attacks continued. The Cobras were attacking from north to south through the big draw separating Coc Muen and Hill 1000 when they began taking fire from a 12.7 mm machine gun emplaced at the southwestern base of Hill 1000.

CPT Goates and Company A were waiting in reserve on the western slope of the hill, looking down on CPT Stanton's attack on the bunkers down in the draw. Goates ordered Alpha one, led by 1LT Richard Driver, to find and destroy the 12.7mm gun firing on the Cobras. He told LT Kwiecien's Alpha Two to advance on a mortar position firing from somewhere near the big machine gun. Kwiecien was annoyed because Goates, an aggressive combat commander, was right at the front telling rifle squads what to do. That was the platoon leaders' job, but Goates was completely ignoring his lieutenants.

Alpha One, leading the move, took out two NVA hiding in 'spider holes' on the crest of a small ridge with frags. Then one of the Cobras took more fire from the 12.7mm as the pilot broke left out of a rocket run and the Cobra gunner fired back with four rounds from its 40mm grenade launcher mounted under the nose of the ship. The grenades missed their target and exploded between Alpha One and Alpha Two. Both platoons had advanced to within two hundred meters of the machine gun. Five men were hit, including platoon leaders Driver and Kwiecien. Apparently Goates had failed to tell Stanton, who was controlling the Cobras, that he had units from Company A who had moved beyond the smoke markers. Or, if Stanton had been told, he had not warned the section leader for the Cobras. Not knowing that they had inadvertently fired up friendly troops, the Cobras kept up their rocket firing runs for B/2-501.

LT Kwiecien had ignored the gunships as his platoon moved toward the enemy. When the grenades suddenly exploded in front of them, he felt something hit his shoulder hard, like a thrown rock. Everyone dropped where they were, trying to see what was happening. Kwiecien reached into his fatigue shirt pocket for a cigarette and found that a piece of grenade shrapnel had gone completely through his plastic cigarette case and badly bruised his shoulder.

LT Kwiecien then realized that the platoon's Kit Carson scout, Chau Ngoc Tu, was down and moaning in pain from a badly mangled left leg. When Kwiecien tried to move him, the scout screamed in pain. SGT Michael McCoy and the platoon's second scout, Kai, came up to help. Kai gave the wounded scout a tongue lashing for acting like a baby as McCoy picked him up and carried him to safety while both Alpha One and Two began pulling back. The big attack had been called off.

Captain Goates had been given a flight of South Vietnamese Air Force A1E Sky raiders to cover Company A's withdrawal back to Triple Hill. The old prop driven aircraft were ideal for close support and they dropped cluster bombs on an NVA unit that had been following in pursuit of Company A. LT Kwiecien, despite being wounded, was still humping his ruck and remembers thinking that the cluster bombs would take care of anything or anyone following them.

LTC Livingston used His Huey C&C bird to fly to the NDP site set up by Companies B, C and Recon a few hundred meters up the ridge from the NVA bunkers at the foot of Coc Muen. At dusk, the NVA dropped mortar rounds on the NDP from the top of Coc Muen. A Huey dust-off that came in to take out Company B's wounded took automatic weapons fire and a round went through the rotor as it lifted off the LZ. Company A's wounded were taken out from the top of Triple Hill.

The next morning BG Sidney Berry flew out to have a conference with LTC Livingston. MG Hennessey had left Vietnam for a twenty-day leave and BG Berry was the acting division commander. Berry's C&C Huey approached the LZ on the narrow ridge, but the small LZ was too cluttered with gear and tree stumps for the Huey to land. The pilot, 1LT John Fox, hovered over the edge of the LZ looking for a safe spot for Berry to jump to the ground. Through his chin bubble, Fox saw a trooper lying on his back at the side of the LZ, firing a CAR-15 with one hand and waving the helicopter away with the other. Fox could not see any other troops or hear any gunfire. At that moment, one of the door gunners saw muzzle flashes in the brush on the side of the ridge and yelled a warning. Fox, a superb pilot, banked hard right and zoomed down into the valley to gain air speed. The maneuver was so abrupt that one of Berry's aides, not strapped down, almost fell out of the door.

BG Berry told Fox to make another try, but again they had to break away from the heavy enemy fire. When they flew back to Camp Eagle to refuel, SP4 Thomas Chase found a bullet hole in the ammo box for his door-mounted M-60. Chase later said, *"It was foolish. It was an unnecessary risk for a general. There had been something like four or five generals killed in 'Nam already at that time. We didn't need a sixth. Berry scared me. He thought he was John Wayne." Ripcord* – page 262.

BG Berry had wanted to land so that he could personally tell LTC Livingston that he was prepared to relieve him of command of his battalion if he did not start using all the firepower against Hill 1000 that he had available. Berry had become angry the day before as he monitored the progress of the failed attack of 14 July. However, Livingston and his officers did not believe the problem lay with the supposed inefficient use of firepower. From bitter experience, they knew that it was the NVA's willingness to die defending a piece of ground that was at the root of their failure to push the enemy off Hill 1000. Given the constraints put on them to take anything but 'light US casualties', they knew they would never be able to take and hold Hill 1000 or any other heavily fortified hill.

Livingston called in artillery on the side of the ridge, hoping to suppress the enemy fire long enough for log birds to bring in the ammo and other supplies he needed for another assault on Hill 1000. One of the first log birds attempting to land had its tail boom blown off by a 12.7mm heavy machine gun, causing it to crash on the side of the ridge below the LZ. The Huey pilot lost his leg in the crash.

The resupply efforts were also plagued by extremely high winds that day. CPT Goates, waiting for resupply on Triple Hill, watched as a Huey on its way to him was blown in a complete 360° circle. The slick was forced to retreat to Ripcord to wait out the winds.

The attack was held up still longer as more tactical air strikes, artillery and ARA were called in to pound known or suspected NVA positions. It was after 1400 hours on 15 July before the 2-501 Recon Platoon began moving toward the bunkers located between Hill 1000 and Coc Muen. During this time, the site of the downed log bird had been secured by a line platoon and a big CH-47 brought in to lift out the crashed Huey. The Chinook attracted such heavy fire that the mission had to be called off. The pilot pulled away with six bullet holes in his aircraft. The escorting Red Team dove in on the NVA, blasting the area with rockets.

At 1600 hours, the recon team made contact at the bunker complex, still held by the NVA even though it had been subjected to a heavy dose of artillery and air strikes. LTC Livingston pulled the platoon back instead of bringing in additional forces and began hitting the bunkers with artillery. Reluctant to spend a second night in the same NDP, Livingston moved the field CP, Companies B, C and the Recon Platoon some four hundred meters up the ridge toward the summit of Coc Muen. Company A, which had begun to move toward Hill 1000 that day, humped a kilometer west of Triple Hill and set up a new NDP. LTC Livingston's cautious moves were in keeping with the orders he was receiving from COL Harrison, himself responding to guidance from BG Berry and MG Hennessey. Livingston recalled that *"We had identified Hill 1000 as being very strongly defended, but we were not directed to make another assault. I think the enemy force on and around the hill was a lot larger than brigade and division had expected. We were up against a formidable, dug in enemy and the concern was that Hill 1000 could become another 'Hamburger Hill'. Nobody wanted to be responsible for that. The division was still in a state of shock over Hamburger Hill, so there was some indecision in the operation at that point, a lull of sorts as the upper echelons sorted the problem out and decided how best to proceed. "* LTC Livingston's belief was that the division leadership hoped that using massive amounts of firepower would drive the NVA off Hill 1000, but, because of the hill's tactical importance, Livingston thought that orders to attack Hill 1000 could come at any time. *"I was ready to go, and so were the troops." Ripcord* – page 263

At daylight on 16 July, an awful accident occurred at Company A's NDP. CPT Goates woke up to the sound of a tree loudly creaking in the high winds. An unusually strong gust of wind came and the tree cracked and began to fall. Goates hastily rolled out of the way, but the tree smashed to the ground on top of PFC Richard Timmons, asleep only ten feet from where Goates had been lying. It took five men to lift the tree high enough for Timmons to be dragged free. The medic was already there and waiting, but Timmons was dead. The tree, heavily damaged by ARA fire, had only needed a strong gust of wind to topple it.

The 2-501 spent 16 July finding a way around the big NVA bunker complex in the draw between Hill 1000 and Coc Muen mountain. LTC Livingston and his field CP, traveling with Company C, were digging in at their NDP site north of the bunkers, with Company B to the south, when Livingston received a message from 3rd Brigade Headquarters that the assault on Hill 1000 had been called off. To Livingston's surprise, he was informed that the entire battalion, including D/2-501 on Hill 805, was to be withdrawn from the Ripcord AO.

"I was very surprised when we were directed to withdraw," said Lieutenant Colonel Livingston. *"I was ready to keep on going, man–there was still a fight out there–but somebody up above had made the decision to not launch any more assaults up Hill 1000." Ripcord* – page 269.

BG Berry was the 'someone' who had made that decision. Berry and LTC Young, the division G3 (operations), had flown to Camp Evans late on 16 July for a rather argumentative meeting with COL Harrison in the 3rd Brigade TOC. Harrison vehemently argued that controlling Hills 1000 and 805 was vital to the security of FSB Ripcord. Enemy mortar and antiaircraft fire from those hills would soon make it too costly to even resupply the base. Harrison told Berry that it was not a good time to be withdrawing forces; instead, they should be bringing in additional troops.

Virtually ignoring COL Harrison's tactical concerns, BG Berry said that those higher up the chain of command had 'expressed displeasure' at the resources being used to keep Ripcord open. There were already more casualties than public opinion would bear, more helicopters lost and more mortar and artillery ammo expended than he (Berry) could justify, given the fiscal cutbacks the army was undergoing due to Vietnamization and the withdrawal from Vietnam.

In a later meeting, a staff officer from division artillery said, approved by BG Berry, that they had to be careful how many 105mm rounds were fired during operations around Ripcord. COL Harrison lost his temper at that statement, but Berry told him that the directive had come down from USARV (United States Army, Vietnam) headquarters in Saigon and, presumably, from the Pentagon and the Secretary of the Army. COL Harrison and his aide, CPT Fred Spaulding, knew then that it was over. They were not going to win any battles when higher command was more concerned with the cost of artillery shells than defeating the North Vietnamese.

When a war correspondent visited the 101st Airborne after the Ripcord battle, he had an interesting conversation with a battalion commander. This lieutenant colonel pulled a 3 x 5 index card from his pocket and handed it to the correspondent. On the card was the exact number of M-16, M-60, 40mm rounds, claymore mines and 81mm shells the battalion could use each month. The card also listed the number of artillery shells the colonel could request. On a second card, the colonel listed the number of hours a day he could fly the helicopters assigned for his use, called the blade-hour or blade-time limitation. In 1970, helicopters were flying roughly one-sixth the hours they could fly the previous year.

The cut-backs made it clear that while the enemy was deeply committed to destroying Ripcord, higher headquarters was not equally committed to defending it. 3rd Brigade was being reined in by division and the 101st Airborne was being held back by XXIV Corps and so on, up the chain of command. No one above brigade level wanted to confront the NVA in a major battle. So, it was decided to let things continue as they were until either the NVA withdrew or it became too costly for the 101st Airborne and the troops around Ripcord were withdrawn.

In his book *Hell on a Hill Top—America's Last Major Battle in Vietnam,* Major General (retired) Benjamin L. Harrison, then the 3rd Brigade commander, states that *"The enemy force on Hill 1000 proved too strong, too determined, and too well-fortified to be dislodged without the cost in American lives becoming too great. The Brigade did not want to experience another* 'Hamburger Hill' *and called off [LTC] Livingston's planned attack." Hell on a Hill top*—page 92.

Chapter 15
HILL 805 – A DESPERATE BATTLE

"The enemy didn't hunt us. We hunted them. I was very concerned, then, when we dug in atop 805 because we were giving up the initiative right at the start to the North Vietnamese." Captain Christopher C. Straub, commanding D/2-501, July 1970.

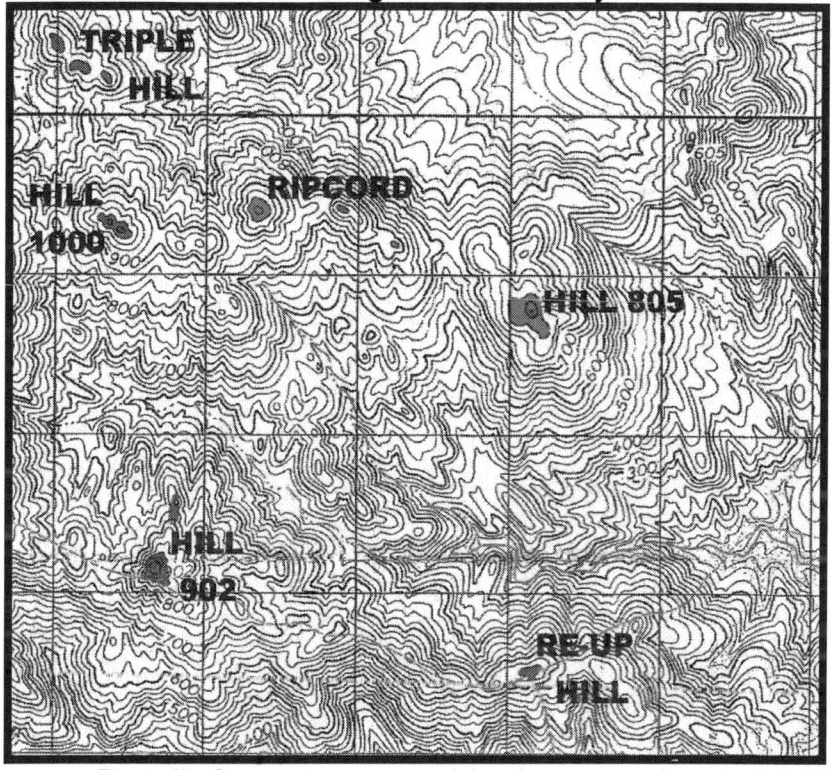

Detail from topographical map sheet 6441-4 Series L-7014 A Luoi District, Thua Thien Province. US positions outlined in blue, known or suspected NVA positions and trails outlined in red. Original map from author's collection.

After the failure of Companies C and D, 2-506 Infantry, to push the NVA off Hill 1000, attention shifted to another hill about two klicks southeast of FSB Ripcord. Shown on tactical maps as Hill 805, this rocky prominence sat at the southeastern end of a three klick-long winding ridge with Ripcord in the center and Hill 1000 at the western terminus.

On 11 July, COL Benjamin Harrison, the 3rd Brigade Commander, pulled LTC Otis Livingston's 2-501 Infantry (minus D/2-501 which was OPCON to the 2-506) back to Camp Evans to prepare for a CA to the back side of Hill 1000. On 12 July, COL Harrison moved the 2-501 (-) to an LZ west of Hill 1000 to get ready for another assault on that hill.

In preparation for the assault on Hill 805, LTC Lucas moved A/2-506, led by CPT Charles 'Chuck' Hawkins to an LZ near YD 349194 about six hundred meters east of Ripcord already secured by the still under-strength C/2-506. As the slicks carrying Company A came into the hot LZ marked by red smoke, Company C boarded the Huey's as Company A jumped off. NVA snipers on the south slope of the ridge fired at the slicks as they lifted off carrying Company C. Hawkins called in artillery to silence the snipers as his lead platoon moved east down the ridge from the LZ looking for a good NDP site.

Chuck Hawkins' mission was to move along the ridge to the LZ on the western slope of Hill 805 that had previously been held by B/2-506 on 2 July. The hill had been hit hard by numerous air strikes and artillery tear gas shells but LTC Lucas had good reason to believe that 805 had been re-occupied by the aggressive NVA.

Around mid-day of the following day, Company A reached the knoll at the end of the ridge near YD 353193, about one klick northwest of Hill 805. Alpha Three, led by 1LT James Noll, found a booby trap on the LZ that was disarmed by Noll. Company A set up their NDP around the LZ on the knoll. Their objective on the slope of Hill 805 was in sight and they settled down to wait.

On 11 July D/2-501 received a re-supply of extra ammo. The log birds also flew in sodas, watermelons and a hot meal for the surprised grunts. Many of the Company D men thought the hot meal and the treats were a bad omen of what was to come. SGT Raymond 'Blackie' Blackman of Delta Three remembers thinking that it was *"kind of a last meal for us. After eating, we split up into platoons and NDP'd in separate locations down separate trails from the LZ. At first light, we met at the LZ and waited for the birds. We didn't talk much. We knew this wasn't going to be a typical mission." Ripcord* – page 214.

The slicks came in and carried D/2-501 to an LZ at YD 357196, a knoll on the ridge about one klick north of Hill 805. Company D, commanded by CPT Christopher Straub, had orders to move overland to the top of Hill 805 and occupy it. The company moved out at a fast pace, everyone on edge as they progressed up the ridge. SGT Blackman remembers, *"You could feel the gooks. I walked rear security and never felt so alone in my life. We could hear them prepping 805 in the distance and the explosions were getting louder as we got closer." Ripcord* – page 215.

At about the same time, Company A moved off the knoll west of Hill 805 and started down into the saddle between the two hills. CPT Hawkins started the move with Alpha Three, led by Hawkins' most experienced platoon leader, 1LT James Noll, an OCS graduate. Noll told his platoon that they would probably make contact and that they should be ready to instantly return fire. He explained that as soon as they took fire, he wanted to put the platoon online and assault into the enemy positions, firing as they went forward. He warned that if they did not do that, the NVA would trap them down in the saddle and chop them up. Noll was concerned about how his men would react when they came under fire because Alpha Three had a lot of replacements filling its ranks.

1LT Noll was so sure they would make contact that placed himself right behind the point and slack men as they moved down the narrow trail. Noll turned out to be right. At about 1015 hours while moving up over a small knoll, the point man walked up on an NVA trail watcher. Noll heard a burst from the enemy soldier's AK and then silence. Expecting to find the point man dead, Noll rushed forward and found the man still alive. The excited soldier told Noll that a "*little gook*" had shot at him. An exasperated Noll asked the trooper, one of his veterans, why he had not shot the NVA. The man told Noll that the encounter was so sudden that he had just ducked, forgetting to shoot back.

Noll hurried back down the trail to the platoon and found they had taken cover instead of getting online for an assault as he had ordered. Angry that they had failed to follow orders, Noll snapped at them, telling his reluctant men to get on their feet and move up the hill. They responded so slowly that Noll grabbed some of them and pulled them into place.

As 1LT Noll ran back up the hill, his RTO scurrying behind, enemy fire crackled past his head. Locating where the fire was coming from, Noll fired at the spot. Noll's M-16 was loaded with nothing but tracer rounds to mark the target and the platoon was supposed to fire at the spot where the platoon leader aimed the tracers. There was no fire from the platoon because no one had followed the lieutenant up the slope into the enemy fire.

Cresting the top of the little hill, Noll suddenly realized that no one had followed him except his RTO. A surprised NVA jumped from behind a log and Noll raised his M-16 and pulled the trigger. The NVA ducked but nothing happened; Noll had forgotten to replace his empty magazine. By the time he jerked a fresh magazine from his bandolier and reloaded, the very lucky NVA had vanished among the trees.

Noll rushed back down the hill and began jerking his new men to their feet, forcing them to move up the hill. As Noll turned to his RTO, a single shot sounded and he was knocked backward into a bomb crater. Feeling no sensation in his left leg below the knee, he ran his hand over his calf and felt a small bullet hole. Looking at his hand, he saw blood and a piece of flesh on his finger. Frightened, he yelled for a medic.

The platoon medic crawled forward and into some brush. From this concealment, the medic yelled at Noll asking what was wrong. Noll called out that he was hit and ordered the medic to get his ass out of the brush and come get him. The medic, SP4 Mark Draper, yelled back that Noll was okay and to crawl back to him. The lieutenant did so and, as he crawled, realized that he was not that seriously wounded.

After Draper had bandaged him, Noll took cover in an old foxhole and called CPT Hawkins to request Cobra gunships. At that point, the NVA began tossing grenades down on them and Noll's RTO took a fragment in his hand.

The Cobra's came on station and Noll threw a smoke grenade to mark Alpha Three's position. The Cobra's made their pass, rippling off a barrage of rockets. The NVA apparently got away into the jungle during the Cobra attack.

The wounded were moved back to Company A's NDP for evacuation while the artillery FO dropped 81mm mortar fire on the NVA's likely retreat routes. LTC Lucas, orbiting overhead in his C & C bird, urged Hawkins to continue the assault out of the saddle without delay.

Lucas had also been in touch by radio with CPT Straub from D/2-501 to coordinate the movement of the two companies onto Hill 805. Straub told Hawkins that they had detected one or two NVA who were following Company D and he expected to be attacked at any moment.

Nothing happened; there was no further contact. Company A took no fire as they moved onto the LZ on the western slope of Hill 805. Company D moved onto the rocky summit of 805 at about the same time and found nothing but a few destroyed bunkers, showing that the NVA had been there. They found two dead NVA still in their foxholes, probably killed by a minigun-armed LOH. The dead enemy were dragged away before they could start to stink.

CPT Straub was senior to CPT Hawkins by date of rank, so he became the *de facto* commander of the two companies on the boulder-strewn hill. Straub was in control of all the supporting arms (artillery, gunships and tactical air) except for the 81 mm mortars on Ripcord that Hawkins would use in case of a ground attack. LTC Lucas told both company commander that they should expect an attack that night. With that in mind, Straub placed his company CP in the big boulders at the top of the hill that offered protection on three sides.

That afternoon, a log bird hovered over the hill and dropped off shovels, picks, axes and sandbags. They also received enough extra ammo for each man to have sixty M-16 magazines with a case of grenades for each two-or-three man fighting position.

The hilltop was so small that there was barely enough room for the company around the military crest of the hill. The positions were almost elbow-to-elbow as the men struggled to dig foxholes in the rocky soil. Many of them, exhausted after the up-hill assault carrying 80-pound rucks, settled for scooping shallow fighting positions from the old, partially-filled foxholes left by other units. CPT Straub later recalled that his greatest mistake that first night was not ordering the men to dig deeper holes.

The troops had been ready for a tough fight to take the hill and when that did not happen, they let their guard down. Most of them did not really believe that an attack was coming, so they did not set out any more trip flares and claymore mines then they usually did. Some of the men expressed uneasiness because they had never established an NDP on a hill completely devoid of natural cover and concealment. SGT Blackman recalled that downed trees and tree limbs covered the hillsides, giving an attacking force a myriad of places to hide. There was a thick wall of jungle at the bottom of the hill where the NVA could stage an attack so Blackman knew they were very vulnerable as darkness fell on the windswept hill.

■ ■ ■

CPT Hawkins and Company A had set up their NDP about two hundred meters west of Company D around an old LZ. While they were digging in on the afternoon of 12 July, SSGT Gerald Singleton, Alpha One's platoon sergeant, suggested to Hawkins that he be allowed to implant some newly-issued sensor devices along the trail they had used to reach the LZ. These devices resembled railroad spikes and came in a kit of four sensors, a receiver and a headset. Each spike contained a transmitter which, when activated by the ground vibrations caused by footsteps, gave a series of beeps heard in the headset.

Hawkins, curious about the devices, gave permission and Singleton along with 1LT William Pahissa, Alpha One's platoon leader, and two grunts, set out the devices at forty-meter intervals along the trail beginning about two hundred meters west of the NDP on the LZ. Hawkins was not sure the devices would work but decided to allow SSGT Singleton to try them out.

So, at about 2200 hours that night, Singleton reported to Hawkins that the sensors were "*chirping like crickets*" through the headsets. Singleton and Pahissa told Hawkins that they had heavy movement coming up the trail toward them. Hawkins turned to the artillery FO, 2LT Stephen Olsen, and told him to have the 81mm mortars on Ripcord "fire for effect" without using the customary adjusting rounds which would have warned the enemy they were about to be mortared. Hawkins then called CPT Straub up on 805 and told him they had a lot of movement to their west. Straub replied that one of their mechanical ambushes had just gone off. Just as the mortar rounds came crashing down to Alpha One's front, the NVA hit Company D from three sides with RPG fire. The NVA force moving up the trail to attack from the west was broken up by the sudden mortar barrage and was not able to press home their attack. The NVA may not have known that there was a second company in place to Company D's west.

The main attack began about 2220 hours when a green star cluster flare popped overhead and, within seconds, RPG's were exploding all over the hill. 1LT James Potter, the artillery FO attached to Company D, was standing at the northern edge of the perimeter calling in corrections for defensive fires to the artillery FDC on Ripcord. When the RPG's began exploding all around him, Potter fell flat and then crawled frantically uphill to the CP. When he reached the CP, he noticed that his air mattress, where he would have been sleeping, was full of shrapnel holes.

SGT Blackman of Delta Three remembers that everyone was already awake when the first RPG's came in on the northern sector of Company D's perimeter. They had been enjoying the quiet night and the pleasant coolness after the sweltering hot day. The sudden barrage of RPG's exploding all over the hilltop took them all by surprise.

1LT John Shipley, Delta Two's platoon leader, was slightly wounded in the opening barrage. Shipley, along with many others, had not taken LTC Lucas' warning of a coming attack seriously. They had gotten such warnings before and nothing had happened. The sudden rain of RPG's onto Hill 805 caught them off guard. The fury of the attack was stunning.

SGT Blackman recalls a lot of confusion at first because not enough fighting holes had been dug and the men were scrambling for cover. Company D recovered from the suddenness of the attack quickly and was fully engaged by the time Blackman had crawled to his foxhole and began firing back. All weapons were firing, with the M-16's and M-60's putting out maximum fire. Red tracers poured from the hilltop, ricocheting from boulders and logs into the sky. Blackman was greatly impressed by the amount of firepower put out by the one hundred men of Company D. The gunfire was earsplitting and got louder as 1LT Potter called in 81mm fire as close to Company D's perimeter as he could safely bring it.

The mortar battery on Ripcord fired flares as quickly as they could because the high winds blew the parachute-borne illumination away almost as soon as they ignited. The moving flares cast weird, flickering shadows across the hillside, making it difficult to spot individual targets.

CPT Hawkins, from his position ten meters below and two hundred meters west, spotted NVA soldiers scrambling up both the northern and southern slopes of the embattled hill. From Company A's position, the enemy was easy to spot as they fired their AK-47's into Company D's perimeter, the green tracers glancing off the boulders into the sky.

CPT Hawkins was puzzled because the NVA had left their flanks open to fire from his company in its position on the LZ. Again, Hawkins thought the enemy did not know they were there. As Hawkins said later, *"It was one of the few times I'd ever seen them attack without conducting adequate reconnaissance. We were in a position to devastate them. We had, in fact, prearranged sectors of fire with Straub to interlock with his defensive position[s]. My machine gunners and grenadiers knew where to fire and where not to fire if we had to provide support." Ripcord* – page 220.

A problem quickly developed because no one in Company A was firing. The troops were in shock, perhaps because they had never seen so many enemy troops in one place before. Hawkins ran to Alpha Three's sector which faced the south slope of 805. Finding an M-60 crew, he pointed at the NVA and asked the gunner if he could see them. *"That's the enemy attacking your buddies up there,"* he snapped. *"You've got targets. You know where the friendlies are. Shoot to the right of the hill." Ripcord* – page 220.

CPT Hawkins next rushed to an M-79 man and asked if he could put a grenade on the south slope every fifteen seconds. The trooper said he certainly could so Hawkins told him to start firing, right now.

Hurrying over to Alpha Two, Hawkins collared the platoon leader, 1LT Lee Widjeskog. Alpha Two had a good view of the north slope of Hill 805 and Hawkins told Widjeskog to get his men firing to the left of the hill. Hawkins warned Alpha Two to keep up a continuous fire and to get their M-79's firing.

With his troops putting out a continuous fire into the enemy's flanks, Hawkins cautiously made his way onto the open LZ for a look around. He saw that many RPG's, trailing sparks, were being launched from a jungled depression a couple of hundred meters north of Hill 805. Grabbing a LAW from a position close by, he tried to fire it but it was a dud. He tried another LAW and this one fired, the rocket exploding on target with a good, solid **CRUMP**. Silence followed, but then a surprised Hawkins heard the pop-pop-pop-pop-pop sound of a lot of RPG's firing at once. Racing to the nearest foxhole, Hawkins fell in on top of 1LT Pahissa and SSGT Singleton, still busy directing 81mmm fire onto the trail leading out of the saddle to the LZ. As Hawkins rolled into the hole, fifteen RPG's, counted by Singleton, exploded in a rippling blast about twenty meters in front of Alpha One, causing the started troopers to exclaim "*Goddamn*" and "*what the fuck. . .*" In the understatement of the night, SSGT Singleton looked at CPT Hawkins and gravely said, *"I wouldn't do that again if I were you, sir." Ripcord* – page 221. Hawkins did not, but he later said that at least those fifteen rockets were not used against Company D.

The NVA, taking cover among the boulders about fifty meters downhill from Delta Two's sector, pushed their attack forward against 1LT Shipley's men under a heavy barrage of RPG's. Trying to prevent the enemy from crawling up under cover of the rockets, the 2nd Platoon kept up a terrific rate of fire. Shipley's M-60 gunners, firing without let-up, burned out the barrels of their guns. Blistering their hands, they replaced the red-hot barrels and kept firing. One man with a seriously torn-up arm was bandaged by a medic and shot full of morphine. The potent pain killer did not stop him from getting back into the battle; he was soon tossing grenades down the slope, screaming curse s at the enemy.

Cobra gunships, called for by CPT Straub, arrived overhead about fifteen minutes into the fight and the NVA began to disengage. Company D kept pouring out a heavy fire for another hour while three artillery batteries put a wall of shrapnel around the little hill. The shooting finally slowed and then stopped. Utter silence reigned for a moment, then calls for a medic began to sound, at first softly and then louder.

About a dozen Company D troopers were hit badly enough to be evacuated after daybreak the next morning, while an equal number, wounded less seriously, remained on the hill. SGT Blackman, who had escaped injury, stayed awake the rest of the night in a crowded foxhole with two others.

CPT Straub ordered security patrols to move forward of the perimeter at dawn. The patrols found piles of bloody bandages, plus a few AK magazine and RPG's missed by the enemy as they withdrew. LTC Lucas landed to confer with Hawkins and Straub and Hawkins was given a new mission; they were to move down the draw west of Hill 805 and recon the low ground south of FSB Ripcord. The company was prepared to move out on their new mission when Lucas called Hawkins and told him he had assigned a pair of F-4 Phantom fighter-bombers for his exclusive use. Hawkins told the colonel that he did not have a target but Lucas told him to pick a target and use the Phantoms.

Following orders, Hawkins picked a spot on his map near YD 353186, about six hundred meters southwest of his position on the LZ. Said Hawkins, "*It was on my planned route into the valley and, because the spot was not in line of sight with Ripcord, but was down low on the finger [ridge], I figured it was as good a place as any for the enemy to have a cache." Ripcord* – page 222.

The FAC, buzzing down in a steep dive, fired white phosphorous marking rockets and the first F-4 dived and released his bombs. *". . .and **KA-BOOM**, we had smoke and flame and debris shooting into the air two or three hundred feet above the treetops. The FAC told us it wasn't the bombs doing that, but secondary explosions. We'd lucked out and hit an enemy ammo bunker. . .and the FAC went nuts watching all the secondary's. He said you could tell what you'd hit by the color of the explosion. Reddish-yellow meant munitions. My troops and I enjoyed a ringside seat, looking right down on the area from the LZ. Guys were cheering. It was a pretty awesome sight."* Ripcord – page 222.

■ ■ ■

The decision had been made to hold on to Hill 805 to deny the NVA high ground from which to observe and direct fire on to FSB Ripcord. Company D's new mission was to draw the NVA to Hill 805 so they could be subjected to the massed firepower that could be called upon by the 101st Airborne Division. As CPT Straub explained it, *"I was basically told to go sit on a bald hilltop and wait to be attacked. I didn't accept that order with good cheer. I wasn't the way we operated. We weren't a company that did obvious things and set up in obvious places. The enemy didn't hunt us. We hunted them. I was very concerned, then, when we dug in atop [Hill] 805 because we were giving up the initiative right at the start to the North Vietnamese."* Ripcord – page 223.

All through the day of 13 July, log birds came and went as Company D labored to get ready for another night on the hill. Teams of grunts, sweating in the 100° heat, worked to clear fields of fire all around the hill. Bunkers were excavated chest deep, some big enough for six men, covered with sand bags and tree limbs. Log birds delivered crate after crate of ammo and grenades, all of which had to be hauled up the slope of Hill 805 from the LZ two hundred meters to the west. Extra claymores and trip flares were set up, hidden among the fallen trees on the hillside. Additional movement sensors and mechanical ambushes were put in place along suspected avenues of approach. Coils of concertina wire were delivered and staked out in a single row around the entire hilltop, thirty feet below the row of bunkers and foxholes.

1LT Joseph Guerra was flown from Camp Evans where he had been convalescing from wounds to take over as platoon leader for Delta Three. Guerra's platoon held the ground from ten to two; 1LT Shipley's men from two to six and 1LT Terry Palm's troops covered from six to ten, facing the shallow saddle between Hill 805 and the resupply LZ to the west.

As the troops labored to build their positions, a 12.7mm (.51 caliber) machine gun, in place on the slope below Hill 805, began to fire on the CH-47's approaching Ripcord. 1LT Potter, the artillery FO, called in 8-inch artillery in a vain attempt to silence the gun. The NVA gunners would just move the gun a few meters and fire again as the big Chinooks hovered over the firebase.

Potter spent the day plotting defensive targets all around the hill. He *"adjusted selected targets with live fire. This allowed the [artillery] batteries supporting us to record firing data – deflection, elevation, powder charge and fuse setting – and assign target numbers for quick reaction if we had contact."* The FO was given priority for supporting fire on 13 July, and he *"spent four hours adjusting 81mm rounds over the surface of the hill in twenty-five-meter increments. Each time we adjusted on a piece of terrain from which we had received fire during the night, I recorded a target number on my map and the mortar section on Ripcord recorded the firing data. I also refined my artillery adjustments, calling for close-in fire from [Firebases] Ripcord, O'Reilly, and Rakkasan." Ripcord* – page 223.

1LT Palm, leading Delta One, decided against bunkers with overhead cover. Instead, he had his platoon dig deep foxholes and prone fighting positions rather than bunkers covered with big piles of sandbags. As Palm was killed in action on 14 July, no one knows whether he thought it foolish to advertise his positions with big mounds of sandbags or if he just decided the NVA would not launch an attack across the bare-from-cover LZ. SP4 Richard Soubers of Delta One remembers that they dug sleeping positions that angled back into the hillside, but only a few foxholes. Neither he or his buddies felt any sense of urgency even though the other two platoons had been attacked the night before. Soubers did not know why they were on the hill or how long they would be there.

The night of 13-14 July was cool and the tension could be felt all along the foxhole/bunker line on 805. The troops had trouble hearing over the ceaseless winds. Occasional flares popping overhead were quickly carried away by the wind and showed nothing but shifting shadows to the stressed-out grunts. The sappers creeping up the hill expertly used the fallen trees and boulders as cover and concealment to get close to D Company's positions. Many of the sappers were within twenty meters (sixty-five feet) or less of the perimeter when one of them set off a trip flare.

SGT Blackman remembers what happened next, *"By the time we were attacked, we were pretty tired. We'd been digging all day, then standing in our bunkers for a long time, trying to stay awake and alert. When the attack came, it seemed to happen all at once around the hill. The hill just exploded with incoming fire. . ."* Ripcord – page 226.

It was about 0203 hours on 14 July when SP4 Dennis Belt, occupying a position on Delta One's right flank, saw a sapper in the concertina wire only thirty feet beyond his hole. Belt yelled a warning and fired half a magazine at the sapper. Rolling behind a log, the sapper fired back with his folding stock AK-50. SGT William Jones, sitting on the ground near Belt, had failed to dig a fighting hole that day. Jones was Regular Army-not a draftee-on his second tour and should have known better. Jones began to fire and, moving forward to get a better firing angle on the sapper behind the log, took an AK round through his helmet and died instantly.

LT Palm and Delta One's platoon sergeant, SSGT Mike Cooksley, scurried along the perimeter, yelling encouragement and telling the men to blow their claymores. There was so much outgoing fire that it was hard to hear where the NVA fire was coming from. All the men could do was look for muzzle flashes and shoot at them. CPT Straub and LT Potter called for artillery support and soon the big shells were roaring in, adding to the general noise and confusion. CPT Straub later called it *"the most intense combat experience of my Vietnam service. . ." Ripcord* – page 227.

LT Potter called in 105mm artillery from Ripcord and adjusted it to fall as close to the west and south sectors of the perimeter as was safe. He adjusted 81mm mortars, also from Ripcord, to fall even closer to the perimeter, especially on the west where the main attack was coming in. Potter called in 155mm rounds from the ARVN battery on FSB O'Reilly to hit two hundred and fifty meters from the south edge of the perimeter. He was afraid to bring it in closer because Hill 805 was between the guns on O'Reilly and the target. He used the big 8-inch guns on FSB Rakkasan, adjusting them to fall in the valley to the south of Hill 805.

CPT Straub called for fire from the Quad-50 on Ripcord and the line of red tracers flowing in an arc from one hill to the other made a spectacular show. The big bullets rained down onto the deadfall in front of Delta One, tracers ricocheting high into the air.

About a half-hour into the fight, Cobra gunships from Camp Evans came on station. CPT Straub had a strobe light placed on top of 805 to mark the center of the perimeter and serve as a reference point from which to give the Cobra pilots firing instructions. Potter and Straub, working in close coordination with the three platoon leaders, sometimes had as many as eight fire missions underway at the same time. Potter later recalled that he had never been under such stress and that they owed their lives to the pilots and gunners of the Cobras. The troops marked targets with a steady stream of tracers from an M-60 and the Cobras came in very low and dumped their ordnance as close as fifty meters from the perimeter.

The NVA on the west side, Delta One's sector, were so close as to be inside the ring of mortar, artillery and Cobra 2.75-inch rocket fire. So near that some of the satchel charges lobbed at the line of foxholes on the perimeter overshot their targets and exploded in the CP ten meters behind the perimeter. Potter later wrote that *"At one point, four satchel charges exploded against the inside edge of the boulder about six feet to my left. I didn't expect to see the sun rise in the morning. We were that close to being overrun. . ." Ripcord* – page 228.

Many individual battles were happening at the same time. In a three-man foxhole in the center of Delta One's sector, SP4 Jack Godwin had a foot and lower leg blown off by a satchel charge. The two other men, their ear drums ruptured and bleeding, abandoned the hole and ran uphill to shelter among the boulders. To plug the gap, the squad leader on the left flank sent two of his men to cover the hole. One of the men, SP4 John Keister moved beside PFC Martin Cirrincione-SSGT Cooksley's RTO-who had moved up beside the wounded Godwin. Keister asked where he should go and the RTO told him to stay with him. Both troopers had just begun to fire at the sappers below them when Keister took a round right under the rim of his helmet, killing him instantly.

Dennis Belt, in a very personal battle, was still fighting it out with the sapper firing the AK-50 from behind the log. *"He had me cold,"* remembers Belt who, unable to raise his head to fire his rifle, feverishly tossed grenades at the man. Belt had a case of grenades and he *"threw almost all of them that were in there. . ." Ripcord* – page 229.

Over in Delta Three's sector, SGT Blackman's M-16 had jammed and he was rolling grenades down the hill and re-loading magazines for the other men at his position. Blackman recalled that the M-60 gunner to his left fire fired so long that the barrel of the gun was bright red and he could clearly see the bolt moving back and forth inside the barrel. The night was surreal, with flashes from explosions creating brief images of the battle. The noise was mind-numbing: gunfire, artillery rounds whooshing overhead to explode, grenades, satchel charges, miniguns ripping, RPG's and Cobra rockets all combined to create an unceasing roar of noise. And yet, even in the face of tremendous fire power, the NVA kept coming.

LT Joseph Guerra, who had been wounded while serving with 'Hard Luck Alpha' (A/2-501), jumped into SGT Blackman's hole and wanted Blackman to point out where the NVA were. The men in the hole pointed out a few spots and Guerra climbed onto the bunkers' overhead cover and began firing LAW's down into probable NVA positions. Blackman remembers thinking how crazy that was but then, it was a crazy night.

LT Palm of Delta One continued to expose himself as he moved from foxhole to foxhole in his sector. He was trying to help Jack Godwin when he was hit. Badly wounded, Godwin was hunched in the bottom of his hole when he heard Palm calling his name. Just as Palm reached Godwin, he was shot in the chest, collapsing into the hole on top of Godwin.

CPT Straub got Delta Two's LT Shipley on the radio and told him, because Delta Two was only lightly engaged, to send four men to help Delta One. The platoon sergeant, SSGT James Hembree picked four men, one of whom was a machine gunner. Hembree changed his mind when he saw fear flash across the young man's face. Hembree took the M-60 and told the kid to never mind, that he would go himself.

SSGT Hembree, burdened with extra ammo for Delta One and the 23-pound M-60, led his reinforcements to the western slope of Hill 805. While he was getting into position to fire on a pocket of NVA in the boulders on the side of the hill, he was shot through the neck and killed. Hembree was a Regular Army NCO and the one man in Delta Two everyone relied on from the platoon leader down to the newest PFC.

While moving up, PFC Keith Utter, one of Hembree's men, took a bullet in the head. Both Utter and Hembree were awarded posthumous Silver Stars for exposing themselves to heavy fire while going to the aid of the hard-pressed Delta One. Jones, Keister and Palm, like Hembree and Utter, had probably been shot by the sapper behind the log in front of Dennis Belt's position. This sapper, lying low and firing only when he had a clear target, killed his enemies without 805's defenders even being aware that an NVA had gotten so close to their perimeter.

SGT Warren Hanrahan was another of SSGT Hembree's reinforcements. He crossed over the crest of the hill and found a foxhole. Right below him was SP4 Ron Grubidt, Delta One's medic, yelling for covering fire while he moved a wounded man. Hanrahan jumped up to help Grubidt and was immediately shot in the neck, the bullet going between his jugular vein and neck vertebrae, bruising the spinal cord. Hanrahan dropped, his right arm temporarily paralyzed. Helping each other, the other wounded man and Hanrahan slowly crawled back up the slope, sliding in the loose dirt. Hanrahan's M-16 had gotten smashed, so he tried firing the other man's weapon left-handed but his marksmanship was so bad that the man told him he might as well go over to the NVA's side for all the good he was doing.

The center of Delta One's line was anchored by the M-60 team of SP4 Roger Myles and his A-gunner, PFC Angel Arimont. They kept up a continuous fire until the gun barrel, heated red-hot, became warped and the bolt jammed in the barrel. Myles yelled out that he had a jam and needed a new barrel. The M-60 gunner on Delta One's right flank, SP4 Paul "Rat" Guimond, jumped up to try and help. He ran fully erect and SP4 Drew Gaster tried to trip him, yelling for him to get down.

As Guimond passed behind Dennis Belt's foxhole, the sapper behind the log shot him. He fell and rolled about twenty feet down the hill, ending up lying in no-man's land, just above the concertina wire. Belt and SP4 Richard Soubers, after waiting for the overhead flares to blow away, ran downhill to get Guimond. Belt was hit in the stomach, the round chipping his spine as it exited his back while another bullet crushed his right hip. Soubers, hoisting Belt over his shoulder, hardly noticed the bullet that grazed his steel pot. Soubers moved as quickly as he could up the steep hillside, slipping in the loose earth. Soubers later said that Belt was. . .." cussing *a blue streak as I carried him up the hill, since the pain of his stomach wound was so intense. After I got him to a level spot above our position, I wrapped a poncho liner around him while at the same time yelling for a medic. I then went back to our position on the line, hesitant to go back after Rat given the intense fire we were getting. . ." Ripcord* – page 232.

Doc Grubidt scurried quickly from one casualty to another, treating them as best he could. Grubidt and several other troopers carried the wounded to the collection point that the other medics had set up in the boulders on top of the hill. Grubidt dragged LT Palm out of Godwin's foxhole but the lieutenant was already dead.

Even with their heavy casualties, Delta One was holding its own. SP4 Myles had gotten his M-60 going again and SP4 Gaster, with the help PFC Rodger Collins, had put Rat Guimond's gun back into action.

Rod Soubers moved into a position with SP4 David Beyl, his best friend. Beyl was firing M-79 grenades out into the downed logs and firing at the muzzle flashes coming from the tree line. SSGT Cooksley, though wounded, moved around Deltas One's sector, helping where and when he could, taking charge of the platoon after LT Palm's death.

CPT Straub received a radio call from six US Marine A-6 Intruders, specially designed to operate at night or in bad weather. The six Intruders, homing in on the navigation beacon on Ripcord, dropped a total of forty-two tons of 500-pound bombs. Straub gave the pilots the range and direction from Hill 805 and the bombs hit the targets with uncanny accuracy. Straub remembers that *"It was a spectacular sight and it broke up the attack on us." Ripcord* – page 232-233.

After the devastating bomb drops, the NVA fire slacked off and quit altogether about 0320 hours. SSGT Raymond Dotson of Delta Three showed up at Ray Blackman's bunker and told them that Delta One had been hard hit and needed help. Dotson wanted one man to come with him. Blackman, who had just cleared his jammed M-16, crawled out of the bunker and followed Dotson over the top of the hill and down to Delta One. Blackman noticed three poncho-covered figures lying side-by-side and knew they were dead. Dotson pointed to a prone fighting position and told Blackman to stay there and keep his eyes open. Worried that his M-16 would jam again, Blackman regretted that he had not brought more grenades.

During the lull, SSGT Cooksley and SP4 Soubers planned how to recover Rat Guimond. Cooksley told Soubers that he and the whole platoon would put out covering fire while Soubers and one other man got Guimond. Cooksley and Soubers crawled along the line, explaining the plan at each position.

Basically, they would wait until burning flares were directly overhead before they moved. Cooksley had noticed that the NVA took cover when flares were overhead, so they would use the bright light of the flares being dropped by a CH-47 flare ship to their advantage. Soubers stopped at Blackman's hole and told him he wanted him to go with him to get Rat. Blackman could not see where Guimond was lying, so Soubers pointed out the spot, just above the row of concertina wire.

The flares popped into light and the cover fire began. Blackman looked around and saw Soubers running downhill toward Guimond. Blackman hesitated and Soubers, seeing this, yelled for him to get some balls and come help him. Blackman moved then. Reaching Guimond, they each grabbed an arm and dragged him up the steep hillside, laying him near Dennis Belt. Doc Grubidt put a bandage on the wound in Guimond's temple and told Blackman to hold it in there until a medevac arrived.

A dust-off arrived about 0340 hours and lowered a basket while hovering over the hill, using a strobe light as a point of reference in the wind-shipped darkness. The senior company medic Sp4 Gary Fowler, loaded Rat Guimond into the basket first then put Dennis Belt on top. Everyone worked quickly, afraid the NVA would fire an RPG at the vulnerable dust-off.

A second medevac arrived and lowered its basket. To save time, Fowler loaded Jack Godwin alone into the basket and the second Huey was soon on its way. As the first medevac approached Camp Evans, Belt could feel Rat Guimond's labored breathing as he lay atop the gravely wounded machine gunner. As they flared for landing on the hospital LZ, Belt felt Guimond give a last big gasp and then he died.

As the second medevac came on station, so did an air force C-130 carrying big parachute flares. CPT Straub kept the big aircraft orbiting overhead until dawn, dropping its large flares and keeping Hill 805 well lit. When the sun finally rose, all the claymores that had not been detonated during the attack were set off so that new mines could be safely emplaced.

Many of the frag grenades lobbed down the hill during the battle had not exploded. Some of these duds were now cooking off in the fires burning among the downed trees. PFC 'Chip' Collins was wounded by one of these cook offs and had to be evacuated.

Security patrols, sent out to check the slopes below the perimeter, found a sack full of satchel charges and an RPG rocket. Five badly shot-up bodies were left behind by the retreating NVA, an indication that the enemy had been hit hard. The NVA always made every effort to remove their dead and wounded from a battlefield. One of the abandoned bodies was that of the sapper who had been behind the log in front of Dennis Belt's hole, his right hand blown off.

CPT Straub sent a squad to secure the LZ to the west so that a dust off could land to take on the wounded. Doc Fowler then checked the remaining wounded and decided who needed to go in for treatment and who could be treated in the field. Six additional wounded were flown to Camp Evans, included those with ruptured ear drums along with SGT Hanrahan, a large field dressing around his neck. Those who had relatively minor shrapnel wounds, and there were a lot of them, stayed behind on the hill.

Said CPT Straub, *"I wouldn't let anyone be medevacked unless he had a really serious wound. Anybody who could pull a trigger and throw frags was going to be of immense value when the next attack came. I didn't get any resistance on this. Nobody complained, nobody pleaded to be sent out. They were willing to stay with their unit until this mess was over." Ripcord* – page 235.

OP's were sent out all around the perimeter. Log birds came in laden with ammo, water, more claymores, trip flares and concertina wire. Twenty replacements came out, not all of them trained as Infantry. The log birds took out the dead, who had been carried to the LZ in body bags. LTC Lucas came out with his artillery liaison officer, bringing mail, medical supplies and two starlight scopes for the CP. Lucas, apparently noting CPT Straub's depression over his many casualties, took him aside and re-emphasized how important it was to the security of Ripcord to hold onto Hill 805. Straub recalls about Lucas. . ." *he gave me a good little pep talk, which I needed. He got me thinking positively and made me stop feeling sorry for Delta Company . . .he went around to every position and talked to everybody, sat in foxholes and talked with the troops. That was super." Ripcord* – page 236.

Company D had indeed held onto the hill but it had cost the lives of six men: 1LT Terry A. Palm; SP4 Paul G. Guimond; SSGT James T. Hembree; SGT William E. Jones; SP4 John L. Keister and PFC Keith E. Utter.

■ ■ ■

CPT Straub, while LTC Lucas was visiting Hill 805, had tried to get permission to move Company D off the battered hilltop. Lucas denied Straub's request; he wanted the hill occupied to prevent the NVA from using it as an observation post or a base for mortar attacks on Ripcord. It was a perilous situation for D/2-501; the NVA had them under observation and could count the number of casualties evacuated from the position. CPT Straub knew it was only a matter of time, if the situation remained as it was, before they were overrun.

The men of Company D were, as was CPT Straub, exhausted by the time the third attack came. Said Straub, "*I basically stopped eating and sleeping after the first night. I couldn't stop checking on things and thinking about what else we could do to prepare for the next attack. I forced myself to eat. There was zero hunger. I was just going on water and cigarettes and a very intense desire to get the company through this.*" Straub took heart from the excellent fire support they were getting and the courage of his troops. The men fought hard and took care of each other. *Ripcord* – page 257.

At around 1330 hours on 14 July, Company D's executive officer, 1LT Ralph Selvaggi, flew onto the beleaguered hilltop with twelve replacements. The company had evacuated twenty-nine men from the hill since 12 July. Seven of the replacements were cherries, but every man was needed to fill a foxhole. LT Selvaggi himself stayed to serve as the platoon leader for Delta One, replacing the dead 1LT Terry Palm.

The long day finally ended and the OP's were brought in at dusk as the company went on 50 percent alert. When the first RPG's came in at 2253 hours, Straub fired a red star-cluster flare, a pre-arranged signal to CPT Ray Williams, the artillery liaison officer on Ripcord. Williams put the fire plan into action and within three minutes, Company D was receiving pre-plotted defensive fire from the 105's, 155's, 81mm's and Quad-50's on FSB Ripcord. A wall of artillery, machine gun and mortar fire ringed the top of Hill 805.

The troops responded to the attack by throwing frags out into the wire and putting out sheets of fire from their M-16's, M-79's and M-60's. The third NVA attack came in from the south and southeast, primarily against 1LT Shipley's Delta Two. Someone had thought to send out two 90mm recoilless rifles and Straub had one of them facing the LZ and the second with Delta Two.

LT Shipley loaded the weapon for the gunner who then fired off flechette rounds, called Beehives. Each of these rounds blasts out thousands of little steel darts in an expanding cone from the muzzle. They could go right through a small tree and would shred any attackers coming up the slopes of Hill 805.

The NVA regular infantry attack was shattered. Straub and his artillery FO, 1LT Potter, were too close to the dangerous back blast coming from Shipley's 90mm. Straub's steel pot, chin strap in place, was blown to the side of his head after each shot while Potter said it was like standing in the exhaust from a jet engine.

The sappers were a different story. Despite the heavy fire put out by Delta Two, the NVA sappers moved forward from boulder to boulder, covering each other with bursts of AK-50 fire. When the sappers got close enough, satchel charges began to come into the perimeter, exploding with eardrum-bursting blasts. One satchel charge, thrown at Delta Two's CP, was accidentally deflected by the platoon medic when he happened to raise his arm. The charge bounced off the medic's arm and exploded harmlessly.

SP4 Gary Schneider from Delta Two was firing his M-60 from a four-man bunker. M-60's were prime targets for RPG gunners and Schneider's position took a direct hit, blowing all four men up and out of the bunker. Schneider and one other man were wounded, Schneider seriously. The other two were unhurt due to their flak jackets but one of them went temporarily insane from the effects of the blast, screaming and crying hysterically.

Then the enemy hit Company D with tear gas. There was no gas cloud and they did not know where the gas came from. Some of the many satchel charges thrown into the perimeter may have been impregnated with CS crystals. Very quickly, some of the troops on the perimeter began choking and crying. Unable to see or breathe, they could not fire their weapons until they managed to get into their gas masks. Luckily the ever-present high wind soon blew the choking gas away from the hill. Ripping off the hated gas masks, the troops resumed firing at a furious rate.

Crazy things happened. An explosion started a fire in the downed trees, lighting up all the positions on that side of the hill. Troops grabbed some five-gallon water cans and, still under fire, ran down the hill and put out the fire.

The Red Team that had been scrambled from Camp Evans began making rocket and miniguns firing runs at about 2314 hours. The troops kept up their heavy fire, throwing grenades and screaming and cursing at the NVA. Said 1LT Shipley, *"The enemy must have thought we were a bunch of idiots, screaming down the hill at them like that, but it worked on them psychologically. They were so close, we thought we were going to have hand-to-hand combat. We'd already made up our minds that we'd fight to the last man. We weren't going to be captured. In the midst of the firefight, fear was not a problem. We had complete control, most of us. It was before, and after [the fight], that we were scared."* Ripcord – page 259.

As flare ships came on station and began to light up the area, the NVA fire died down and the enemy began to withdraw. CPT Straub called for a night medevac for Gary Schneider who, bleeding heavily, was slipping into shock. Delta Two's medic pumped Schneider's heart while the senior medic, Doc Fowler, did mouth-to-mouth, barely keeping him alive. The medevac arrived at about 0112 hours and tried for forty minutes to hold a hover while lowering a basket, but the gusty winds made it impossible. The pilot finally had to break station to refuel. The pilot radioed Straub that there was only one pilot able to hold a helicopter steady in such blustery conditions. The pilot encouraged them to hang on and that they were going to call for him.

While they were waiting for the second medevac, the NVA began firing 75mm recoilless rifles at them. Most of these rounds missed, exploding harmlessly on the hillside. Then more accurate 82mm mortar fire began dropping on the hilltop. 1LT Potter wrote later that *"the enemy would bracket our position. One short, one long and then one in the middle. It was nerve-wracking because our overhead cover could not stop the direct hit of a mortar shell. . ." Ripcord* – page 260.

The Cobras dove on the NVA firing positions and the incoming stopped. The two medics had continued to work on Schneider the whole time, ignoring the incoming mortar rounds. Doc Fowler wrote about the experience, *"He was bleeding internally and each time I breathed into him, I got a mouthful of blood. I cannot describe in words what that was like. I spit the blood out and continued the artificial resuscitation. When the second medevac arrived, we still had a pulse." Ripcord* – page 260.

The second medevac arrived overhead at 0241 hours. The NVA began firing on the hovering Huey with automatic weapons, ignoring the flares and suppressing fire put out by the mortars on Ripcord. The gunships dove, firing volleys of rockets while the grunts poured out a furious fire. The pilot told Straub that the winds were gusting up to 60 knots (about 70 mph) but he kept the dust-off at a steady hover over the strobe light marking the spot where Schneider lay, barely alive. The basket was lowered, Schneider strapped in and the basket went back up.

The medics heroic efforts to keep Schneider alive were in vain. The NVA fire on the unarmed medevac killed SP4 Gary Schneider. 1LT Shipley wrote, *"The medics kept him alive for hours, but he was killed while being hoisted up in the basket. They found several bullet holes in him when the medevac landed at Camp Evans." Ripcord* – page 260.

After the medevac left, a heavy, tense silence descended over the hill. Flares still lit the night as CPT Straub peered through a starlight scope. The exhausted troops waited in their holes, chewing on C-ration Tootsie Rolls, afraid to let their guard down enough to sleep. About 0400 hours, three trip flares suddenly ignited around fifteen meters to the west of Delta One. Instantly, all three platoon's individual weapons put out a heavy volume of fire. Artillery and ARA pummeled the terrain west of 805. The NVA withdrew without returning fire. LT Potter remembers that Company D had nearly exhausted their ammo supply by that time. *"If the NVA had pressed the attack, they would have had us. . ." Ripcord* – page 261.

At first light, security patrols were sent out. The patrols found a lot of blood trails and drag marks, left by the NVA as they removed their casualties. Shredded uniforms and equipment lay scattered about and a wallet was found holding documents and personal photos but no indication of the NVA unit they had been fighting. The fallen trees in the area in front of Delta One and Delta Two were studded with hundreds of flechette darts. One patrol found a wide, bloody trail leading southwest. They followed the trail until it faded away.

As the sun rose higher, Huey log birds began to come in loaded with everything they needed for another day on the hill – ammo, claymores, grenades, flares, C-rations, PRC-25 batteries and five-gallon cans of water, flavored by the iodine water purification tablets.

While the exhausted troops began to get organized, CPT Straub quietly took Doc Fowler aside and asked him to wash his face. Fowler had a small mirror in his personal gear and, after a quick look, he saw that *"the horror of war was all over me. I had dried blood all around my lips and nose, my teeth were red, my hands were stained, my uniform had blood all over it. I washed myself, got some other clothes and tried to put it behind me. We were staying on the hill and we knew we were going to get attacked again when the sun went down. . ." Ripcord* – page 261.

Around mid-day on 15 July another dust off was called when medics found that a man they had thought only lightly wounded had developed a collapsed lung. The soldier, James Plenderleith, was flown off the hill without incident.

Company D spent most of Monday, 15 July, laying down more concertina wire, setting out more claymores and trip flares, reinforcing bunkers and fighting holes and doing everything they could think of to get ready for another attack. LT Potter contacted CPT David Rich, the 105mm battery commander on Ripcord and asked for one howitzer to be specifically dedicated to neutralizing a clump of boulders on the south slope of hill 805. The NVA had used these boulders as cover from which to launch numerous RPG's during the three previous attacks. Potter got Delta Two down in their holes because the clump of boulders was only fifty meters out from the perimeter. Rich and Potter then walked shells up the slope until they fell right on the boulders. CPT Rich then gave orders for the howitzer not to be touched so the settings on the gun would remain intact, then waited for the next attack to begin.

A log bird received enemy fire as flared for landing on the LZ at about 1525 hours. When the pilot applied power to pull away, the engine failed and the Huey made a hard landing on the slope of the LZ. A squad from Delta One secured the downed bird as they waited for a Chinook to extract the crippled Huey. About twenty minutes later, the CH-47 arrived and the Huey was rigged for extraction. When the Chinook started to lift the Huey, it received heavy small arms fire. As the weight of the Huey came onto the strap, it broke. The Chinook made it out safely but the Huey had to be left in place. The radios were removed and the two pilots flown to the rear. The enlisted crew members had to spend the night on Hill 895. The very pissed-off crew chief and door gunner were put into position with Delta One, their machine guns from the downed Huey covering the trail to the LZ.

In the early evening, the NVA dropped three 82mm mortar rounds on Hill 805 that fell on the slope forty meters west of Delta One. No other rounds fell on the hill and the three may have been registration rounds for a barrage to be fired later.

The fourth attack against Company D started at about 0246 hours on 16 July, when sappers set of a mechanical ambush in Delta One's sector. The NVA were only fifty meters from the perimeter when the mechanical went off and a heavy exchange of small arms fire started. A trip flare on the southeast slope ignited and revealed the enemy's approach from southwest, south and southeast in front of Delta Two. CPT Straub and LT Potter began calling in close fire support all around the hill – mortars, artillery and brilliant streams of red tracers from the Quad-50's on Ripcord.

As RPG's began to zoom in, fired from the rocky outcrop south of the perimeter, Straub had the men of Delta Two get down in their holes as Potter called in the pre-registered fire from the single howitzer on Ripcord. The first 105 shell came in a few seconds later and, after a dozen more, they received no more RPG fire from that spot.

The attack lasted no more than twenty minutes and Company D took no casualties. When the first flare ship came on station at 0315 hours and dropped the first flares, the sudden light showed a large group of NVA moving up the north slope of 805, a direction the NVA had not attacked from before. The Cobras that had just arrived dove on the NVA attackers and, with a barrage of rockets, broke up the attack about 250 meters from the perimeter.

There was a pause lasting almost sixty minutes before the blast of a mechanical ambush signaled the start of another attack from the north in Delta Three's sector. The NVA were still trying to make their way up the slope. Delta Three opened up with all the firepower they could muster; thump guns, M-60's, M-16's and the powerful 90mm recoilless rifles, blasting out flechette rounds. A few minutes into that attack, US Marine Intruders roared overhead, dropping 500-pound bombs to the south and southeast of Hill 805. The attack never gained momentum, but the men of Delta Three tossed grenades down the slope every few minutes just to make sure.

The rest of the night was quiet, but the Cobras and flare ships remained on station, orbiting overhead until daylight. The log birds began to come in, bringing more ammo and other supplies. Tactical air strikes went in on the hills and in the valley around Hill 805. As the security patrols fanned out from the perimeter, they found two dead NVA on the south slope, where they recovered weapons, satchel charges and grenades. SP4 Richard Soubers remembers that when a patrol checked out the downed Huey on the LZ, they found that the NVA had taken the metal plate with the helicopters logo as a souvenir.

NVA forces began moving into attack positions around Hill 805 at about 2030 hours, as soon as it became fully dark. Movement and voices could be plainly heard about one hundred meters out from the perimeter. CPT Straub and LT Potter called in ARA and organized the release of flares from several flare ships orbiting overhead. The troops began throwing frags down the slope and M-79 gunners lobbed HE grenades on the hillsides south and southeast of the perimeter.

A movement sensor was activated north of the perimeter and shortly after that, a mechanical ambush went off to the west in front of Delta One. The pilot of a LOH saw flashlights in the darkness three hundred meters out from the east and northeast sectors of the perimeter. The LOH pilot called in artillery and 81mm mortars from Ripcord. One Cobra from a Red Team fired a barrage of 2.75-inch rockets east of the hill and got secondary explosions.

At about 2055 hours, CPT Straub received a message from LTC Lucas on Ripcord stating the TOC had monitored radio traffic in the clear between NVA units, coordinating movement for a mass attack on Hill 805. CPT Raymond Williams, the battalion S3 on Ripcord, remembers, *"It just so happened that one of the radios in the TOC was set to the same frequency the gooks were using that night, [and] a Kit Carson Scout was called over, and he listened to it. These guys were talking in the clear, no radio security at all, and the Scout said they were coordinating for a big attack later on that night against Hill 805." Ripcord* – page 272.

Just before midnight, a mechanical ambush went off about one hundred fifty meters west of Delta One's sector. Artillery and 81mm mortars fire was called in on the suspected enemy movement. Shortly after midnight, enemy movement was seen to the north and west of the perimeter. ARA, artillery and 81mm mortars were called in.

The main attack did not begin until 0230 hours on 17 July, nearly six hours after the first probes of Company D's positions were detected. A mechanical ambush and several trip flares went off in front of Delta One. The whole company opened fire and the NVA immediately responded with AK-47 fire and a shower of satchel charges at Delta One and Two's sectors.

It seemed that the fight had been taken out of the NVA while they struggled for six hours, enduring artillery fire and Cobra attacks, to get into position. They had been blasted repeatedly by ARA, artillery and 81mm mortars while they maneuvered to begin the attack. When the attack finally got started, they were greeted by over whelming fire from M-16's, M-60's, M-79's, 90mm's, 81's, 105's, 155's, ARA and Quad-50's. The fifth attack just melted away in the face of all the firepower. SGT Drew Gaster recalled that after five attacks in five nights, *"you was totally burned out. There was nothin' left in you…" Ripcord –* page 272.

The security patrols went out from the perimeter at first light and found nothing; the NVA had thoroughly cleaned up the battlefield. Later that morning and into the early afternoon, the usual Huey log birds came out with needed resupply. Company D then received orders to move to an LZ at YD 358190 about seven hundred meters away on the northwestern base of Hill 805.

The company began the work of tearing down the defenses they had built. As SGT Ray Blackman of Delta Three said, *"We busted our asses filling in our bunkers. We wanted to get off the hill before they changed their minds and made us stay another night."* Ripcord – page 272. The company piled everything that could not be carried away on top of the hill with Delta Two remaining behind to destroy the surplus. The other two platoons moved off the hill to wait for Delta Two at a spot a little northwest of the resupply LZ at YD360188.

A slick came in and hauled out the 90mm recoilless rifles and other valuable gear that could not be destroyed. Delta Two rigged the extra ammo and surplus equipment left on the hill with demolition charges and hurriedly moved off the hill just before the demo charges went off with a huge **B-O-O-O-M**.

Delta Two joined the rest of the company where it was waiting astride a trail just inside the jungle below the resupply LZ. LT Shipley wrote that what happened next *"scared us and made us mad, too. We were trying to sneak away with the woods full of NVA. Along came a helicopter, no warning, no radio message to us. It tried to land first on the LZ with the downed chopper, took fire, then came over to where we were trying not to be seen and lowered a ladder to us."* Ripcord – page 273.

The first man to try climbing down the flexible ladder lost his grip and fell from a height of about fifty feet. The man dazzled everyone by jumping to his feet before immediately collapsing with a broken foot. Several more heavily-laden men made it safely to the ground. LT Shipley explained that *"It turned out to be a communications team that had been dispatched to set up sensors around the hill. We told them they were crazy, to go ahead if they wanted to, but without us. They decided to stay with us."* Ripcord – page 273.

Company D held its position while CPT Straub called in a medevac for the injured team leader, a lieutenant. The medevac soon arrived and lowered a basket for the injured man. One of the escorting Cobras took AK-47 fire as it circled above the south slope of Hill 805. After a conference with his platoon leaders to map out the next move, Delta Three began to move through Delta One to take the point at about 1800 hours. Suddenly, there was a huge explosion back at the company CP. Everybody hit the dirt and put out fire. Straub, wounded in his left elbow, radioed Lucas and reported they were under attack; everyone thought an RPG had hit the CP.

There were several casualties. SP4 Soubers was knocked off his feet by the concussion but otherwise unhurt. He quickly shrugged off his rucksack and began to fire into the jungle with his M-16 on full automatic. Looking around, Soubers saw his friend SP4 David Beyl sitting on the ground. Beyl calmly told Soubers that he was hit and needed a medic. Rushing over to help his friend, Soubers saw he had a hole in his chest. Beyl had not zipped his flak jacket closed all the way because of the terrible heat (105° and 85% humidity on 17 July). Beyl quickly went into shock and then became unconscious. Frothy blood was bubbling from the hole in Beyl's chest and from his mouth. Soubers ripped his shirt up to make rough bandages for Beyl. Not knowing that Doc Grubidt, the platoon medic, had been severely wounded in both legs, Soubers began screaming for a medic, but the other medics were busy treating the severe casualties in the CP.

Soubers writes, *"As I looked up the trail, I saw two or three different colored smoke grenades filling the air with smoke. I continued to hold my torn shirt over Dave's wound and continued to yell for a medic until I was hoarse. . .."* Ripcord – page 273.

LT Selvaggi from Delta One ran back down the trail to Straub who yelled for him to find out what was going on. Everyone was completely confused; except for the first explosion, there had been no further fire. Selvaggi ran from man to man, asking what they had seen. Realizing they were not under attack, he yelled for everyone to cease firing.

Investigation revealed that the Kit Carson Scout called Kim had dropped a live grenade between his feet and the explosion had set off the three other grenades he carried on his web gear. Kim was killed instantly, blown to pieces. His assigned buddy, SP4 Wilfred Warner, was badly wounded in the chest.

Why the scout Kim did what he did will never be known. Some believed that Kim, feeling guilty about the many former comrades who had been killed during the five attacks on Hill 805, had tried to kill CPT Straub as well as himself. Most of the men felt that Kim had only wanted to kill himself, believing that Company D was going to be overrun while they moved to an LZ for pickup. They thought that Kim was so crazy with fear over what would happen to him as a *"chieu hoi"* (a defector) if he were captured that he pulled the pin with no thought of the men around him. It was well known that Kim, complaining of sore feet, had tried to get himself evacuated before Company D left the hill. Some of the men remembered Warner telling Kim that if he did not keep up, He (Warner) was going to leave Kim behind for the NVA. No one knows if fear of capture or of being left behind is what drove the scout to suicide.

The story of the scout's suicide passed quickly among the men. Several grunts from Delta Three went back up the trail to secure a little clearing for a medevac. Doc Fowler had finally gotten Dave Beyl bandaged, so Soubers and a few others carried him to the clearing which was too small for a dust off to land. When the Huey arrived overhead, the pilot did not want to hover while he lowered a basket because they were in enemy territory. Straub pleaded with him to stay, assuring the pilot they were not in contact. Beyl and another badly wounded man, peppered from head to foot with shrapnel, were loaded into the basket and winched up through the trees.

Shortly after that, another medevac arrived as well as a LOH, small enough to skip between the trees and land in the clearing. Between them, the three helicopters took out seven men of the nine who had been hit. CPT Straub and LT Potter elected to stay with the company until it was over. SP4 David Beyl and SP4 Wilfred Warner later died of their wounds in the hospital at Camp Evans.

CPT Straub ordered LT Selvaggi to get the body of the scout evacuated. Kim's body had been blown in several pieces, so they gathered the parts in a poncho and wrapped them up. They carried the poncho to the little clearing, leaking blood onto the trail along the way. Another LOH came in but hovered about three feet above the LZ, unwilling to land in case they took fire. Selvaggi tried to tell the pilot that the body was in pieces but he did not understand. As they slung the body aboard, the pilot started to move forward. When they let go the poncho came unwrapped and body parts slid across the deck of the little helicopter. The pilot took off without ever looking back at what they had placed into his LOH.

By the time the medical evacuations were completed, it was too late in the day to reach the extraction LZ before dark. Company D moved a few hundred meters down the trail and set up their NDP in an old NVA bunker complex at YD358190 that had once been seeded with a type of persistent CS gas. The gas crystals had weakened over time but they were still strong enough to make the NDP uncomfortable. They decided not to dig foxholes because of the noise they would make, so they set up claymores and trip flares and tried to get comfortable. SP4 Soubers noticed that the entire company was now about the size of a normal infantry platoon.

After a restless, though uneventful, night, Company D moved to an LZ at YD353192, about a klick northwest of Hill 805. The slicks came in and Delta One went out first then Delta Two. By then, those left on the LZ could see NVA running down from the top of Hill 805, probably trying to get into position to fire on the slicks as they climbed away from the LZ. The enemy had gotten within AK-47 range by the time the last few men of Delta Three were being flown out. SGT Raymond Blackman remembers, "*I think the group I was with went out on the second or third to last chopper. When it came in, we started running toward it from behind. As I passed the door gunner, the bird took three rounds, maybe more, in its' tail, very close to where I was. The pilot started to take off as I was climbing in the chopper. [SSGT]Jerry Bull and another guy pulled me in. Just as I turned to sit down, the bird, having reached treetop level, banked and dove to pick up speed. I started to slide out the door. I remember trying to grab ahold of something – anything. What a helpless feeling. As I slid out, Bull grabbed my rucksack frame and pulled me back in. He saved my life.*" Ripcord – page 276.

Soon after the slick carrying Blackman landed at Camp Evans, the last two helicopters came in with the remainder of Delta Three. The air crews shut down, got out of their slicks and started counting the bullet holes. Blackman was told that the last slick had to circle the LZ a few times before it could land due to the heavy enemy fire. The last slick load of men said they could see the NVA running up the hill after them when that last pilot braved the fire to pick them up.

That same day the whole of the 2-501 Infantry was lifted out of the Ripcord AO. The battalion was moved by truck down QL (highway) 1 from Camp Evans to Phu Bai where CPT Straub went to the 85th Evacuation Hospital to have his elbow treated. While Straub was lying on a gurney next to one of his machine gunners with infected shrapnel wounds on both hands, a doctor marched in and took one look at the gunner's swollen hands and demanded to know who had kept him in the field for so long. "*It was me, Doc,*" barked Straub. "*Send me the bill,*" too tired to explain the ordeal they had just gone through. Ripcord – page 277.

Later that day, while Straub was visiting the wounded from his company, BG Berry arrived to present the men with their Purple Hearts. Straub and Berry had worked together before at The Infantry School at Fort Benning where Straub had been Berry's speechwriter. The General was impressed with the way Straub had handled Company D on Hill 805 and tried to congratulate him. Straub, exhausted and in pain, became angry and told Berry he did not want to talk to him, but then the dam burst and Straub told Berry, "*You people forsake me and my soldiers, you put us out there and just left us. We were statistics to you people, nothing but numbers, but I lost a lot of good men on that hill.*" Ripcord – page 277.

Straub went on to tell Berry he was going to resign his commission because he did not want to be part of an army as poorly lead as the one in Vietnam. BG Berry did not lose his temper; he understood what Straub had been through. He told Straub to think it over before he resigned because the army needed leaders of his caliber to help put it back together after Vietnam was over.

Berry went out of his way to visit Straub again. Straub had cooled off by then and the two officers had a long discussion about US versus NVA tactics in the Ripcord AO. After their second talk, Straub finally realized that Berry had done the best he could for the 2-501 and the 2-506. Considering the limitations placed on Berry by USARV and MACV in Saigon, it was surprising that they had as much support as they did.

The grunts from Company D, minus those few who had re-enlisted to get out of the field, were sent to the in-country R&R Center at Eagle Beach, near Tan My, to recuperate from their ordeal on Hill 805. Most of the men had a good time swimming in the South China Sea and partying long into the night. SP4 Soubers was not one of them; he was much too depressed over the death of Dave Beyl on 18 July. Soubers wrote, "*I had lost the best friend I ever had. I suddenly felt all alone . . .Instead of joining the rest of the guys, I would spend much of my time sitting on the beach, just staring out at the South China Sea. I kept asking myself why, why did Dave have to die? Dave had so much to live for, if anyone deserved to live it was Dave. Why couldn't I have been the one to take that piece of shrapnel? I felt there must have been something I could have done after he was hit to help him survive. We had depended on each other to get through the year, so for the longest time I felt that I had somehow let him down. I would take years before I would be able to put this feeling of guilt behind me, but the pain of his death will stay with me the rest of my life . . .*" Ripcord – page 278.

Chapter 16
RIPCORD UNDER SIEGE
PART TWO

"We've now reached a point when we must question the continued use of Ripcord. Is it worth the casualties for the purpose it is serving? If we decide no, how do we get out of Ripcord? If we vacate Ripcord, then what do we do?" Brigadier General Sidney B. Berry in a letter to his wife, 22 July 1970. *Hell On A Hill Top* – page 120.

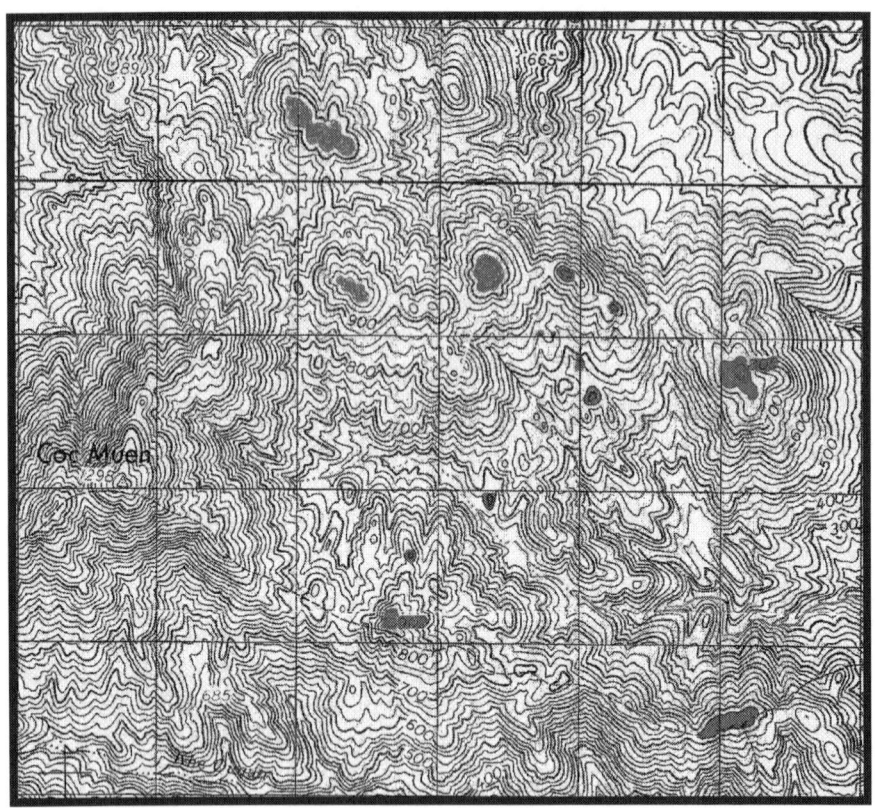

Color-enhanced detail from Map Sheet 6441–4, Series L-7014, A Luoi District of Thua Thien Province showing Firebase Ripcord outlined in blue. Known NVA mortar and 12.7mm machine gun firing positions shown outlined in red. Original map from author's collection. Color-enhanced map ©2017.

The NVA build-up continued into mid-July with the number of mortar rounds falling on Ripcord steadily increasing. The use of large caliber machine guns against incoming resupply helicopters also increased. On 12 July, a CH-47 coming into Ripcord took fire from a 12.7mm gun in position less than a thousand meters southeast of the base near YD 351188. The 81mm mortar platoon quickly dropped rounds onto the site and the gun grew silent. Later that same morning, three mortar rounds came in, two of which were CS gas rounds.

To reduce the amount of incoming fire coming from that area, A/2-506 and D/2-501 (OPCON to the 506th Infantry) moved onto hill 805 about two-thousand meters southeast of Ripcord. Since there was not room for both companies to occupy the small hilltop, Company A dug in on an LZ two hundred meters west of the hill while Company D occupied the rocky summit itself. Both companies set out trip flares, claymore mines and set up mechanical ambushes, while the FO's registered pre-planned artillery fires against the attack they all knew would come that night.

On Ripcord that night, starting at about 2222 hours, the 105's, 155's and 81's fired hundreds of rounds in support of A/2-506 and D/2-501 under attack on Hill 805. The 81mm mortar platoon alone fired a total of five hundred sixty-eight rounds that night.

On the morning of 13 July, the firebase came under fire from at least two AK-47's from only one hundred fifty to two hundred meters east of the perimeter near YD 346194. Again, the 81mm mortars were called on to silence the fire. Just after noon, snipers peppered away at the base, this time from the south. Both 81 and 105mm direct fire was used against the snipers. In just six hours, the 81's fired six hundred twenty-five HE rounds against various targets around the base.

Later that afternoon, a CH-47 took heavy fire from the vicinity of YD 354184 and YD 357186. Half an hour later, a Huey Log bird took fire from these same locations. Both helicopters completed their missions.

The enemy was so close to the firebase that CPT Rich's artillery battery fired frequent Charge One missions. This meant only one of the seven powder bags (charges) that came packed in the shell canister were used. The unused powder charges were thrown in a pit dug for that purpose. When the build-up of excess charges became dangerous, a work party would destroy them by burning them in a 'burn pit.'

Again, that night, D/2-501 came under attack on Hill 805. The artillery and mortar batteries on Ripcord, as well as the batteries on O'Reilly and Rakkasan, fired all night in support of Company D. In the twenty-four hours between noon on 13 July and noon on 14 July, one thousand forty-six 81mm HE rounds were fired from Ripcord against NVA mortars and machine guns as well as in support of D/2-501 on Hill 805.

Early on the morning of 14 July, Ripcord began receiving 75mm recoilless rifle rounds. Most of the rounds exploded in the wire and those that hit the firebase itself caused no casualties. Later that morning, a medevac was shot down on Ripcord and late that afternoon, Huey log birds began taking fire from a 12.7mm gun located near YD 357183. This gun was in the valley southwest of Hill 805, only fifteen hundred meters from Ripcord. The guns' location gave the gunners a straight shot up the gradually sloping valley at the helicopters as they approached Ripcord. Direct fire from the 105's was brought against the gun. Finally, around 1715 Hours, the 105's scored a direct hit on the 12.7mm position causing secondary explosions, destroying the gun.

Late on the night of 14 July and into the morning of 15 July, D/2-501 was attacked on Hill 805. The artillery and mortar batteries on Ripcord fired all night during the attack. Between 1200 hours on 14 July and 0600 hours on 15 July, the 81's blasted out nearly one thousand four hundred HE rounds at targets around Ripcord and in direct support of D Company.

At about 1800 hours on 15 July, another heavy machine gun began firing on the helicopters approaching Ripcord. This gun was located only about three hundred meters to the south of the base. Ripcord did not receive any incoming mortar rounds during the day on 15 July but D/2-501 received nearly forty 82mm rounds on Hill 805. The NVA gunners seemed to have switched their fire to Hill 805 as Company D was a definite obstacle to their attempts to surround and destroy FSB Ripcord.

About three hours after midnight on 16 July, Hill 805 came under heavy attack and the artillery batteries on Ripcord fired until daylight in support of the battered Company D. The mortars and 105's had fired thousands of rounds and the build-up of un-fired powder charges reached a hazardous level.

A burn party was organized to get rid of the dangerous charges. During the burn, the high winds constantly blowing across Ripcord blew sparks from the burn pit into the ready ammunition in the 105mm gun positions. A big explosion followed, which blasted the XO (executive officer or second-in-command) for B/2-319, 1LT Thomas Brennan, clear across the battery area, badly burning him. He was replaced by his West Point classmate, 2LT Sheldon Wintermute, who was flown out from Camp Evans where he had been recovering from wounds received while serving as an artillery FO with the 1-506 Infantry.

Once again during the night of 16 July and the early morning of 17 July, D/2-501 was attacked in their position on Hill 805. Company D was ready and waiting for this assault on their rocky hilltop. Up on the firebase, a Kit Carson Scout assigned to B/2-506 had intercepted NVA radio traffic describing plans for an all-out attack on Hill 805. The attack began at 2124 hours and once again the artillery and mortars on Ripcord fired hundreds of rounds in support of D Company and were instrumental in breaking up the attack. The 81's alone fired over eight hundred rounds at the enemy forces around Hill 805.

Shortly after 0700 hours on 17 July, as the artillery gunners moved around cleaning up the debris left after firing all night, FSB Ripcord received more than a dozen 82mm mortar rounds. The NVA gunners had shifted their attention back to Ripcord. These rounds all fell short of their intended target and caused no damage or casualties. The fire came from two mortar tubes positioned on a ridge near YD 342188, only about six hundred meters south of the base.

At about 0737 hours, two larger than normal explosions occurred, one outside the wire and one inside. While checking the area for damage, a trooper found the oversized, badly twisted tailfin from a 120mm mortar round. This added a whole new dimension to the siege and, according to the army photographer Chris Jensen, *"That got everybody's attention big time. That ratched [sic] everything up a little." Ripcord* – page 290.

Manufactured in Russia and China, the M-43 120mm mortar was the most powerful mortar in Hanoi's inventory of weapons. The tube, base plate and bipod weighed over six hundred pounds and each projectile weighed in at thirty-four pounds. It took a crew of six to operate it and a well-drilled crew could put out ten to fifteen rounds per minute. The weapons sustained rate of fire was closer to six rounds per minute and it had a maximum range of fifty-seven hundred meters, or about three and a half miles. Because of the weapons size, it was not normally used in such rugged terrain as that found around Ripcord. The NVA's use of the big weapon sent a clear signal to Ripcord's defenders that the enemy fully intended to destroy the base.

As the suspected mortar firing positions were identified, air strikes were called in and the 81's, 105's and 155's put out a heavy counterbattery fire. At about 0822 hours, two more 120mm rounds impacted on Ripcord and eighteen minutes later, two more hit the hilltop. The last two 120mm projectiles exploded in the 155mm battery manned by gunners from Battery B/2-11 Field Artillery, lightly wounding two crewmen. Chris Jensen decided to get off the hill while he still could and, as he climbed onto a Huey, he was given a big piece of 120mm mortar shrapnel with orders to deliver it to a division intelligence officer who would meet him on the LZ at Camp Eagle. When Jensen reported to the Camp Eagle PIO office, he was given a reprimand for having taken his team out to Ripcord without orders.

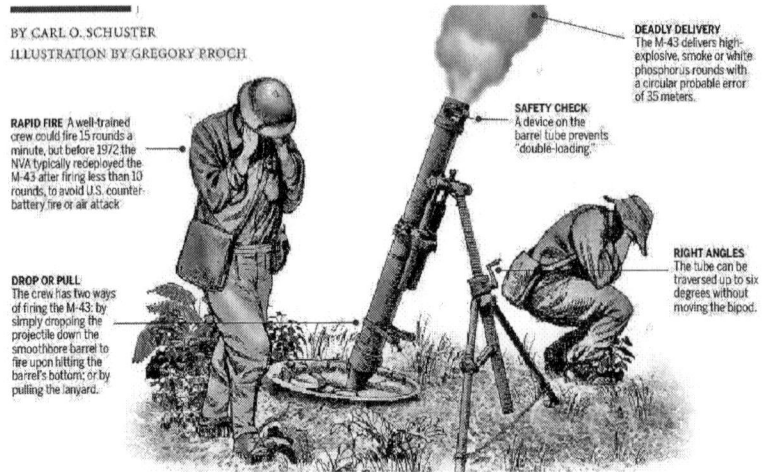

The firebase came under heavy bombardment at about 1230 hours when sixteen 60mm mortar rounds and twelve 120mm shells came in all at once, impacting on top of the firebase hill. CPT Rich was supervising a fire mission with B/2-319 FA when some of the 120's exploded inside the artillery positions. Eight gunners were wounded, plus CPT Rich, who took several shrapnel hits in his legs, slightly fracturing one leg. The gunners kept firing even as the big mortar rounds exploded in their position. 2LT Wintermute, the newly-arrived XO of the battery, remembers what he saw. *"The men never left their guns. I saw one round impact very close to one of the howitzers, literally blowing a crewman out of the position. He did a black flip . . . but immediately popped back into the position, loaded the howitzer, and continued firing. They were all like that. They did an absolutely fantastic job. For all the stuff you read about bad morale in Vietnam, quite frankly, I never saw it."* Ripcord – pages 290-291. All eight of the wounded artillery crewman went out on a medevac.

    The big mortars were now firing on Ripcord from positions to the northwest, southwest and south, one of them firing from the back side of Coc Muen mountain near YD 305178. Tactical air strikes were called in and one strike caused secondary explosions at a mortar firing from near YD 303211, down in a river valley some forty-five hundred meters northwest of Ripcord. The resulting fires cooked off rounds for over an hour

After receiving his seventh wound, a serious shrapnel hit to his groin area, CPT Rich was ordered off Ripcord by LTC William Walker, CO of the 319th Field Artillery. CPT Phillip Michaud, CO of Battery A/2-319 on FSB Rakkasan was ordered to Ripcord to take command of Rich's battery. Michaud arrived on Ripcord in a LOH and went directly to the 105's for a hasty briefing from CPT Rich. Just as they left Rich's small bunker to check the guns, a 120mm shell scored a direct hit on the bunker, destroying it. After this last close call CPT Rich, by then functioning solely on adrenaline, left Ripcord aboard LTC Walker's Huey.

CPT Gordon Baxendale, CO of the 155's was also evacuated on 17 July so that a piece of shrapnel stuck in a bone in his neck could be removed. Command of the battery (A/2-11 FA) fell to 1LT J. Robert Kalsu. Described as fearing *"absolutely nothing"* by CPT Michaud, Kalsu had played a season with pro football's Buffalo Bills and was their Rookie of the Year in 1969. Kalsu had an ROTC commission and was called to active duty in time to serve on Ripcord.

Ripcord was also receiving increasing amounts of small arms sniper fire along with the mortar and recoilless rifle fire. CPT Michaud was hit by sniper fire only a few hours after taking over from CPT Rich. The bullet, a ricochet, hit him in the thigh and went in sideways, penetrating all the way to the femur. The medics wanted to evacuate Michaud so the bullet could be removed surgically, but he refused, remaining on Ripcord until the wound became infected, turning his leg an alarming black.

Even with all the mortar rounds and sniper fire, casualties on the firebase were very few, with only a few men having been killed. That all changed on 18 July when the battle became a siege in fact. COL Harrison, 3rd Brigade CO, flew onto Ripcord during a lull in the shelling late that morning. The colonel was standing at the entrance to a bunker near the TOC, leaning against a stack of dirt-filled ammo crates that protected the entryway to the bunker, talking with a sergeant. A 120mm round hit at the base of the ammo crates and blew Harrison and the sergeant backwards into the bunker. The sergeant had to be evacuated with blood leaking from both ears and a sniper, SP4 William Rollason, from E/2-501 who was standing nearby was killed instantly. Six other men were wounded and COL Harrison was nearly deaf for hours afterward.

After Harrison left, several Chinooks delivered supplies to the logistics LZ on the southeast side of the base where they were protected by the top of the hill from a 12.7mm that had been firing from down in the valley to the southwest. One of the CH-47's, piloted by WO1 Robert Barrocliff from A/159th Aviation out of Phu Bai, arrived over the firebase at about 1330 hours, carrying a sling load of 105 ammo. Barrocliff's Chinook was diverted from the logistics LZ to the ammo supply point for the 105 battery, another fifty feet from the logistics LZ. The pathfinders controlling the flights had vigorously objected to the diversion because the big Chinook hovering over the ammo supply point would then be open to fire from the machine gun in the valley below the firebase. LTC Lucas, in his role as King of the Hill, had over ruled the pathfinders. Lucas wanted to protect the troops who would have had to carry the big ammo canisters up the hill from the log pad to the ammo storage area, a dangerous job because of the incoming mortar fire. Because Chinook pilots were usually able to quickly position and drop their loads, Lucas took the chance that the load could be delivered before the enemy had time to fire on the helicopter. The Chinooks did not have radio communications with the firebase and were guided to their drop-off points by smoke grenades.

WO1 Barrocliff was just lowering the helicopter into a thirty-foot hover when the door gunner on the left side of the aircraft behind the pilot, SP4 Terry Stanger, saw three men wearing strange uniforms and odd-looking helmets. They were down in the brush at the base of the hill and pointing some type of weapon at the Chinook. The gunner swung his M-60 toward the group and, as regulations required, asked his pilot for permission to open fire. Stanger remembers that, *"We had been informed that there were friendlies outside the wire. I could tell those three weren't Americans, but I thought they might be ARVN's."* Stanger's delay in opening fire (he had been in-country only two weeks) proved fatal. *Ripcord* – page 294.

The NVA gun crew opened fire at that moment. 1LT Fred Edwards, the leader of the engineer platoon on Ripcord, was under the hovering Chinook and, along with several other men, was guiding the net holding the artillery ammo into the trench in front of the ammo bunker when he saw the 12.7mm bullets strike the CH-47.

LT Edwards later wrote, *"If you have ever been near a hovering helicopter, you know that the noise is deafening. It's so deafening, in fact, that there was absolutely no sound as several bullet holes spontaneously appeared in the side of the Chinook. It was almost surreal—one second it was a perfectly routine resupply mission, the next, there were these big bullet holes two to three inches wide. I was dumbfounded for a second before it registered that the Chinook had taken direct hits from a .51 cal."* *Ripcord* – page 294.

When the 12.7mm opened fire on Chinook tail number 68-15810 the flight engineer, SP4 Michael Walker, was lying on his belly looking through the 'hook hole' in the center of the helicopter's deck. He was ready to push the button that would release the sling load once it was positioned correctly on the ground. 810's crew chief, PFC Charles Holmen, was on the M-60 at the right door, directly across from Stanger.

The bullets passed completely through the helicopter and started a fire in the engine on Holmen's side of the ship but, as Holmen said later, the crew did not at first know they were in trouble. Holmen saw a pathfinder running toward them waving his arms and pointing, so he leaned out the door to check the side of the helicopter. He saw that the right engine was on fire and as he leaned back inside the fuselage, he saw that the cabin had filled with thick smoke. Holmen yelled into his radio mic that they were on fire just as the auxiliary fuel tank ignited. Sp4 Walker quickly released the sling load of ammo so that the pilot could move away from the dangerous cargo before he crash-landed the flaming helicopter. Burned by the quickly spreading fire, Walker shoved past Holmen and climbing through the crew chief's door, jumped to the ground from the still-hovering helicopter.

The intense heat melted SP4 Stanger's helmet visor as he scrambled into the cockpit, yelling that they were on fire. WO1 Barrocliff and the co-pilot, CPT Edwin Grove, had just realized that something was wrong when Stanger rushed into the cockpit. The cockpit filled with smoke as the Chinook lurched forward, knocking Stanger down and into the forward windshield. The gunner was tangled up with the controls and Barrocliff was not able to guide the crippled aircraft away from the load of ammo they had just dropped. He had no choice but to drop the ship straight down where they were and hope that they could all escape before the main fuel tanks blew.

Before he could do that, the big helicopter suddenly tilted to the right and Stanger toppled onto CPT Grove, who managed to pull the emergency door release for his door. The whole door, plus Stanger, fell out of the Chinook. Stanger remembers his sudden fall from the helicopter: *"It was just boom, out goes the door with me in tow. I fell about fifty to a hundred feet down the mountain and landed on some empty ammo crates that had been thrown down the side of the mountain as trash. I hit pretty hard. The visor on my helmet slammed into the bridge of my nose, and I was half-blind for all the blood in my eyes. . . when I stood up, my flak vest had ammo crate lids hanging all over it. The nails had embedded themselves in the metal plate in the vest. . . All I could think of was my instructors at helicopter school who told us to get the hell away from a chopper's [rotor] blades when you crashed. I took off downhill. . . until I thought I was clear of the blades. When I looked back up, I saw that the aircraft had come to rest on its side. The rotors had flayed themselves off against the ground. I tore my helmet off. . . and started climbing back up the mountain as fast as I could. . ."* *Ripcord* – page 296.

The men from the artillery battery had barely survived the crash of the Chinook. They watched as the back of the helicopter caught on fire and then dove for cover as the rear wheels crashed straight down onto the roof of the ammo bunker. The front wheels came to rest in the trench in front of this bunker and then the helicopter rolled to the right onto its side. The twin sixty-foot-wide rotor disks, still turning at operating speed, beat themselves to pieces against the ground, the chunks slicing through the air like shrapnel and destroying everything in their path.

Pilot WO1 Barrocliff and the co-pilot, CPT Groves, waited for the rotors to destroy themselves against the ground then managed to climb out of the aircraft through Grove's emergency exit door. The crew chief, PFC Holmen, got out through the door gunners window, now facing up. As SP4 Stanger joined them, they ran to help SP4 Walker who had been hit and knocked face down by the Chinook as it rolled onto its right side. Walker was found lying on his stomach at the edge of the trench, pinned to the ground by the crew chiefs window frame and the main fuel tank lying across the back of his thighs. The rear section of the aircraft, lying on top of the ammo bunker, was blazing furiously. The fire was spreading quickly along the length of the fuselage toward Walker. The skin of the helicopter, made from an alloy of magnesium and aluminum, burned with an intensity rivaling the sun, nearly impossible to extinguish.

Men from the artillery battery and the near-by TOC ran to help and began building a sandbag wall between Walker and the fire, trying to shield him from the flames. Barrocliff pulled off Walker's flight helmet as soldiers tried to pull him free. Others frantically dug at the rock-hard soil around his legs with shovels. Stanger remembers that, *"Walker was begging us to help him. We were beside ourselves."* Ripcord – page 297.

Crew Chief Holmen crawled back inside the flaming aircraft to find the escape ax. Using this ax, Holmen split the skin of the fuselage around Walker's thighs, but he was still pinned down by the metal frame of the door. Despite repeated blows, the ax only bounced off the frame. During these frantic attempts to free Walker, the NVA began to drop mortar rounds around the fallen Chinook.

CPT Michaud, CO of the endangered 105mm howitzer battery, did what he could to help the trapped crewman. *"I remember jumping into the trench and crawling under the helicopter—there was just enough clearance under the nose—to see if there was any way I could get that crewman's legs loose from underneath. I thought if I clawed enough dirt away, he could pull himself free, but I got soaked with boiling hydraulic fluid that was pouring out of the helicopter, and quickly gave up that attempt. . ."* Ripcord – page 297.

The pathfinders brought up two chemical fire extinguishers and emptied them trying to keep the flames away from Walker as others frantically attempted to free him. The fire extinguishers temporarily put out the fires closest to Walker, but they erupted into flames again when the extinguishers were emptied. The machine gun ammo aboard the aircraft began to cook off as heat from the growing blaze finally caused everyone to run for their lives. The rescuers were forced to leave Walker behind, still pinned to the ground by the metal door frame.

Finding safety, CPT Michaud remembers looking back at Walker. *"All we could do was watch as he cooked inside his flame-retardant Nomex flight suit. You could see the steam coming out of his flight suit. It was the most terrible thing I've ever witnessed in my life. I even considered pulling my .45 and just ending it for him, but I couldn't do it. He was finally consumed by the flames. . ."* Ripcord – page 298.

The situation became desperate as the heat began to cook off the ammunition in the trench under the helicopter. Burning JP4 began to run in a stream into the artillery positions and chunks of flaming metal rained down. 105 shells, blown into the air by explosions, detonated when they hit the ground. Many of the troops, driven out of their bunkers around the artillery battery, found shelter in the TOC. The big bunker trembled and shook but held together as artillery shells, blown out of the ammo dump, exploded when they hit the roof.

The wooden ammo crates filled with sand around the communications bunker caught fire and the flames spread to the battalion aid station right next door. Captain/Doctor Harris and his medics barely escaped from the aid station before it burst into flames, finally finding shelter in the TOC. There was a large ammo dump dug into the slope of the hill just above the aid station. When those shells detonated, the aid station was destroyed with nothing remaining but a huge crater.

White phosphorous shells were stored in the ammo dump and when they cooked off, the WP splattered down all over the firebase, igniting more fires. Tear gas from exploding CS shells rolled in choking clouds over the southeast section of the firebase and into bunkers, including the TOC, where men were sheltering. Many of the troops did not have their gas masks with them and survived by breathing through water-soaked cloth held over their nose and mouth.

It took over three hours for all the ammunition stored in the ammo supply point to burn itself out. There had been more than two thousand 105mm shells and their powder charges stored there. The huge explosions literally lifted men and equipment off the ground and slammed them back down, leaving the troops bruised and shaken. One soldier, asleep in his bunker on top of the hill, ran in terror downhill when the base began exploding around him. His uniform was ripped off him as he struggled down the slope through the concertina wire barriers. Naked except for his boots, he finally reached the jungle at the base of the hill. Moving on foot around to the northern slope, he made his way uphill to the base while dodging grenades thrown at him by GI's who thought he was an NVA. When these troops, men from B/2-506, realized he was an American, they retrieved him from the wire and took him to the medics for treatment of his many cuts and scrapes.

COL Harrison orbited over the firebase in his C and C bird in radio contact with LTC Lucas. Ripcord was covered by a haze of smoke and CS tear gas while a column of black smoke rose straight up from the burning Chinook. Lucas and Harrison called in protective artillery fire from firebases Barbara, Rakkasan and O'Reilly to fall in a ring around Ripcord. As the tear gas blew away and it became safer to land, COL Harrison dispatched Huey's carrying firefighting equipment to the base, evacuating wounded when they left.

The colonel was amazed to learn that no one had been killed or even seriously wounded by the tons of exploding ordnance. The 105 battery had been destroyed, taking away Ripcord's ability to quickly respond to calls for artillery support from infantry units in contact. The 155 battery was undamaged, but its rate of fire and adjustment were too slow to give artillery support to units in the field. COL Harrison called BG Berry, also aloft in his command helicopter, and asked for FSB Gladiator to be reopened so that a 105 battery could be put in place to support ground troops operating in the Ripcord AO. Harrison also asked Berry for an EOD unit to be attached to 3rd Brigade's recon platoon to check the hill for booby traps before the engineers and artillery arrived to open the base. Berry agreed and gave Harrison operation control of the 1-501 Infantry to provide security for Gladiator.

FSB Gladiator, located at YD 416211 on Hill 316, was about eight klicks northeast of Ripcord and had not been in use for several months. After the hill had been secured by an infantry company from 1-506, B Battery 2-320 Field Artillery manning 105mm howitzers landed on the hill. It took only forty minutes from the time the first gun was put in place for the battery to be ready to fire. After firing a few registration rounds, the guns began firing at known targets around Ripcord, two hundred rounds per gun, the battery's entire basic load of ammo. The guns fired all night, putting out more than four hundred rounds per gun, all aimed at known NVA mortar and 12.7mm positions on the hills and ridges around Ripcord. Chinook's flew twenty-nine resupply sorties to keep the guns firing.

On Ripcord, the fires had finally been brought under control and damage assessment began. All six 105mm guns from Battery B 2-319 had been destroyed. Nothing remained of three of the guns but the tubes, their wheels and frames burned away. It had not been decided by division if replacement guns would be flown in, so CPT Michaud and 2LT Wintermute acted as artillery spotters on the perimeter and the gun crews were put into infantry positions or used as replacements for wounded gunners from the 155's of Battery A 2-11 Field Artillery.

While the troops were trying to clear up some of the wreckage and rebuild their positions, the NVA continued to drop in mortar rounds. At about 1800 hours on 18 July, a twenty-round barrage of 120mm fire came in, wounding several men and killing PFC Burke Miller, a 155 gunner. Some of the hot 105mm shells that had been scattered all over the base by explosions continued to randomly cook off, causing havoc with the work crews. 82mm CS gas rounds also came in among the 120mm HE shells. The men suffered until the gas cleared; most of their equipment, including their gas masks, had burned. The gas caused the men to vomit uncontrollably while their noses and eyes overflowed with mucus.

Because of the damage Ripcord had suffered, COL Harrison and LTC Lucas expected the NVA to launch a ground attack against the firebase that night. Lucas and Harrison arranged for and coordinated supporting fire from Firebases Gladiator, Barbara, Rakkasan and O'Reilly. Marine A6 Intruder fighter/bombers blasted the hills around Ripcord all night. Chinooks with all-volunteer crews made run after run carrying ammo borrowed from other firebases for use on Ripcord. The constant counter battery fire from the 155's and 81's on Ripcord suppressed most but not all the fire from NVA mortars in the hills around the beleaguered base. The ground attack, perhaps because of the tremendous amount of out-going fire from Ripcord and the other firebases, did not materialize.

BG Berry paid a visit to Ripcord on 19 July, By then, landing a helicopter at one of the four LZ's on Ripcord was a dangerous affair. All helicopter flights into and out of Ripcord were controlled by the pathfinders, known as Black Hats (they wore black baseball caps), who did not communicate with pilots of an approaching Huey or Chinook by radio, assuming the NVA were monitoring the radio frequencies in use on Ripcord. Berry's Huey pilot, 1LT John Fox, remembers that at the last possible second, a Black Hat would jump out of his bunker and indicate which landing pad to use. Once on the ground, all passengers exited the aircraft very quickly and the aircraft took off immediately because there was probably an incoming mortar shell aimed at that LZ.

The situation on Ripcord was a nightmare come to life for the men of the 287th Explosive Ordnance Disposal Team, sent out from USARV headquarters at Phu Bai. The three-man team was completely unprepared for what they found on Ripcord. The whole hill was strewn with damaged and unexploded ordnance: hand grenades, 40mm shells in armed condition, HE rounds, WP rounds and small 'bomblets' from an artillery shell called a 'firecracker' that were designed to spring six feet into the air before exploding when stepped on. Many of the artillery rounds were still too hot to handle without gloves and were extremely sensitive to jostling. Others were cracked open by the heat with their powder leaking out.

There were shell craters everywhere, so the team began stacking the damaged ordnance in the nearest crater before blowing them up with C4. They used everything they had brought with them so more C4 had to be flown out from Camp Evans. When the C4 ran out, they used blocks of TNT until more C4 could be rounded up and sent out. There was so much damaged ordnance to be destroyed that the team, working until dark, could not finish the job on the 19th and were flown back to Phu Bai for the night.

All the cleanup and demolition work was carried out under a near-constant rain of mortar rounds. The EOD teams used the many shell craters scattered everywhere as cover during the barrages. There was sniper fire coming in and the team could sometimes hear bullets zipping past their heads. One of the EOD team was lightly wounded by mortar fragments on three different occasions.

The 326th Engineer Battalion at Camp Eagle sent out an M450 'mini' bulldozer for use in clearing the debris from the 105 battery area. The 'dozer crew drew heavy enemy fire, so the three operators took turns using the machine to shove the destroyed guns and unexploded shells over the side of the hill to make room for replacement guns. Each of the three operators later received the Silver Star, including one engineer who refused to leave his post on the 'dozer even though NVA sniper bullets ricocheted off the machine all around him.

The 2-320 Field Artillery sent volunteer working parties out to Ripcord to help with the cleanup. During the day, they helped clear debris, carried ammo to the infantry positions on the perimeter or humped supplies off the LZ's as they came in on the log birds. There were snipers firing from among the boulders on the ridges around Ripcord and the men of the working parties fired back when they spotted smoke or muzzle flashes.

After dark, they helped man the 155's or formed chains to pass mortar rounds to the 81's that fired counterbattery missions all night. The NVA would drop in a mortar salvo every twenty minutes or so and the men dove for cover in the nearest shell hole or bunker.

One night, one of the grunts from B/2-506 caught a Kit Carson Scout shining a flashlight out into the wire and calling out in Vietnamese. Many of the scouts had been caught in the act of yelling to the enemy on the other side of the wire. Since no one knew if they were trying to surrender or pass information to the NVA, LTC Lucas had them all rounded up and confined to a bunker under guard.

During the cleanup, casualties continued to mount. Two members of LTC Lucas' staff were badly wounded on 19 July by a 120mm mortar round that came in as the officers were gathering for the evening staff briefing. The NVA had observed this nightly gathering and habitually dropped one or two rounds on the TOC and this time they scored. On 20 July, two members of LT Edwards engineer platoon were killed. SP4 Durl Calhoun and SP4 Dennis Fisher were caught in the open by a 120mm barrage while clearing debris on top of the hill. Calhoun, a much-admired veteran of the original combat assault onto Ripcord on 1 April, had just extended his tour to stay with the platoon while they were on Ripcord.

■ ■ ■

Life under the continuous rain of mortar shells and sniper fire began to take its toll and morale suffered. The troops could not understand why the brass at division did not either reinforce them or pull them out. COL George S. Patton III, the son of WW II General George S. Patton, Jr., had a motto for his 11th Armored Cavalry 'Black Horse' Regiment: *Find the bastards, then pile on.* The troops of the 3rd Brigade, 101st Airborne Division had found the enemy and they could not understand why they were not 'piling on.' They became numb to the danger; some grunts casually going about their duties as if there were no mortar fire while at all while others refused to leave their bunkers, not even for chow.

SSGT Thomas Rubsam of Bravo One remembers that *"It was terrible picking people for the working parties that had to go topside. You could hardly look 'em in the face. We spaced it out as reasonably as we could so a guy didn't have to go up top every day."* Ripcord – page 310.

The troops were emotionally and physically exhausted, not only from the hard work under the hot sun and the rain of mortar fire but from lack of sleep. Because of the heavy casualties, the infantry defensive positions around the perimeter were now manned by only two men each. This meant two hours on duty and two hours off all night long which quickly wore a man down. Then it was up at daylight the next day to begin all over again. Troops would abandon their work assignments when a mortar barrage came in to take shelter in a bunker, then refuse to come out when the attack ended.

Replacement guns for the destroyed 105 battery were not flown at as expected. Commanders at brigade and division level decided there was too great a chance that the NVA would shoot down a Chinook as it hovered while putting a new 105 howitzer in place. It was not unusual for a CH-47 on a resupply mission to leave Ripcord with shrapnel or bullet damage even though they hardly slowed down as they unhooked the sling loads of cargo. Engineer lieutenant Fred Edwards' diary entry on 21 July speaks volumes. *"We're taking 75-80 rounds a day and they're deadly accurate. Medevacs are constantly in and out with the wounded. . .A ground attack is sure to follow as the whole hill is all but wiped out and no supplies can get in. Really feel low. . ."* Ripcord – page 311.

The casualties kept piling up and Edwards himself was injured when a direct hit caved in a corner of the bunker he was sheltering in. The engineer platoon sergeant, SSGT Ronald Henn was hit by fragments from an exploding CS gas shell and had to be evacuated. Edwards remained on the hill.

Sniper fire was a constant danger and on 21 July, Ripcord received fire from the south side of the base. SP4 Al Riddle from Bravo Three returned the fire with an M2 .50 caliber machine gun but the NVA put the gun out of action very quickly with a single 82mm mortar round dropped just behind the gun. PFC 'Chip' Collins wrote, "*Unfortunately, there were five or six guys from the platoon clusterfucked around Al, seeing if they could help.*" Collins was one of several men from Bravo Three who ran to help the wounded and found the scene to be a horrible sight. "*All I saw was a mass of bodies, and we began pulling them out of the position.*" PFC Francis Maune had been killed instantly and five more men were wounded. PFC Larry McDowell was evacuated but died later of his wounds. Riddle, the man on the gun, was at the bottom of the pile of bodies, wounded and in shock. As he was carried to cover, Riddle kept saying "*Those fuckin' gooks. . .Those fuckin' gooks.*" *Ripcord* – page 312.

Sp4 Roberto Flores was killed by a heavy salvo of 82mm rounds dropped into the 155 battery where Flores was part of a working party. Flores, a close friend of Tom Rubsam, had a wife and new-born baby waiting for him back in Texas. The NVA gunners had waited until they saw a work party begin moving a sling load of 155 ammo, hoping to catch a group of men in the open. They did; the salvo wounded seven men and killed SP4 David Johnson of A/2-11 Field Artillery as well as Flores.

That barrage also killed 1LT Bob Kalsu, the tough, popular pro-football player who was serving as acting commander of the 155 battery. Kalsu was standing at the top of the steps leading down into his FDC, talking with Black Hat Nick Fotias and trying to get a breath of fresh air after spending the day in the sweltering FDC bunker. Kalsu was telling Fotias that his wife was due to give birth to their second child that day when an 82mm round exploded just five feet from the two men. Both were blown down the steps, Kalsu landing on top of Fotias. Kalsu was killed instantly, a piece of mortar fragment entering his head just above his left eye.

The deaths of LT Kalsu and SP4 Johnson was a shock to everyone on Ripcord. Kalsu was the only pro athlete killed during the Vietnam War. Kalsu and Johnson, both big, strong men had a contest going despite their difference in rank. Nearly every day, the two men competed to see who could hump the most ninety-seven pound 155 rounds up the hill from the ammo supply point. Most artillerymen could carry only two rounds, one on each shoulder. Johnson and Kalsu, however, carried three per trip, a total of nearly three hundred pounds. They made a game out of the hard work, just to see who would quit first.

1LT Edwards felt himself descending into a deep depression. He wrote, *"Every time a chopper approached, the entire hill headed for cover because we knew incoming was on the way. Cobras would be circling and artillery fire smashing into the adjacent hills, but nothing could stop the incoming. We felt helpless, at the mercy of the enemy. Sustained incoming has to be one of the worst tortures ever inflicted on a soldier. There is an element of humiliation involved, too—you just have to sit and take it." Ripcord* – page 313.

As more and more men were killed and wounded by an invisible enemy who, day after day, defied the US forces supposedly overwhelming fire power, the men felt helpless, humiliated and, above all, very angry.

Edwards at last gave in and succumbed to the resignation and numbness of combat fatigue as he wrote *"I can remember saying to myself, I'm gonna die on this damn hill. It was an awful, apathetic feeling. Finally, near the end, the passivity bordered on indifference to death. Maybe there was no other way to cope with what was happening day in, day out, more incoming every day, almost constant, more body bags stacking up to be evacuated. Who's next? Who cares? Here it comes again. . ."* Ripcord – page 314.

Chapter 17
INTO THE STORM

"There are plenty of NVA in those hills. More of them are moving in from North Vietnam and Laos. . .the mountains seem loaded with 12.7mm AA machine guns. . .The NVA want very badly to inflict a major defeat on US forces." BG Sidney B. Berry in a letter to his wife, July 22, 1970. *Hell On A Hill Top*, page 131.

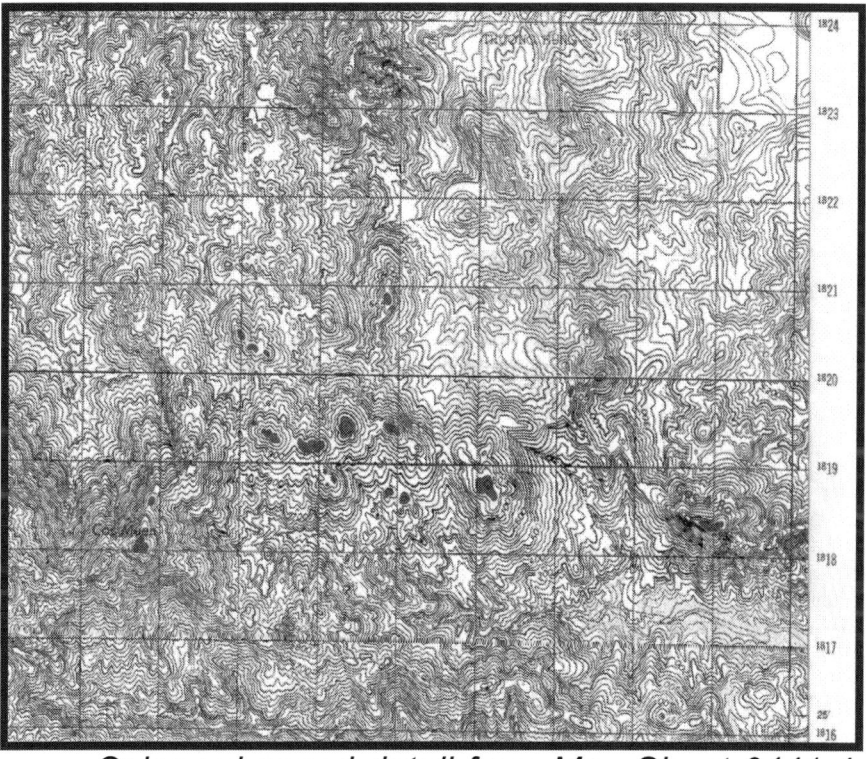

Color enhanced detail from Map Sheet 6441-4, Series L7014, A Luoi District, Thua Thien Province showing US positions after 18 July highlighted in blue, known NVA mortar and machine gun positions in red. Original tactical map from author's collection. Color enhanced map ©2017.

After the lucky hit on the ammo cache by an air strike on 13 July, CPT Hawkins and A/2-506 moved off Hill 805 and began working their way into the deep valley southwest of Hill 805 and southeast of Firebase Ripcord. On 15 July, Company A received a new mission—find enemy graves. Apparently those higher up the chain of command wanted something to show for all the expensive munitions being expended to defend FSB Ripcord.

In compliance with his new orders, Hawkins and Company A moved deeper into the valley southeast of Ripcord. On 17 July, they approached a knoll on the ridge leading into the valley that Hawkins had chosen as a likely NDP site. On reaching the top of the knoll, the point team discovered two newly-constructed log-and-earth bunkers with a pile of fresh human feces beside one of them, indicating that the NVA had very recently vacated the bunkers. It was too late in the day to move to another NDP site, so Hawkins and Company A dug in where they were.

Around three or four AM the next morning, CPT Hawkins woke up with the strong feeling that something was wrong, that they were about to be attacked. Hawkins and his RTO woke up the platoon leaders and the company packed up and moved silently downhill off the knoll. An hour later, after they had moved another five hundred meters down into the valley, they heard a mortar tube being fired. Seconds later the rounds came crashing down on the former NDP site, for total of fifteen to twenty rounds, enough to have caused major problems for Company A had they still been there. After that, many of the men in Company A began to wonder if their captain had a future-revealing crystal ball.

The sudden move before dawn on 18 July caused the NVA to lose track of Company A. As the company moved silently down the ridge, they discovered a great many NVA positions built into the side of the ridge. They were truly in the enemy's country for they found sleeping bunkers, hospital bunkers, mortar and machine gun pits and a complete underground kitchen. The company stopped long enough to blast each position with a jug of crystallized CS gas wrapped in det cord. This impregnated the dirt walls of the positions with gas crystals, making them uninhabitable for a long time.

Company A had never operated in an area that was so obviously the enemy's ground. They moved through the triple-canopied jungle with great stealth, constantly alert for an ambush. Distant gunfire sounded all around them as other units made contact with the NVA. 1LT Lee Widjeskog's Alpha Two was close enough to Ripcord to witness the CH-47 being shot down on the afternoon of 18 July. They heard the fire from the 12.7mm that shot down the Chinook and saw it crash and begin to burn. When the 105 ammo began to cook off, chunks of shrapnel hit the trees between Ripcord and Alpha Two and Widjeskog was certain that a major disaster had befallen Ripcord.

The level of tension was so great among the grunts of Alpha Two that LT Widjeskog and his squad leaders were having trouble finding men who were willing to walk point in the new, dangerous AO. The lieutenant did not want to have to give a direct order to anyone because if the man refused, he would be sent to the rear on the next resupply chopper for a court martial, leaving the platoon even more short-handed. Widjeskog knew there were several men in his platoon who would take a court martial to get out of the field. The lieutenant solved the problem by walking point himself.

He had not moved more than two hundred meters when the sergeant in charge of the problem squad came up and told Widjeskog he had found a man willing to walk point. The lieutenant later found out that none of the sergeants wanted him to get killed or wounded while walking point because they did not want to be given the responsibility of taking over the leadership of Alpha Two. The sergeants saw to it that Widjeskog had no more problems with men refusing to walk point.

On 19 July, CPT Hawkins was ordered by LTC Lucas to move further down into the narrow valley between the foot of Hill 805 and the long ridge running east from Coc Muen Mountain. That morning, the 155's fired an unexpected six-gun salvo that came perilously close to Widjeskog's Alpha Two. Widjeskog hurriedly called Hawkins and asked him to get the fire stopped. Hawkins called the TOC on Ripcord and in a sharp exchange with CPT Bill Williams, the battalion S3, got the fire stopped. The S3 tried to make light of the situation since no one had been hit but Hawkins told him that he had not called for artillery fire into his AO and that he wanted to know before any more missions were fired to insure the safety of his platoons. Williams agreed and the matter was dropped.

CPT Hawkins and his CP groups had been traveling with Alpha Three because there was no lieutenant to run the platoon. After the incident with the 155 salvo, he decided to move his CP to travel with LT Widjeskog and Alpha Two, hoping his presence would help settle down the uptight Alpha Two. Hawkins ordered 1LT William Pahissa who was leading Alpha One to also take control of Alpha Three, then being led by a less-than-eager E-5. LT Pahissa, a West Point graduate, was pleased with the added responsibility and moved off with his new command to locate a good company-sized NDP.

The CO's presence with Alpha Two did not have the effect he wanted. The CP group had eight men: Hawkins and his three RTO's; the FO and his RTO; the senior company medic and SFC Pham Van Long, an ARVN translator attached to Company A. The CP group, out of necessity, was far noisier than the men of Alpha Two were accustomed too. LT Widjeskog wrote, *"There was so much activity because of the radiomen and all the things the CP had to do, that I was immediately getting complaints from my men that these guys were too noisy and were sure to get us into trouble. We could hardly wait till the CP joined another platoon and left us quietly alone in the jungle." Ripcord* – page 320.

Hawkins' CP group was still with Alpha Two when, on the afternoon of 19 July, Hawkins realized he had led the group onto the wrong ridge to reach the NDP being secured by LT Pahissa. Hawkins called a rest halt while he determined how to get to the position being secured by the other two platoons. Hawkins shrugged out of his ruck sack and sat down. He heard someone moving through the brush and saw two NVA wearing fatigues walking toward the halted column, moving at an angle up the side of the ridge. He could not tell if any more troops were following the two he had spotted. They were carrying their AK-50's on a sling over their shoulders, unaware that an American unit was in the area.

Realizing that no one else had seen the NVA, Hawkins picked up his M-16 and shot the lead soldier three times in the chest. Shifting his aim, he shot the second man. Thinking that they might be the point team for a larger unit, Hawkins threw a frag but it hit a branch and bounced back, landing between Hawkins and one of his RTO's. Yelling "frag," Hawkins and the RTO dove away while the grenade exploded harmlessly. The RTO and several others began spraying the brush with M-16 fire until Hawkins, realizing there were no other NVA, yelled for a cease fire.

Back tracking, they finally made it to the overnight position with Alpha One and Three. As Hawkins moved onto the knoll on a ridge falling away into the valley, LT Pahissa and his platoon sergeant, SSGT Gerald Singleton, gave him a round of applause for the two kills.

Hawkins had taken a small brass cigarette lighter as a souvenir from the first man and, as was the custom, had taken the second man's belt with the highly prized red star belt buckle. Called a "hard corps belt", it signified that the soldier in possession had killed his enemy in combat and taken the belt from his body. The lead NVA had been carrying a wallet holding documents, a letter, photos and a few pages from an American skin magazine. SFC Pham, the ARVN interpreter, checked the material and told Hawkins that the NVA with the wallet had been SGT Van Thai and the second man was PVT Thuan, both assigned to the 'K3 Company, D9 Battalion' as recon men. The sergeant had partly healed wounds on his back and legs. One of the documents he was carrying was a supply request from Van's company commander to a higher headquarters. The note further stated that SGT Van was on light duty after having been wounded by ARA shrapnel during the attacks on Hill 805. A letter was also found written by Van to his older brother in Bac Thai, North Vietnam, complaining about the lack of medicine, food and uniforms.

Hawkins was concerned because there was obviously a large NVA force around Ripcord. He wondered why LTC Lucas had ordered a single company into a valley with the enemy all around? In a conversation with Lucas over the secure radio net, Hawkins had learned Ripcord was now taking 120mm mortar fire and that the NVA normally did not employ such heavy weapons unless they were in at least regimental strength. Hawkins did not really know what he was up against but he realized he had no choice but to *"look for the enemy and kill him; find his bunkers and supply caches and destroy them."* He decided to keep his platoons within supporting distance of each other rather than have them operating independently as they usually did. *Ripcord* – page 321.

■ ■ ■

When the 2-501 Infantry was moved by air from the area around Hill 1000, D/2-501 went with them from Hill 805. D/2-501 had been OPCON to the 2-506 and the company's return to its parent battalion left LTC Lucas with only two understrength companies (Hawkins' A/2-506 and Rollison's D/2-506) still in the field. To bolster Lucas' field strength, COL Harrison asked LTC Bobby Porter, commanding the 1-506 Infantry to place one rifle company OPCON to the 3rd Brigade. Porter assigned CPT Donald Workman's D/1-506 to the task and COL Harrison further assigned Company D to the 2-506. Lucas moved them by air to an LZ on Triple Hill. Company D's new mission was to begin patrol operations east toward Hill 805.

LTC Lucas decided to reinforce FSB Ripcord by bringing his Battalion Ready Reaction Platoon from Camp Evans. 1LT John Hall, formerly the XO for Delta One, D/2-506, had been serving as the XO for D Company at Camp Evans. He had the additional duty of organizing and commanding the Ready Reaction Force, made up from about thirty cooks, clerks and other rear area personnel, known as REMF's by the line grunts. These reluctant warriors were moved by air to the firebase where they served until the end of the battle.

With the withdrawal of the 2-501 Infantry from the Ripcord area, the division leadership put its hope of dispersing the NVA holding Hill 1000 on firepower alone. LTC Lucas still hoped to deny the enemy the use of their other strongpoint, Hill 805. When D/2-501 had moved off Hill 805, the NVA immediately took control of the hill. Keeping this in mind, Lucas moved Hawkins and Company A into the valley southwest of Hill 805 and planned to move Workman's D/1-506 onto an LZ on a ridge between Hill 605 and Hill 665, Coc A Bo Mountain.

Quite a few of the grunts with A/2-506 believed that CPT Hawkins had volunteered the company for the dangerous mission into the valley. To them it seemed like a suicide mission, so on the morning of 20 July, Hawkins had to call a medevac for one of his grunts who had 'accidently' shot himself in the foot with his M-16. The medic who treated the man did not believe it had been an accidental discharge. He later told Hawkins, *"He says it was an accident, but It's sure a good way to get out of the field." Ripcord* – page 322.

■ ■ ■

At about 1100 hours that same day, LTC Lucas air assaulted CPT Don Workman's D/1-506 from a PZ at YD333203 on Triple Hill to an LZ at YD376191 in a saddle about eight hundred meters southeast of Hill 605 and fifteen hundred meters northwest of the summit of Coc A Bo mountain, Hill 665. Almost immediately, Company D reported they were taking fire from the west.

The first slick onto the LZ carried men from Delta One, led by 2LT Randall Thompson. The men ran to the southside of the LZ and found concealment from which to provide covering fire for the next five slicks bringing in the remainder of Delta One. As they moved across the open LZ, the men noticed a black commo wire running across the open ground and a few bunkers around the edges of the landing zone.

LT Thompson popped a red smoke grenade on the LZ to indicate a hot landing zone as the slicks came in with green tracers flashing past and the door gunners returning the fire. As each load of six grunts landed on the LZ, they poured out a furious fire, attempting to suppress the incoming AK-47 fire. CPT Workman, known by his call sign 'Ranger', came in with Delta One.

The slicks circled around to the west to pick up 1LT John Smith's Delta Two, waiting at the PZ on Triple Hill. One of the slicks took several hits as it came into the LZ and was forced to break off its approach and come in again. According to the Daily Staff Journal for the 2-506 Infantry on 20 July, two men on the eleventh slick into the LZ were hit by ground fire and flown to Charley Med at Camp Evans.

The enemy fire died away as the last slicks, carrying men from SSGT John Frazer's Delta Three, hit the LZ which lay in a saddle between two small knolls about two hundred meters apart. CPT Workman sent Thompson and Delta One to secure the south knoll and Smith's Delta Two to occupy the northern knoll. Hill 805, the reason LTC Lucas had moved D/1-506 into the area, lay about sixteen hundred meters west of the LZ. Control of Hill 805 was vital to the defense of FSB Ripcord and Lucas wanted to re-occupy the hill as soon as possible.

1LT Smith was getting his platoon ready to move off the LZ when three NVA soldiers walked right on to the LZ, having come down the trail from the northern knoll. The startled and unwary NVA still had their AK's slung over their shoulders. A veteran machine gunner, SGT Bobby Rosas, shouted a warning "*Gooks!*", as he opened fire with his M-60, killing the hapless NVA where they stood. LT Smith wrote" It *boggles my mind that those guys simply walked into our perimeter. I guess they thought that since this was their backyard, they could walk around oblivious to their surroundings. . ." Ripcord* – page 327.

Moments later, the M-60 team guarding the trail to the south knoll spotted someone running down the trail toward the LZ with only the man's brush hat visible, bobbing up and down over the top of the brush. The gun team hesitated briefly, thinking it might be a friendly, but then opened fire. Most of the others on that side of the LZ joined in, blasting away at the jungle. Smith and Delta Two, followed by Delta Three and Ranger with his CP, then advanced to the north knoll, reconnoitering by fire as they went. CPT Workman blasted the knoll with ARA as they moved up the slope. Thompson and Delta One occupied the south knoll without incident. Both knolls had freshly dug enemy fighting positions on them. Ranger's plan was to spend the rest of the day running patrols throughout the area, then for Delta Two, Delta Three and the CP to NDP on the north knoll with Delta One remaining on the south knoll.

PFC James McCoy, a new man in the field with Delta One, was surprised that most of the grunts *"just sat around talking with each other. I occasionally glanced down the trail I was supposed to be watching. It seemed like no one else was paying any attention, and I remember being amazed that they could relax so soon. . ." Ripcord* – page 328.

McCoy took another look down the trail and was startled to see an NVA soldier lying in the trail. McCoy later wrote about his encounter, *"Too scared to yell, I reached down and picked up my M-16."* As he pointed his rifle down the trail, the enemy soldier raised up and looked directly at McCoy, who fired a burst, dropping the man straight down. Everyone began firing and PFC Brian Redfern sent a long burst from his M-60 down the trail. Surprising McCoy, Redfern then stood up and pulled the pin from a frag, letting it cook off in his hand for a couple of seconds before throwing it to get an air burst.

The firing quickly died down and McCoy remembers that the guys from his platoon *"came over to me and patted my now-shaking self on the back in a moment of congratulations for what appeared to be my first kill. For the first time, I actually felt I was one of the guys, but little did they know the turmoil I was feeling inside for killing another person."* McCoy's platoon was very soon to be nearly obliterated and he later wrote that *"the dead and wounded Americans I would see erased any remorse I may have felt at that moment. . ." Ripcord* – page 328.

Also on 20 July, FSB Ripcord received ten mortar rounds and one 75mm recoilless rifle round that caused no casualties or damage. One 60mm CS round exploded at the north end of the base, but the gas quickly dispersed in the high winds.

After securing the southern knoll late that afternoon, LT Thompson from Delta One sent a squad-sized RIF down the south slope of the knoll. Led by SGT Robert Wise, the point man was SP4 Eloy Valle and the slack man was a small soldier named PFC Pat "Little Bit" DeWulf. They had moved about a hundred meters down slope when they came to a small clearing near YD376189. "Little Bit" DeWulf spotted a single NVA soldier and yelled a warning. SGT Wise hit the dirt and opened fire along with Valle. The enemy returned fire as Wise lobbed several frags into the brush in front of them. The squad put out a heavy return fire but the enemy did not withdraw as they usually did. With his squad caught out in the open, Wide figured that the NVA must be in bunkers or they would have withdrawn. Wise ordered his squad to withdraw, crawling on hands and knees under the NVA fire back into the trees; the NVA let them go.

When LT Thompson reported the incident to Ranger, he was ordered to send the patrol out again and to be prepared to reinforce the squad if they hit anything big. Again, Valle led out, followed by DeWulf and, walking third man, SGT Wise. Valle took an alternate route down the hill but came across another clearing, this one about seventy-five feet wide and covered in a low growth of scrub brush.

SGT Wise paused to let Valle and DeWulf cross the clearing before he started across with his RTO, SGT Paul Mueller and the rest of the squad. As they reached the far side of the clearing, Valle and DeWulf did not notice the carefully camouflaged bunker hidden in the thick brush. The NVA waiting inside cut down Valle with a long burst of AK fire and then emptied the rest of the magazine into "Little Bit" DeWulf. Both SP4 Eloy Valle and PFC Patrick DeWulf died of their wounds.

Wise saw the muzzle flash as the NVA shot DeWulf and, after taking cover in the brush, he threw several grenades while Mueller crouched behind a tree and fired up the bushes around the bunker with his M-16. A sudden explosion right next to Wise blew off his glasses and filled his face and shoulder with bits of shrapnel. Nearly blinded by the loss of his glasses and blood from his facial wounds, Wise crawled away hoping he was not moving toward the enemy bunker in his confusion. As he crawled away, Wise saw his M-79 grenadier, PFC John Knott, hiding behind a tree. Knott would become separated from the squad and Wise was probably the last American to see him alive.

LT Thompson had started down the hill with another squad in support of Wise when the NVA began mortaring the south knoll, dropping a total of six 60mm rounds onto the small hill. Wise missed them in his half-blind rush back up the hill to the NDP. As Wise's squad withdrew, the NVA darted out of the bunker to Valle, DeWulf and Knott. Men in the perimeter on the south knoll heard screaming and AK-47 fire. PFC James McCoy wrote that he *"heard screaming, followed by bursts of AK-47 fire, then a faint, muffled scream and another short burst. The NVA were finishing off Valle, DeWulf and Knott. I carry in my head those final screams to this day, and I'm sure for the rest of my days on this earth. . ."* Ripcord – page 334.

LT Thompson had left SGT Elger Sneed in charge of the perimeter when he led his patrol down the slope. Hearing the firing begin, Sneed asked Wise if he could lead him and his men back to the clearing. Without his glasses everything was just a blur and Wise needed all his courage to guide Sneed and his men back down the hill. They found LT Thompson, wounded, sitting beside the trail under the care of a medic. Thompson's patrol had suffered several casualties in their encounter with the NVA. PFC Dale Tauer had been blown down the hill by the same RPG that killed PFC Bill Browning. Browning was SGT Sneed's RTO but as they moved down the hill, he shrugged off the radio and, telling Sneed he could carry his own radio, he took off downhill, shouting that he was going after Valle and DeWulf. Charging ahead, Browning was killed seconds later.

SGT Sneed moved several men on line and pushed slowly forward, blasting the jungle ahead of them to cover the withdrawal of the wounded back up to the NDP. Sneed then joined SGT Mueller behind a big log as Sneed guided ARA and minigun fire closer and closer until shrapnel was buzzing over their heads.

CPT Workman sent a squad led by SSGT Fraser from Delta Three to help Delta One recover their casualties. Sneed and his men tried to advance as he and Fraser's men walked forward while moving the rocket fire back out. They did not get far before they came under very heavy fire from the NVA and decided to break contact. PFC's Brian Redfern and James McCoy put their M-60 into action to cover the withdrawal. When a purple smoke grenade went off behind them, they thought they had been mistakenly marked for the Cobras, so they scrambled back up the hill to the NDP.

Ranger sent LT Smith with a squad from Delta Two to secure the LZ for the medevacs. It was nearly dark when a trooper with a strobe light guided the first medevac onto the LZ. LT Thompson from Delta One. and SGT's Sneed and Wise went out on the first medevac and two other wounded grunts climbed aboard the second dust off, all bound for Charley Med at Camp Evans.

While the medevacs were coming in, several M-60 machine gun teams laid down a continuous sheet of fire down the slope from the LZ. Volunteers crawled out from the perimeter under the fire, attempting to recover the bodies of Browning, DeWulf, Knott and Valle, but it was too dark and the four dead troopers could not be found.

After the medevacs had left, CPT Workman ordered LT Smith to return to the north knoll with his squad from Delta Two and all of Delta One. The men of Delta One were shaken and demoralized by their encounter with the NVA and the deaths of Browning, DeWulf, Knott and Valle. They followed the trail leading uphill from the saddle, guided by artillery flares burning overhead. By the time they arrived at the NDP on the north knoll, it was too late for the men from Delta One to dig in and the other two platoons had not been able scrape out more than shallow depressions in the rocky, root-filled soil of the knoll. The perimeter was nothing more than a circle of troops hidden behind trees and in the thick brush. Claymore mines and trip flares had been set out all around the perimeter and two LP's had been sent out a short way from the NDP. Illumination rounds fired from FSB Granite burned over the knoll all night.

Around midnight, the LP to the north reported a lot of movement to their front and LT Smith felt that the perimeter was being probed in preparation for an attack. The LP's asked several times to come back into the 'safety' of the perimeter but Ranger denied their requests, wanting early warning in case an attack developed. There was no attack and the exhausted men not on guard duty finally fell asleep in the early hours of 21 July.

■ ■ ■

While CPT Workman and D/1-506 was involved in their struggle on the LZ near YD376191, CPT Hawkins and A/2-506 moved further down into the valley south of Hill 805. In mid-afternoon of 20 July, Hawkins received a radio call from LT Pahissa, leading Alpha One, his point platoon. Pahissa told Hawkins he needed to come to the front of the column right away. When Hawkins arrived, Pahissa told him they had found a 'high speed' trail three to four feet wide with an enemy commo wire running through the brush beside the trail. Pahissa said they had tapped the wire and asked for the company interpreter to listen to the tap.

Hawkins wanted to know how they had tapped the wire. Pahissa explained that one of the grunts had an ear plug from a transistor radio—radios were forbidden in the field for reasons of noise discipline—that they had spliced into the line. Pahissa had his Kit Carson Scout listening through the ear plug and taking notes. LT Pahissa then had one of his RTO's cut the cord on a PRC-25 handset and splice it onto the NVA commo wire so that SGT Pham Van Long, Company A's ARVN interpreter, could listen at the same time.

Pham began listening and shortly afterward told Hawkins that the commo wire ran between a mortar unit firing on Ripcord from the eastern slope of Hill 805 and an NVA division headquarters somewhere to the southwest near Hill 902.

CPT Hawkins passed the intelligence directly to LTC Lucas and BG Berry, circling overhead in C & C birds. While the wiretap was in progress, Company A made contact with the NVA several times that day. Alpha Three had moved back up the ridge and established a blocking position while Alpha One set up a perimeter around the wiretap. Alpha Two set an ambush between the other two platoons on a bluff overlooking a swift, rocky stream running between the ridge and the southern base of Hill 805. There was evidence that the NVA was using the stream at the ambush site to refill their canteens.

Alpha Two did not have to wait long. PFC Alan Miller spotted an enemy water detail and opened fire, managing to wound one NVA in the foot before the water detail quickly dispersed into the thick brush along the stream.

Hawkins had moved to the ambush site after the first contact and was talking to LT Widjeskog, Alpha Two's platoon leader, when more firing rang out. PFC Miller had fired on a second water detail with his M-16 and an M-79. Hawkins was surprised that the NVA had returned to the stream so soon after being fired on but then realized that the second water detail must have come from a different enemy unit based on Hill 805.

CPT Hawkins hurried to Miller's ambush position and found a single dead NVA sprawled on a flat rock at the edge of the stream. PFC Miller, one of the few draftees in the unit who really wanted to fight, was grinning from ear-to-ear as Hawkins congratulated him. Miller, because of his college background, had initially been assigned as a clerk but had finagled his way into an infantry line outfit.

After the second ambush, Hawkins returned to the wiretap site where SGT Pham told him that he had determined that there were four NVA regiments (the 803rd, 29th, 812th and the 6th Tri-Thien Regional Forces Regiment) being controlled by the 324B Division headquarters. These regiments were positioned on the high ground to the north, south, east and west of FSB Ripcord. In addition to the infantry regiments, there was an artillery battalion (82 and 120mm mortars), an anti-aircraft battalion (12.7mm and 37mm guns) as well as the 7th Sapper Battalion. Pham informed Hawkins that he had overheard a discussion planning a mass attack on Ripcord that night (20-21 July) but the attack had been postponed because needed reinforcements had not arrived. SGT Pham, pleased by the trick they were putting over on the enemy, grinned at Hawkins as he told him that the enemy was in the area in more than division strength. In addition, the 304B Division was moving into the area with three infantry regiments and two artillery battalions in support of the 324B Division.

In an interview with MG Ben Harrison (3rd Brigade CO in 1970) in Hanoi in June 2001, BG Bui Pham Ky from the NVA 324B Division, confirmed that his forward command post was southwest of Hill 902, co-located with the command post for the 803rd Regiment. The 324B Division's main headquarters was located northwest of FSB Ripcord. *Hell On A Hill Top* – page 46.

The two wiretaps had lowered the signal strength on the commo line and Pham told Hawkins that a repair team had been dispatched to look for the problem. Hawkins at first thought that they would have to break down the wiretap, but then realized that the NVA communicators were only responding routinely to what they thought was a technical malfunction. Hawkins realized that they were in a perfect position to ambush the repair party. LT Pahissa came up with the idea of using the captured AK-50's to fire on the repair party. The distinctive sound of the AK's would confuse the enemy as to who was firing on them.

Hawkins agreed and Pahissa took one of the AK-50's and moved into an ambush position on the trail leading toward the division headquarters near Hill 902. A sergeant named Ross took the second AK-50 and moved to the side of the perimeter that faced the trail leading down from Hill 805.

They did not have to wait long. The repair party came down the trail into SGT Ross's position and Ross shot the lead NVA in the chest with the AK at close range. The man went down but immediately bounced back up and ran into the bushes even as an M-60 team and several grunts fired up the brush with their M-16's on full automatic. LT Pahissa and some others followed a heavy blood trail down to the stream, but the wounded NVA had disappeared.

Hawkins then realized it was time to get out and moved with Alpha Two back up the ridge to join Alpha Three. Hawkins left LT Pahissa and Alpha One at the wiretap site to cover the withdrawal back up the ridge.

It took the NVA over an hour to organize a response to the attack on the repair party. Alpha One briefly engaged the NVA before ripping out a fifty-foot section of the commo line and moving up the ridge to join Hawkins.

Hawkins had his FO, LT Steven Olson call in a heavy artillery barrage on the area of the wiretap as Company A moved cautiously several hundred meters west to set up a new NDP. Both BG Berry and LTC Lucas had praised Hawkins for his coup in tapping the commo line and Hawkins went to sleep *"pleased, excited and feeling very proud of Alpha Company." Ripcord* – page 325.

Hawkins thought it was time to get out of the valley but Lucas wanted a prisoner taken to confirm the intelligence gathered from the wiretap. Berry and Lucas were afraid that the NVA, suspecting the wiretap, may have sent false information to confuse them. Hawkins wrote *"I doubted that, but could not say so in so many words why. If the order to get a prisoner had originated with division, that means there was [a] strong feeling in higher headquarters not to believe how many enemy we were up against, even at that late date. . ." Ripcord* – page 325.

■ ■ ■

Tuesday 21 July began at about 0650 hours with six 82mm mortar rounds exploding on top of the hill at FSB Ripcord. About twenty minutes later, in their NDP at YD376192, D/1-506 reported ten 82mm had fallen on their NDP, fired on an azimuth of 210° from their location. There were no casualties from these rounds, the first of many more to follow.

LT Smith heard the first three rounds being fired—three thumps as the rounds left the tube—and shouted a warning. Smith was surprised that a lot of the men, busy eating their C-ration breakfast, simply stared at him in amazement because they had not heard the rounds being fired. These first three rounds exploded on the LZ as Smith heard two more rounds leave the tube. He again shouted for the men to take cover as the last two rounds impacted halfway up the slope of the north knoll. After that, the grunts belatedly began scrambling for whatever shelter they could find before the enemy could adjust the next salvo on top of them.

LT Smith and his platoon sergeant moved around Delta One's section of the perimeter making sure their men were in what cover there was. Seeing that everyone was down, Smith and the sergeant dove between the big roots of a tall tree as a third salvo came whistling in. Shrapnel from the first round to impact on the top of the hill hit Smith in his lower back. A firestorm of explosions erupted all around Smith and he later recalled *"it seemed the rounds would never stop."* Smith, who had never been subjected to such heavy fire, had been under the impression that the NVA, usually poorly supplied, *"would drop a few mortar rounds on you, then cease fire to conserve ammo. These guys obviously didn't know they needed to save their rounds, they just kept firing and firing after finding the range to our position."* The salvos each took about thirty seconds to land from the time they left the tube. Smith wrote *"There is no scarier feeling in the world then waiting for indirect fire to impact. My stomach still tightens when I think of it. As I came to my senses* [after being hit], *I began to hear cries of pain from all around the perimeter. We were taking casualties." Ripcord* – page 337.

As the mortar rounds continued to fall on Company D, Ranger managed to spot a possible location for the mortar tube at YD371183 about a klick southwest of his position. Workman called in 8-inch tube artillery from FSB Rakkasan on the suspected enemy mortar position as well as airstrikes. CPT Workman and his RTO's managed to squeeze into a narrow enemy-sized slit trench on top of the knoll as the salvos kept coming. According to the 2-506 Infantry Daily Staff Journal for 21 July, a total of eighty 82mm rounds were sent crashing into Company D's NDP.

The mortar barrage seemed to last forever for PFC Jim McCoy. Unable to find cover, McCoy curled up into a ball, his rucksack pulled over his back. The man beside McCoy screamed that he was hit and McCoy bandaged a ragged wound on the man's arm. No sooner had he bandaged that wound when the grunt was hit in the foot but McCoy did not have another field dressing for that wound.

When the mortar rounds began falling, PFC Walter Jurinen dove into Ranger's trench because it seemed to be the safest place, but Workman ordered him to get back to his position on the perimeter. Jurinen obeyed the order and fell into a prone position beside Delta Two's cherry medic, 'Doc' Robert Hays. When the first on-target rounds came in, Jurinen took shrapnel in both legs and Hays was hit in the groin. SGT Handley, a veteran Delta Two squad leader, found Jurinen and Hays as he checked positions between mortar volleys. Hays was not badly wounded but he was hysterical and nearly delirious from fear, mumbling over and over that he was going to die. Handley tried to calm Hays by telling him he was not badly wounded and was going to be okay.

Handley's attempts to reassure Hays did not do any good. Hays kept on repeating that he was going to die and when another salvo impacted on the hill hitting SGT Handley in his buttocks and calf, Hays closed his eyes and went into shock. Handley yelled for help and two other medics, PFC Richard Finley and PFC Barry Marchese ran over and began working on Hays, giving him mouth-to-mouth for several minutes. Hays never regained consciousness, dying either from shock or internal bleeding.

Marchese was devastated; only minutes before, he had failed to save PFC Peter Huk, who died even as Marchese was taping a piece of plastic over Huk's sucking chest wound.

PFC Frank Asher was also killed by the devastating mortar barrage. Asher and Huk were replacements, having been with Company D less than a week when they were killed. SP4 Richard Drury, himself wounded, saw a soldier suddenly jump to his feet, screaming "I can't take it anymore!" The next mortar round blew him down the hill, killing him. Drury did not know if it was Asher or Huk who was killed because they were both so new to the company that he failed to recognize the man.

     Ranger decided to abandon the knoll before his company was blasted to death. CPT Workman stood up in the trench and shouted for his troops to move down to the LZ in the saddle below the knoll. LT Smith recalls that *"By that time, the damned dinks had dropped a few CS rounds in. We abandoned the hill in gas masks, taking our wounded with us and dragging the body of 'Doc' Hays along in a litter made by folding a poncho around two poles."* Ripcord – page 338.

Although wounded in the head, PFC George Pourchot, an RTO with the company CP, stayed behind to cover the retreat, repeatedly spraying the jungle with his M-16 on full automatic. The mortar fire stopped as the company staggered down the hill, but many of the troops were near panic. PFC Jurinen told the man lying next to him that he did not think they were going to make it out of there. SGT Paul Mueller saw a trooper staggering down the hill, dragging his rucksack and M-16 with one hand, his other arm in bloody shreds. Machine gunner Jim McCoy saw his friend PFC John Millard staggering down the hill wounded in both legs. McCoy forced himself to wait for Millard to catch up and, putting his arm around Millard's waist, assisted him down the hill. Millard was wearing his rucksack with a PRC-25 radio strapped to the frame. The radio was shredded by shrapnel, so McCoy told Millard to get rid of it. Millard refused, saying *"No way! It saved my life." Ripcord* – page 339.

McCoy got Millard to the bottom of the little hill, then went back up the slope to help a young soldier holding a field dressing against his face, the ties having worked loose. The grunt let go of the bandage as McCoy reached him. *"I could see that part of his cheek was missing, exposing shattered teeth and gum. I tried not to let him see the sickened look on my face when I tried to put the dangling bandage back. I was unable to reattach the bandage, and simply placed it back against his face, then put his hand to it, and told him he would have to hold it in place. I know it must have hurt him badly to hold it in place. I felt terrible that I was unable to help him. . ." Ripcord* – page 339.

CPT Workman hastily put together a defensive perimeter at the base of the small hill on the northern edge of the LZ. As he worked to organize a defense, Ranger realized he had only forty troops who were fit for duty. Thirty of his men were wounded and three had been killed by the intense mortar barrage they had just endured. Ranger put SGT Terry Handley, himself wounded, in charge of the medevacs and ordered him to evacuate himself on the last dust-off. Workman found LT John Smith, the only officer besides himself still on his feet, and asked how badly he was hurt. Smith told Ranger he was okay; in pain but a medic had looked at the hole in his lower back and assured him the wound appeared to be minor. Wanting to be sure, Workman asked Smith *"Can you stand the pain? If you can't, I'll send you in, but if you can, I really need you—you're the only officer I have left." Ripcord* – page 339.

Smith assured CPT Workman that he was okay and could be counted on but others in the beleaguered perimeter did not feel that way. PFC Ronald 'Kuntz' (a pseudonym), a medic who had earlier diagnosed himself with 'heat stroke', sat in the middle of the trail, mouth hanging open and hands quivering. Workman asked 'Kuntz' what was wrong with him and 'Kuntz' replied that he had "shell shock."

As soon as he had organized the perimeter, Workman sent a five-man patrol back to the knoll to recover an M-60 left behind during the confused retreat. Reaching the top of the knoll, the small patrol came face-to-face with a few NVA soldiers who came over the top of the hill from the north. The patrol fired on them and they quickly scurried back into the trees. Quickly collecting the abandoned machine gun, the patrol hurried back down to the LZ.

The NVA were not far behind. Many short but viscous firefights developed throughout the morning. The enemy attacked in small groups all around the perimeter, withdrawing when Company D responded with heavy fire, but keeping up a steady pressure against the small perimeter. Company D took no serious casualties but they were, Ranger came to realize, surrounded. Neither the steady attacks by Cobra gunships nor the heavy M-16 and M-60 fire from the troops manning the perimeter kept the NVA at bay for very long. 1LT Smith was shocked and dismayed that the NVA held the initiative throughout the battle, even though he was sure that Company D could hold its own. Smith later wrote of the battle *"We were in the middle of an NVA stronghold under attack from all sides by an enemy that was better trained and organized than I'd ever been led to believe from my own training and the war stories I had heard. They had their shit together. They'd had our number, in fact, from the moment we touched down on that same LZ the day before." Ripcord* – page 340.

The fighting became so intense that many of the walking wounded voluntarily helped in the defense of the small perimeter. SP4 Steven DeRoque, a second-tour veteran, ignored his painfully wounded legs and took over an M-60 when the gunner became disabled with wounds in both hands. They fired the gun until the barrel became red-hot, then switched barrels and continued to pour out fire.

1LT Donald 'Ranger' Workman shown at Camp Evans shortly before his promotion to Captain and command of D/1-506. Photo from Virtual Vietnam Veterans Wall of Faces.

y that time, the called-for medevacs began to come on station. 'Dust-Off 91' came into the LZ at about 0820 hours piloted by 1LT Laurence Rosen and WO1 Douglas Rupert of the Air Ambulance Platoon, 326th Medical Battalion, known as Eagle Dust-Off. As the Huey touched down, SGT Handley, assisted by medics Finley, Marchese and several others, ran from the trees carrying Company D's six most seriously wounded in ponchos. The medevac quickly took off without drawing any direct ground fire due to the grunts around the perimeter putting out a heavy covering fire. *Hell On A Hill Top* – page 98

The second medevac to arrive was piloted by 1LT Allen Schwartz who circled above the LZ out of range of small arms fire while being briefed by Rosen, speeding toward Camp Evans, on the best approach and exit route from the LZ. Schwartz landed safely and took aboard six walking wounded and two litter cases as soon as he touched down. Schwartz had pulled up on the collective and climbed a few feet into the air when his windscreen suddenly dissolved in a burst of bullets. The Huey lost lift and fell straight down on the LZ, shuddering violently. An RPG, fired by an NVA in a tree, had blown off the tail boom, taking the anti-torque tail rotor with it and making the Huey uncontrollable. The NVA gunner was quickly dispatched by grunts who spotted him as he fired the rocket.

LT Schwartz, unsure of what had happened, tried to control the violently bucking Huey. The casualties in the cabin, who were not strapped down, were thrown out the open doors as the dust-off shuddered toward the eastern edge of the LZ. Schwartz yelled at his copilot to get out of the helicopter and the man was thrown out his open door as soon as he unfastened his safety harness. Schwartz was also tossed out of his seat before he could shut down the out-of-control turbine engine.

He hit the ground in a heap but scrambled to his feet and ran to the edge of the LZ trying to get away from the slashing twenty-four-inch-wide rotor blades where two of the grunts on the perimeter took him into their foxhole. Schwartz remembers that *"I didn't know I'd been injured until the grunt in the foxhole asked me what had happened to me and pointed to my face. I wiped my gloved hand across my mouth and it was immediately saturated with blood; at some point, I must have gotten slammed into some component of the aircraft, and my lower teeth had penetrated right through the skin between my chin and lower lip."* Ripcord – page 341.

Most of the wounded from Schwartz's dust-off made it back to SGT Handley's position. Two of the wounded, confused by the sudden crash, crawled to the edge of the LZ where they could see NVA in the downed trees below them shooting at the crippled Huey trying to set off the fuel tanks.

Trying to cut down the amount of NVA fire coming into the LZ, Ranger worked the Cobras in very close to the perimeter, shouting at his men to get their heads down while the gunships came in on their strafing runs. LT Smith remembers that the explosions from the big seventeen-pound warheads on the rockets literally lifted him off the ground while shrapnel slammed into the earth around him. Smith was astonished to see individual NVA soldiers stand up out in the open to fire their AK's at the diving Cobras, an incredible act of bravery.

When LT Rosen flew back to the embattled LZ for another load of wounded, he was distressed to see that the engine on the downed Huey was still running, revved up to a dangerous speed. When Rosen touched down, LT Schwartz ran up to the ship and was hauled aboard by Rosen's medic, SP4 Brent Law. Law then ran across the LZ and climbing aboard the still-running Huey, shut it down by hitting the fuel cut-off switch. The medic then rushed back to his own dust-off, arriving in time to help SGT Handley and his crew load nine wounded aboard. Rosen pulled pitch and the heavily loaded Huey struggled into the air, skimming the tops of the jungle trees on the way out. This time there was no enemy fire, the Cobras having discouraged the NVA from shooting at the medevacs.

1LT Rosen and his crew were back at Company D about a half-hour later. The heavy suppressive fire from the infantry and the Cobra gunships kept the NVA from firing at the unarmed medevac as it flared for landing on the LZ. SGT Handley and his men loaded five more wounded as the rest of LT Schwartz's crew clambered aboard, one of them shouting *"That's it, I'm aviation. I'm not a grunt! I'm getting my ass outta here." Ripcord* – page 343.

The 'shell shocked' medic Ron 'Kuntz', instead of helping the wounded, was trying desperately to get himself evacuated. As LT Rosen's dust-off came in on its third trip, 'Kuntz' literally begged SGT Handley to allow him to be medevacked, that he was "really sick". Handley refused, telling 'Kuntz' he was one of the only medics left and even if he was 'sick', he was needed there. 'Kuntz', now in an absolute panic, wouldn't give up and Handley finally agreed to call CPT Workman with his request.

Handley told CPT Workman he had a man claiming to be physically ill who wanted to be medevacked. Ranger asked who the man was and Handley told him it was Doc 'Kuntz', who was not wounded and that, as a trained medic, was needed in the field. Workman agreed, telling Handley that if 'Kuntz' was not wounded, he had to stay.

When Handley told 'Kuntz' he had to stay in the field, he demanded to talk to Ranger, but Handley, finally losing his temper, told 'Kuntz' that the answer was 'no', he had to stay in the field. However, Doc 'Kuntz' was so overcome by fear that he was next to useless when it came to helping the wounded.

Doc Ronald Kuntz had already served six months with the 199th Light Infantry Brigade 'Red Catchers' down in the III Corps Tactical Zone and was transferred to the 101st when the 199th was sent back to the US during the troop reductions brought on by Vietnamization. Arriving in the 101st about two months before the Ripcord battle, 'Kuntz' had already earned his Combat Medics badge with the 'Red Catchers.' Assigned to the relative safety of the battalion aid station for the 1-506 Infantry at Camp Evans, 'Kuntz' was a pot-smoking trouble-maker who spent a good deal of his time in the aid station helping malingerers find medical 'profiles' to keep them out of the bush. Fed up with his activities, the battalion surgeon ordered a disciplinary transfer back to a line company. 'Kuntz' felt he had been screwed over by the system and it was his bad luck that he arrived in Company D just one day before the company went OPCON to the 2-506 and moved into the deadly FSB Ripcord AO. As SGT Terry Handley later explained, *". . .you've got to work with the cards that are dealt you. 'Kuntz' didn't."* Ripcord – page 343.

During a pause in the ground attacks, Ranger sent another small patrol to the north knoll to make sure that no one had been left behind during the confused retreat earlier that morning. As the patrol neared the top of the knoll, one of the men found the body of PFC Frank Asher, already swollen by the July heat, about a hundred feet from the top of the knoll. Instead of dragging Asher's body back with them, the soldier took Asher's wallet and gave his ID card to CPT Workman when they returned to the LZ. Upset because they had not brought the KIA back with them, Workman ordered SGT Paul Mueller to take a squad-sized patrol back up the hill to bring back Asher's body. No one wanted to go back up the knoll, so their advance was slow and very cautious. Soon, the point man thought he saw movement ahead of them and Mueller moved his squad on line and reconned the ground ahead of them by fire. There was no return fire, but Mueller, suspecting an ambush, called CPT Workman and asked permission to return to the NDP. Mueller was very reluctant to take his small patrol any further up the slope and told Workman *"it's just some equipment up there and a guy who's already dead."* CPT Workman had no sympathy and said *"You're not in contact. Now, move up, secure the area, and bring back that KIA."* Mueller answered the order with *"No fuckin' way!"* and after a moment of silence on the radio, Ranger ordered Mueller to return to the LZ. *Ripcord* – page 344.

The ground attack continued all around the perimeter and many of the men began to think that they were going to be overrun. During one such attack, veteran SGT Gilbert Rossetter was checking his squad's positions along the perimeter when he saw an NVA throw a satchel charge at two of his men in a close-by foxhole. Rossetter shot the NVA then scooped up the live satchel charge to throw it back. The charge went off just as Rossetter threw it, the blast leaving him deafened, dazed and confused but otherwise unhurt.

Just minutes later, some of the men saw an NVA with an RPD machine gun scramble into position behind a large tree just fifteen feet beyond the edge of the perimeter. SP4 James Fowler began a duel against the RPD gunner with his M-60 while LT John Smith and several other pelted the NVA gunner with grenades. During the exchange of fire, the confused Rossetter walked past Smith straight at the RPD mumbling about *"getting the goddamned machine gun."* Smith grabbed the dazed Rossetter and dragging him back to cover, ordered a man there to hold Rossetter down even if he had to sit on him. The RPD gunner was finally killed, one of eight NVA known to be killed by Company D during the desperate fight on the LZ.

Company D began to run low on small arms ammo so, at about 0940 hours, a single slick from the 158th Aviation Battalion came in, quickly unloaded the ammo resupply and picked up casualties, including SSGT John Grazer, Delta Three's platoon leader. The NVA unleashed a storm of small arms fire and RPG's at the Huey as it lifted off. One of the RPG's hit the tail boom but did not explode. SP4 Richard Drury, a wounded RTO on the log bird, remembers the tail shaft of the rocket sticking out of the tail boom. He expected the RPG to explode at any time during the flight back to Camp Evans, but it never did.

1LT Rosen (now Doctor Laurence Rosen), making his fourth trip to the LZ, was about ten minutes behind the log bird. Rosen later wrote *"We all knew that the repeated use of the same approach and departure routes to the same landing site was practically suicidal. We all knew that we had already pressed our luck beyond our wildest hopes."* Because of the heavy fire they had flown through on their previous three trips, Rosen asked his crew—copilot Douglas Rupert, medics Brent Law, Donito Deocales and James Weiler—if they were willing to go into the hot LZ again. They all agreed that *"we would keep going in until there were either no more wounded or we were shot down. We were all of one mind. . ."* Ripcord – page 345.

LT Rosen brought Dust-Off 91 in hot, dropping into a two-foot hover above the LZ. Since all the other wounded had been evacuated, SGT Handley, and medics Rosas and Marchese ran for the medevac, the last of the wounded to get out. Only Rosas could dive onto the hovering medevac before an NVA soldier popped up from the downed trees on the western edge of the LZ and fired his AK right into the left front of Dust-Off 91. A blizzard of bullets blew out the windshield and wounded WO1 Doug Rupert, sitting in the left seat. Rosen pulled sharply up, then banking hard to the right to get out of the hail of fire, exited the LZ the way he had come in. Medic Brendan Law, also wounded, started to fall out of the Huey, but James Wieler managed to grab his safety strap and pull him back in.

Rosen pushed the shaking Huey as fast as it would go toward Charley Med at Camp Evans. Rupert sat beside him in agony, his left arm almost severed above the elbow. The bullet that hit Rupert had also hit Brendan Law and medics Deocales and Wieler worked desperately to keep him alive. The AK bullet, deflecting off the armor plate of Rupert's seat, had hit Law just below the armored chest protector worn by air crew and had lacerated his liver. Law bled to death on the deck of Dust-Off 91 before they could reach Charley Med.

In the confusion, no one aboard the damaged medevac knew about the additional drama involving their helicopter. SGT Handley and the medic Barry Marchese had been about to climb aboard when the shooting began and the damaged Huey abruptly pulled up. Both men fell to the ground to avoid the tail rotor as a desperate Ron 'Kuntz' rushed past, reaching up with both hands to grab the right skid as the Huey rose and turned 180°. Handley's first thought was that 'Kuntz" was deserting, but CPT Workman may have given him permission to leave with the last of the wounded.

Handley remembers that *"At first, 'Kuntz' had both his arms and legs wrapped around the skid [as] the helicopter went into a dive down the side of the ridge. The wind was blasting 'Kuntz' so strongly that his legs came loose, and he was just hanging on with his hands. The helicopter started pulling up at that point, going full throttle, and that's when 'Kuntz' was blown off the skid. The helicopter must have been several hundred feet up and going in excess of a hundred miles an hour when he lost his grip. I watched him fall. He just went straight down into the jungle, almost as if in slow motion. There was no way he could have survived. . ." Ripcord* – page 346.

LTC Lucas sent Company D/2-506, commanded by CPT Rembert Rollison, to support Workman's battered D/1-506. Moving by air from a pick-up zone on Coc Bai Mountain at YD330240 to an LZ on Hill 605 at YD372198, Rollison immediately began to move toward Workman's position some eight hundred meters to the southeast. The move was led by 1LT John Flaherty and Delta Three, the only platoon of D/2-506 still commanded by an officer.

Even after the LZ prep by the Cobras, the lead slick took fire from the left. As the helicopter touched down, CPT Rollison and his RTO, Rick Rearick, scrambled off and ran toward what they thought was a large bush on the edge of the LZ. Rollison later wrote that ". . .*it wasn't a bush, it was a camouflage net, and we slid into an enemy gun position.*" They found a 12.7mm machine gun mounted on a dirt mound in the middle of the circular trench. They later discovered that the big gun was inoperable due to a broken firing pin. The NVA gun crew were scrambling into a tunnel even as Rollison and Rearick pushed through the camouflage net. Rollison later said "*I saw the ass end of the last guy as he went into the tunnel. I pitched a frag in there after him, let it go off, then rolled back, stuffed my shotgun in the opening, and pumped off three or four shells. With all the dust, I couldn't tell if I hit anyone or not. It appeared that the tunnel led into a fairly large bunker where I assume the gunners kept their ammo and took shelter whenever we hit 'em with artillery and air strikes.*" *Ripcord* – page 348.

LT Flaherty and Delta Three secured the LZ On the peak of Hill 605 after a brief firefight with two men lightly wounded. CPT Rollison called LT Flaherty to the 12.7mm gun pit and pointed out something unusual regarding the captured gun. The gun was ideally situated to fire on the Chinooks as they made their approach to Ripcord and, amazingly, the NVA had taken the trouble of cutting a V-shaped notch in the trees lining the summit of the next ridge to the west between the gun's position and FSB Ripcord, almost three klicks to the southwest. The notch seemed to be about ten feet across and nearly six feet deep. The only thing the gunners had to do was aim the gun at the notch to put 12.7mm fire directly on to Ripcord, visible in the distance and outlined by the notch.

Delta Three took the point as D/2-506 started down the ridge which ran south for about four hundred meters then took a dogleg to the southeast, leading directly into Workman's position at YD376191. As Delta Three moved down the trail, they passed numerous unoccupied enemy bunkers and found six 75mm recoilless rifle rounds in one of them. Shortly before noon, the point team set off a booby trap which wounded two more men, one of whom had part of one of his feet blown off,

When D/2-506 moved down the trail over the north knoll, they found the bodies of Frank Asher and Peter Huk which they gathered up and took with them. As D/2-506 neared the perimeter manned by D/1-506, shouts of 'Currahee, Currahee' rang through the jungle as one company of very nervous grunts approached another. There were no 'friendly fire' incidents and Rollison joined Workman at about 1220 hours, 21 July.

After Rollison and D/2-506 moved off Hill 605, LTC Lucas moved CPT Kenneth Lamb and C/2-506 by air from FSB O'Reilly to Hill 605 to help stabilize the situation. Lucas then landed at Workman's LZ to hold a conference with Rollison and Workman where he told them they would be spending the night of 21-22 July on the LZ they now occupied. When LT Smith of D/1-506 heard the news, he told his men to dig in deep as they could expect to be hit again with mortar barrages and ground attacks.

CPT Workman felt that D/1-506 had been rendered combat ineffective by their two-day ordeal and tried to persuade LTC Lucas to pull them out. Workman's men had been counting on being relieved and the news that they were remaining in place sent their already low morale plummeting even further.

CPT Rollison began to put D/2-506 in place to secure the southern section of the perimeter. The ground attacks had stopped with the arrival of Rollison's company, but Workman told Rollison about the mortar tube to the southwest with a time in flight of the projectiles to the LZ of about thirty-five seconds. Deciding to test this for himself, Rollison stepped onto the open LZ and began waving his arms and making obscene gestures in the direction of the mortar tube. The enemy responded. Hearing the *bang-bang* as two rounds left the tube, Rollison ran for the cover of the trees. Sure enough, two 82mm mortar rounds impacted in the middle of the LZ about thirty-five seconds later.

With Workman's information confirmed, Rollison began moving his men across the LZ two at a time. Every time the NVA spotted two men running across the LZ, they would fire one or two rounds. PFC Bruce McCorkle, an RTO with D/2-506, was dumbfounded by the way Workman's exhausted men responded to the regularly-spaced mortar barrages. McCorkle recalls that Ranger's ". . .*glassy-eyed troops were to the point where they wouldn't take extreme measures to seek cover when we had incoming on the way. They seemed catatonic. They would just duck a little, like, well, if it hits me, it hits me. Running across an open LZ with eighty pounds on your back, knowing mortar rounds were coming in, was a real fun feat, but we all made it. We immediately began digging in.. ." Ripcord* – page 350.

CPT Rollison took control of the operation at that time and called in artillery and 81mm fire on the suspected mortar position to the southwest. He then brought in a medevac to take out the last of Workman's wounded and some of his own. When a dust-off arrived, it was forced to abort the landing by heavy AK fire from the southwest. Rollison called in Cobras and a second medevac successfully landed just before 3PM and the reliable SGT Handley was finally able to get out for treatment of his wounds.

After the second medevac left, LTC Lucas called Rollison and Workman and told them that plans had changed and they were to prepare for extraction from the LZ. Lucas had wanted to stay and fight it out but BG Berry, overhead in his command helicopter, had let COL Harrison know that he thought it best to pull the troops out. Berry told Harrison that there were two priorities: one; to get the battered D/1-506 out and, two; get everyone else out of the area before dark because they were on the enemy's ground and the NVA had the advantage.

COL Harrison, also circling overhead in *his* command helicopter, agreed with BG Berry's assessment of the situation and had ordered LTC Lucas to begin the extraction. To discourage the enemy before the extraction slicks began to come in, Harrison had CS tear gas missions flown along the western slope of the ridgeline. The gas canisters were tossed out of low-flying slicks while simultaneous air strikes went in on suspected enemy mortar positions on and around Hill 805.

LT Flaherty and some of his grunts from Delta Three 2-506 pushed LT Schwartz's damaged medevac Huey completely off the LZ to clear the way before the first extraction slicks arrived to take out D/1-506. What was left of Workman's company were organized into four-man helicopter loads, loaded down with the extra weapons and equipment left behind by the wounded. LT Smith and three men from Smith's Delta Two 1-506 got ready to dash out to the helicopter as soon as it settled onto the LZ to minimize the time spent on the ground. Because there were known enemy positions to the west of the LZ, the first bird picked up to a hover and moved backwards before turning and accelerating away to the east.

The first two Huey's landed and took off safely. As the third slick flared for landing, it drew AK-47 fire. The grunts assigned to that slick rushed out of the tree line and dived aboard, the ship immediately taking off. The fourth also took fire but made it out safely.

The fifth slick landed safely but was hit with AK fire as it sat on the LZ waiting for troops to board. The slick began to sway from side to side, so the door gunners waved the approaching grunts away as they ran toward it. CPT Workman had assigned himself to go out on the fifth bird and had approached the Huey with his two RTO's. Unable to hear the AK fire over the rotor noise, Workman and his men had just begun to move back when the slick suddenly flipped over onto its side with the rotors running at take-off speed. The main rotor struck Workman at an angle, cutting him in half downward across his chest. His head and shoulders flew under the helicopter and the rest of his body flew the opposite way.

■ ■ ■

While D/1-506 was fighting for its life on the LZ below Coc A Bo mountain, CPT Hawkins and A/2-506 continued to move unnoticed through the valley southwest of Hill 805. Ordered to take a prisoner to help confirm the intelligence received from the wiretap, Company A, led by Alpha Three, moved along an enemy trail deeper into the valley. The point team ran into two NVA coming up the trail toward them and fired on them. One enemy soldier went down while the other, leaving behind a heavy blood trail, disappeared into the brush.

The NVA who lay on the trail was still alive but had suffered a catastrophic head wound. Alpha Three's medic, Doc Mark Draper, checked the NVA and reported to Hawkins that the man could not live. Disappointed that he could not take him prisoner, Hawkins confirmed that the man was dying and could not be interrogated before he told Doc Draper to end his suffering. Seconds later, a single rifle shot echoed through the jungle.

Company A then moved back to the bluff overlooking the stream where they had ambushed the NVA water details and found the body they had left on the rock was gone. Seeing no fresh signs of NVA movement through the area, the company moved west to find an NDP site on higher terrain. To ensure they were not being followed, Hawkins told LT Widjeskog, leading Alpha Two at the rear of the column, to post two men as an OP at YD355178, about a hundred meters out from the NDP site.

A short time later, one of the grunts at the OP, SP4 Robert Journell, fired on two NVA who were apparently trailing Company A. Journell's fire killed one NVA and wounded the other who fled back down the trail. Fortunately for Hawkins and Company A, the dead soldier was carrying documents as well as cigarettes butts, tins of C-ration peanut butter and sugar packets probably scrounged from a previous NDP site. A note, translated by SFC Pham Van Long, the ARVN interpreter, identified the dead man as SGT Son, a member of an NVA recon team ordered to find the best approach through Ripcord's defenses for a two-battalion assault on the firebase. The dead recon sergeant also carried a French-made topographical map on which the sergeant had made notes and drawn arrows showing the route of the proposed attack on Ripcord.

Hawkins was pleased; now they did not need to try and capture a live prisoner for interrogation. Captain Hawkins and Company A were ready to get out of the valley. Hawkins later said, *"We had killed numerous enemy soldiers but too many had also escaped during these encounters for me to feel safe. We were pushing our luck." Ripcord* – page 347.

■ ■ ■

After the crashed slick had come to rest, LT Flaherty ran to the wreckage and knelt behind the tail boom. When he raised up and peered over the tail, he found himself looking right into the muzzle of a .38 revolver held by the pilot, who thought he was being overrun by the NVA. Seeing an American officer, the pilot put his revolver away, then told Flaherty one of his crew was trapped under the helicopter. CPT Rollison ran up to help and saw that the crewman was being choked by the cord for his helmet radio that had gotten wrapped around his neck. Rollison cut the mic cord and the crewman began to plead with them not to let him burn if the helicopter caught fire.

The weight of the helicopter was pressing down on the man's chest, so Corporal Mike Mann and SP4 Robert Gutzman from D/1-506 moved, under fire, over to the Huey with entrenching tools. They tried to dig out the trapped door gunner but the soil was rock hard and it was slow going. Rollison and Flaherty, concerned that the longer it took to free the trapped door gunner, the more likely it was there would be a fuel fire, began to rock the heavy tail boom up and down. They managed to move the boom high enough for SP4 James Fowler to drag the door gunner out from under the Huey. Flaherty then removed the radios from the ship and destroyed them with rifle fire so the NVA could not use them.

Medics dragged the severely injured door gunner to cover and did what they could to help him. He had suffered broken ribs and probably had internal injuries, so he moaned and screamed in his pain-induced delirium. His almost constant loud moaning became so unnerving that a nearby grunt, exasperated, shouted *"Will somebody shut that guy up?" Ripcord* – page 352.

LTC Lucas canceled the extraction from that LZ, so Rollison moved D/2-506 back across the clearing so that all the troops were on the north side. CPT Rollison began organizing the move back up the ridge to the LZ on Hill 605, already secured by C/2-506. It was the only way out at that point and Rollison fully expected the NVA to contest their move back up the ridge. Not wanting to use men as litter bearers who would be needed if a fight developed, Rollison asked permission from Lucas to leave behind the bodies of Asher, Hays, Huk and Workman. Lucas consulted BG Berry and was given permission to leave the KIA's behind.

As dusk approached the column moved slowly up the ridgeline, burdened by the ammo and equipment left behind by the wounded. The speed of the march was further slowed by the men carrying the injured helicopter crewman in a make-shift poncho litter. The NVA did not attack the column, possibly because of the Cobras that strafed along the flanks of the straggling line of men.

The extraction lift began as soon as Rollison linked up with C/2-506 on Hill 605. The slicks came in with one following closely behind another, taking out the remnants of D/1-506 first. D/2-506 followed and finally C/2-506. LT James Campbell of Charley Two described the helicopter lift off Hill 605, *"Those last few ships were coming in to a pitch black LZ. I had my strobe light out. It was hairy as shit."* Ripcord – page 353.

CPT Hawkins and A/2-506 were the only ground troops left in the Ripcord AO after the other companies were extracted. When they began to set up their NDP for the night, Hawkins decided to use a ruse he had learned while in Ranger School at Fort Benning. He had the company settle into a fake NDP late that afternoon and then, after darkness fell, they silently moved into the real NDP site some five hundred meters past the decoy site. A small patrol had gone ahead to recon the real NDP and then served as guides for the rest of the company. They did not dig in and stayed very quiet that night.

The only sound they heard that night was the explosion of the booby-trapped body that had been killed by the OP that afternoon. It seemed that the NVA were out in the darkness, attempting to locate the Americans who had sneaked into their valley. SP4 Frank Marshall recalled *"It was that kind of thing that had the whole company convinced that we had to get out of there. We weren't glory fighters. There were a couple of guys in the outfit who wanted to fight, but most of us just wanted to get the hell out of that valley before the enemy caught up with us."* Ripcord – page 353.

The NVA caught up with Hawkins and Company A the next day. LTC Lucas had notified CPT Hawkins via the secure radio net that they were to be extracted from the valley southwest of Hill 805. Preparing for the move to the extraction LZ, Hawkins sent out small security patrols to check the area around their NDP at YD353178. The patrols did not see or hear anything, but some of the more experienced grunts said they could smell the enemy, a sort of fishy smell coming from the 'nouc mam', a fermented fish sauce the Vietnamese poured over their rice. But because the company was carrying a lot of captured NVA equipment, it was thought the smell must be emanating from the gear.

CPT Hawkins made plans to extract from an LZ on a ridge near YD356181, about eight hundred meters to the northwest of his current location. That morning, he sent LT Pahissa and Alpha One to recon and then secure a crossing over the stream running below the NDP site.

During Pahissa's move, a friendly fire incident occurred when Alpha One's second squad opened fire on the point squad. The Kit Carson Scout leading second squad took them off course so that they ended up to one side of the point squad instead of joining them from the rear. Not expecting anyone to be on their flank, second squad opened fire when they heard movement in the heavy brush. The point squad quickly returned fire.

The firefight ended as quickly as it started when both squads heard orders being shouted in English. When second squad realized they had been shooting at their own point squad, the Kit Carson Scout, who had fired first, ran away and disappeared into the thick jungle. It is not clear whether the Kit Carson Scout had set up the incident so he could escape and rejoin the NVA or if he had just gotten lost and became afraid the Americans would not believe he was lost and would later shoot him 'by accident.' Frank Marshall later commented, *"We never trusted those Kit Carsons." Ripcord* – page 361.

Shortly after the friendly fire incident, LTC Lucas contacted Hawkins, again over the secure net, and told him to move to the knoll on the ridge just east of Ripcord at YD349194 for extraction. Lucas did not give a reason but Hawkins felt that Lucas wanted Company A to be in position to support B/2-506, then securing Ripcord's perimeter, in case the firebase was attacked. To reach that hill, Company A would have to move back up the same ridge they had used to move into the valley. It was not a safe move considering all the trouble Company A had stirred up in the Valley. It was a long march, about two klicks, to the LZ Lucas wanted them to use. The company could do it before dark, but they would have to sacrifice security for speed.

Just as Hawkins started to tell Lucas that he wanted to use an LZ he had located at YD346182, his secure net radio suddenly went dead. Hawkins and his RTO had to take the time to compose and encrypt a message to Lucas, then send it over the unsecure PRC-25 radio. It took ten minutes to encrypt and send the message —*Want to move to LZ grid 346182. Most secure for me. Your LZ tactically unsound. Please advise*--and additional time for the RTO's at the TOC to decode it. By that time, Lucas had left his headquarters on Ripcord and was headed to a conference at Camp Evans. When the message was finally decoded, there were no staff officers available to read the request and relay a decision to Hawkins. Hawkins had to decide whether to follow his instincts and move to the safer LZ or to follow Lucas' order. He chose to obey orders.

Hawkins moved LT Pahissa's Alpha One back from the stream and put LT Widjeskog and Alpha Two on point. The change in the direction of march disturbed the grunts who knew the NVA had been following them and that the new route would probably take them right into the enemy.

It took the company until 1300 hours to get themselves re-oriented for the move. When they finally moved out, LT Widjeskog was walking fifth in the seventeen-man column of Alpha Two, following a narrow trail through the thick jungle. They had not moved more than 150 meters from the NDP when the point man scurried back to report that he had seen several NVA setting up a mortar tube right on the trail. Widjeskog passed the word to his small platoon and they began to move up to attack the mortar crew.

They had not moved very far up the trail when the ominous silence of the jungle was shattered by an RPG hitting a tree beside the point man, knocking the tree down. The platoon fell flat on the trail as the column was raked by AK-47 and RPD fire from both the front and the right flank. Widjeskog's RTO took a bullet in his leg as he lay on the trail trying to raise CPT Hawkins on the radio. LT Widjeskog could hear the *bang!* *a*s mortar rounds left the tube on the trail ahead of them, the shells falling on Alpha Two and Three back at the NDP.

Widjeskog dragged his crippled RTO back into the little defensive circle formed by his platoon with the trail running down the center, but lost the RTO's rucksack with the radio in it in the process. Alpha Two lost radio contact with Hawkins but it did not matter. Hawkins could not have helped Alpha Two then due to the ferocious attack his two platoons were then trying to fight off. Hawkins remembers mortar shells bursting in the trees overhead while others came through the canopy to explode among the troops. The captain was immediately hit by small shell fragments in his upper back, neck and shoulders. Casualties mounted quickly as tear gas shells began to fall among the high explosives. The choking gas clouds caused many of the grunts to run down the north and west sides of the hill, taking their weapons but, in their hurry to escape the gas, leaving rucksacks and ammo bandoliers behind. *"Everybody just went in their own direction,"* said Frank Marshall, hit in one of his legs as he tried to escape the shelling. *"We became totally clusterfucked."* Ripcord – page 363.

CPT Hawkins took shelter behind a large tree as his company began to disintegrate around him. When the last shell came in, enemy soldiers popped out of the brush around the small hill and charged, their leaders wearing distinctive blue pith helmets. Some of the NVA were as close as fifty meters, having moved in under cover of the mortar barrage. They charged in a rush, a mass attack running through the underbrush, shooting and shouting as they came.

A few of the attackers were wounded or killed by those few defenders still on top of the hill. The return fire lasted only seconds; there were just too many NVA for them to resist. Hawkins stood up and shouted for the CP to rally at a little knoll about fifty meters to the north, then took off running as RPG's began impacting inside what was left of his perimeter. Followed by his company and battalion RTO's, Hawkins made it to the little hill, taking more shrapnel in his leg as he ran. During the frantic scramble to the new position, he lost track of the other members of his CP.

Only later would Hawkins find out that his CP had been nearly wiped out. Artillery FO, 2LT Steven Olson had been killed early in the fight when an RPG blew off his left arm. The CP's secure radio net operator was blinded by an exploding satchel charge. SFC Pham Van Long, the ARVN interpreter, was killed by AK fire. 1LT William Pahissa, Alpha One's platoon leader, took an RPD round through the head and SSGT Gerald Singleton, Pahissa's platoon sergeant, was killed rushing to help his lieutenant. The CP's medic, SP4 Mark Draper, was shot and killed while defending a wounded man. He was found clutching his .45 pistol in one hand and an IV bag in the other.

On the small hill, Hawkins caught his breath and forced himself to calm down. Getting his location straight, he got on the radio and requested Cobra gunships and tactical air strikes, hoping that LT Olson would soon be calling in artillery and mortars. The NVA soon spotted their radio antennas and RPG's came in on them. To get away from the RPG's, they slid down the slope of the knoll as far as they could and still maintain radio contact.

Left: *Captain Charles F. Hawkins and,* **Right:** *1LT Lee J Widjeskog of A/2-506, shortly after the battle for FSB Ripcord. Photos from Charles Hawkins and Lee Widjeskog.*

A pair of Cobras on their way to another mission diverted to Company A's location, arriving in minutes. By then, Hawkins and a half-dozen others had put together a small defensive circle on the slope of the hill. The captain crawled up to the top of the knoll and, shouting at his fragmented company to get an idea of where they were, brought the Cobras in so close that Hawkins was hit by a rocket fragment in his left shoulder.

SP4 Frank Marshall had initially joined up with two guys from Alpha Three, but enemy fire from the top of the hill killed or wounded both the Alpha Three guys. Marshall managed to scramble away unhurt, yelling *"First platoon, where are you?"*

Marshall's buddy, SP4 Ronald Janezic, answered *"Over here!"*

Marshall began crawling toward Janezic's voice, only to come under fire before he had gone very far and he yelled *"Don't fire. It's me, it's me."*

Janezic answered, *"It wasn't us. There's a gook in between us."*

Diverted, Marshall then hurried to PFC Danny Fries, Alpha One's medic who, badly wounded, was screaming for help. Marshall later wrote that he found Fries with his *"ass half blown off."* As Marshall was bending down to help him, *"a satchel charge was thrown down on us, hitting him [Fries] in the back as he laid there [,] blowing up and knocking me down the hill. I was blinded for a few seconds and my ears were ringing,"* but Fries was killed. After he came to his senses, Marshall made his way to Hawkins, where, after *". . .a few minutes, I was fine except for some facial burns. . ."* Ripcord – page 364-365.

There were still men up on the NDP hill. SP4 Floyd Alexander, LT Olson's RTO, was trying to help the blind secure net radio operator when the NVA overran the NDP. Seeing them coming, Alexander fell on top of the blind man, covering him with his body and playing dead. As he watched through half-open eyes, Alexander saw NVA soldiers move up to the wounded grunts on the hill and shoot each one in the head. When an enemy soldier stopped next to him, Alexander felt sure he was about to die. All Alexander could see were the man's feet wearing Ho Chi Minh sandals. The NVA suddenly kicked the radioman hard in the forehead then, after getting no response, he moved away. SP4 Alexander and the blind radio operator played dead, surrounded by the enemy, for the rest of the battle.

The two men survived but ten others did not. 2LT Steven Olson and SFC Pham Van Long from the CP; 1LT William Pahissa, SSGT Gerald Singleton, PFC Danny Fries, SP4 Donald Severson and PFC Robert Brown from Alpha One; Sp4 Mark 'Doc' Draper, PFC John Babich and PFC Virgil Bixby from Alpha Three all died on the NDP hill.

SP4 Rick Isom from Alpha Three remembers that the NVA rummaged through the abandoned rucksacks on top of the hill and threw their own grenades at them. Isom was hidden in a thick growth of brush close to the top of the hill and he could hear the NVA officers and NCO's yelling at their men as they placed them in position around the hill. All the NVA that Isom could see were wearing pressed fatigues, green pith helmets and carried AK's. The leaders wore blue pith helmets. A very young enemy soldier took up a security position behind a large tree not more than ten meters up the hill from Isom's hiding place. The young soldier kept peeking around the tree and Isom knew it was only a matter of time before the boy spotted him. Aiming carefully, Isom shot him in the head the next time he peeked around the tree. Jumping up, Isom ran down the hill screaming "Currahee, Currahee," so his own men would not shoot him as he crashed through the brush. The NVA threw satchel charges and grenades at him and fired their AK's but the brush was too thick for the enemy to get a clear shot at him. Isom made his escape and joined a group of ten or twelve other grunts further down the slope.

LT Widjeskog and Alpha Two had escaped the mortar barrage and had fewer initial casualties than the other platoons but they also faced a large force of NVA. The main NVA assault charged right past Alpha Two's right flank but a second, smaller force moved in behind Widjeskog so that Alpha Two, already out of radio communication with Hawkins, was now physically cut off as well.

Surrounded, the grunts in Widjeskog's small platoon fought like demons and Widjeskog, generally an easy-going, soft-spoken man proved himself under fire. SGT John Brown, Alpha Two's platoon sergeant, had been walking drag when the fight started. Shot through both cheeks, the bullet took some teeth and part of his jaw bone when it passed through his face. Brown had to hold his head down so the blood would not drain down his throat and choke him. With the platoon sergeant out of the fight, it was left to PFC Alan Miller, SSGT Whitecotton and Brown's RTO to hold off the NVA as they charged up the trail. Putting out a heavy fire, the three grunts knocked down at least ten NVA. Unable to face the devastating fire from the three men, the rest of the NVA force darted off the trail and began sniping from behind trees. The RTO was wounded but kept shooting as Whitecotton threw every grenade the little group had, wounding and killing so many that the NVA fire died down. Taking advantage of the lull, Miller and Whitecotton, followed by the wounded RTO, dragged the bleeding SGT Brown down the trail into Widjeskog's tiny perimeter. PFC Miller, his own weapon destroyed, was now armed with an AK-50, taken from a dead NVA.

LT Widjeskog had hoped to use SGT Brown's PRC-25 radio but the RTO had lost his rucksack when he was hit. They had a third radio that was not working, so Widjeskog put the wounded RTO to work trying to get the radio up and running. The RTO broke the radio down into its component parts even as the firefight raged around him.

Alpha Two's young medic, PFC Martin Glennon, had frozen up at the start of the battle, but when he saw Brown and his terrible wound, he pulled himself together. Glennon saved Brown's life by starting an IV and giving him a blood filler to keep him out of shock, then a transfusion of dextrose. 'Doc' Glennon literally kept him alive by consoling and encouraging him when he began to slip away into unconsciousness.

Widjeskog used a brief lull in the fighting to take stock of Alpha Two's situation. He had two men seriously wounded and SP4 Thomas Schultz was missing. One of the other men told the lieutenant that Schultz had lost his glasses in the opening burst of fire. They had found cover together, but several satchel charges had exploded all around them. When the dust and smoke cleared, SP4 Schultz was gone. He had probably decided to make a run for what he thought was the safety of the NDP on the hill. Schultz's body was found later in the jungle between Alpha Two and the rest of Company A. Schultz had been a member of the squad that had refused to walk point a week before and Schultz had even approached his squad leader about getting a rear job. Widjeskog later said, *"Everybody was nervous, but Schultz more so than anybody else. . .Maybe he was getting premonitions that he was going to be killed. Sometimes those kinds of things are self-fulfilling, I think."* Ripcord – page 367.

Widjeskog's men, on their bellies facing outward with visibility no better than fifteen or twenty feet, fired short, well-controlled bursts whenever they saw or heard movement in the brush or they took fire. The lieutenant controlled his men from the center of the tiny perimeter, the only one on his knees. When one of his men fired, he would move quickly to the man and ask what he had seen. More than one man could tell Widjeskog that he had gotten an NVA square in his sights and had seen the enemy go down when he fired.

The NVA suddenly loosed a shower of grenades and satchel charges at the perimeter but most of them fell short or flew completely over the small position to explode on the other side. The enemy rushed the perimeter behind the grenade shower from all sides, firing their AK's as they came. The enemy hit a wall of M-16 and M-60 bullets. The fight lasted only five brief but intense minutes during which Widjeskog was wounded in his left arm, shoulder and thigh by grenade fragments. A large chunk from the same grenade hit machine gunner SP4 Anthony Galindo in his right cheek and his right eye instantly swelled shut. Galindo just switched over to his left side and continued to fire his M-60.

SP4 Robert Journell, screaming curses at the enemy, cut down the brush in front of him as he fired his M-16 on full automatic. Journell was knocked down by a burst of enemy fire and 'Doc' Glennon could do very little for him except comfort him and administer morphine to control his pain. Bleeding internally, it took Journell forty-five long minutes to die.

Widjeskog spotted a muzzle blast from behind a tree; Whitecotton also saw it. Shouting to the lieutenant to give him cover fire, Whitecotton grabbed a frag. Widjeskog fired rapid single shots, keeping the enemy pinned down while the sergeant let the grenade cook off before throwing it so the enemy could not grab it and throw it back. The grenade killed the enemy soldier, but a small fragment shattered one of Widjeskog's teeth and glanced up into his gum. He felt the impact but adrenaline masked the pain and he did not realize he was hurt until one of his men asked about the blood on his face.

Whitecotton yelled for more grenades, so 'Doc' Glennon pulled a grenade from his cargo pocket and, without thinking, pulled the pin before handing it to the sergeant. When he realized what he had done, Glennon yelled a warning that the grenade was live. Whitecotton immediately threw the frag and it rolled down the hill before exploding. No one in the little perimeter was hurt.

With rifle fire crackling all around him, Widjeskog began to realize that they would eventually be overrun, that they were not going to get out of there alive. Things got better when the wounded RTO managed to get their radio working after about ninety minutes of tinkering. Finally contacting CPT Hawkins, Widjeskog learned that Company A had been split into three or four small groups that seemed to be holding their own. Hawkins thought Alpha Two had been overrun, but when Widjeskog pinpointed an enemy troop concentration only a hundred meters from his tiny perimeter, Hawkins called in artillery and Cobra gunships on them which quickly reduced the pressure on them.

■ ■ ■

Captain Hawkins remembers that when the Cobras came on station and he began speaking with the pilots, he stopped being afraid. The gunships stopped the enemy assault and Hawkins felt his confidence growing. When the F-4 Phantoms arrived, Hawkins became angry at the enemy commander and started to fight his [Hawkins'] way instead of letting the NVA commander call the shots. As Hawkins said," At *that point, it was him and me, his will against mine. He had thrown his best punch and we were still standing. Now I set out to destroy him."* *Ripcord* – page 369.

Hawkins organized the incoming supporting fires—81mm mortars, artillery and ARA—so they all hit the enemy at the same time. The Air Force FAC, MAJ 'Skip' Little, overhead in his small propeller-driven aircraft, fired his white phosphorous marking rockets along the enemy's most likely routes of reinforcement, giving the fast-moving F-4's clear targets to hit with their napalm and 250-pound high-drag bombs. Hawkins and Little worked the Phantoms along the enemy lines most of the afternoon. However, MAJ Little did not have authorization to put any ordnance closer than five hundred meters from American troops. Realizing that Company A was in serious trouble, MAJ Little moved the 'danger-close' line to three hundred meters but it was still not close enough. The NVA were aware of the safety margin and most of them were only fifty to a hundred fifty meters from Company A's positions. At times, they moved even closer and the 82mm mortar on the trail in front of Alpha Two's position was still periodically putting out rounds.

The men knew they were in trouble and several times a trooper in position near Hawkins caught his attention and yelled over the gunfire, *"Charlie Oscar, we got to do something!" Ripcord* – page 369

Hawkins knew the man was right but the only way to recapture the NDP hill was by a frontal assault So, Hawkins and his men moved up the north slope of the hill while SGT John Kreckel of Alpha One provided covering fire with a half-dozen stragglers he had pulled together. Kreckel had also gone out and dragged several wounded men to safety while under very heavy fire and Hawkins little assault group ran into some of that fire. An RPG impacting close by hit Hawkins in his cheek bone with a small piece of shrapnel and another man was grazed across his face by an RPD bullet, so they had to move back.

During the aborted assault, SP4 Frank Marshall took a piece of shrapnel in his right arm, the wound penetrating nearly to the bone. Still able to function, Marshall caught up an abandoned M-16 and threw aside his M-79, useless in the heavy brush. When his attack stalled, Hawkins sat down and began to talk on the radio. He then spotted an NVA silhouetted on the hilltop, aiming an RPG at the command group. Hawkins picked up his M-16 and took aim at the center of the man's chest, but the bullet went high and struck the gunner in the neck, knocking him flat on his back.

Hawkins tried another assault up the north slope while SGT Kreckel's group moved up the west side of the hill. PFC Buster Harrison from Alpha Three laid down a heavy covering fire from his M-60. SP4 Lowell Webster, the acting platoon leader for Alpha One since the death of LT Pahissa, led a dozen troopers up the slope closely followed by Hawkins and his CP group. Leapfrogging from tree to tree, the grunts faced fire from AK's, RPD's and RPG's. Hawkins got on the radio and demanded that MAJ Little ignore the danger-close restrictions and put a bomb or napalm on the NVA mortar, still dropping shells around them. Little did not answer but the next F-4 came in lower and closer than usual and dropped two high drag bombs. One, a dud, hit the top of the hill but the other landed almost directly on the mortar position. When the smoke and dust cleared, they could see deep into the surrounding jungle, most of the trees having been cut down by the blast. That single bomb ended the NVA threat to Hawkins position.

After the bomb blast, wounded NVA soldiers could be heard screaming and their fire nearly stopped. SGT Kreckel, SP4 Webster and their men, coughing and gagging from the high explosive fumes left by the bomb, made it into the NDP site. They could see enemy soldiers dragging their wounded away and they shot some of the NVA in the back as they ran off the hill. Dead GI's, dead NVA and abandoned equipment from both sides littered the hilltop.

The NVA's retreat was being covered by an RPD gunner, firing from the northeast. Unaware of the threat, a grunt walked into the machine gun's beaten zone. SGT Kreckel, noticing this, ran over and pushed the man away just as the RPD fired. Kreckel was hit in the head and died a few minutes later, surrounded by his men. SGT John Kreckel was awarded the Distinguished Service Cross posthumously.

Hawkins attack stalled as the enemy abandoned the hill. Few of the men wanted to chase the NVA down the far side of the hill but because he was a squad leader, SP4 Rick Isom decided he had to set the example. As he moved to the far side of the hill, Isom became silhouetted against the evening sky. An NVA in place further down the slope fired two shots from an AK-47, one round grazing Isom and the other penetrating his chest, knocking him down. Isom immediately knew he was in deep trouble. The NVA who had shot him was only twenty meters away and a Cobra gunship was coming in on a rocket firing run. Isom had suffered a sucking chest wound and, barely able to breathe could not crawl to cover. Isom later wrote, *"when the rockets came ripping through the trees above me, I received shrapnel wounds in the hip and back, one piece hitting me in the spine and paralyzing me from the waist down. . ."* Ripcord – page 371.

Looking around, Isom spotted a young grunt behind a nearby tree and asked him to go find his friend PFC 'Buster' Harrison and bring him back to help him. Isom, by then drowning in his own blood, remembers that *"The kid didn't move. He was frozen with fear. I emphasized over and over to him that I was going to die if he didn't go get Buster, and he finally crawled off across the hilltop to find Buster. . ."* Ripcord – page 371.

Harrison cautiously crawled forward with the young soldier. No one else would join them. When he saw where Isom lay, Harrison crawled to him, covered by the other GI. and asked if he could move. Isom said he could not move so Harrison rolled him on his side and began dragging him away, yelling for a medic as they moved.

Right about that time, CPT Hawkins joined SP4 Webster on top of the hill. An NVA gunner, spotting the radio antenna's clustered around Hawkins, fired an RPG at the group. Instead of blowing them up, the rocket hit a tree branch as it came in, exploding above them instead of at their feet. That tree branch saved them, though Hawkins caught a piece of shrapnel right in his throat, knocking him onto his butt. Thinking he was badly injured, Hawkins was ready to pass command to Widjeskog when he realized that he could breathe and was just barely bleeding. The shrapnel had sliced through his windpipe and out the left side of his neck but had missed his jugular vein, carotid artery and his spine.

LT Widjeskog now had a good view through the shattered trees around his position. He spotted an NVA running away carrying an RPD by the handle. Still kneeling, the lieutenant was the only one who could see the enemy soldier because everyone else was still on their bellies. Opening fire with his M-16, he squeezed off single shots but could not get a good sight picture as the enemy zigged and zagged around the broken tree trunks. The NVA finally darted into some brush and vanished, the lucky one who got away. Widjeskog called in a Cobra on the bushes and they all hugged the ground as the gunship fired a volley of rockets. SGT Whitecotton raised his head to watch and a spent rocket fragment struck him right in the nose. Whitecotton would later tell Widjeskog that he just could not take his eyes off the fragment even as it was about to hit him. It bloodied his nose and slowed him down as they moved back up the trail to rejoin the rest of the company.

After a brutal five-hour battle, Company A tried to regroup on the little hilltop as darkness began to fall. Men dragged some of the sounded into the perimeter while others limped or crawled in under their own power under weirdly flickering shadows cast by the artillery flares burning overhead. Men desperately rummaged through the rucksacks scattered across the hill, looking for urgently needed water, grenades and ammo that might have been missed by the North Vietnamese. CPT Hawkins called in a ring of artillery fire around the remnants of his company as the exhausted men dug in as well as they could and assigned fields of fire. Everyone fully expected to be attacked again before morning.

'Doc' Martin Glennon and SP4 Ian Hailstones were the only medics still on their feet. They used all their albumin, bandages and morphine taking care of the fifty-one wounded. Fifteen of them were hurt so badly that they would have been judged as urgent medevacs if there had been men available to clear an LZ. Squad leader Rick Isom was one of these men. His buddy Buster Harrison, who spent the night assisting the two medics with the wounded, draped a poncho over a medic and Isom so the medic could use a flashlight while he sealed Isom's sucking chest wound. Isom later wrote about that long night. *"He [the medic] told me to lay with the wound down. That helped a lot, at least it didn't feel like I was drowning anymore. The medic, of course, couldn't do anything for my spinal injury, and not only did I grow progressively weak from loss of blood, but I also became very sick because my bladder was paralyzed and urine was backing up in my system. I was awake all night and pretty much on my own, but the thought that I would be going home helped me hang on."* Ripcord – page 373.

There were only twenty men available to CPT Hawkins who could still get around or fight and fourteen of those were wounded in some way. There were just not enough men to form a perimeter large enough to include all the casualties. Hawkins made the very tough decision to leave the most seriously wounded off to one side, outside the tiny perimeter. The men understood the necessity of such a decision. They placed the wounded in groups of two or three between tree roots or anywhere else where they would have some cover and a chance of making it through another attack. Some of the wounded were in shock or terrible pain, but quite a few could still use a weapon and were ready to put up a fight if the need arose. The men on the perimeter who had wounded placed in front of their position planned their defensive fire sectors around them.

Those men who thought that Hawkins had volunteered the company for the mission into the valley still blame him for what happened. Others who feel Hawkins was only following orders believe differently. As Hawkins checked positions around the perimeter that night, one of the grunts told him, *"You did a good job, sir. Without you, we'd all be dead." Ripcord* – page 373.

Just about everyone was traumatized to some extent, laughing and crying in the same breath. One partially paralyzed grunt, propped against a tree with his rifle and ammo held across his lap, told Hawkins, *"Let 'em come back. We'll whip the shit out of 'em again." Ripcord* – page 373.

LTC Lucas got CPT Hawkins on the radio late that night and told him, *Raffles Four-three, this is Black Spade. We're going to evacuate tomorrow. Deal Four-three—Rollison and D/2-506—will be inserted to assist you."* Hawkins acknowledged the transmission and Lucas then asked him, *"What's your status? How are your men?"*

The casualty list that Hawkins recited was far worse than that reported earlier that night. The colonel's self-control gave way as the terrible numbers sank in. Lucas was bothered by the fact that if Hawkins had moved northwest as he wanted to and not northeast as ordered, he might have avoided the enemy attack altogether. Under great pressure, Lucas briefly lost his composure and sobbed, *"Chuck, I'm so sorry. I'm so goddamned sorry."*

Embarrassed, Hawkins replied, *"It's okay. We'll be fine. Currahee, sir."*

"Roger," answered Lucas, recovering his control. *"Currahee. Out."*

Aware that the North Vietnamese knew their exact location anyway, Hawkins fastened a strobe light to a long pole and set it up in the middle of the perimeter as a reference point for the Cobras that circled the hill all night. Hawkins then spent most of the rest of the night moving among the wounded outside the perimeter until one of his RTO's realized Hawkins was about to collapse. The radioman dragged his captain back inside the perimeter and forced him to lie down. Hawkins fell asleep immediately and slept until first light when he awoke to find himself staring into the face of a dead NVA soldier.

LTC Andre Lucas was up at 0430 hours on Thursday, 23 July. During a conference held at Camp Evans the day before, the decision had been made to evacuate the Ripcord AO and the firebase itself. After a quick tour of the firebase to ensure that everything was ready for extraction, Lucas boarded a C&C bird sent from Camp Evans for his use that day. The colonel was accompanied by his artillery liaison officer, CPT Ray Williams who immediately set to work coordinating the prep fires around a knoll near YD349186. The LZ on that knoll was about one klick southeast of Ripcord and one klick northwest of Company A's NDP at YD353177. LTC Lucas planned to move CPT Rollison's D/2-506 into that LZ from the Currahee Pad at Camp Evans. They would then move overland to the relief of CPT Hawkins and Company A.

Lucas had attempted to insert Company D onto the knoll during the night of 22 July, but brush fires started by the air strikes supporting Company A had spread to the area of the LZ on the knoll and the LZ had been obscured by smoke. The lift ship carrying Company D had been forced to return to Camp Evans, much to the relief of the grunts on board. They had not relished a kilometer-long night march through a jungle full of North Vietnamese soldiers.

BG Berry and COL Harrison, in separate C&C birds, arrived in the Ripcord area a half hour before LTC Lucas left Ripcord. Harrison assisted Lucas in coordinating the massive amount of artillery fire from every gun tube within range that began impacting onto all the hills surrounding FSB Ripcord. The AO had been divided into sectors, some covered by artillery and others by Cobra gunships. Low-flying Huey's smothered known NVA firing positions with choking clouds of tactical CS gas.

The seventeen Huey slicks carrying D/2-506 made their approach in a long trailing formation from the east, the rising sun behind them. The Huey crews were under orders to maintain strict radio silence so the NVA could not determine the assault plan by listening to the radio chatter.

The lead slick was flown by CPT Randolph House of Company C, (Phoenix) 158th Aviation Battalion. House began his hovering descent into the small LZ at 0625 hours while it was still dark under the jungle canopy. House had to hover straight down into an LZ hemmed in on all sides by huge trees, the forty-foot rotors barely clearing the trees. The NVA fired on the slowly descending Huey and the rotors struck a bare-limbless tree on the ships right side. House managed to safely land the badly vibrating Huey and off-load CPT Rollison and his CP group before struggling back into the sky.

The sixteen Huey's following CPT House came in with door guns blazing at the AK-47 fire coming from the trees. A 12.7mm machine gun began firing on the slicks from atop Hill 805 and LTC Lucas directed Cobra gunships on to that target. Air strikes from F-4 Phantom fighter-bombers also went in on the hills surrounding the LZ.

When CPT Rollison had enough troops on the ground, they fired a 'Mad Minute' into the jungle surrounding the LZ to discourage an attack. He then took a compass heading and led off cross-country, staying off trails to avoid any ambushes that might have been set by the NVA. Rollison set a fast pace, relying on speed as his security. They moved right through the enemy, ignoring the NVA they could hear moving through the jungle around them. They paused briefly to return fire when the drag platoon was attacked, but otherwise kept moving.

In their beleaguered NDP, Hawkins and his men could hear the distant gunfire as Company D drew closer. Hawkins knew Company A could not survive the day without help, but did not believe that Rollison would be able to fight his way through to them. Lucas had told Hawkins that intercepted enemy radio messages had revealed that Company A had been attacked by a full battalion the day before. Hawkins believed Rollison would run into the same or another battalion and be delayed by another big fight.

Rollison and Company D had previously been in the area through which they now moved, but the familiar ground had been so altered by air strikes that they were not sure of their exact location. Rollison radioed Hawkins and asked him to fire three shots from his M-16 rifle for him to guide on. A little later, Rollison asked for three additional shots and then three more. Nervous that the repeated rifle shots would attract the enemy, Hawkins told Rollison to just follow the trail of enemy bodies to his position.

CPT Rollison did just that—sixty-one bodies by actual count—scattered through the bomb-blasted jungle that ended at Company A's NDP. When they were about fifty meters out from the link-up with Hawkins, a disturbing message came over the battalion radio net that the 2-506 operations officer had been killed and the battalion commander gravely wounded. Bruce McCorkle and Rick Rearick, Rollison's RTO's, looked at him in astonishment. Rollison instantly ordered them to remain silent about what they had heard, fearful of the effect such news would have on the troops. Rollison did not even tell Hawkins the bad news about Black Spade when he finally reached Company A's perimeter about 0925 hours, 23 July.

When Rollison learned that Hawkins had only twenty troops fit for duty, he told Hawkins they could serve as security while Company D built a new LZ from which they could all be extracted. Rollison then told Hawkins, *"This is lieutenants work, Hawk. You an' me are going to have a cup of coffee."*

The coffee was brewed and served in a canteen cup, 'boonie rat' style. Trying to get Hawkins to relax, Rollison joked, *"Dang, Hawk, y'all bleedin' in the coffee,"* referring to Hawkins throat wound. (For the recipe for 'boonie rat' coffee, see *Mighty Men of Valor- With Charley Company on Hill 714* – page 187.) Rollison then took a minute to tell Hawkins that his company had rescued Don Workman's D/1-506 two days earlier and that Workman, Hawkins' West Point classmate, had been killed.

While the LZ was being built, the NVA dropped a few mortar shells in the direction of the hill, but they all fell short. In case of a full-scale attack by the NVA on Rollison and Hawkins, BG Berry had placed a full battalion, LTC Chuck Shay's 2-502 Infantry (the author's battalion), on stand-by at Camp Eagle ready to assault into the Ripcord AO.

A hole big enough for a single helicopter had been blown in the jungle by 1000 hours and a medevac arrived and hovered over the stumps of the dynamited trees while Hawkins ten most seriously wounded were loaded on board. Those evacuated included Rick Isom and SP4 Harvey Neal, who had waited for eighteen hours with a serious stomach wound. The long delay before hospitalization proved fatal for Neal who died from his wound on 27 July.

The work on the LZ continued. 1LT Flaherty had knocked down nearly enough trees so a Huey could land safely when he reported to Rollison that he was almost out of C-4. Rollison told him to use the company's LAW's to knock down the rest of the trees. Flaherty did, later writing, *"I fired probably twenty LAWs'. They'd blow a nice little hole in the trunk. You'd pack it with plastic explosives [C-4] and you could knock down a good-sized tree with less than a pound of C-4. Normally,"* explained Flaherty, *"you'd daisy-chain the explosives around the trunk and it'd take ten or twelve pounds to do the job. The only problem with firing so many LAW's was that I couldn't hear a thing in my right ear for something like two weeks afterwards. I've still got a sixty per cent hearing loss in that ear. We were working fast. We had no idea what was going on, but from the bits and pieces we were catching on the radio, it sounded like the world was coming to an end up on Ripcord."* Ripcord – page 393.

The LZ was finally ready and the extraction of Companies A and D began at about 1300 hours. Once again. CPT Randolph House's slicks from Company C, 158th Aviation Battalion were called in to hover straight down into a 150-foot hole in the jungle. Until all the dead were gotten out, each slick carried two body bags and four live grunts. It took thirty minutes to get all of Company A out with Company D to follow immediately. As the extraction of Rollison's Company D began, three Huey's took hits from a 12.7mm that began firing from only a hundred meters away. NVA soldiers had also moved in as close as thirty-five meters on the LZ's north side. WO1 Steve Wandland and CPT Frederick Spaulding, flying a LOH, went in very low and marked targets with smoke grenades for the supporting Cobras to hit. The Cobras' 2.75-inch rockets armed with seventeen-pound warheads splintered and knocked down trees all around Company D. The enemy fire quickly died away.

CPT Rollison flew out on the third-to-last slick and LT Flaherty went out on the second-to-last ship. After checking the area for any stragglers, SSGT George Strasberg, Flaherty's platoon sergeant, climbed aboard the last Huey out of the valley below Hill 805.

There was a mob scene on the Currahee pad at Camp Evans as each load of troopers came in. Everyone was hugging everyone else with relief, the men almost overcome with joy at making it out of the valley in one piece. Rollison's joy was shattered when he learned that LTC Lucas had died of his wounds. Rollison had loved and respected Lucas and as he told LT Flaherty of the Colonel's death, he broke down while still standing on the pad and cried and cried. LTC Andre Lucas was later posthumously awarded the Medal of Honor.

With the extraction of Companies A and D 2-506 Infantry from the valley, there were no more troops left on the ground in the Ripcord AO. Bowing to pressure from higher command to keep casualties down and reduce the expenditure of ammunition and equipment, the 101st Airborne had decided to cut its losses and abandon the ground the men of the division had fought so hard for.

Chapter 18
RIPCORD UNDER SIEGE
THE FINAL DAY

"After analyzing the situation, the division commander decided that this might be an enemy deception operation, and that the enemy was firing off all his remaining artillery shells as part of a plan to evacuate Base 935 [FSB Ripcord]." – From North Vietnamese Records.

The intelligence gleaned from the A/2-506 wiretap operation in the valley below Hill 805 played a pivotal role in the decision whether to 'pile on or pull out.' Should the 101st Airborne reinforce an operation that had already chewed up an entire infantry battalion, two additional companies from another battalion plus an artillery battery? Or, should the division cut its losses and get out while they could? Pressure from higher command at MACV headquarters in Saigon to keep casualties and equipment losses to a minimum played an integral part in reaching a decision.

BG Berry, the acting division commander, wrestled with the decision. Early on the morning of 22 July, he marshalled his thoughts in a letter to his wife:

"We've now reached a point where we must question the continued use of Ripcord. Is it worth the casualties for the purpose it is serving? If we decide "no", how do we get out of Ripcord? If we vacate Ripcord, then what do we do? Where will we place our artillery to support the attack we want to make into the NVA base camp and cache area?

Today we must decide on a course of action that differs from what we are now doing. Now we are taking constant casualties on Ripcord from incoming mortar rounds, particularly among our artillerymen on top of the hill. We are taking constant casualties among the rifle companies operating in the mountains and jungles around Ripcord trying to locate and destroy the enemy mortars and AA machine guns that attack our helicopters and people. Daily our artillery fire from Ripcord grows less effective as enemy mortar rounds make it more difficult for the artillerymen to fire their howitzers.

There are plenty of NVA in those hills. More of them are moving in from North Vietnam via Laos. They are well equipped and supplied. The mountains seem loaded with 12.7mm AA machine guns. The NVA want very badly to inflict a major defeat on US forces.

MACV's hopes for some kind of successful summer 1970 offensive depend on the Screaming Eagles, but we cannot afford to take heavy casualties." Hell On A Hill Top – page 121.

Sometime later that day, BG Berry made the difficult decision to close Ripcord and evacuate A/2-506, then in heavy contact with an NVA battalion, the only line company still on the ground in the Ripcord AO.

A planning session was convened at 3rd Brigade Headquarters, Camp Evans where Berry asked his commanders what was necessary to conduct the extraction on 23 July. COL Harrison immediately asked for OPCON of the 2-17 Cavalry, direct support from the 4-77 Artillery (ARA), direct support from the 101st Aviation Group and priority from all division and XXIV Corps artillery units. Harrison also asked for forty-eight sets (each set consisting of two to four aircraft) of close-in fighter-bomber support.

With the decision to close Ripcord made, extensive planning went into formulating a workable plan. One of the first priorities was the extraction of CPT Chuck Hawkins and A/2-506 from the valley below Hill 805. CPT 'Gabe' Rollison and D/2-506 were given the mission to combat assault into an LZ near Company A, then to move overland to Company A's position and assist in building an LZ for the extraction of both units.

LTC Lucas startled his staff when he returned from Camp Evans with the news that Ripcord was being closed. The operation was scheduled to begin at dawn the next day, so Lucas and his staff were up most of the night organizing the evacuation. CPT Vasquez-Rodriguez, the battalion supply officer; LT Gabino Caballero, pathfinder platoon leader and a liaison officer from the 159th Aviation Battalion all came out to Ripcord to help Lucas survey the base and determine how many Chinook sorties would be needed to lift out all the equipment then on Ripcord. Teams of riggers from DISCOM (division support command) began to prepare the loads for pick up the next day.

CPT Thomas Austin's crews from the 2-11 Field Artillery began firing off the thirteen hundred 155mm rounds left on Ripcord so the big guns could be gotten ready for extraction. NVA observers around the firebase were confused by the sudden, random (to them) firing of the big guns. According to North Vietnamese records:

"*Meanwhile enemy artillery barrages blanketed the perimeter of the enemy base. The chief of division artillery reported that enemy artillery was firing heavily toward the east, but the fire was haphazard and uncoordinated. There did not seem to be any rhyme or reason in the direction of the enemy fire. One gun was even firing shells with different charges and settings, one right after another. . .The division commander sent a cable to Military Region Headquarters to report the enemy activities and the division's preliminary assessment of the situation. The Military Region commander responded with an order: 'Overrun Base 935 and do not allow the enemy troops to escape!'" Hell On A Hill Top* – page 123.

Some non-essential personnel were extracted that night; CPT Phillip Michaud and his 105mm crews from Battery B/2-319 Field Artillery and 1LT Fred Edwards and his men from the 326th Engineer Battalion were all lifted out during the evening of 22 July. Michaud's six 105mm howitzers, damaged in the Chinook crash of 18 July, were left behind after the artillery crews had rendered them useless.

After only two hours sleep, LTC Lucas was up at 0430 hours and spent about an hour touring the base, checking that everything was rigged and that all personnel understood the plan of evacuation. Lucas left in his C&C bird, an OH-6 LOH, accompanied by his new operations officer, MAJ Kenneth Tanner. Near dawn, the colonel inserted seventeen Huey slicks carrying D/2-506 into an LZ southeast of Ripcord to help with the extraction of A/2-506.

At about 0545 hours, the first airlift began with fourteen CH-47 aircraft hovering one or two at a time over the base amid incoming mortar rounds and 12.7mm fire coming in from many locations surrounding Ripcord. The Chinooks flew twenty-two sorties and had successfully removed six 155mm howitzers, two M450 bulldozers, tons of commo equipment and one M55 Quad 50 machine gun by 1214 hours. Enemy 12.7mm fire had brought down a Chinook at about 0740 hours. The aircraft made an emergency landing amid the ruined 105mm howitzers and the crew escaped safely. Before the damaged CH-47 could be rigged for recovery, it took a direct hit from a mortar round that caused the big helicopter to catch fire then explode.

CPT Alton Caldwell from the 2-319 Artillery had been sent to Ripcord with orders to render the damaged 105 mm battery inoperable in case the guns could not be evacuated. He arrived with a three-man crew and a pack full of thermite grenades. When the damaged Chinook crash-landed in the battery, Caldwell knew the howitzers could not be evacuated and he and his men set to work. His plan was to close the breech locks on the guns and then drop a live thermite grenade down the barrel. The tremendous heat generated by the grenade would fuse the breech closed and the guns would be useless. Caldwell and his men had time to damage only one 105 before the mortar round set the Chinook on fire and drove Caldwell and his men to cover. Caldwell believed that the two fires (18 July and 23 July) had so damaged the gun tubes that they could not be safely fired.

LTC Lucas had to land at his battalion headquarters at Camp Evans to refuel his C&C helicopter. While there he took the time to run into his office to sign the efficiency report on MAJ Herbert Koenigsbauer, his former operations officer. The extraction of Rollison and Hawkins was still in progress, so Lucas wasted no more time in getting back into the air, returning on station in the Ripcord AO at about 0740 hours. On Lucas' return to the area, both BG Berry and COL Harrison diverted to Camp Evans to refuel their C&C ships.

Slicks from the 101st and 158th Aviation Battalions began extracting the troops from Ripcord at about 0830 hours. WO1 Kenneth Mayberry from Company C/158th Aviation Battalion remembers that "the *beginning of the evacuation was a nightmare. Flights of ten [slicks] were orbiting everywhere you looked over the flats in the Firebase Jack area just below the mountains. Mass confusion reigned. The air mission commander's radios were breaking up and he had trouble communicating with us."* Ripcord – page 381.

Hearing the confusion, CPT Randolph House broke off from his flight and took over as commander of the air mission. His radios were working perfectly and he turned chaos into order quickly. He used a big waterfall three klicks northeast of Ripcord, a landmark well known to pilots, as the final checkpoint between Evans and Ripcord. House sent the recovery slicks into Ripcord in groups of three, reducing the number of aircraft and crews exposed to the heavy enemy fire at any one time and making it easier for the over-worked Cobras to cover them. The slicks landed on three different helipads, guided by pathfinders wearing day-glow vests and using hand and arm signals. Several of the pilots had to abort their landings at the last second due to incoming mortar rounds on or near the helipads.

The NVA gunners began firing all the ammo they had stockpiled for a siege at a furious pace when they realized that the base was being evacuated. The incoming mortar fire was so constant that the troops stopped getting on those slicks that did manage to land. The troops did not want to leave their bunkers, foxholes and trenches to run through the explosions and board the Huey's. CPT House recalls that, *"Our aircraft were going in empty and coming out empty. They could only sit on those pads for a matter of seconds, then they had to take off whether anyone got on board or not because of the heavy fire."* Ripcord – page 381.

CPT House made a test run in his own Huey to confirm the pilots' reports then called LTC Lucas and told him he could not keep sending slicks into the heavy fire if nobody was going to board them.

At about 0845 hours, the radio Lucas was using to talk to MAJ Tanner, his new operations officer on Ripcord, stopped working. Lucas had planned to land on Ripcord only after the extraction had been completed to check that all the support troops had gotten off before he extracted the last loads of troops. Using another radio, he told COL Harrison that the air mission commander had advised that the troops were not boarding the extraction helicopters. He explained that he had lost commo with the firebase and that he was going to land and take charge on the ground.

The heavy incoming forced Lucas' pilot to abort several attempted landings onto the VIP helipad, closest to the TOC. He was finally able to set down for a few seconds on the POL pad on the opposite side of the base. Even as the command ship rose into the air and banked steeply away, the NVA dropped a salvo on the pad, sending CPT Raymond Williams—the artillery liaison officer with Lucas—diving headfirst into the nearest foxhole. Completely ignoring the incoming, Lucas walked around Ripcord talking with the troops huddled in bunkers and trenches, looking for the infantry command post.

Lucas ran into his operations officer MAJ Tanner and 1LT Henry Bialosuknia who was helping coordinate the airlift. While they were talking, they noticed that much of the incoming mortar fire was coming from a 120mm mortar in place on Hill 805, clearly marked by a puff of smoke visible every time the weapon fired. The three men watched as 1LT Gary Watrous called in air strikes trying to take out the mortar on Hill 805. The gun tube was emplaced in a deep, narrow gully that was difficult to hit from the air. A Cobra rolled in on the hill and fired a long minigun burst. The hilltop disappeared in a cloud of dust as thousands of bullets struck home but the big mortar continued to fire.

An F-4 Phantom appeared and dove in at the correct angle to hit the mortar but the two high-drag bombs it dropped sailed right over the hilltop and exploded in the valley below. Lucas ordered Watrous to concentrate everything on destroying that mortar. Watrous answered that he intended to and warned the colonel to take cover because, *"there's nothing for you to do out here except get killed." Ripcord* - page 383.

LTC Lucas shrugged off the advice and about 0915 hours, he was seriously wounded by a 120mm shell that exploded only three feet behind him, probably launched by the seemingly indestructible mortar tube up on Hill 805. The same shell instantly killed MAJ Tanner and PFC Gus Allen from A/2-506 who happened to be walking by when the round came in. CPT Williams and his RTO, protected by the sandbag wall in front of the artillery FDC bunker, were knocked unconscious by the concussion.

CPT James Harris, the battalion surgeon sheltering in the FDC bunker, rushed outside and grabbing Lucas by the collar, dragged him inside the bunker. Harris got Lucas to safety just as four other rounds exploded right outside the bunker entrance.

Harris did not recognize Lucas until he unzipped his flak jacket and saw the black oak leaf rank insignia on his collar. The doctor immediately got an IV started and began giving Lucas albumin but that was about all he could do. Lucas had been protected from the waist up by his flak jacket but his legs were so mutilated that Harris could not bandage them with what he had available. The backs of the colonel's legs and his buttocks were full of shrapnel, one kneecap was blown away and the tibia dislocated from the socket. The wounds were barely bleeding because the white-hot shrapnel had cauterized them but it was obvious to Doctor Harris that Lucas's legs would probably have to be amputated to save his life.

Lucas woke up about ten minutes later and asked what had happened. Harris told him he had been seriously wounded by a mortar round. At that point CPT Benjamin Peters, commanding B/2-506 on the firebase, having been summoned when Lucas was hit, came into the FDC. As the next highest-ranking infantry officer on the firebase, command fell to him when Lucas was put out of action. Handing Peters his blood-spotted map, Lucas told him he was now in command of the firebase. Peters answered that he thought he could handle it and Lucas replied that he knew Peters could do it.

CPT House, who respected and admired Lucas, came in to get him escorted by four Cobras. House got Lucas to the hospital pad at Camp Evans in record time but it was too late. He had apparently gone into shock during the flight and took his last breath as they lifted him from the Huey.

News of the death of the battalion commander was a shock to many but the operation had to go on. CPT Jeffrey Wilcox, relieved of command of C/2-506 by Lucas on Hill 1000, was now assigned to the 3rd Brigade TOC at Camp Evans. Still angry and bitter over his relief, Wilcox remarked, *"Well, listen, I've discussed losing people with Colonel Lucas, and he thinks casualties are all just in the game."* Wilcox later wrote that, after his statement," *No one said anything, and we all just slowly got back to work."* Ripcord – page 385.

■ ■ ■

The Huey slicks came in very low and fast, flying along a ridge that led southwest from the waterfall landmark directly to Ripcord. Cobras flew along the flanks and Phantoms zoomed past above them as the lift ships flew through a gauntlet of NVA fire. The battlefield was partly hidden under billowing clouds of dust and smoke from friendly and NVA fire. The slicks flew through these clouds before landing on Ripcord amid explosions and green tracers.

It was confused and organized at the same time. Flight corridors had been set up so that helicopters going into the firebase would not collide with those going out. The air was crowded with Cobras and scout ships looking for targets, Huey's on tear gas missions and fast-movers on bombing and napalm runs. All these aircraft also had to avoid the trajectories of friendly artillery fire coming in from supporting firebases around Ripcord.

CPT House, still acting as air mission commander, was in constant contact with LT Bialosuknia, controlling the evacuation of the support troops who had all been moved to the TOC. The men went out in groups of five, most of them from the VIP pad adjacent to the TOC. When the slicks came in, three would run from the TOC and two others would dash from foxholes on the opposite side of the pad. As the foxholes were vacated, others would scramble across the LZ and into the foxholes to await the next slick. Bialosuknia also sent men up the hill above the TOC to the 105mm battery's log pad.

CPT Steven Austin, who had commanded the 155mm howitzer battery, was in radio contact with his fire direction officer who had assembled the battery personnel in a bunker. When Austin managed to get five men out on a slick, he would call his FDO who would send five more men up to the pad. CPT House was playing roulette with his helicopters by then because the incoming fire was so heavy. He would send the lift ships in one at a time so the pathfinders could direct the pilot to the pad that was taking the least amount of fire at that moment. Once the troops had dived aboard, the Huey would lift off and move backwards to the edge of the hill, make a quick pedal turn then literally fall down the northeast slope of the base to gain speed and avoid most of the enemy fire coming in from the west and southeast. House later wrote, *"You got out of there right on the deck. People literally had tree limbs stuck in their skids when they landed at Camp Evans." Ripcord – page 386.*

None of the lift ships were shot down on Ripcord. Four were badly damaged by mortar fragments, including the slick piloted by WO1 Ken Mayberry from C/158th who later wrote a lengthy account of his ordeal:

"I had begun my flare when another mortar round landed between my aircraft and the five troops I could see to my front, waiting to board. There was a puff of smoke and dust, and they were knocked flat like bowling pins. At the same instant, my aircraft was splattered with shrapnel, and it felt like someone had stuck a burning hot poker into my left leg. Someone yelled over the intercom to "go around"—to abort the mission and get back in line—but when I saw those guys go down, I felt responsible, and knew I couldn't leave them there. I said we had to get the wounded first, and set down.

When the skids hit the ground, my crew chief SP5 John T. Ackerman, and my door gunner, SP4 Wayne E. Wasilk, jumped from the aircraft and ran forward to get to the wounded, an act of tremendous courage given the machine gun and mortar fire impacting all around. . .

I don't know how long it took them to carry and drag the wounded on board, but it seemed like forever. More than one aircraft making its final approach to the pad I was sitting on had to make a go-around, and Captain House was calling to ask what my situation was. I couldn't answer. I just stared straight ahead at the scene before me. Everything was happening in slow motion. I was afraid if I moved I'd break the spell and the next mortar round would kill us all. . .

Finally, all the wounded were loaded and Ackerman yelled, "All clear." The spell was snapped and I pulled pitch.

As I made my call, "Chalk 1 is coming out." My throat was so dry from fear that I didn't even recognize my own voice.

I began to relax on the way back and watched my instruments to detect anything amiss. I knew we'd taken some hits, but didn't know the extent of the damage. Another aircraft from our company, piloted by WO1 David J. Wolfe, flew all around us so his crew chief could check us over visually. He didn't see any major damage, but thought he detected some smoke, so Wolfe escorted me all the way back to Charlie Med at Camp Evans in case the engine quit.

I called ahead, and there were medics waiting on the pad with stretchers for the wounded when we landed. One of the doctors stuck his head through my window to ask if we were okay. I told him we were fine. It was rather comical as he looked at the holes in the aircraft and down at my chin bubble, which also had a shrapnel hole in it, and asked me, "Are you sure you're okay?" My leg stung, but it wasn't a big deal. I would have been embarrassed to go into Charlie Med where the really seriously wounded guys were so I pulled pitch and flew over to Phoenix Nest, our company area at Camp Evans. I parked outside the hanger so maintenance could check me out. Maintenance took one look and Red-X'd my aircraft. We had over forty shrapnel holes and had sustained structural damage. Maintenance was preparing for a long day of battle damage, and didn't want to give me one of their replacement aircraft, but I eventually got one and got back in the air near the end of the evacuation. . ." Ripcord – pages 386-387.

The courageous and professional airmanship of the air crews was amazing. Cobra pilots flew their ships in between the lift ships approaching Ripcord and NVA 12.7mm AA guns to draw their fire while firing rockets and miniguns. All the pilots who flew the evacuation except one was awarded the Distinguished Flying Cross while every door gunner and crew chief got an Air Medal with V-device for valor.

The only exception was a young, new warrant officer in Company C who, forced to abort his landing on Ripcord, did not rejoin the queue of slicks orbiting the base but headed for Camp Evans. CPT House, who thought he had been wounded or needed fuel learned later that ". . .he had cracked. As I understand it, he climbed out of his aircraft in shock after he landed and just walked into his quarters. He was a good kid, and was absolutely ashamed when I talked to him after the mission. He got it together, as I recall, and started flying again after Ripcord." Ripcord – pages 387-388.

It was equally nerve-wracking for the support troops still on Ripcord as they waited for a ride out on one of the slicks coming in through the mortar and AA fire. PFC Frank Parko from the 2-320 Field Artillery describes his trial by fire:

"There were beaucoup people in the TOC. We were all crunched together, standing room only. An officer with a PRC-25 radio [LT Bialosuknia] was at the doorway, calling out names from a list as the choppers came in. Somebody had a transistor radio off to one side and the Lovin' Spoonful came out in the middle of all this with, 'It's A Beautiful Morning'. Everybody in the bunker started laughing and snickering; you should be here!

When my group was called up to the door, the officer with the PRC-25 said, 'You know where the 155 pits are? Go down this road, get in the 155 pits, and the slick will be right there.'

He tapped us on our backs— 'Go!'—and we hauled ass down the road to the 155 area. I was wearing my flak jacket and had my helmet in one hand and my M-16 in the other. Mortar rounds were coming in, and there were some zings going by, so I figured we were getting sniped at, too.

We got down to the empty 155 pits—there was nothing there—no chopper—and we just kind of looked at each other and headed for cover—and all of a sudden, the chopper dropped straight in from out of nowhere. The pilot must have come right up the side of the firebase. He hovered about two feet off the ground, and we all ran to climb aboard. One of the guys was having trouble getting in, so me and another guy who had our feet on the skid just grabbed him by the seat of his pants, threw him in, and piled in right behind him.

We were on the floor of the chopper, holding on to each other and the webbing of the seats as the pilot lifted off and put the pedal to the metal. We were flying over the valley below the firebase when we started taking fire, and the pilot banked hard to the right to avoid it—and everybody said, 'Holy shit, look at that,' because [of] the way we were tipped, we were looking straight down at fifteen or twenty NVA. They were hauling a 120 mortar. Three of them had the tube over their shoulders like a log. The rest of them were ammo bearers with mortar shells strapped to their backs. They were going down the side of a hill, like they were changing positions or something. Most of them were shooting up at us with their AK-47's. We swept right over them. . ." Ripcord – pages 388-389.

The grunts from B/2-506 were under orders to hold the perimeter until all the support troops had been evacuated. As the helicopter evacuation progressed, they came under fire from NVA who had moved up the hill into the debris below the wire barrier. The men threw grenades and fired LAW's down the hill, firing their M-60's until the barrels grew red-hot and burned out.

CPT Benjamin Peters, put temporarily in charge of the base when LTC Lucas was evacuated, had been relieved by MAJ James King, the operations officer for 3rd Brigade. When King arrived on the firebase, Peters re-joined his men on the perimeter, firing at muzzle flashes down in the fallen logs with an abandoned M-60 he had picked up.

The heavy mortar barrage continued to fall all over the hill. 1LT Stephen Wallace of Bravo Three was checking his sector of the perimeter with his RTO, PFC Donald Colbert, when he found one of his troops, SP4 Andre Rice, with one leg blown off. The stump had been cauterized by the white-hot shrapnel but Rice was going into shock. Wallace told Rice to lie still and he would get somebody to help. Rice just nodded weakly and lay back.

Rice was not the only wounded man waiting for help. There were so many wounded that LT Caballero and his pathfinders found themselves carrying wounded to safety as well as guiding aircraft onto one of the three helipads on the base. The pathfinder section leader, SSGT Samuel Williams, had two men assisting him; CPL Jimmy Howton and PFC William Kohr. Caballero and Williams stumbled upon a group of wounded men sheltering below Impact Rock. They appeared to have been abandoned in the confusion so Williams began carrying them on his back up the hill, ignoring the incoming. SSGT Williams had been a professional boxer before joining the army and had kept himself in great shape.

After taking care of the wounded, Williams himself was hit when a mortar round exploded behind him, shredding one arm and blasting a big chunk of muscle from the back of a thigh. Though wounded himself, LT Caballero pushed a towel into the gaping thigh wound and, tying on a tourniquet, got Williams out on the next Huey.

Caballero's wounds did not even slow him down. SSGT Thomas Rubsam from B/2-506 helped the lieutenant to *"drive some people out of the mortar pits and onto the slicks. They were incoherent, just at the end of their rope, I suspect."* Caballero, on the other hand, was just the opposite. Noted Rubsam, *"Caballero was doing one hell of a job, man, and loving it, too. He was totally in charge, totally up to the task at hand. That's what he had been trained for, and now he was doing it. He was completely in his element. He was just reveling in it." Ripcord* – page 390.

CPT Thomas Austin was supervising the evacuation of the last of his 155 crewmen when he was knocked down by a mortar shell. He was hit by fragments in his hip and the right armpit when shrapnel went through the armhole of his flak jacket. The pain was so severe that Austin thought he must be dying. 'Doc" Lanny Savoie pulled him into a bunker where his wounds were found to be minor. Feeling better, Austin got the remainder of his people off Ripcord. After a careful check to make sure he had not missed anyone, he went to report to the base commander at the FDC bunker.

Two sergeants were standing at the bunker's entrance and Austin was greeting them when he was sent sprawling by an explosion on the slope of the hill behind and below him. As soon as he landed, someone grabbed the back of his collar and began shouting for him to get up. Gasping from the pain, Austin managed to say that he could not get up or move his legs—his right calf was badly lacerated and the Achilles tendon above his left foot was gone—then he passed out.

When he woke up, he found himself on a stretcher being rushed toward a Huey that was just landing. Austin was so big and heavy that the litter bearers had trouble lifting him onto the cargo deck of the slick. He was banged against the side of the helicopter before they managed to get him inside. After another stretcher case came sliding in next to him, the pilot pulled pitch and then turned away, ending CPT Austin's—a self-described REMF—short but eventful forty-hour combat tour.

1LT Gary Watrous, the artillery FO, had several near-misses before he was finally hit. He had been running back and forth from one side of the hill to the other, calling in air strikes on mortar and AA machine gun positions. Watrous would call in air strikes on an NVA position and when they stopped firing, he would run to another vantage point and call in tac air on a new target, only to find that fire was again coming from a target he had previously hit.

The mortar round that landed behind Watrous knocked him out. When he came to, he was on his back, both legs folded under him. His steel pot, flak jacket and the PRC-25 radio on his back had absorbed a lot of the shrapnel from the waist up—the radio was destroyed—but when he pulled his legs out straight, he discovered that he was seriously injured from his waist down. In terrible pain, both legs shredded, bleeding badly from a big hole behind his right knee, he ripped a strip from his fatigue shirt and tied off the wound behind his knee. He could not move, so he just lay there, praying he would not be hit again.

Looking around, Watrous spotted two men watching him from a foxhole close-by. The men, obviously terrified, just looked at him as he repeatedly yelled for them to come get him. Finally, they did, quickly dragging him to the TOC. Watrous was placed on a litter and rushed out to the next Huey that came in. He had only two weeks left on his tour and he was very worried that he would not get off the hill before the enemy fire became so heavy that no more helicopters could land. He made it, but has no memory of the flight from Ripcord to Charlie Med at Camp Evans.

With the death of LTC Lucas, COL Harrison had ordered his operations officer, MAJ James King to take command of FSB Ripcord, now a firebase in name only. King was close to the end of his tour and he had qualms about his return to combat, especially when he was so 'short.' King met the LOH sent for him and climbed aboard carrying a case of fragmentation grenades. When the LOH arrived over Ripcord, the hill was covered in so much smoke and dust that CPT Fred Spaulding, 3rd Brigade S-3 for air, had to lean out the door of the aircraft and guide the pilot to the ground with hand signals. MAJ King jumped out of the LOH carrying the case of grenades, the weight of which caused him to fall to the ground just as three mortar shells came in. The fall saved him. King was unhurt and the LOH lifted off safely.

MAJ King arrived on Ripcord at about 1045 hours when the evacuation was about half completed. LT Bialosuknia had gone out with the last of the support troops, leaving LT Stephen Wallace in charge of the extraction of B/2-506, still manning the perimeter.

When MAJ King assumed command, the incoming fire was so heavy that King shut down Ripcord to all incoming air traffic at about 1105 hours. The official estimate is that between six hundred and a thousand mortar shells fell on Ripcord during the evacuation. Closing the airspace around Ripcord to Huey slicks allowed the Cobra gunships and F-4 Phantoms to operate more freely. The Cobra pilots reported that NVA troops, glimpsed through rolling clouds of dust and smoke, were moving up the sides of the Ripcord hill in squad and platoon strength. Most of the enemy troops were still five hundred meters or more from the wire barrier. Tactical CS gas was dropped on a mortar crew that had started to fire on Ripcord from only two hundred meters away.

The NVA were attempting to 'hug' the perimeter, a standard enemy tactic to get away from US firepower and to put troops in position to break through the wire barriers. There was almost no vegetation left on the upper slopes of the Ripcord Hill, but the NVA took cover among the stumps and fallen logs. The F-4's dropped low-drag bombs and napalm on enemy troops farther away from the perimeter while Cobras hit the enemy troops closest to the wire.

MAJ King had CPT House from the 158th Aviation Battalion resume the extraction for a brief time but had to shut it down again at 1145 hours because LT Caballero told King it was too dangerous to use the log pad on the upper tier of the base. The Chinook that had gone down earlier in the 105mm battery area was now fully engulfed in flames and the fire had spread to the TOC. Caballero had sent out his last two pathfinders with all the secure commo equipment on the base, leaving no one to evacuate on the upper level of the base.

When the Chinook fire spread to the TOC, it prevented the evacuation of the radios in the TOC bunker and the 81mm mortar tubes that had been left there by the mortar platoon from E/2-506 when they were evacuated. The twenty-five men left on the base with LT Caballero moved down to the lower tier and set up a rough perimeter near Impact Rock.

Maj King was already there as was CPT Peters, CPT Williams and LT Wallace. Several men from B/2-506 had moved in from the perimeter, including Chip Collins, RTO Don Colbert, SGT Phil Tolson and machine gunner Chris Hinman. Tolson had fragment wounds all over his body and Hinman had burns on his face and shrapnel in an arm and leg. Hinman had been firing his M-60 at the NVA down in the debris below the wire when a 12.7mm round had hit the ammo can he was feeding his gun from, causing it to explode. The enemy had begun dropping CS rounds and noxious gas clouds drifted across the base. Black smoke rose from the burning CH-47, the TOC and refueling bladders as well as smoke from brush fires started by detonating claymores and Phou gas barrels set off by grunts from B/2-506 as they withdrew from their positions on the perimeter.

LT Caballero began to bring slicks onto the POL pad on the lower level of the base, but there were long intervals between the Huey's as ARA and tactical air had to be called in to suppress enemy fire before each slick could come in. PFC Don Colbert wrote in a letter home, *"After I left there, were 8 men left. Man, I was scared. There were Gooks coming up the hill when I left. They were trying to shoot our chopper down. We had to leave our rucks up there plus a lot of weapons, etc.. ." Ripcord* – page 395.

Chip Collins got out on the second-to-last slick. For safety reasons, grunts were not supposed to fire their weapons from inside a Huey, but as Collins' slick passed over the edge of the hill, everyone aboard spontaneously began to fire at the NVA coming up the slope.

The last Huey left what remained of FSB Ripcord at about 1214 hours, 23 July. The record is not clear as to who was on board, but MAJ King's Silver Star citation and SGT Phil Tolson's Bronze Star citation credit them with being the last men off Ripcord. The RTO's in the 3rd Brigade TOC at Camp Evans confirmed that King was the last man to step aboard that last Huey. Tolson remembers, however, that the only other passenger with him was an enlisted grunt, not an officer. CPT Williams, the artillery liaison officer recalled that there were six passengers aboard that helicopter and MAJ King was not one of them.

CPT Raymond Williams remembers the last moments of the evacuation in this way:

"By the time we were down to the last few loads, there were enemy soldiers coming up into the 105 battery area on the other side of Ripcord. I could see them with my binoculars. They were rummaging around, looking for whatever they could find. They didn't seem to be in any big hurry to get over to our side of the base, and they basically laid low after some of the infantrymen took them under fire with M-60's.

I was the last person to leave that firebase. They tried to get me to go on an earlier chopper, but I refused. Somebody had to stay and coordinate the fires. I found a place where I could see everything, and called in fire until the last Huey arrived. There was a lieutenant from the infantry company [Wallace], myself, and four enlisted men on that last chopper out. He touched down, we jumped on—and we were gone in a flash, Cobras laying down fire all around us. . ." Ripcord – pages 395-396.

CPT Benjamin Peters, commanding B/2-506 recalls that *he* and LT Wallace were the last two officers to leave Ripcord:

"After the second-to-last helicopter got out, myself and another individual were the only people left on Ripcord. I cannot definitely remember who that other individual was. I remember that he was wearing a radio. It might have been my RTO, but I think it was probably Lieutenant Wallace. He was wearing a radio by that point, and he was the kind of officer who would have insisted on being the last to leave.

Whoever it was, we went around to all the fighting positions on the base to make sure we weren't leaving anyone. We were hollering, 'Is anyone still here, is anyone still here?' but no one answered There was absolutely nothing going on when we called the last helicopter in—no incoming, no nothing. When the two of us disembarked at the Currahee Pad back at Camp Evans, there had been enough of a lull between our helicopter and the second-to-last helicopter that the guys thought we had been left behind. I remember there was a group of people going from helicopter to helicopter, trying to get one of the pilots to take them back to get us. . ." Ripcord – pages 396-397.

There is no official record of the fact that two people—one dead, one still alive—had accidentally been left behind in the confused muddle of those last few minutes on Ripcord. The dead trooper was SGT Stanley Diehl, a mortarman who had been attached to D/2-506, killed on 22 July. His body had been placed in a body bag and moved to the TOC to await evacuation. When the TOC caught fire, SGT Diehl's remains were inadvertently left behind, lying on a stretcher next to the bunker's entrance.

The living one was a young Kit Carson Scout, attached to Bravo One, B/2-506. The man's GI handler, a Vietnamese speaker, had been wounded several days earlier and medevacked to Camp Evans. Left behind with no other friends and unable to speak English, the scout had taken cover in a bunker and remained there. He emerged only when it suddenly got very quiet. COL Harrison describes what happened next:

"An Air Cavalry Scout pilot called my frequency telling me there was a man in jungle fatigues still on Ripcord wildly waving his arms. I flew in for a very close look to verify and pick up the man. A small shot of wisdom hit me on final approach saying it might be a ruse by an NVA soldier. I directed the Air Cav Team to give cover as CWO2 Leslie Rush, an artillery spotter, picked him up using his LOH. I followed Rush back for the drop-off at Camp Evans. The man was a non-English speaking Kit Carson who had been taking cover deep, deep in one of the bunkers." Hell On A Hill Top – page 127.

Air Force forward air controller MAJ 'Skip' Little was still orbiting over the battlefield in his little Cessna L-19 'Bird Dog' as the evacuation of Ripcord came to an end. Army 1LT James McCall was a passenger in the FAC's aircraft because he was very familiar with the layout of FSB Ripcord and MAJ Little had specific orders to destroy the TOC. There were concerns at the 101st Division's higher command levels that some secure commo equipment might have been left behind in the TOC. To make sure that the NVA did not capture these items, Little put white phosphorous marking rockets right on the TOC. After bombs had destroyed the bunker, McCall and Little marked other key targets for destruction, including the damaged 105's on the top level of the base.

After the bombs had hit each specified target, the small aircraft would zoom down for a bomb damage assessment and to make sure the bombs had hit where they would do the most good. LT McCall remembers one thing that confused them was that ". . .*we could see footprints in the dust that had settled across the firebase from the air strikes. We were getting right down on the deck, and we could see footprints going from one position to another inside the perimeter. We called back to confirm that there were no friendlies still on the ground, and were told that everyone had been accounted for, and to continue the mission.*" It was McCall's belief that the NVA, having got through the razor wire barriers, were hiding in the abandoned bunkers. *"I think every time we rolled in hot, they would take cover, so we never actually saw anybody. But there was definite evidence that somebody was running around up there, and more than one. . ."* Ripcord – pages 400-401.

Of course, the North Vietnamese have their own version of the evacuation of FSB Ripcord. COL (later major general) Harrison obtained some records pertaining to the battle from Major General Chu Phuong Doi, who had commanded the NVA 324B Division during Operation Texas Star and the Ripcord battle. Chu told Harrison that the 324B Division had been committed to the battle on 19 May 1970 with orders to "*concentrate its main forces to attack and destroy Operating Base 935* (the NVA name for Ripcord)."

During a conversation with General Chu in Cao Bang, Vietnam on 26 May 2004, General Harrison asked what Chu would have done if the 101st had not evacuated Ripcord on 23 July? His reply was a very candid admission, unusual for a Vietnamese, that his division had begun the battle with nine infantry battalions but by the end of the battle, he had only one fully combat capable battalion left, the other battalions having been destroyed or rendered combat ineffective.

General Chu went on to explain that he would have continued the battle using strategies he had learned as a young man against the French at Dien Bien Phu in 1954 and later put into practice against the US Marines at Khe Sanh in 1968. He told Harrison that he would have moved his troops closer and closer to Ripcord, digging tunnels as they had at Dien Bien Phu.

General Chu had recently been honored at the 50th Anniversary celebration of the history-making victory over the French by the Viet Minh in 1954. But General Harrison says, *"I am not sure those were his true thoughts in July 1970 after losing thousands of his soldiers to our troopers and our truly superb air and artillery support."* Hell On A Hill Top – pages 128-129.

An excerpt from the records of the 324B Division states the following:

"At 12:30 P.M. on 23 July there were no more enemy troops left on Hill 935. At 1400 hours that same day U.S. B-52 bombers bombed and destroyed Base 935. 324B Division's campaign to besiege Operating Base 935 and attack enemy forces in the field was over. During twenty-three days and nights of continuous combat 324B Division had killed more than 1,700 American troops, shot down 97 helicopters, and captured or destroyed sixteen 105mm and 155mm howitzers together with large quantities of weapons, military equipment, and supplies. Our attacks had inflicted serious losses on five battalions of the U.S. 3rd Brigade, and three battalion command posts had been destroyed. For the first time in the history of the Tri-Thien battlefield *a heavily fortified U.S. battalion-sized base camp located on high ground had been attacked and destroyed by one of our divisions."* Hell On A Hill Top – page 127.

The North Vietnamese claims are, of course, greatly exaggerated. The NVA attacked with firepower only and were never able to penetrate the wire barriers around Ripcord. During the part of the battle lasting from 1 July through 23 July, the US forces lost 75 KIA, six (a battery) 105mm howitzers and three helicopters. No battalion command posts or the base itself were destroyed until the 101st did it themselves with close-in air strikes, artillery and B-52 bombing. Later, persistent CS gas was sown over the site of FSB Ripcord, making the hill uninhabitable for years to come.

Chapter 19
PICKING UP THE PIECES

"The decision to withdraw from Ripcord had been the right move. Harrison had gotten a tiger by the tail during the siege, though, and he didn't let go." LTC Charles 'Shamrock' Shay, CO of the 2-502 Infantry, 101st Airborne.

Brigadier General Berry held an awards ceremony on 25 July, only two days after the evacuation. Silver Stars were presented to COL Harrison and about a dozen other officers and men from the 2-506 Infantry. When Berry pinned the medal on Harrison's shirt pocket, he told him that, in his opinion, the evacuation of Ripcord was *"The most brilliantly planned and executed airmobile operation of the war."* Ripcord – page 403.

BG Berry was very concerned about morale in the 3rd Brigade and spent a great deal of time talking with men from the 2-501 and 2-506 Infantry, the battalions that had borne the brunt of the battle from 1 July until the firebase was closed. Berry tried the best he could to present the Ripcord battle as a U.S. victory. The general told the men that the 155mm battery on the base had done so much damage to the NVA supply lines that they [the NVA] had to commit an entire division to the battle. By concentrating his forces in one area, the enemy had been vulnerable to the massed firepower of the division and, as a result, had suffered heavy casualties. Berry did mention that political considerations had forced the 101st to hold back the additional ground forces needed to push the NVA back into Laos. He told the men that they had held out as long as they could to maximize the enemy's losses before being withdrawn. Berry usually concluded his pep talks by telling the troops that operations were then being planned to attack the supply areas of the North Vietnamese units that had attacked Ripcord.

Although the officers were impressed by the concern shown by Berry during his visits with the troops, the grunts did not feel the same. The chaplain for the 2-506 Infantry, CPT Leroy Fox, remembers that *"The troops didn't receive him very well. There was a lot of anger from the troops at that time." Ripcord* – page 403.

As the line grunts viewed it, they had been used as live bait to draw the enemy in, then hung out to dry when the enemy closed in around them. The troops did not understand or care about the 'big picture' and most of their anger was due to the perception that they had not received the support they should have from higher up the chain of command. Because of the perception of lack of support, numerous troops came to Chaplain Fox and told him they were going to refuse to return to the field when the 2-506 began a new operation. Fox spent a lot of his time counseling the bitter, angry troops, trying to keep them from committing a court martial offense. It took a lot of persuasion but, in the end, almost all the men did go back out with their units. All that most of them had needed was a little time to come to terms with what they had just gone through.

During one of BG Berry's visits to 3rd Brigade, he asked COL Harrison his opinion of a proposed posthumous award for LTC Andre Lucas and Harrison suggested that Lucas be given the Distinguished Service Cross. Berry then asked if Lucas was not more deserving of the Medal of Honor. Harrison agreed that he was, but said he was not sure that they could make that kind of a case because Lucas had not been involved in any one action that by itself would merit the award of the country's highest award for valor. Berry told Harrison that, even so, he wanted to try and explained that he would base the recommendation on Lucas' gallantry over the length of the operation rather than on just a single incident. In a letter home, Berry noted that *"Over the entire 23-day spasm of Ripcord that I observed, Lucas was magnificent. He was utterly and courageously devoted to his mission and his men. . .Medal of Honor recommendations take a long time to go all the way, but I believe this one will make it."* Ripcord – page 404.

The recommendation did go all the way and LTC Andre Lucas became the only infantry officer above the rank of captain and one of only two battalion commanders—the other recipient was an artillery officer—to be awarded the Medal of Honor during the Vietnam Conflict.

The recommendation for the award caused a great deal of controversy. The general opinion was best described by a squad leader who said that "[LTC] *Lucas' handling of the battalion was a fiasco. He got his people in bad situations and didn't know what to do. It was the kind of situation where if he had lived, he probably would have been brought up on charges, but since he got killed, he ended up with the Medal of Honor." Ripcord – page 404.*

Captain's Chuck Hawkins and 'Gabe' Rollison both agreed that Lucas deserved the medal of Honor. So did his former operations officer, MAJ Herb Koenigsbauer, who noted that the criticism of the award was mainly from junior personnel who did not have all the information needed to formulate such critical conclusions about Lucas. COL Harrison believes that Berry sought to do more than recognize Lucas' personal courage; he meant the award to be a testimony to all the soldiers who served at Ripcord and in Operation Texas Star. It was General Berry's way of letting the country and the world know that something important had occurred at Ripcord.

Something big had indeed occurred at Ripcord. The 101st Airborne lost 74 KIA and more than 400 WIA during the fighting from 1 July through the evacuation on 23 July. The public information office press release listed the number of KIA's at 61, making the losses appear less than they were. Trying to avoid a scandal in the press, the memo did not mention the 13 MIA's who were still out on the hills and in the jungle around Ripcord.

The actual number of enemy losses will never be known. Since the 101st did not inflate body counts, the 125 NVA KIA's listed in the Daily Staff Journals of the units involved reflects only those enemy dead physically present and counted on the battlefield. The actual figures were certainly much higher considering the tremendous amount of firepower that had been brought to bear on the NVA. During the weeks following the evacuation, the most likely routes of withdrawal had been subjected to a relentless pounding by artillery, tactical air strikes and B-52 'Arc Light' raids. During one of his visits, BG Berry told assembled troops that at least 500 North Vietnamese had been killed.

The long-awaited Operation Chicago Peak finally began on 25 July when LTC Charles 'Shamrock' Shay's 2-502 'Strike Force' Infantry opened FSB Maureen on Hill 980 just east of Co Pung Mountain. After an artillery battery had been airlifted onto Maureen on 30 July, elements from the ARVN 1st Infantry Division moved by air onto the summit of Co Pung. The NVA, after some initial resistance, elected not to defend Co Pung and avoided major contact with both the ARVN and the 2-502 Infantry. Instead, the NVA attacked FSB O'Reilly on 6 August, using the 6th NVA Regiment to surround the firebase.

MG Hennessey, having returned from his leave, cancelled Chicago Peak to allow the ARVN to concentrate their forces for the defense of FSB O'Reilly. The abbreviated operation resulted in 97 NVA KIA and 32 weapons captured, but no major cache sites or supply depots were found.

In the meantime, COL Harrison was anxious to recover his 13 MIA's from the hills and jungle around Ripcord. Harrison determined that there was no point in risking men to search for PFC Stephen Harber from C/2-506 missing on Hill 902, since all that had ever been found was a jungle boot with his foot inside and one of his dog tags attached. He also felt that it would be useless to look for the remains of SP4 Lewis Howard and PFC Charles Beals from D/2-506, left on Hill 1000. To Harrison, it seemed likely that the three men had been blown to pieces during the respective battles. So, on 3 August, Harrison sent the 3rd Brigade recon platoon to the site of D/1-506's struggle to look for the body of the medic, PFC Ronald 'Kuntz', who had fallen from the helicopter skid but his body was never found. The remaining eight MIA's from D/1-506—SP4 Eloy Valle; PFC Bill Browning; PFC Patrick DeWulf; PFC John Knott; CPT Donald Workman; PFC Frank Asher; PFC Robert Hays and PFC Peter Huk—were located and placed in body bags for the flight back to Camp Evans on board COL Harrison's C&C helicopter. Harrison later wrote of the gruesome flight *"The odor was overwhelming. We had difficulty flying and not throwing up. Ripcord* – page 405.

Another three weeks went by before the weather allowed COL Harrison to launch an operation to recover the remains of SGT Stanley Diehl from D/2-506, the last of the 3rd Brigades MIA's, left behind on Ripcord during the hectic evacuation of 23 July. By that time, the firebase bore no resemblance to its former appearance, having been turned inside out by air strikes. After LTC Otis Livingston's 2-501 had secured the high ground around the former firebase on 27 August, a LOH from the 3rd Brigade aviation platoon, covered by Cobra gunships, darted in to touch down on Ripcord. SGT Diehl, still in his body bag, was located and loaded onto the LOH. When the LOH tried to take off, it took fire and crashed back onto Ripcord. A platoon from B/2-501 moved on foot onto Ripcord and secured the crash site long enough for a Huey to come in to pick up the Diehl's body and the crew of the downed LOH. An aero rifle platoon from B/2-17 Cavalry was moved by air onto Ripcord to secure the area and get the LOH ready for extraction. After the LOH was recovered on 29 August, the 2-501 Infantry was also withdrawn from the Ripcord area.

Estimates by the 101st Airborne's intelligence analysts put the size of the enemy force arrayed against the 3rd Brigade at six battalions. Since NVA battalions were smaller than their U.S. counterparts, it was estimated that at least 2,300 NVA had taken part in the battle. That figure, however, does not accurately convey the tremendous advantages enjoyed by the enemy. The concealment and cover afforded by the double-and-triple canopy jungle and the rugged terrain plus the innumerable bunker complexes that were virtually immune to artillery or air strikes gave the NVA an advantage almost impossible to overcome by one or two battalions, no matter how well-supported they were.

Both General Berry and (later) General Harrison cite Chuck Hawkins wire-tap intelligence as proof that the enemy brought an entire division to the Ripcord battle. This later became an accepted fact after Berry said in a speech at a Ripcord reunion, *"There were for sure three, and probably four regiments. . .So let's say there were nine to twelve thousand* [NVA soldiers around Ripcord]." *Ripcord* – page 430. Many people believe that Berry was attempting to justify his decision to withdraw on the overwhelming numbers the enemy had amassed around Ripcord, but this information was not fully known until years after the battle.

CPT Christopher Straub, who had commanded D/2-501 on Hill 805, came to view BG Berry's decision to close Ripcord as both militarily and politically necessary, but the decision to close the firebase also cast doubts on the original decision to open a firebase deep in the heart of an area controlled by the NVA. Straub wrote that *"The decision to evacuate confirms my view that from the start the 101st's push into the Ripcord AO was not in consonance with what the U.S. was trying to accomplish in Vietnam in 1970."* Ripcord – page 411.

CPT Chuck Hawkins has often said that he does not understand why the 101st did not use their air mobility to keep the NVA off balance. *"We could have choppered into Ripcord, built a base, waited for signs of enemy activity, then choppered over to the next mountain to continue harassing their lines of communication with artillery fire. Can you imagine the effort. . . [the NVA] put into preparing for the Ripcord siege? What if they had to do that all over again in order to ring the next mountaintop we occupied?"* Ripcord – page 411.

The fact that the 101st built a hardened, semi-permanent base deep in enemy territory implied that the division wanted to draw the North Vietnamese into a major confrontation. That decision puzzled Chris Straub who wrote *"The people down in Saigon were biting their nails every night, wondering who was going to get involved in the next Hamburger Hill. . .Why did the 101st commit itself to a grandiose operation out on the edge of the A Shau Valley. . .if the division leadership was aware that once they'd taken a certain number of casualties, they'd have to pull out because of pressure from MACV and USARV?" Ripcord* – page 412.

MAJ Herb Kornigsbauer, LTC Lucas's operation officer during a large part of the battle, wrote that it had never occurred to him that the 101st Airborne's senior leadership did not have the will to engage the North Vietnamese and destroy them. Lucas and Koenigsbauer made many requests for the division to commit additional battalions to the battle. The existence of Ripcord in the heart of the NVA's 'Warehouse Area' had forced the enemy to concentrate their units around the base, making them vulnerable to the division's air mobility and air power.

At the time, there were no other major actions in the division's AO to divert resources away from Ripcord, so if they division was going to 'pile on', then was the time. The opportunity existed to hurt the enemy, but higher command (division, corps and higher) was not ready to follow through and commit the resources needed to win the battle. Koenigsbauer later said that he became somewhat disillusioned that "...*after all the sacrifices that had been made to take and hold Ripcord, we just turned around and gave it back to the North Vietnamese...There had been no change in the political situation from the time we were ordered to take Ripcord and the time we were ordered to evacuate. To write Ripcord off made clear to those of us fighting the war that there was no national commitment to fight and win...The evacuation saved U.S. lives, but it was also one more step towards our tactical, operational, and strategic defeat in Vietnam." Ripcord* – page 412.

In the months after the battle, when their flights from one base to another took them near Ripcord, BG Berry would order his C&C ship pilot, 1LT John Fox, to circle the destroyed base. Berry would stare down at the cratered hilltop and the blasted hills and ridges around it with an angry look on his face. Wrote Fox *"He might have been evaluating the battle in professional terms. You could see that he was in pain over what happened. It weighed on his mind for a long time that we'd had to pull out of Ripcord. He wouldn't say anything as he looked out the helicopter window, and, finally, he would just give me a quick hand signal to continue on." Ripcord* – page 413.

Chapter 20
FIREBASE BARNETT
AND 'COME BACK RIDGE'

From North Vietnamese records... *"304B Division will attack and destroy the enemy base at Da Ban (FSB Barnett) in Quang Tri Province."*

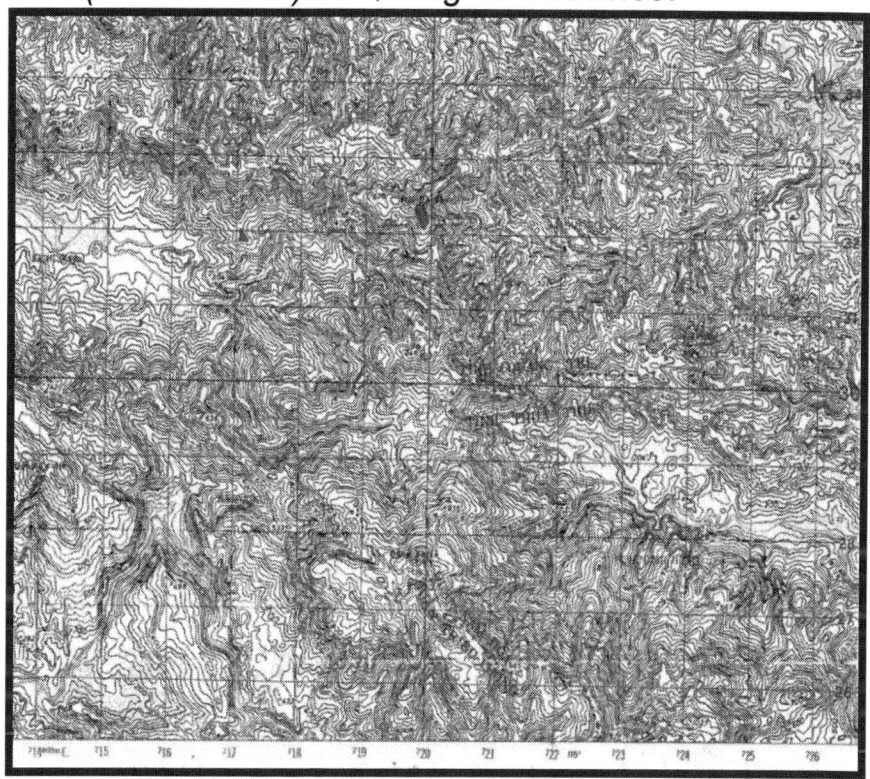

Enhanced detail from Map Sheet 6442-3 Series L7014, Ba Long District of Quang Tri Province. FSB Barnett and 2-502 Infantry positions on 'Come Back Ridge' highlighted in blue, with Khe Ta Laou River valley (The 13th Valley) in upper left quadrant of map, five kilometers west of FSB Barnett. Original map from author's collection. Color enhanced map ©2017.

After  the 2-502 Infantry was relieved by the 1-327 Infantry on Hill 882, the 'O-Deuce' moved by air to a new AO around Firebase Bastogne and QL (highway) 547. The battalion operated around Bastogne with light enemy contact while integrating replacement troops into the battalion. On 9 July, the 2-502 was moved by truck on QL-547 to Camp Eagle. The entire battalion was then flown by CH-47 to Quang Tri and then by UH-1H to the vicinity of FSB Shepherd in Quang Tri Province at XD 936410.

An old firebase built on a low hill by the 3rd Marine Division in 1969, Shepherd overlooked QL-9 and was surrounded on three sides by the Quang Tri and Da Krong Rivers. After arriving in the new AO. The 2-502 Infantry became OPCON to COL Benjamin Harrison and the 3rd Brigade. The 'O-Deuce' remained in the Firebase Shepherd AO until 15 July with no contact with the enemy. On 15 July, the 2-502 was again moved by CH-47 back to Camp Eagle and returned to the OPCON of 1 Brigade.

On 17 July, the whole battalion was moved by air from Camp Eagle to FSB Veghel. The battalion then moved by air to various LZ's near YC 493981 along a large terrain feature known as Dong A Tay Ridge about eight klicks southwest of FSB Veghel. Dong A Tay had been the scene of fierce fighting in March and April 1969 between elements of the 1-502 Infantry, the 2-327 Infantry and an NVA battalion that had attacked FSB Veghel. The NVA battalion was broken up, suffering ninety confirmed KIA's.

The 2-502 operated near Dong A Tay Ridge until 21 July with no contact. Numerous bunkers, food caches and bamboo shelters were located and destroyed. On 21 July, the battalion returned to Camp Eagle and was placed on stand-by to be moved by air to the FSB Ripcord AO. Company C was placed on thirty-minute alert with the rest of the battalion on two-hour alert.

As Firebase Ripcord was being evacuated on 23 July, Company C moved to the Strike Force LZ on one-hour stand-by with Charlie One (the author's platoon) on thirty- minute stand-by for air movement to the Ripcord AO to support A/2-506. That afternoon, the 'O-Deuce' was taken off alert status and stand down training resumed in preparation for the next operation in the FSB Maureen AO.

■ ■ ■

On 25 July under OPORDER Chicago Peak, the 2-502 Infantry moved by air from the Strike Force LZ at Camp Eagle to Firebase Maureen at YD 429122. Maureen was first built in 1968 on Hill 980 or Dong Tam Hanh as it was known to the Vietnamese. Maureen was the scene of several firefights between CPT (then 1LT) Donald Workman's D/1-506 and an NVA unit on 5 May and again on 6 May.

A 155mm howitzer battery on FSB Maureen, looking southwest. The flat-topped peak on the horizon at center is Co Pung Mountain on the eastern side of the A Shau Valley. Photo by Bill Maxey, A/2-501 Infantry.

When D/2-502 began landing on their LZ at YD400115, the fourth Huey into the LZ came under AK-47 fire and took hits in the left door. Troops already on the LZ spotted twelve NVA southwest of the LZ out of range of small arms fire, so artillery and air strikes were called in with unknown results.

At about 1200 hours on 25 July, an air strike came in near YD 443121 and nearly hit a platoon from Company C. No one knew who had called for the airstrike and the battalion TOC on Firebase Maureen was unable to raise the Air Force FAC, call sign Bilk 16, to determine who had called for the air strike. Fortunately, there were no casualties on the ground from the air strike.

As the combat engineers from Company D, 326th Engineer Battalion began to prepare positions on the firebase, they found a grave holding one NVA killed by small arms fire. The body had been dead about three months and may have killed by D/1-506 in early May. The next day, two more graves were discovered on the firebase, one killed by artillery or an air strike and the other by small arms fire.

Over the next six days, the line companies from the O-Deuce spread out over the AO and began finding many bunkers, food and ammo caches. The weather was very hot and humid (105°, 85-90% humidity) and Company C had to request a medevac for two men down with heat exhaustion. When the dust-off arrived, it was fired on from a near-by ridge as it hovered to hoist up the two heat casualties. A Pink
Team responded to support the medevac and was also fired on from the same ridge. Troops from Company C fired on the area with small arms, but received no return fire. There was no further contact with the NVA by O-Deuce ground troops as the month of July ended.

As the month of August began the O-Deuce continued operations in the FSB Maureen AO. There was no contact with the NVA but troops continued to uncover extensive bunker complexes (including hospital and mess hall bunkers), tunnels and ammo, weapons and food caches. Many of these installations were located by markings carved into tree trunks along the trails.

Helicopters were used to drop persistent and non-persistent CS gas crystals on known or suspected enemy positions. On the evening of 8 August, the helicopter covering for a Huey dropping CS gas was fired on by five to ten NVA on a ridge above the Rao La River near YD 424098. The Huey was not hit and air strikes were called in on the ridge.

On 10 August, a division PSYOPS Huey broadcasting over loud speakers took fire and received hits in the transmission. Apparently the NVA did not like what they were hearing! The Huey was forced down near YD382138. An aero-rifle platoon from the 2-17 Cav was scrambled to protect the helicopter and crew until they could be extracted by CH-47 the next day.

Since the 2-502 Infantry had been unable to initiate significant contact with the enemy in the Firebase Maureen AO, the decision to move the battalion was made on 11 August to terminate OPORDER Chicago Peak and the O-Deuce was moved by air to Camp Eagle on 12 August. Company C from the O-Deuce remained on Firebase Maureen to secure the base under the OPCON of the 2-506 Infantry. The new AO would be around FSB Barnett and the Khe Ta Loau River in Quang Tri Province and the O-Deuce would again come under the OPCON of 3rd Brigade.

■ ■ ■

At mid-afternoon on 13 August, the 2-502 (-) moved by air from Camp Eagle northwest to Quang Tri Province and the FSB Barnett AO. Firebase Barnett, on the peak of Nui Da Ban Mountain at YD199324, overlooked the eastern end of the Khe Ta Laou River valley, later made famous in John Del Vecchio's novel *The 13th Valley*. The firebase was manned by the 2-502 TOC, D/2-502(-) as base security, Battery B 2-11 Field Artillery and 81mm mortars from E/2-502. Communications were supplied by the VHF section of the 501st Signal Battalion.

As A/2-502 came into their LZ at YD195340 two hundred meters west of the peak of Hill 848, they found two dead NVA, killed by the LZ artillery prep earlier that morning. The dead soldiers were wearing olive drab fatigues and Ho Chi Minh sandals. Company A also found a damaged RPD machine gun, an RPD drum magazine, ammo, both US and NVA grenades and assorted field equipment. While still on the LZ, Company A received several 60mm mortar rounds that caused no casualties.

Two hours later, about one klick northeast of the firebase at YD204328, the Recon Platoon made contact with four NVA at fifteen-meter range. Recon's point man, PFC Russell Bahrke, was killed instantly by the first volley and three other Recon men were wounded. Recon's return fire killed three of the NVA who were apparently defending a freshly dug log-and-earth bunker.

On a hill about six hundred meters west of Hill 848, Company A overran an NVA headquarters bunker complex. In one of the bunkers was found a typewriter and a mimeograph machine. A dead NVA was discovered in one of the bunkers wearing a T-shirt and a loin-cloth. His shirt had the red letter 'B' on it. Nearby were one hundred fifty fighting positions scattered across the hillside.

B/2-502 and LTC Shay, the battalion commander overhead in a C&C Huey, spotted an 82mm mortar tube and sixty to seventy bunkers along a ridgeline near YD172322 about two and a half klicks west of Firebase Barnett. A White Team, F-4 Phantom fighter-bombers and 8-inch tube artillery were called in on the bunkers. At about 2145 hours that night, a Night Hawk armed reconnaissance aircraft spotted a sampan moving west on the Khe Ta Laou river about five klicks west of Barnett. The boat was destroyed.

On the morning of 15 August, C/2-502 returned to the OPCON of the 2-502 Infantry and was moved by air from FSB Maureen to Camp Eagle to prepare for the move by air from Camp Eagle to the FSB Barnett AO.

Aerial view of FSB Barnett looking southwest toward the Khe Ta Laou River valley behind the ridge just above the hovering CH-47 Chinook. Photo by Randy Kirby, Company C, 159th Assault Helicopter Battalion.

Early that same morning, a LOH from a White Team was checking a ridge near YD170330 when they were fired on, wounding one crewman. A Pink Team, checking a ridge above a branch of the Khe Ta Laou river near YD173298 found thirty-three bunkers and fifty fighting positions capable of housing about one hundred men. Company A, while moving along a trail about two klicks southwest of Barnett near YD 183311 found the following markings carved into trees: TD, K18, CT5 and 13V. Company B's Bravo Three received AK-47 fire followed by about fifteen rounds of 82mm fire at YD171319, near a ridge that would later become known as 'Come Back Ridge.' Bravo Three took two casualties and called in tube artillery and ARA. They spotted eight NVA moving away from the contact area and took them under fire with unknown results. A sweep of the contact area by Bravo Three found one dead NVA and they captured small arms ammo, two AK-47's, first aid supplies and clothing items.

A Pink Team checking the area for NVA found a foot bridge across the Khe Ta Laou River and destroyed it with rocket fire. Early that same evening, Firebase Barnett received twelve 82mm mortar rounds, six impacting inside the wire. The NVA mortar tube was spotted at YD193310 and tube artillery from Barnett fired on that position.

At about 1930 hours, Bravo Three and Delta Three in separate NDP's near YD170325, received thirty-eight rounds of 82mm mortar fire. Bravo Three had two wounded while Delta Three had one wounded trooper and one wounded Kit Carson Scout. When the medevac came on station and went into a hover to hoist up the wounded, a 12.7mm machine gun on Hill 478 two klicks to the north, fired about fifty rounds but did not hit the dust-off. All the wounded were successfully evacuated to the 18th Surgical Hospital at Camp Evans.

Sunday 16 August began with Company B's Bravo Two and Bravo Three and Company D's Delta Three reporting probes of their NDP's near YD170325. Four trip flares went off in front of Bravo Three's positions at about 0057 hours. Grenades were thrown at movement around the NDP and 81mm mortar fire from Firebase Barnett was called in. At around 0100 hours, the three platoons came under ground attack while receiving about seventy 60mm mortar rounds and over one hundred satchel charges and grenades thrown at their positions. This fight last over three hours until the NVA broke contact at about 0430 hours.

Twenty-five minutes later, the enemy pelted the battered NDP perimeter with more satchel charges and AK-47 fire. At about 0600 hours, Bravo Two and Three received a ground attack which was thrown back. Twelve minutes later, the NVA launched a second attack which was also broken up by small arms fire and artillery. Then, at 0628 hours, a third ground attack came at Company B which lasted until about 0650 hours when the enemy finally withdrew. The three platoons had suffered eleven wounded and SGT Frederick Huttie from Delta Three was killed. A sweep of the area after the attacks ended revealed at least sixteen NVA killed by small arms fire and twenty NVA killed by artillery or mortar fire. Ten AK-47's and an RPG launcher were captured.

The three platoons asked for an emergency resupply of ammo and a log bird flew out five cases of frags, five cases of M-79 grenades, two cases of M-60 ammo and four cases of M-16 ammo. Shortly after the log bird left the O-Deuce LZ at Camp Eagle, Company C was moved by air to a staging area at Camp Evans to wait for insertion by UH-1H slicks into the Barnett AO.

At mid-morning, The Recon Platoon made contact about two hundred meters southwest of the peak of Hill 606 near YD214332. The platoon's Kit Carson Scout, who was walking point, received a minor wound during the brief exchange of fire before the enemy withdrew. Company B's Bravo Two and Three continued their sweep of the contact area and recovered weapons, ammo and equipment abandoned earlier by their attackers.

At about 1030 hours on 16 August, Company C moved from Camp Evans aboard UH-1H Huey slicks on the way to an LZ at YD 175330. As the third slick came into the LZ carrying men from Charlie One, it received fire from NVA positions to the west of the LZ. The enemy fired RPG's, AK-47's and threw satchel charges at the men on the open LZ. Charley One returned fire while two men were wounded as they exited a slick that had just landed on the LZ. Shortly after that, the enemy withdrew leaving behind one dead NVA and one wounded NVA who was taken prisoner. Subsequent interrogation of the POW revealed that he was a member of the 6th Company, 1st Battalion, 56th Regiment attached to the 304B Division, elements of which had recently fought at FSB Ripcord.

Bravo One, operating about fourteen hundred meters northwest of 'Come Back Ridge', overran a bunker complex containing a field hospital. Captured were an RPD machine gun, two AK-47's and several blood-stained medical kits. Various documents were found, among them firing tables for 82mm mortars, a doctor's hand book and numerous personal diaries. A recently killed NVA soldier was found in one of the bunkers. It appeared that the field hospital had been treating wounded from the attack on elements of Companies B and D. At 'Come Back Ridge', Delta Three was moved by air to FSB Barnett to join the other two platoons of Company D as firebase security.

In the early morning of 17 August, a white team making an aerial reconnaissance of the Khe Ta Laou valley found several large fields of rice and corn near YD146324. Some of the rice had been harvested and was stacked in shocks in the field. The White Team also found evidence of enemy base camps in the valley near the rice and corn fields.

Company B finished their search of the large bunker/hospital complex they had found on 16 August. They had found a large pile of bloody bandages and torn and bloody clothing for at least twenty-five men. They also recovered bags of rice, shovels and picks, new uniforms and ruck sacks, tents, hammocks and ammunition and weapons. All of this was destroyed in place except for the weapons which were flown to Camp Eagle.

Company B left the bunkers and moved about five hundred meters southeast to YD171321 where they ran into an NVA unit of unknown size. Shots were exchanged and the NVA quickly broke contact. Company B followed a heavy blood trail but the enemy had disappeared. This action took place only about two hundred meters north of 'Come Back Ridge.'

The Recon Platoon received twelve 60mm mortar rounds that impacted near their NDP at YD215334 near the top of Hill 606. The platoon then had movement in the brush on three sides of their perimeter but the enemy did not launch an attack. Recon quietly packed up and moved about two hundred meters northwest of the NDP site and called in ARA from a Pink Team onto Hill 606.

On 18 August, the O-Deuce continued to uncover enemy bunker complexes and supply caches. Company B found a cache at YD169320 with four Russian-made electrical generators, tools, new uniforms NVA-style jungle boots and Ho Chi Minh sandals. As Company B searched the bunkers, several NVA ran from the area without firing at US troops. About 75% of the bunker complex had been destroyed or damaged by air strikes.

The Recon Platoon made a brief contact at YD216334 on the east side of Hill 606. They killed one NVA and followed two blood trails southwest until the trails were washed out by a sudden rain shower.

Company B's Bravo Two found a commo wire running along a three-foot wide trail. They followed the commo wire and trail until it merged into a four-foot wide trail known as a 'freeway.' The platoon found a tree with a carved arrow pointing east and the word 'HUE' carved into the bark beneath the arrow. On either side of the 'freeway', they discovered fighting positions with overhead cover that had been occupied as recently as twelve hours prior to discovery.

On 19 August, Company B returned to the area of 'Come Back Ridge' at YD170320 and made contact with an estimated company-sized NVA unit out in the open. A vicious fight developed that lasted for several hours with ARA being called in to attack the NVA as they tried to withdraw. LTC Shay briefly considered sending in another company to reinforce Company B but eventually decided not to make the move.

Company B killed nine NVA with small arms fire, a White Team killed five NVA and the ARA Cobras accounted for another four. Air strikes killed four NVA and artillery fire killed an additional three enemy . A wounded enemy soldier was taken prisoner and became the second POW of the Barnett Operation.

PFC Frank Fratellenico was killed while assaulting an enemy position. He was getting ready to throw a live grenade at the NVA when he was hit by small arms fire and dropped the grenade. Realizing the grenade was a danger to his squad, he pulled the grenade next to his body and held it until it exploded, protecting his squad mates. Fratellenico was posthumously awarded the Medal of Honor for his actions. Eight other men from Company B were wounded. The company captured an RPD machine gun, two RPG launchers, twelve AK-47's and an 82mm mortar tube.

Up on the high ridge at YD174328 about a klick north of 'Come Back Ridge', Company C found and interesting set of markings carved on a large tree beside a trail they were following. The markings are illustrated below:

```
          ■  ■
           ■
           X
          TD
DD2     2 – 1
           A
          ■ ■
           X
```

Authors' rendition of the trail markers carved into the tree on the ridge above the area known as 'Come Back Ridge' on 19 August. Authors collection ©2017.

Company C continued to move down the long narrow ridgeline above 'Come Back Ridge' and set up their NDP for 19-20 August at YD177328. At around midnight, three mortar rounds exploded in the trees above the NDP and the shrapnel blew downward onto the sleeping men below. SP4 Bruce Scott describes what happened after the mortar shells exploded, "*I was a short-timer and had only two weeks left to go home. At that time, the 101st would not take people out of the field until they had four days left. We had been humping on a ridgeline for a while and it was starting to get dark. We had passed an LZ and were trying to make it to another. . .the decision was made to back track to the last LZ we had passed. . .I woke up Dave Kingery for his turn on guard duty and I gave him my watch. I think it was about midnight when I heard three large explosions. I later learned there were three 81mm mortar fins [found] the next day. I got up and expecting an [ground] attack tried to fire off the claymore mines. I remember clicking [the firing mechanisms] them but nothing seemed to happen. I suddenly realized that I could not breathe very well. I had a sucking chest wound from shrapnel which I still have pieces of in my body today. I remember going towards a bright light and I really thought I was dying and going to heaven but the light turned out to be [the light on] a medevac helicopter.*" Might Men of Valor – page 168.

Seventeen men from Company C were wounded with ten needing evacuation. SP4 Marshall Jones and SP4 Paul Miller were killed. A controversy arose over who had fired the three mortar rounds. The three tail fin assemblies were recovered the next morning and they were found to 81mm of US manufacture. A rumor began that the three rounds had been fired by the 81mm mortar platoon from E/2-502 on FSB Barnett and some of the men from Company C vowed to get even with the men from the mortar platoon.

The rounds were most probably fired by the NVA. Because their mortar tubes were 82mm they could, and often did, fire captured 81mm rounds from their tubes. Tom Boyce, a member of the Recon Platoon then in their NDP at YD192325 about seven hundred meters northwest of Company C, told the author in a phone conversation in December 2014 that he heard a mortar tube fire three rounds at about midnight and the shots fired had not come from the direction of FSB Barnett.

In an e-mail to the author dated November 7, 2012, SGT Jim Brinker, a Recon team leader, described a confrontation at the next stand down, "*Some Charley Company guys came to the Echo Company bar to confront Echo Company 'mortar fuckers' about the incident. Denials were made and no fights took place.*"

Early on the morning of 20 August, Company B was still in their NDP at YD169319 overlooking the Khe Ta Laou river valley when two NVA walked right into their perimeter. Company B opened fire, killing one enemy soldier and wounding the other who managed to escape. While sweeping the area, Company B discovered a small bunker complex and weapons cache. Later that day, Bravo Company moved by air to FSB Barnett and assumed responsibility for firebase security.

In the early evening of 20 August, what remained of Company C was moved by air to FSB Barnett. The company then moved north on foot from Barnett to YD 198325 where an NDP was established. Company A/2-501 became OPCON to the O-Deuce and was moved by air to an LZ near 'Come Back Ridge' to begin patrol and ambush operations.

The morning of 21 August began with one 75mm recoilless rifle round being fired at FSB Barnett causing no damage or casualties. At about 1100 hours, two men from Company A left the company's perimeter at YD200311 to defecate. The NVA were watching the company and fired on the two men with an RPD machine gun and AK-47's. The NVA were within sixty feet of the two men when they opened fire and both men were hit. The RPD gunner fired at Company A's perimeter and wounded a third man before they broke contact and fled southeast. One of the company medic's, SP4 Ben O. Johnson was killed; SP4 Michael Snotts and PFC William B. Hern were wounded and required evacuation. Later that afternoon, Company A was notified that within the next two days, they would be moved by air to Camp Evans and become OPCON to the 2-501 Infantry.

That same morning, the author returned to the field from Camp Eagle where he had been recovering from an injury to his right foot and joined Company C at their NDP at YD198325. Upon re-joining his platoon, Charley One, the author remembers, *"I got off the helicopter at Charley Company's LZ and went to find Charley One. Almost immediately, I noticed a change in the way the men were behaving. Charley One was normally very alert, with good dispersal and noise discipline. However, on that day they were sitting in groups in the open talking among themselves, and I saw several men just staring off into space. Evidently the mortar attack and the heavy casualties had done great damage to Charley One's morale."* Mighty Men of Valor – page 170.

That night, the O-Deuce TOC was notified that ten men from Company D; seven men from A/2-501; two men from Recon, twenty-five men from Company B; ten from Company C; three from Company E and five men from Battery B/2-11 Artillery would be moved by air to Barnett and from Barnett to Camp Eagle to view the Miss America Show at the Eagle Bowl at Camp Eagle. The 101st always made a great effort to get as many men as possible from the field to Eagle Bowl to view special events such as the Bob Hope Show and other celebrities who came to entertain the troops.

Shortly before 7 PM that evening, FSB Barnett received twelve 82mm mortar rounds but only one round fell inside the perimeter and caused no casualties. The mortar was spotted firing from a position near YD184298, about three klicks southwest of the firebase. 82mm, 155mm and ARA from a Pink Team blasted the area and no further fire was received from that location

At mid-morning on 22 August, Company A's Alpha Two spotted four NVA in the distance and opened fire with unknown results. During a sweep of the area, the platoon was fired on by an unknown number of NVA and one trooper was lightly wounded. Alpha Two found four bunkers on the east slope of Hill 848 at YD201306. The bunkers had been partially destroyed by artillery, but the platoon found seven 82mm mortar rounds and nine fuses.

Later that day, FSB Barnett received eleven 60mm mortar rounds spaced out over a forty-minute period. All the rounds impacted outside the firebase perimeter and caused no damage or casualties.

LTC Chuck Shay, the O-Deuce battalion commander, spotted four NVA out in the open from his C&C helicopter and called in 155mm fire from Battery B/2-11 Artillery on Barnett. Two of the NVA were killed and the other two fled.

23 August was quiet with FSB Barnett receiving one round of 75mm recoilless rifle fire and one round of 60mm mortar fire. The back blast from the recoilless rifle was spotted and 81mm rounds were called in on the location. Cobra gunships on a recon mission spotted thirty to forty bunkers at YD220305 near the Border of Quang Tri Province with Thua Thien Province. They also spotted mortar pits and 12.7mm emplacements. The ARA ships received small arms fire but took no hits. One of the helicopters from a White Team on a bomb damage assessment mission took hits from a 12.7mm machine gun and had to return to base. The other ship strafed the location and killed one NVA.

On 24 August, an element from Company A ran into an unknown-sized NVA unit. They were fired upon by an RPD machine gun, AK-47's and several hand grenades were thrown at them. The unit's Kit Carson Scout had been on point when he walked into a newly-constructed NVA bunker complex. The startled NVA open fire with an RPG. When the Company A men returned fire, the enemy broke contact and ran southwest, leaving two heavy blood trails and abandoning their new bunkers. Six men from Company A were wounded; all of them were evacuated to the 18th Surgical Hospital at Quang Tri.

The next day, Company D's Delta Three was following a fresh trail near YD194305 when the point man spotted a lone NVA moving toward him on the trail. The trooper shot the NVA but Delta Three began receiving AK-47 fire from less than eighty feet away. Delta Three moved on line and began recon by fire. They received more AK fire and several RPG's came in on them. Delta Three moved into a defensive perimeter, still receiving sporadic small arms fire from the southwest slope of Hill 848. Shortly after noon, a man was wounded and a medevac was called in. When the dust-off arrived and began to hover, it took several hits from AK fire and had to make an emergency landing on FSB Barnett. The Huey was disabled and remained on Barnett waiting for a Chinook to extract it. A second medevac responded an hour later and the wounded man, by then in shock from loss of blood, was successfully evacuated. Company D continued to receive sporadic AK and RPG fire from Hill 848 until nearly 1500 hours when the enemy withdrew.

Beginning at about 1900 hours that evening, FSB Barnett took twelve 60mm mortar rounds all of which exploded outside the perimeter wire. A White Team came on station and, while searching for the mortar position, found thirty to forty bunkers at YD178318. The White Team expended all their ordnance load on these bunkers and called in 8-inch artillery fire as it grew dark.

Shortly after 5 AM on 26 August, Company D received about fifty 60mm, 82mm and RPG rounds into and around their NDP at YD189304. The troops were well dug in and no one was wounded. The perimeter was probed but a full-scale attack did not develop. At about 0600 hours, the NVA withdrew and a sweep of the area proved negative for the enemy, but several escape trails leading west were found.

Later that morning, Company A spotted eight NVA moving across an open area about two hundred fifty meters to the west of YD203306. 81mm mortars were called in but the enemy ran into the jungle and disappeared. M-72 LAW's were fired into the area with unknown results.

Company A then moved to an LZ northeast of Hill 848 at YD99308 for a re-supply. When the log bird approached the LZ, it was driven away by six to eight bursts of AK fire. The Huey circled around and came in for a second attempt at landing on the LZ and again received small arms fire but took no hits.

Shortly after 8 PM that night, a squad from Company A's Alpha One set up an ambush at YD196309 on the north slope of Hill 848. A single NVA soldier walked into the ambush kill zone and was killed by a claymore mine. No other enemy was seen.

At about 1145 hours on 27 August, two NVA walked into an ambush set by an element from Company D at YD 190304. Both NVA were killed and their two AK-47 rifles captured. About seven hundred meters northwest of the ambush site, another Company D element found an 82mm mortar position and recovered three mortar rounds. The brush had been cleared from around the mortar to provide a good view of FSB Barnett.

In the late afternoon of 27 August, a patrol from Company A was returning to the main company position at YD201306 when they spotted a single NVA soldier armed with an AK-50 that had probably been the one that had fired on the log bird the day before. The NVA was killed and the AK-50 captured.

At around the same time, another Company A element on an ambush patrol at YD199306 fired on two NVA soldiers and killed them both. The element moved about three hundred meters northwest and set up another ambush on the northwest slope of Hill 848 at YD199308. After waiting only six minutes, they killed another NVA soldier and captured his AK-50. The soldier was probably the point man for a larger NVA unit that fled to the east when the ambush was sprung.

Friday 28 August was generally a quiet day through-out the O-Deuce AO. In the early evening of that day, Company D's Delta Two was moving down a trail to the northwest, using a dog team from the 42nd Scout Dog Platoon as the point for the column. The dog alerted and Delta Two moved off the trail and set up a hasty ambush. A single enemy soldier was seen moving southeast toward Delta Two. The NVA was killed by M-16 fire. When Delta Two began moving up the trail, they received small arms fire from three or four enemy who ran away after the initial burst of fire. Delta Two continued to move up the trail and found a newly-constructed, empty mortar pit.

At about 0213 hours on 29 August at YD189305 near Hill 848, one of the OP's sent out by Company D reported movement to their front. The OP fired their M-16's and set off their claymore mine, then began to withdraw to Company D's main NDP. A man on guard on the perimeter heard them coming and fired at them, wounding one man in the abdomen and leg. A medevac responded and evacuated the man to the 18th Surgical Hospital at Quang Tri.

Later that same morning, an element from Company D moved to the northwest slope of Hill 848 near YD187304 to check a report of enemy movement in that area. The point man walked to within five feet of a single NVA soldier before he saw him. The point man killed the NVA but came under fire from ten to twelve other NVA. The element from Company D tried to flank the enemy position but were driven back by heavy small arms fire. ARA was called in and the area hit by 81mm mortar fire from Barnett and the enemy fled to the west. Five men from Company D were wounded and evacuated to the 18th Surgical Hospital.

About mid-day on 29 August, the 2-502 received word that the battalion would be relieved by the 4th Battalion, 3rd Regiment of the ARVN 1st Infantry Division on 30 August. The O-Deuce would be moved by air from the Barnett AO to Camp Eagle for a stand down and refresher training.

Firebase Barnett received ten rounds of 75mm recoilless rifle fire over a two-hour period that afternoon. The enemy marksmanship remained poor; all the rounds passed over the firebase to explode outside the wire to the northwest, causing no casualties or damage.

On 30 August, the 2-502 Infantry was extracted from the Barnett AO and flown to the Strike Force LZ at Camp Eagle. At that time, the O-Deuce became the division ready reaction force with Company A being the first to go out if the need for an emergency deployment arose. At the end of the FSB Barnett deployment and as Operation Texas Star ended, the 2-502 Infantry had lost thirty-seven men killed in action and suffered two hundred ninety wounded. The battalion had accounted for two hundred eighty-nine NVA killed in action with an unknown number of wounded and had captured two POW's.

Chapter 21
"BUT WHAT GOOD...?"

"But what good came of it at last," quoth little Peterkin?" Why, that I cannot say," said he. "But 'twas a famous victory." Robert Southey (1774-1843) *The Battle of Blenheim*

A lot has been learned about the PAVN and the way they fought during Operation Texas Star and the battle for FSB Ripcord, but there is much we still do not know. It is likely we will never know the truth or, at least, not the whole truth about the PAVN side of the battle. The Socialist Republic of Vietnam is a totalitarian state and, as such, its citizens live in ever-present fear of their own government. There is no mandate for the production and preservation of an accurate historical record. But there is a mandate to "*alter, obfuscate, change and distort both history and reality to serve the needs of the* Lao Dong *Party (the Communist Vietnam Worker's Party)."* Hell On A Hill Top – page 213.

The so-called "official" records of the PAVN units that fought against the 101st Airborne during Operation Texas Star fail as true historical documents. Even in their distorted reporting, they still provide insight into the battles we fought during that long summer of 1970. The *324B Unit History* clearly acknowledges the importance of FSB Ripcord. "*Hill 935 (FSB Ripcord) . . .was the key to opening our route back down to the lowlands."* Hell On A Hill Top – page 213.

The only battles ever immortalized by the Vietnamese are ones in which they won, or at least claim to have won, a big victory. These battles—Ap Bac in 1963; Dong Ap Bia in 1969; the '72 Easter Offensive and the final '75 Ho Chi Minh Offensive that ended the war—are celebrated by the government of Vietnam. The fact that the Ripcord battle remains largely unreported indicates that it proved to be a complete and embarrassing failure for the North Vietnamese government and the People's Army.

Even though North Vietnamese records are distorted and often misleading, U.S. historians have learned several important facts regarding the PAVN. These are:

The 324B Division and the 6th Thua Thien Regiment operated in strength in the Ripcord, Coc Muen, Hills 805, 902 and 1000 area long before the first air assaults by the 3rd Brigade in March 1970.

The PAVN in the general Ripcord AO had already established underground bunker complexes, gun and mortar emplacements, supply caches and medical facilities.

The 324B Division was given a division mission. . .to 'up-root' and destroy FSB Ripcord with all division assets reinforced by the 6th Thua Thien Regiment and the 7th Sapper Battalion with the 304B Division in support.

Hanoi's leaders never wavered from their conviction that the United States would fold and eventually leave South Vietnam.

Hanoi believed it imperative to take the offensive against the Americans to accelerate their withdrawal no matter the cost to themselves in human lives.

They greatly feared our helicopter gunships and respected our airmobile tactics.

Their primary strategic concern focused on maintaining the flow of men and materials down the Ho Chi Minh Trail and keeping open the supply chain from the coastal lowlands [of South Vietnam] to the highlands to feed their troops.

The North Vietnamese **could not** *have won [even] in the next several decades without the support of the Soviet Union and China.*

The PAVN with its great concentration of men, supporting firepower and its singular mission, **never once** *penetrated the defensive perimeter of FSB Ripcord.*

The [324B's] mission to destroy FSB O'Reilly, a less formidable firebase than Ripcord, was also a failure of the significantly weakened 324B Division. . ." Hell On A Hill Top – pages 214-215.

That the leadership and the men of the 101st Airborne wanted to win the Battle of Ripcord but were prevented from doing so by the official policy of withdrawal and keeping down U.S. casualties is a forgone conclusion. The battle **was** a victory for the U.S. because the North Vietnamese were denied the political and military victory they wanted at a critical time in the war. If the NVA had been able to take Ripcord with a ground attack, the political repercussions would have greatly sped up the troop withdrawals and the Vietnamization process would have been cut short, which was the goal of the North Vietnamese.

The Hanoi government wanted the U.S. out of South Vietnam so badly that they expended vast amounts of treasure and human lives to force the withdrawal. After the severe mauling they received at the hands of the 1st and 3rd Brigades of the 101st, the 324B Division was in no shape to reoccupy the lowlands around Hue that was their ultimate strategic objective. The 324B Division was rendered so combat ineffective that they were withdrawn from offensive operations. This gained critical time for the ARVN who failed to take advantage of this.

The 101st Airborne and its supporting units lost far too many of America's finest young men during Operation Texas Star and the Battle of Ripcord. COL (major general, ret.) Harrison estimated that the twenty-one NVA units and their several thousand support troops who took part in the Battle of Ripcord suffered at least 2400 killed and several thousand wounded. The additional casualties suffered by NVA units who fought against troopers from the 101st Airborne's 1st Brigade on Hills 714, 882 and at FSB Barnett add up to a strategic set back in the summer of 1970 for the PAVN.

We still do not, and probably never will, know the exact details of how the PAVN soldiers and their leaders fought the Battle of Ripcord during Operation Texas Star. No PAVN documents or histories **ever mention** their losses in any of their battles. We do know that the 101st Airborne and its supporting units lost 243 men during Operation Texas Star and the Battle of Ripcord combined. These men fought valiantly for their buddies, their individual units and their country. They were the best America had. As General George S. Patton, Jr. once said, *"It is foolish and wrong to mourn the men who died. Rather, we should thank God that such men lived."*

INFANTRY WEAPONS of the VIETNAM WAR

UNITED STATES ARMY AND MARINE CORPS

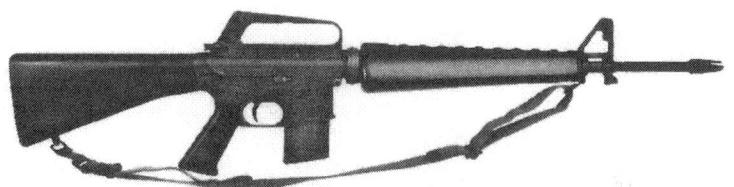

Standard infantry assault rifle during much of the Vietnam War was the M-16, caliber 5.56 x 45mm with a twenty-round magazine. The manufacturer overcame jamming in early models by providing a chrome-plated bolt and slowing the rate of fire.

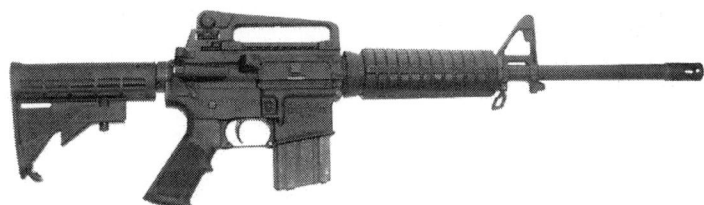

The light weight (6 lbs.) compact version of the M-16 is known as the CAR-15 caliber 5.56 x 45mm with a twenty-round magazine. This weapon could be fired semi-automatic, a three-round burst or full automatic.

The M-79 40 x 46mm grenade launcher replaced the rifle-launched grenade after the Korean War and was used extensively in Vietnam. It fired an HE round, buck shot, illumination, WP and flechette rounds.

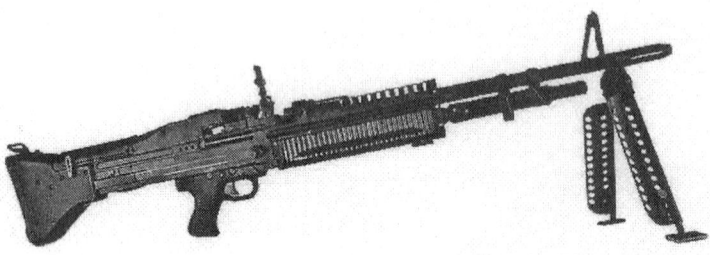

The M-60 gas operated machine gun, modeled after the German MG-42, is a 7.62 x 51mm belt-fed light machine gun. The weapon fires 100 round disintegrating link belts of ball, tracer and armor-piercing ammunition at a 650 round per minute rate of fire.

The M-72 Light Anti-Tank Weapon replaced the Bazooka of WW II and Korea. It is a shoulder fired 66mm fin stabilized rocket with a range of 200 meters that can penetrate up to 8 inches of armor plate. It is not reloadable in the field. It was used mainly against bunkers and entrenched troops.

The M-67 90mm recoilless rifles weighed 37.5 pounds and was most often used for perimeter defense using the M-590 flechette round. This weapon was used in the defense of Hill 805 by D/2-501 to great effect against NVA troops in the open.

The M1911A1 Automatic Pistol with a 7-round magazine fired a .45 caliber round at 852 feet per second. The weapon was carried extensively as a back-up weapon by medics, machine gunners, M-79 gunners and some officers.

PEOPLE'S ARMY OF VIETNAM – NVA

A very reliable weapon, the AK-47 assault rifle caliber 7.62 x 39mm with a 30-round detachable magazine was carried extensively by NVA and Viet Cong soldiers during the Vietnam War. Some models had a fold-down bayonet, shown above.

The AK-50 variant of the standard AK-47 had a fold-down wire stock but otherwise was the same weapon. Its compact size made it a favorite of the NVA's infamous sapper troops.

This Russian-made RPD gas-operated light machine gun fires a 7.62 x 39mm cartridge from a non-disintegrating 100 round belt loaded into a drum magazine as shown above with a 700 round per minute rate of fire.

The Russian-designed SKS semi-automatic carbine fired a 7.72 x 39mm cartridge from a 10-round internal box magazine loaded from a stripper clip. Some models were equipped with a fold-down bayonet. It was sometimes used as a sniper weapon.

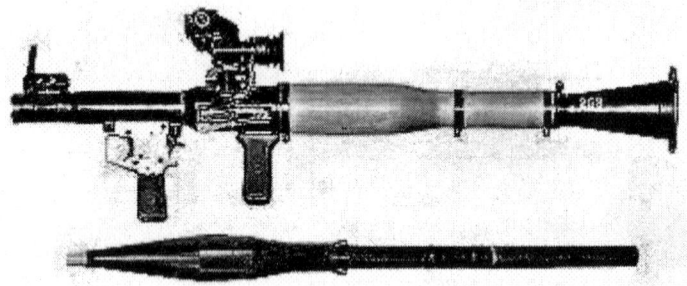

The Russian-designed reloadable, shoulder-fired RPG 7 fired a 40mm fin- stabilized rocket grenade out to an effective range of 200 meters and a maximum range of 500 meters. It is deadly when used against hovering helicopters, bunkers and infantry that has not dug foxholes.

BIBLIOGRAPHY

ARTICLES

The Delta Raiders of Vietnam Association – "July 1970, A Hill Called 805" Delta Raiders 1995

Hawkins, Charles F. – "Hell Night at Henderson" *VFW Magazine* August 2010

Higgins, William – "C/1-506 on FSB Granite"

Matkin, Ralph 'Doc' – "Reflections on [the] 1st Battle at Firebase Granite"

Mitchell, James E. – "The Battle of FSB Granite"

Mitchell, James E. – "The Battle of FSB Henderson"

Mitchell, James E. – "The Battle of Reup Hill"

McCormick, Ted W. – "Hill 882"

McCoy, Jim – "Eighteen - D Co, 1st BN, 1970-1971"

Miller, Eric W. – "A Hill to Remember"

BOOKS

Brinker, James P. – "West of Hue: Down The Yellow Brick Road" Charleston: Book Surge Publishing, 2009

Harrison, Benjamin L. – "Hell On A Hill Top – America's Last Major Battle In Vietnam" Lincoln: iUniverse, Inc. 2004

Johnson, Frank – "Diary Of An Airborne Ranger – A LRRP's Year in the Combat Zone" New York: Ballantine Books 2001

Lucero, Eraldo – "Echoes Of A Distant Past-Screaming Eagles-A Vietnam War Memoir (Revised Edition) Pena Blanca: 2012, 2014

McBain, Richard L. – "Reluctant Warrior-Memories of a Viet Nam Combat Soldier" San Bernardino: 2013

Nolan, Keith W. – "Ripcord-Screaming Eagles Under Siege, Vietnam 1970" Novato: Presidio Press, Inc. 2000

Roberts, John G. – "Mighty Men Of Valor-With Charley Company on Hill 714, Vietnam 1970" North Charleston: CreateSpace 2012

REFERENCE BOOKS

Kelley, Michael P. – "Where We Were In Vietnam-A Comprehensive Guide To The Firebases, Military Installations and Naval Vessels Of The Vietnam War 1945-75" Central Point, OR: Hellgate Press 2002

Olson, James S. Ed. – "Dictionary of the Vietnam War" New York: Peter Bedrick Books 1987

Stanton, Shelby L. – "Vietnam Order of Battle" Washington, D.C.: U.S. News Books 1981

DOCUMENTS

"Combat Operations After Action Report, Operation TEXAS STAR, 1 April 1970- 5 September 1970" 101st Airborne Combat Operations by Major General John J. Hennessey.

"Daily Staff Journal or Duty Officer's Log, 1-327 Infantry, May 1970"
"Daily Staff Journal or Duty Officer's Log, 1-327 Infantry, June 1970"
"Daily Staff Journal or Duty Officer's Log, 2-501 Infantry, 12 July through 17 July 1970"
"Daily Staff Journal or Duty Officer's Log, 1-502 Infantry, April 1970
"Daily Staff Jpurnal or Duty Officer's Log, 1-502 Infantry, May 1970"
"Daily Staff Journal or Duty Officer's Log, 2-502 Infantry, May 1970"
"Daily Staff Journal or Duty Officer's Log, 2-502 Infantry, July 1970"
"Daily Staff Journal or Duty Officer's Log, 2-502 Infantry, August 1970"
"Daily Staff Journal or Duty Officer's Log, 2-502 Infantry, September 1970"
"Unit History of the Strike Force - Vietnam '70, 2-502 Infantry"
"Daily Staff Journal or Duty Officer's Log," 1-506 Infantry, 12 July through 23 July
"Daily Staff Journal or Duty Officer's Log, 2-506 Infantry, 12 July through 23 July 1970"
"Office of Information Headquarters MACV Monthly Summary, April 1970"
"Office of Information Headquarters MACV Monthly Summary, May 1970"
"Office of Information Headquarters MACV Monthly Summary, June 1970"
"Office of Information Headquarters MACV Monthly Summary, July 1970."

Printed in Poland
by Amazon Fulfillment
Poland Sp. z o.o., Wrocław